HIDDEN IN PLAIN SIGHT

HIDDEN
IN PLAIN
SIGHT

What Really Caused the
World's Worst Financial Crisis
and Why It Could Happen Again

PETER J. WALLISON

Encounter Books
New York • London

First American edition published in 2015 by Encounter Books, an activity of Encounter for Culture and Education, Inc., a nonprofit, tax-exempt corporation.   ·
Encounter Books website address: www.encounterbooks.com

Manufactured in the United States and printed on acid-free paper. The paper used in this publication meets the minimum requirements of ANSI/NISO Z39.48-1992 (R 1997) (Permanence of Paper).

FIRST AMERICAN EDITION

LIBRARY OF CONGRESS CATALOGING-IN-PUBLICATION DATA
Wallison, Peter J.
Hidden in plain sight : what really caused the world's worst financial crisis and why it could happen again / by Peter J. Wallison.
pages cm
Includes bibliographical references and index.
ISBN 978-1-59403-770-2 (hard cover : alk. paper) —
ISBN 978-1-59403-771-9 (ebook)
1. Housing—Finance—Government policy—United States.
2. Mortgage loans—Government policy—United States. 3. Subprime mortgage loans—Government policy—United States. 4. Financial crises—Government policy—United States. 5. United States—Economic policy—2001–2009. I. Title.
HD7293.Z9W35 2015
332.7'20973090511—dc23
2014005179

PRODUCED BY WILSTED & TAYLOR PUBLISHING SERVICES
Copy editing: Nancy Evans
Design: Yvonne Tsang
Composition: Nancy Koerner
Charts: Evan Winslow Smith

For my amazing grandchildren, with love

Skylar
Allegra
Alex
Henry
and
Elodie

CONTENTS

PREFACE

Far from being a failure of free market capitalism, the
Depression was a failure of government. Unfortunately,
that failure did not end with the Great Depression. . . .
In practice, just as during the Depression, far from
promoting stability, the government has itself been the
major single source of instability.

MILTON FRIEDMAN

Political contests often force the crystallization of answers to difficult
political issues, and so it was with the question of responsibility for
the financial crisis in the 2008 presidential election. In their second
2008 presidential debate, almost three weeks after Lehman Brothers had filed for bankruptcy, John McCain and Barack Obama laid
out sharply divergent views of the causes of the financial convulsion
that was then dominating the public's concerns. The debate was in a
town-hall format, and a member of the audience named Oliver Clark
asked a question that was undoubtedly on the mind of every viewer
that night:

> Clark: Well, Senators, through this economic crisis, most
> of the people that I know have had a difficult time. . . . I
> was wondering what it is that's going to actually help these
> people out?
>
> Senator McCain: Well, thank you, Oliver, that's an excellent
> question. . . . But you know, one of the real catalysts, really

the match that lit this fire, was Fannie Mae and Freddie Mac
... they're the ones that, with the encouragement of Sen.
Obama and his cronies and his friends in Washington, that
went out and made all these risky loans, gave them to people
who could never afford to pay back ...

Then it was Obama's turn.

Senator Obama: Let's, first of all, understand that the biggest problem in this whole process was the deregulation
of the financial system. . . . Senator McCain, as recently as
March, bragged about the fact that he is a deregulator. . . .
A year ago, I went to Wall Street and said we've got to rereg-
ulate, and nothing happened. And Senator McCain during that period said that we should keep on deregulating
because that's how the free enterprise system works.

Although neither candidate answered the question that Oliver
Clark had asked, their exchange, with remarkable economy, effectively framed the issues both in 2008 and today: was the financial
crisis the result of government action, as John McCain contended, or
of insufficient regulation, as Barack Obama claimed?

Since this debate, the stage has belonged to Obama and the
Democrats, who gained control of the presidency and Congress in
2008, and their narrative about the causes of the financial crisis was
adopted by the media and embedded in the popular mind. Dozens of
books, television documentaries, and films have told the easy story of
greed on Wall Street or excessive and uncontrolled risk-taking by the
private sector—the expected result of what the media has caricatured
as "laissez-faire capitalism." To the extent that government has been
blamed for the crisis, it has been for failing to halt the abuses of the
private sector.

The inevitable outcome of this perspective was the Dodd-Frank
Wall Street Reform and Consumer Protection Act,[1] by far the most
costly and restrictive regulatory legislation since the New Deal. Its
regulatory controls and the uncertainties they engendered helped

produce the slowest post-recession U.S. recovery in modern history. Figure P.1 compares the recovery of gross domestic product (GDP) per capita since the recession ended in June 2009 with the recoveries following recessions since 1960.

Unfortunately, Dodd-Frank may provide a glimpse of the future. As long as the financial crisis is seen in this light—as the result of insufficient regulation of the private sector—there will be no end to the pressure from the left for further and more stringent regulation. As this is being written, proposals to break up the largest banks, re-instate Glass-Steagall in its original form, and resume government support for subprime mortgage loans are circulating in Congress. These ideas are likely to find public support as long as the prevailing view of the financial crisis is that it was caused by the risk-taking and greed of the private sector.

For that reason, the question of what caused the financial crisis is still very relevant today. If the crisis were the result of government

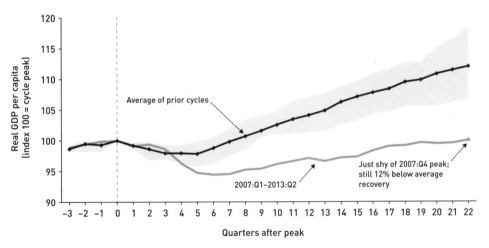

Sources: Bureau of Economic Analysis; Census Bureau; authors' calculations. Adapted from Tyler Atkinson, David Luttrell, and Harvey Rosenblum, "How Bad Was It? The Costs and Consequences of the 2007–09 Financial Crisis," *Staff Papers* (Federal Reserve Bank of Dallas) no. 20 (July 2013): 4.

Note: The gray area indicates the range of major recessions since 1960, excluding the short 1980 recession.

FIG. P.1. Current rebound in GDP per capita compared to previous cycles

policies, as described in this book, the Dodd-Frank Act was an illegitimate response to the crisis and many of its unnecessary and damaging restrictions should be repealed. Similarly, proposals and regulations based on a false narrative about the causes of the financial crisis should also be seen as misplaced and unfounded.

As demonstrated by Dodd-Frank itself, first impressions are never a sound basis for policy action, and haste in passing significant legislation can have painful consequences. During the Depression era, it was widely believed that the extreme level of unemployment was caused by excessive competition. This, it was thought, drove down prices and wages and forced companies out of business, causing the loss of jobs. Accordingly, some of the most far-reaching and hastily adopted legislation—such as the National Industrial Recovery Act and the Agricultural Adjustment Act (both ultimately declared unconstitutional)—was designed to protect competitors from price competition. Raising prices in the midst of a depression seems wildly misguided now, but it was a result of a mistaken view about what caused the high levels of unemployment that characterized the era.

In the 1960s, Milton Friedman and Anna Schwartz produced a compelling argument that the Great Depression was an ordinary cyclical downturn that was unduly prolonged by the mistaken monetary policies of the Federal Reserve. Their view and the evidence that they adduced gradually gained traction among economists and policy makers. Freed of its association with unemployment and depression, competition came to be seen as a benefit to consumers and a source of innovation and economic growth rather than a threat to jobs.

With that intellectual backing, a gradual process of reducing government regulation began in the Carter administration. Air travel, trucking, rail, and securities trading were all deregulated, followed later by energy and telecommunications. We owe cell phones and the Internet to the deregulation of telecommunications, and a stock market in which billions of shares are traded every day—at a transaction cost of a penny a share—to the deregulation of securities trading. Because of the huge reductions in cost brought about by competition, families don't think twice about making plane reservations for visits to Grandma, and we take it for granted that an item we bought over the Internet will be delivered to us, often free of a separate charge, the next day. These are the indirect benefits of a revised theory for the causes of the Depression that freed us to see the benefits of competition.

We have not yet had this epiphany about the financial crisis, but the elements for it—as readers will see in this book—have been hidden in plain sight. Accordingly, what follows is intended to be an entry in a political debate—a debate that was framed in the 2008 presidential contest but never actually joined. In these pages I argue that, but for the housing policies of the U.S. government during the Clinton and George W. Bush administrations, there would not have been a financial crisis in 2008. Moreover, because of the government's extraordinary role in bringing on the crisis, it is invalid to treat it as an inherent part of a capitalist or free market system, or to use it as a pretext for greater government control of the financial system.

I do not absolve the private sector, although that will be the claim of some, but put the errors of the private sector in the context of the government policies that dominated the housing finance market for the fifteen years before the crisis, including the government regulations that induced banks to load up on assets that ultimately made them appear unstable or insolvent. I hope readers will find the data I have assembled informative and compelling. The future of the housing finance system and the health of the wider economy depend on a public that is fully informed about the causes of the 2008 financial crisis.

ACKNOWLEDGMENTS

Anyone who reads this book will realize that it couldn't have been written without the invaluable research and housing market knowledge of my American Enterprise Institute colleague Edward Pinto. Although I had been a critic of Fannie Mae and Freddie Mac as early as 1999, it was Ed who showed me in 2009 that Fannie and Freddie had been taking serious credit risks since 1992, when the affordable-housing goals were enacted by Congress. Until that time, I and all the scholars and government economists I consulted had assumed that the GSEs' principal risks were interest-rate risks, stemming from their accumulation of huge portfolios of mortgages.

As far as I can tell, Ed is the only person—even now, almost seven years after the financial crisis—who has been able to piece together the haphazard records and eccentric data standards of the housing finance industry to create a coherent narrative about the growth of non-traditional mortgages and the contribution of deteriorating underwriting standards to the 2008 financial crisis. If there are errors in this book, they are mine.

Over the fifteen years I have been fortunate enough to have a niche at AEI, I have also had some excellent research assistants. Those who have made real contributions to this book include Karen Dubas, Steffanie Hawkins, Emily Rapp, Andre Gardiner, and Brian Marein.

When I was a member of the Financial Crisis Inquiry Commission, one staff member and investigator, Bradley J. Bondi, now a partner at Cadwalader, Wickersham & Taft in Washington, D.C., provided important research assistance.

Then, too, there were all the colleagues, friends, and acquaintances who understood and deplored the fact that the public has so little knowledge of what actually caused the financial crisis. They encouraged me to take the time necessary to get this book into print. To all of them, I am grateful.

Finally, I owe a lot to the assistance of my wonderful wife, the inestimable Frieda, who took time from her many other projects to read and critique the first draft. Thanks, sweetheart.

HIDDEN IN PLAIN SIGHT

The Basics

A summary of the argument, important distinctions
among mortgages, other explanations for the financial crisis,
and a short history of government housing policies

1

Introduction

What Really Caused the World's Worst
Financial Crisis and Why It Could Happen Again

Who controls the past controls the future.

GEORGE ORWELL, *1984*

The 2008 financial crisis was a major event, equivalent in its initial scope—if not its duration—to the Great Depression of the 1930s. Government officials who participated in efforts to mitigate its effects claim that their actions prevented a complete meltdown of the world's financial system, an idea that has found many adherents among academic and other commentators. We will never know, of course, what would have happened if these emergency actions had not been taken, but it is possible to gain an understanding of why they were considered necessary—that is, the likely causes of the crisis. The history of events leading up to the crisis forms a coherent story, but one that is quite different from the narrative underlying the Dodd-Frank Act.

Why is it important at this point to examine the causes of the crisis? After all, the crisis is six years in the past, and Congress and financial regulators have acted, or are acting, to prevent a recurrence. Even if we can't pinpoint the exact cause of the crisis, some will argue that the new regulations now being put in place will make a repetition unlikely. Perhaps. But these new regulations—specifically those authorized in the Dodd-Frank Act adopted by Congress in 2010—

have slowed and will continue to slow economic growth in the future, reducing the quality of life for most Americans. If these regulations were really necessary to prevent a recurrence of the financial crisis, then there might be a legitimate trade-off in which we are obliged to sacrifice economic freedom for the sake of financial stability. But if the crisis did not stem from a lack of regulation, we have needlessly restricted future economic growth.

In the wake of the crisis, many commentators saw it as a "crisis of capitalism," an inevitable consequence of the inherent instability—as they see it—of a free-market or capitalist system.[1] The implication was that crises of this kind will be repeated unless we gain control of the financial and economic institutions that influence the direction of our economy. That was the unspoken impulse behind the Dodd-Frank Act and the underlying assumption of those who imposed it.

But it is not at all clear that what happened in 2008 was the result of insufficient regulation, deregulation, or an economic system that is inherently unstable. On the contrary, there is compelling evidence that the financial crisis was the result of the government's own housing policies. These policies, as we will see, were based on an idea—still popular on the left—that underwriting standards in housing finance are excessively conservative, discriminatory, and unnecessary. If it is true that the crisis was the result of government policies, then the supposed instability of the financial system is a myth, and the regulations put in place to prevent a recurrence at such great cost to economic growth were a serious policy mistake. Indeed, if we look back over the last hundred years, it is difficult to see instability in the financial system that was not caused by the government's own policies. The Great Depression, now more than eighty years ago, probably doesn't qualify as a financial crisis; although financial firms were affected, it was a broadly based economic recession, made worse and prolonged by the Federal Reserve's mistaken monetary policies. One would have to go back to the Panic of 1907 to find something comparable to what happened in 2008, and few would claim that a financial system is inherently unstable if its major convulsions occur only once every hundred years.

How, then, did government housing policies cause the 2008 financial crisis? Actually, "cause" is too strong a word. Many factors were involved in the crisis, but the way to think about the relationship between the government's housing policies and the financial crisis, as I will discuss in this book, is that the crisis would not have occurred without those policies; they were, one might say, the *sine qua non* of the crisis—the element without which there would not have been a widespread financial breakdown in 2008. In this sense, throughout this book, I will say that the U.S. government's housing policies caused the crisis.

The seeds of the crisis were planted in 1992 when Congress enacted "affordable-housing" goals for two giant government-sponsored enterprises (GSEs), the Federal National Mortgage Association (Fannie Mae) and the Federal Home Loan Mortgage Corporation (Freddie Mac). Before 1992, these two firms dominated the housing finance market, especially after the savings and loan (S&L) industry—another government mistake—had collapsed. The role of the GSEs, as initially envisioned and as it developed until 1992, was to conduct what were called secondary market operations. They were prohibited from making loans themselves, but they were authorized to buy mortgages from banks, S&Ls, and other lenders. Their purchases provided cash for lenders and thus encouraged homeownership by making more funds available for additional mortgages.

Other government agencies were involved in housing finance, notably the Federal Housing Administration (FHA), the Veterans Administration (VA), and the Department of Agriculture's Rural Housing Service (RHS), but the GSEs were by far the most important. By the mid-1980s, they were acting as conduits by packaging mortgages into pools and selling securities backed by these pools to investors in the United States and around the world. For a fee, they guaranteed that investors would receive the principal and interest on these securities that they had been promised. The increasing dominance of the housing market by the GSEs and the government is well illustrated in Figure 1.1, which covers both the mortgage pools they guaranteed and their portfolios of mortgages and mortgage-backed securities (MBS).

Although Fannie and Freddie, as they were called, were owned

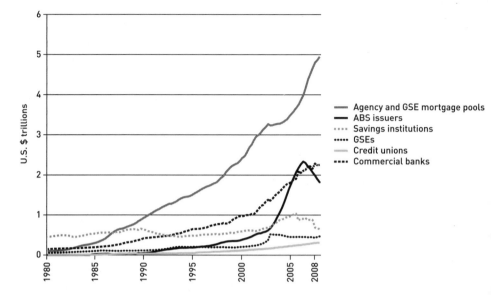

Source: U.S. Flow of Funds, Federal Reserve, 1980–2009. Adapted from Tobias Adrian and Hyun Song Shin, "The Changing Nature of Financial Intermediation and the Financial Crisis of 2008–09," Federal Reserve Bank of New York, Staff Report no. 439, revised April 2010, p. 2.

FIG. 1.1. Total holdings of U.S. home mortgages by type of financial institution

by public shareholders, they were chartered by Congress and carried out a government mission by maintaining a liquid secondary market in mortgages. As a result, market participants believed that the two GSEs were government-backed and would be rescued by the government if they ever encountered financial difficulties. This widely assumed government support enabled them to borrow at rates only slightly higher than the U.S. Treasury itself; with these low-cost funds they were able to drive all competition out of the secondary mortgage market for middle-class mortgages. Between 1991 and 2003, the GSEs' share of the U.S. housing market increased from 28.5 percent to 46.3 percent.[2] From this dominant position, they were able to set the underwriting standards for the market as a whole; few mortgage lenders would make middle-class mortgages—by far the predominant market—that could not be sold to Fannie or Freddie.

THE DEVELOPMENT OF UNDERWRITING STANDARDS

Over time, the GSEs had learned from experience what underwriting standards kept delinquencies and defaults low. These standards required down payments of 10 to 20 percent, good borrower credit histories, and low debt-to-income (DTI) ratios after the mortgage was closed. These were the foundational elements of what was called a prime loan or a traditional mortgage, discussed more fully in chapter 2. Mortgages that did not meet these standards were called "subprime" if the weakness in the loan was caused by the borrower's credit standing, and were called "Alt-A"* if the problem was the quality of the loan itself. Among other defects, Alt-A loans might involve reduced documentation; negative amortization; a borrower's obligation to pay interest only; a low down payment; a second mortgage; cash-out refinancing; or loans made to an investor who intends to rent out the home. In this book, subprime and Alt-A mortgages are together called nontraditional mortgages, or NTMs, because they differ substantially in default risk from the mortgages that Fannie and Freddie had made traditional in the U.S. housing finance market. Many observers of this market believe that tight underwriting standards—occasionally called a "tight credit box"—adversely affect the homeownership rate in the United States; however, even though the GSEs insisted on tight underwriting standards before 1992, the homeownership rate in the United States remained relatively high, at 64 percent, for the thirty years between 1965 and 1995.

The GSEs were subject to some statutory restrictions on their activities. In addition to the prohibition on direct lending to homebuyers, they could not acquire mortgages that were larger than a certain size (this was known as the "conforming loan limit," a statutory formula that allowed loan size to grow as housing prices rose), and

---

*The term Alt-A is said to derive from the market practice of referring to the GSEs as "Agencies." Alt-A mortgages were said to be "Alternative to Agencies" or mortgages that the GSEs wouldn't buy. Ironically, in order to meet the affordable-housing goals, the GSEs eventually became the biggest buyers of Alt-A loans.

after 1992 they were subject to prudential regulation by the Office of Federal Housing Enterprise Oversight (OFHEO), an agency of the Department of Housing and Urban Development (HUD). HUD was also their "mission regulator," with power to ensure that they were performing the role that the government had assigned to them. Most important, as mission regulator, HUD was given authority under the 1992 legislation to administer the affordable-housing goals, which are discussed at much greater length in later chapters of this book.

THE AFFORDABLE-HOUSING GOALS AND THE DECLINE IN UNDERWRITING STANDARDS

In a sense, the ability of the GSEs to dominate the housing finance market and set their own strict underwriting standards was their undoing. Community activists had had the two firms in their sights for many years, arguing that their underwriting standards were so tight that they were keeping many low- and moderate-income families from buying homes. Finally, as housing legislation was moving through Congress in 1992, the House and Senate acted, directing the GSEs to meet a quota of loans to low- and moderate-income borrowers when they acquired mortgages. At first, the low- and moderate-income (LMI) quota was 30 percent: in any year, at least 30 percent of the loans Fannie and Freddie acquired must have been made to LMI borrowers—defined as borrowers at or below the median income in their communities.

Thirty percent was not a difficult goal. It was probably true at the time the affordable-housing goals were enacted that 30 percent of the loans Fannie and Freddie bought had been made to LMI borrowers. But in giving HUD authority to increase the goals, Congress cleared the way for far more ambitious requirements—suggesting in the legislation, for example, that down payments could be reduced below 5 percent without seriously impairing mortgage quality. HUD received the signal. In succeeding years, HUD raised the LMI goal in steps to 42 percent in 1997, 50 percent in 2001, and 56 percent in 2008. Congress also required additional "base goals" that encompassed low- and very-low-income borrowers and residents of minority areas described as "underserved." HUD increased these base goals between 1996 and 2008, and at a faster rate than the LMI goals. Finally, in 2004, HUD added subgoals that provided affordable-housing goals credit only when the loans were used to purchase a home (known as a home purchase mortgage), as distinguished from a refinancing. As discussed later, it was much more difficult to find high-quality home-purchase mortgages than loans that were simply refinancing an existing mortgage.

As HUD increased the goals after 1992, it became considerably more difficult for the GSEs to find creditworthy borrowers, especially when the quota reached and then exceeded 50 percent. To do so, Fannie and Freddie had to reduce their underwriting standards. In fact, as we will see, that was explicitly HUD's purpose. As early as 1995, the GSEs were buying mortgages with 3-percent down payments, and by 2000 Fannie and Freddie were accepting loans with zero down payments. At the same time, they were compromising other underwriting standards, such as borrower credit standing and debt-to-income ratios (DTIs), in order to find the NTMs they needed to meet the affordable-housing goals.

New, easy credit terms brought many new buyers into the market, but the effect spread far beyond the LMI borrowers whom the reduced underwriting standards were intended to help. Mortgage lending is a competitive business; once Fannie and Freddie started to loosen their underwriting standards, many borrowers who could have afforded prime mortgages sought the easier terms now available so they could buy larger homes with smaller down payments. As early as 1995, Fannie's staff recognized that it was subsidizing homebuyers who were *above* the median income, noting that "average pricing of risk characteristics provides insufficient targeting of the subsidy. The majority of high LTV [loan-to-value] loans go to borrowers with incomes above 100% of the area median."[3] Thus, homebuyers above the median income were gaining leverage, and loans to them were decreasing in quality. In many cases, they were withdrawing cash from the equity in their homes through cash-out refinancing, further weakening the quality of the mortgages. Although the initial objective had been to reduce underwriting standards for low-income borrowers, the advantages of buying or refinancing a home with a low down payment were also flowing to high-income borrowers. Fannie never cured this problem. By 2007, 37 percent of loans with down payments of 3 percent or less went to borrowers with incomes above the median.[4]

Because of the gradual deterioration in loan quality after 1992, by 2008 half of all mortgages in the United States—31 million loans— were subprime or Alt-A. Of these 31 million, 76 percent were on the books of government agencies or institutions like the GSEs that were controlled by government policies.* This shows incontrovertibly where the demand for these mortgages originated. Table 1.1 shows where these 31 million loans were held on June 30, 2008.

THE GSES' FAILURE TO DISCLOSE THEIR RISK-TAKING

Even today, the numbers and dollar value of the NTMs in Table 1.1 are considerably larger than the numbers for subprime or Alt-A loans in most academic and government papers or reports. This discrepancy is explained by the fact that, after the affordable-housing requirements were adopted, the housing finance market underwent a radical change that was never fully grasped or understood by most market observers. Before 1992, it was relatively easy to tell the difference between a subprime loan and a prime loan. Subprime loans were a niche market, perhaps 10 percent of all mortgages; they were made by specialized lenders. The GSEs seldom acquired these loans. A subprime loan, therefore, was one made by a subprime lender, or a loan that Fannie and Freddie wouldn't buy. After the enactment

---

*Throughout this book, for ease of reference, I refer to institutions that were compelled to acquire NTMs by government regulations as "government agencies." Many of them, such as FDIC-insured banks and even Fannie Mae and Freddie Mac, are not government agencies in the sense that they are funded by the government. However, they played a role in the financial crisis because their activities with respect to mortgage underwriting were subject to government control and regulation. FDIC-insured banks, for example, were subject to the Community Reinvestment ACT (CRA), which required them to make loans in their service areas that did not meet their regular underwriting standards.

TABLE 1.1. Entities holding credit risk of subprime
and other high-risk mortgages as of June 30, 2008

Entity	Subprime and Alt-A loans (millions)	Unpaid principal amount ($ trillions)	
Fannie Mae and Freddie Mac	16.5	2.5	$151,515/Loan
FHA and other federal[a]	5.1	0.6	117,647/Loan
CRA and HUD programs	2.2	0.3	136,363/Loan
Total federal government	23.8	3.4	
Other[b]	7.5	1.9	253,333/Loan
Total	31.0[c]	5.3	

Sources: The data in this table and others throughout this book are drawn from research by Edward J. Pinto of the American Enterprise Institute. This table reflects the results of the analysis in Studies 1 and 2 in Pinto's "Three Studies of Subprime and Alt-A Loans in the U.S. Mortgage Market," September 29, 2014, http://www.aei.org/publication /three-studies-of-subprime-and-alt-a-loans-in-the-us-mortgage-market/.

[a]"FHA and other federal" includes Veterans Administration, Department of Agriculture, Federal Home Loan Banks, and others.

[b]"Other" includes subprime and Alt-A private MBS issued by Countrywide and Wall Street.

[c]Figure rounded.

of the affordable-housing requirements, however, the GSEs began to acquire loans that were subprime or Alt-A by their characteristics— that is, they might not have been originated by a subprime lender or insured by the FHA, but they had the same deficiencies as traditional subprime or Alt-A loans, and they performed the same way.

However—and this is a key point—even after they began to acquire large numbers of subprime mortgages, the GSEs continued to define subprime loans as mortgages that they bought from subprime lenders or that had been sold to them as subprime mortgages.[5] This misleading definition allowed them to maintain for many years that their exposure to subprime or Alt-A loans was minimal. In addition, when lenders reported their loans to organizations such as First American LoanPerformance, Inc. (now CoreLogic), a well-known data aggregator and publisher in the housing market, loans that had been sold to Fannie and Freddie were classified as prime loans. The GSEs took adantage of this highly misleading classification system, failing to acknowledge loans with subprime characteristics as subprime or Alt-A, even though these loans would inevitably have much higher rates of default than prime loans. LoanPerformance and other data aggregators such as Inside Mortgage Finance (IMF), not in the business of classifying loans, simply assumed that loans sold to the GSEs were prime loans and carried them in that category. IMF noted, "Some subprime and Alt-A originations were likely reported by lenders as conventional conforming mortgages if they were sold to Fannie Mae or Freddie Mac."[6] For that reason, many respected academic, government, media, and professional commentators who discuss the financial crisis did not at the time of the crisis—and still do not—understand that the number of NTMs in the financial system was far higher in 2008 than what LoanPerformance's data showed, and the number of prime loans, accordingly, was much lower.[7] In December 2011, three top officers of both Fannie and Freddie were sued by the Securities and Exchange Commission (SEC) for failing to disclose that they had been acquiring subprime loans in substantial numbers. This was confirmed by Fannie and Freddie in nonprosecution agreements with the SEC, discussed in chapter 3.[8] The NTM numbers used in this book will include loans that should properly be labeled subprime or Alt-A because of their characteristics, not because the GSEs or the originators of these loans happened to label them that way. Indeed, after they were taken over in a government conservatorship, Fannie and Freddie disclosed the extent of their exposure to NTMs.

The failure of the GSEs to report the full extent of their NTM acquisitions is only one of the factors that might account for the general failure of risk managers, rating agencies, regulators, and housing market analysts to recognize the dangers that were building up in the mortgage market through the mid-2000s. Other elements were the growth of the bubble, which (as discussed below) tends to suppress delinquencies and defaults; the fact that no one could imagine a decline in housing prices nationally of 30–40 percent, or indeed a decline of 30–40 percent anywhere;[9] and the misplaced belief that automated underwriting had made it possible to eliminate much of the risk in subprime lending.

Unfortunately, some of the largest financial institutions were victims of the same misapprehensions as regulators and academics about the quality of the mortgages outstanding and the safety of the mortgage market, but they have been blamed by the government, the media, and ultimately the American people for excessive risk-taking. This view, a product of both the absence of accurate data and the government's efforts to avoid blame, has led to calls for what are essentially pubic hangings of the alleged malefactors—principally banks and their managers. Although placing responsibility for the financial crisis where it belongs may be seen by some as a defense of the banks and their officials, it is not.[10] Clearly, the private sector made serious errors in the crisis, but one fact is difficult to dismiss: the banks and investment banks got into serious trouble because they kept—they did not sell—the mortgage-backed securities, based on NTMs, that declined so sharply in value in 2007 and 2008. Two academics, Viral V. Acharya and Matthew Richardson, argue that the banks held onto the AAA-rated tranches (the levels most protected against loss) of these disastrously risky securities in order to evade the Basel capital regulations,[11] but at some level they must have believed that these instruments were safe. Ironically, if the banks had sold these securities, the losses would have been distributed more widely throughout the global financial system, where there was more capital to absorb them; instead, the losses were concentrated in the largest financial institutions in the United States and abroad, creating a financial crisis when these firms were so weakened that they could not continue to supply liquidity to the financial system.

THE GREAT HOUSING BUBBLE, 1997–2007

With all the new buyers entering the market because of the affordable-housing goals, together with the loosened underwriting standards the goals produced, housing prices began to rise. By 2000, the developing bubble was already larger than any bubble in U.S. history, and it kept rising until 2007, when—at nine times larger than any previous bubble—it finally topped out, and housing prices began to fall. Figure 1.2, based on Yale professor Robert Shiller's data, shows the extraordinary size of the 1997–2007 housing bubble in relation to the two other significant bubbles of the postwar period.

The growth and ultimate collapse of the 1997–2007 bubble seems consistent with economist Hyman Minsky's model for what eventually becomes a financial crisis or panic; many economists and policy makers have commented on this similarity.[12] Although Minsky posited a wholly private sector–driven financial crisis, his theory neatly fits the government-driven financial crisis of 2008. It begins with a "displacement"—some kind of shock to the market that creates unusual profit opportunities. As described in Charles Kindleberger and Robert Aliber's *Manias, Panics, and Crashes*: "Assume an increase in the effective demand for goods and services. After a time, the increase in demand presses against the capacity to produce goods. Market prices increase, and the more rapid increase in profits attracts both more investment and more firms."[13]

The shock to the market in the case of the 1997–2007 bubble was the newfound and strong interest by Fannie and Freddie in NTMs, beginning in 1993. The GSEs' demand, pressing against the existing supply, created new profits for subprime lenders such as Countrywide, as well as realtors, homebuilders, and banks. Minsky also

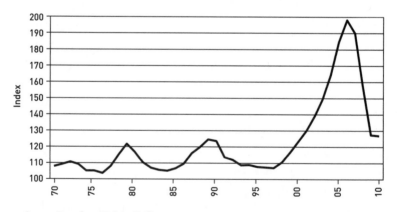

Source: Data from Robert Shiller.

FIG. 1.2. Real home prices from 1970 to 2010 per the Shiller home price index

posited that there must be a continuing injection of new funds in order to maintain the necessary euphoria. The gradual increase in the affordable-housing goals and the growing size of Fannie and Freddie as financing sources appear to satisfy this requirement between 1997 and 2007, accounting for the continued growth of the bubble. Figure 1.3 shows that between 1983 and approximately 1997 the trend in home prices tracked rental values as calculated by the Bureau of Labor Statistics (BLS). Then, beginning somewhere between 1995 and 1998, home prices began a sharp rise. The figure shows a correlation between the beginnings of the bubble and what might be called a Minsky event—the displacement or shock in the form of a sudden rise in the GSEs' appetite for lower-quality loans, reflected in their acceptance of DTI ratios greater than 38 percent and down payments of 3 percent or less. Low down payments were of particular importance here. If a potential buyer has a down payment of $20,000, he or she could buy a $200,000 house if the required down payment is 10 percent. But if the required down payment is 5 percent, as it quickly became after the adoption of affordable-housing goals, the same buyer could buy a $400,000 house. In this way, lower down payments made much more credit available for mortgages and thus enlarged the market for more expensive houses.

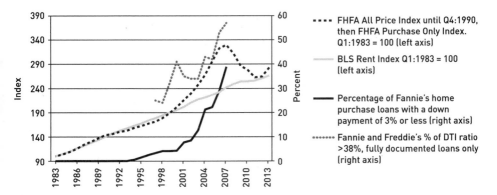

Sources: Federal Housing Finance Agency; Bureau of Labor Statistics; Department of Housing and Urban Development; Consumer Financial Protection Bureau.

FIG. 1.3. The Minsky event implicit in the 1997–2007 housing bubble

The principal beneficiaries of these policies were the realtors, and they joined community activists as cheerleaders for lower underwriting standards. The principal victims, in addition to the taxpayers, were the low-income homebuyers who lost their homes when the inevitable recession arrived.

Housing bubbles tend to suppress delinquencies and defaults while the bubble is growing. As prices rise, borrowers who are having difficulty meeting their mortgage obligations are able to refinance or sell the home for more than the principal amount of the mortgage. In these conditions, potential investors in mortgages or in mortgage-backed securities receive a strong affirmative signal; they see high-cost mortgages—loans that reflect the riskiness of lending to a borrower with a weak credit history—but the expected number of delinquencies and defaults have not occurred. They come to think that "this time it's different," that the risks of investing in subprime or other weak mortgages are not as great as they'd thought. At the same time, Fannie and Freddie were arguing that the automated underwriting standards they had developed allowed them to find good mortgages among those that would in the past have been considered subprime or Alt-A. For example, in a 2002 study, two Freddie Mac officials reported: "We find evidence that AU [automated underwriting] systems more accurately predict default than manual underwriters do. We also find evidence that this increased accuracy results in higher borrower approval rates, especially for underserved applicants."[14] The superiority of new technology, rather than the existence of a bubble, was thus used to explain the lower rates of default observed in the market.

These factors brought many new investors into the market, looking to invest in securities backed by NTMs. These were private mortgage–backed securities (PMBS), also called private label securities, or PLS, which were securitized and sold by commercial banks, investment banks, subprime lenders, and others. Although never before a large part of the mortgage market, PMBS (denoted as ABS issuers in Figure 1.1), much of them backed by subprime and Alt-A mortgages, became a booming business, especially from 2004 through 2006, as private securitizers discovered ways to compete with securitizations by Fannie and Freddie. Still, although the private securitization system challenged Fannie and Freddie during these years, the NTMs securitized by the private sector were only 24 percent of the NTMs outstanding in 2008, showing that PMBS and the financial institutions that held them were not the major source of the bubble or the crisis.

Housing bubbles are also by definition procyclical. When they are growing they feed on themselves to encourage higher prices, through higher appraisals and other mechanisms, until prices get so high that buyers can't afford them no matter how lenient the terms of a mortgage. But when bubbles begin to deflate, the process reverses. It then becomes impossible to refinance or sell a house that has no equity; financial losses cause creditors to pull back and tighten lending standards; recessions frequently occur; and low appraisals make it difficult for a purchaser to get financing. As in the United States today, many homeowners suddenly find that their mortgage is larger than the value of the home; they are said to be "underwater." Sadly, many are likely to have lost their jobs because of the conditions in the economy brought on by the housing decline but cannot move to a place where jobs are more plentiful because they can't sell their home without paying off the unpaid mortgage loan balance. In these circumstances, many homeowners simply walk away from the mortgage, knowing that in most states the lender has recourse only to the home itself. This, of course, weakens the banking system, with many banks left holding defaulted mortgages and unsalable properties. These banks are then required to reduce their lending in the hope of restoring their capital positions, which diminishes the credit available to consumers and business and impedes a recovery.

With the largest housing bubble in history deflating, and more than half of all mortgages made to borrowers who had weak credit, high debt ratios, or little equity in their homes, the number of delinquencies and defaults in 2008 was unprecedented. One immediate effect was the collapse of the market for private mortgage-backed securities. Investors, shocked by the sheer number of defaults that seemed to be under way, fled the market. Mortgage values fell along with housing prices, with dramatic effect on the PMBS market, as

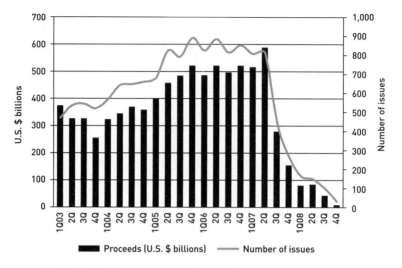

Proceeds (U.S. $ billions) ———— Number of issues

Source: Adapted from Thomson Reuters, *Debt Capital Markets Review,* Fourth Quarter 2008, available at http://thomsonreuters.com/products_services/financial/league_tables /debt_equity/ (accessed July 30, 2009).

FIG. 1.4. Quarterly residential ABS, MBS, and CDO volume

shown in Figure 1.4, which reflects the combined effect of the decline in the markets for asset-backed securities (ABS), private mortgage-backed securities (PMBS), and collateralized debt obligations (CDOs). These are all ways that mortgages and other obligations are securitized. Sponsors of securitizations form pools of thousands of such individual obligations and issue securities backed by the stream of principal and interest that these obligations produce.

THE EFFECT OF BANK CAPITAL AND ACCOUNTING RULES

The abrupt fall in housing and mortgage values during 2007 had a disastrous effect on financial institutions, particularly banks. Since the adoption in the 1980s of the internationally agreed risk-based capital requirements for banks known as Basel I (after the Swiss city in which the bank regulators convened), mortgages had been a favored investment for banks.[15] As outlined in more detail later, the initial capital rules known as Basel I treated mortgages and highly rated MBS as safer investments than commercial loans, requiring banks to hold less capital against a residential mortgage (4 percent) than they held against a commercial loan (8 percent). In 2002 the Basel rules were changed so that highly rated PMBS required only 1.6 percent capital, making PMBS even less costly in terms of capital than whole mortgages and high-quality corporate loans. This equalized the treatment of GSE and private mortgage-backed securities that were rated AAA or AA. These regulations encouraged banks to favor the acquisition of PMBS, which made them particularly vulnerable to the decline in housing and mortgage values that occurred in 2007 and 2008. If the Basel rules had not put a regulatory thumb on the scale, pushing banks in the direction of residential mortgages and PMBS, the consequences of the housing value collapse would have been much less significant for the world's economy than it turned out to be. Score this as another unforced error for the government's role in the financial crisis.

The effect of the decline in housing and mortgage values was also exacerbated for all financial institutions by accounting rules that, since 1994, had required financial firms to use what was called "fair-value accounting" in setting the balance sheet value of their assets and liabilities. The most significant element of fair-value accounting was a requirement that financial institutions carry assets and liabilities at current market value instead of using amortized cost or other traditional valuation methods. This system worked effectively as long as there was a market for the assets in question, but it was destructive in the market collapse precipitated by the vast number of delinquent and defaulting mortgages during 2007. In that case, buyers fled the market, and the market value of PMBS plummeted. Although there were alternative ways for assets to be valued in the absence of market prices, auditors—worried about their potential liability if they permitted their clients to overstate assets in the midst of the financial crisis—were reluctant to allow the use of these alternatives. Accordingly, as described in chapter 12, financial firms were compelled to write down significant portions of their PMBS assets, taking operating losses that substantially reduced their capital positions.

Moreover, because most PMBS held by financial institutions were rated AAA, they were used by many banks and other financial firms for short-term collateralized borrowing through repurchase agreements. Suddenly, no one wanted these securities as collateral, and many firms were left without sufficient liquidity to meet demands for cash by customers and creditors. The asset write-downs and the liquidity constraints created great anxiety among market participants, who did not know whether the affected firms were solvent or insolvent. The Federal Reserve adopted a number of programs to provide liquidity to banks and some investment banks, but while that allowed them to meet withdrawals it did nothing to improve their capital positions or compensate for their operating losses. Also, the natural effect of a fall in asset values is to reduce liquidity; with asset values lower, leverage rises, and intermediaries pull back on their willingness to lend.

Through the early part of 2007 and into early 2008, the news was uniformly frightening for investors and creditors. Formerly healthy firms that held large portfolios of PMBS were illiquid or insolvent and were declaring bankruptcy. On August 9, 2007, BNP Paribas, a major French bank, suspended redemptions from funds it was managing because it could no longer be sure of the value of the PMBS assets that the funds were holding. This event shook the market and caused a sharp rise in indicators of market unease. Still, Ben Bernanke, the chair of the Federal Reserve, and Henry ("Hank") Paulson, the U.S. treasury secretary, continued to assure the markets that the problem of subprime mortgages was manageable and the current troubles only temporary. In substantial part their position was the result of the fact that neither they nor anyone else outside of the GSEs knew that Fannie and Freddie had not disclosed their NTM holdings in full.

In March 2008, however, Bear Stearns, the smallest of the five major Wall Street investment banks, was unable to fund its operations; it had lost the confidence of the market and was bleeding cash. Paulson and Bernanke were faced with a choice between letting Bear Stearns fail or taking extraordinary steps to rescue it. They chose the latter. Bear Stearns was sold to the giant bank JPMorgan Chase with the Federal Reserve providing $29 billion in financial support as an inducement to the acquiring bank. This was a fateful move.

THE ARRIVAL OF MORAL HAZARD

Although the Bear rescue temporarily calmed the markets, it created substantial moral hazard. Market participants now believed that the government had established a policy of rescuing large failing financial institutions. This perception substantially affected subsequent decisions. Firms with weak cash or capital positions did not take the opportunity to raise as much new equity as their parlous condition required; with the government likely to protect their creditors, there was little reason to dilute their shareholders further in order to foster creditor confidence. Firms that might have been willing to accept acquisition offers from stronger buyers thought they could drive harder bargains, and erstwhile buyers backed away. Potential acquirers for Lehman, noting the $29 billion support that JPMorgan Chase received from the Federal Reserve, were probably unwilling to buy a firm even larger than Bear with no financial support or risk-sharing from the U.S. government. Yet, the U.S. treasury secretary was telling anyone who would listen that there would be no government risk-sharing. Most specifically, the Reserve Primary Fund, a money market mutual fund, decided to retain Lehman Brothers commercial paper in its portfolio, probably assuming that if Lehman went under, its creditors, like Bear's, would be bailed out.

Paulson and Bernanke seemed not to recognize any of this. They apparently thought that during the relatively calm period after the Bear Stearns rescue, financial firms were taking adequate steps to prepare themselves for future challenges—improving their liquidity positions and selling shares to shore up their capital. To encourage these steps, Paulson decided at some point that the government would not bail out any other firms, and jawboned individual firms to sell more equity, but this had only a marginal effect; market participants had seen the government act and did not believe that it would allow a major financial firm to fail. In addition, Paulson's insistence, with Bernanke's apparent concurrence, that no government funds would again be employed for a Bear-like rescue, probably discouraged other potential buyers. Thus, the key government decision makers had very different perceptions of reality than market participants.

Despite the fact that both Paulson and Bernanke had extensive financial experience (Paulson in particular had been a chair of Goldman Sachs), neither seemed to understand that their strategy was both discouraging actions by weakened firms that would improve their capital position and making a buyer for Lehman more difficult to find. The moral hazard created by the rescue of Bear Stearns, plus the fact that the U.S. government had been willing to share JPMorgan's risk of acquiring Bear, trumped all.

2008: GROWING WEAKNESS AMONG THE LARGEST BANKS

Also during this period, the biggest banks were compelled to take back onto their balance sheets hundreds of billions of dollars in mortgage-backed securities, largely based on subprime loans, that the Federal Reserve had allowed them to park in off-balance-sheet asset-backed commercial paper (ABCP) conduits.[16] By 2007, the commercial paper issued by these conduits was the largest money market instrument in the U.S. financial markets; the second largest were Treasury bills, with about $940 billion outstanding.[17] The failure of these ABCP conduits is a major reason that the financial crisis was so severe, but it had little media coverage either at the time it occurred or since. One of the characteristic activities of banks is maturity transformation—turning short-term deposits into long-term assets like loans. It is highly risky because of the danger that depositors—if they lose confidence in a bank's soundness—may demand the return of their deposits when the bank has already lent the cash to borrowers. In this case, the bank must have a way of obtaining cash to meet withdrawals. This was one of the reasons for establishing the Federal Reserve System, which was intended to be a lender of last resort for solvent banks that needed cash in these circumstances. The theory was that the Federal Reserve would accept or "discount" (hence the "discount window") illiquid bank assets such as loans or securities in exchange for cash. When the cash crunch was over, the bank could redeem its assets from the Federal Reserve for the cash it received, plus interest. It turns out, however, that banks are reluctant to use the discount window, especially during periods of liquidity shortage, beause it signals weakness to the market.

One of the ways that banks are supposed to be able to withstand losses and withdrawals is to hold sufficient capital to allay depositors' fears about the banks' solvency and their ability to supply sufficient cash to meet withdrawals. That's why banks are required to hold capital. However, the ABCP conduits, which were not on the banks' balance sheets, had no capital; they attracted short-term investors, mostly money market mutual funds, because they were backed by liquidity guarantees from the associated banks. In other words, the Federal Reserve had permitted some of the largest U.S. banks to ignore the Basel capital requirements so they could engage in the risky but profitable business of maturity transformation, using short-term funding to support long-term assets. Former Treasury Secretary Geithner confirmed all this in his 2014 book *Stress Test* when he noted that Citibank "had stashed . . . $1.2 trillion in assets off its balance sheet in ways that allowed it to hold virtually no capital against losses in those assets . . . [and] financed some of its off-balance-sheet securities by issuing asset-backed commercial paper, while providing assurances that it would buy the paper if no one else wanted it. When markets ran from asset-backed commercial paper—the market shrank 30 percent in the second half of 2007—Citi had to shell out $25 billion to make good on its assurances."[18] Although $1.2 trillion is far larger than Citi's actual contribution to this activity, what Geithner didn't say is that the Federal Reserve (and probably the New York Federal Reserve Bank, which he headed) had permitted this evasion of the capital requirements otherwise applicable to banks.

When the mortgage market began to weaken in 2006 and 2007, many money market mutual funds refused to renew their loans by rolling over the commercial paper they had previously acquired. The only alternative for the banks was to take much of this paper back on their balance sheets, with an immediate adverse effect on their capital. So as the financial crisis approached in September 2008, the largest U.S. banks were already weakened and strapped for cash. As one academic paper noted: "Our main conclusion in this paper is that, somewhat surprisingly . . . the crisis had a profoundly negative effect on commercial banks because they had (in large part) insured outside investors in ABCP by providing explicit guarantees to conduits, which required the banks to pay off maturing ABCP at par."[19]

CHAOS

Thus, when Lehman Brothers was required to file for bankruptcy on September 15, chaos ensued. Market participants, investors, and creditors who had assumed that the government would not allow any large financial institution to fail now had to reevaluate all their counterparties. This outcome was not conducive to calm reflection. Uncertainty about the financial condition of many firms caused investors and creditors to seek cash. In turn, financial institutions, including the biggest banks, afraid of rumors that they were not able to meet the withdrawal requests of creditors and depositors, hoarded cash, not willing to lend to one another even overnight. This caused a virtual collapse of liquidity and the market panic that we know as the financial crisis.

Filling out the details about how the government's housing policies led to the crisis will be the principal focus of the balance of this book. I will show that the 2008 financial crisis would not have occurred without the government's housing polices, which fostered the creation of 31 million NTMs. Three-quarters of these deficient mortgages were on the books of government agencies, and their failure in unprecedented numbers caused housing prices to fall throughout the United States. The sudden decline in housing values immediately affected the value of mortgages, particularly those—with a value of approximately $2 trillion—that were held by private financial institutions, such as banks, in the form of PMBS. This process would not have been as frightening, and might not have induced a panic, were it not for mark-to-market accounting, which required financial institutions to take substantial asset write-downs and operating losses that sharply affected their earnings and their capital positions.

Ultimately, there was nothing exceptional about the government actions that led to the crisis. They were disastrous, to be sure, but also to be expected when the government controls the distribution of an important good like housing. Daily, we see how difficult it is to stop government spending. Equally if not more difficult is preventing the government, once it controls an activity, from using it to provide benefits to favored constituencies and then charging the taxpayers for the inevitable losses. As this book is written, there is a debate in Washington about reform of the housing finance system. Fannie and Freddie, which were driven into insolvency by the government's policies, will probably not survive. But, as shown in chapter 14, many participants in the debate want to erect another government-controlled system in their place. If this $11 trillion plaything is not taken out of the government's hands, another financial crisis awaits us in the future.

By 2010, many of the strongest supporters of affordable-housing as enforced by HUD had recognized their error. In an interview on Larry Kudlow's CNBC television program in late August, Representative Barney Frank (D-Mass.)—the former chair of the House Financial Services Committee and previously the loudest congressional advocate for affordable-housing—conceded that he had made a mistake: "I hope by next year we'll have abolished Fannie and Freddie . . . it was a great mistake to push lower-income people into housing they couldn't afford and couldn't really handle once they had it." He then added, "I had been too sanguine about Fannie and Freddie."[20] Barney Frank has taken a lot of criticism for his unqualified support for the affordable-housing goals during much of his career in Congress, but at least he had the courage and intellectual honesty to admit in the end that he had erred. As we will see, others have not. And as discussed fully in chapter 14, the supporters of weakened or nonexistent mortgage underwriting standards are trying again.

Succeeding chapters will fill out with data and examples the points made in this Introduction. Chapter 2 outlines the key differences between prime and nontraditional mortgages, and why these differences are important. Chapter 3 discusses the report of the Financial Crisis Inquiry Commission, of which I was a member and from which I dissented, and details why other explanations of the crisis are deficient. Chapter 4 is a short history of government housing policy since the Depression era and the significant change that occurred with the adoption of the affordable-housing goals in 1992. Chapters 5 through 8 explain how the affordable-housing goals forced a decline in mortgage underwriting standards that spread to the wider market, show that this was a deliberate policy of the Department of Housing and Urban Development under both the Clinton and George W. Bush administrations, and make clear that Fannie and Freddie led the market into perdition because of the goals and not for profit or market share. Chapters 9 through 12 discuss factors that exacerbated the problems initially created by degraded underwriting standards, particularly the role of the housing price bubble, mark-to-market accounting, and the susceptibility of a securities market to panic behavior. Finally, chapters 13 and 14 show how the bumbling of government officials made a bad situation considerably worse, and why the false narrative about the causes of the crisis has both saddled the financial system with the Dodd-Frank Act and made it likely that the same mistakes in housing policy that were responsible for the crisis will be repeated in the future.

2

The Difference between Prime and Nontraditional Mortgages

The Importance of Sound Underwriting Standards

> First, we must recognize that the financial crisis was triggered by a reckless departure from tried and true, common-sense loan underwriting practices.
>
> Traditional mortgage lending worked so well in the past because lenders required sizeable down payments, solid borrower credit histories, proper income documentation, and sufficient income to make regular payments at the fully-indexed rate of the loan. Not only were these bedrock principles relaxed in the run-up to the crisis, but they were frequently relaxed all at once in the same loans in a practice regulators refer to as "risk layering."
>
> [T]he long-term credit performance of a portfolio of mortgage loans can only be as sound as the underwriting practices used to originate those loans.
>
> SHEILA BAIR, remarks at the
> Wharton School, June 18, 2010

This chapter will explain the crucial relationship between mortgage underwriting standards and mortgage defaults. After years of experience with good and bad results, it is clear beyond doubt that good underwriting standards as outlined in this chapter produce a stable housing market during normal (non-stressed) times, while deviations from these standards produce instability and high rates of mortgage default. With this background, a decision to loosen under-writing standards as a matter of deliberate government policy was a serious error.

The difference in performance between a traditional prime mort-gage and a nontraditional mortgage, or NTM, is crucial to the ar-gument presented in this book. Traditional prime mortgages have historically had low rates of default. NTMs, on the other hand, usu-ally have rates of default that are multiples of the prime loan default rate. In periods of economic stress, such as the one that occurred in the period between 2007 and 2009, even prime mortgage defaults might substantially exceed 1 percent, but the performance of NTMs became disproportionately worse. That difference was crucial be-tween 2007 and 2009, when the large number of NTMs in the finan-cial system began to default in unprecedented numbers.

In this book, I will use data developed by Edward Pinto, my col-league at the American Enterprise Institute, on the number of NTMs outstanding in the U.S. financial system on June 30, 2008, immedi-ately before the financial crisis. Pinto's data and analysis are available on the American Enterprise Institute website in "Three Studies of Subprime and Alt-A Loans in the US Mortgage Market."[1] These stud-ies cover the total number of NTMs outstanding on June 30, 2008, the total number held by government agencies on that date, and the increase in the number of NTMs between 1992 and 2008.

Pinto's analysis establishes the total number of NTMs outstand-ing on June 30, 2008, by adding together two separate categories of subprime loans—those identified by lenders as subprime (6.7 mil-lion), which Pinto called "self-denominated subprime," and those made to borrowers with FICO credit scores of 660 or less (9.2 mil-lion), which Pinto—following the definition used by the U.S. bank regulators—called "subprime by characteristics." (The support for counting loans with FICO scores of 660 or less as subprime is cov-ered later in this chapter.) These totaled 15.9 million. Pinto then added the total number of Alt-A loans outstanding on June 30, 2008 (15.3 million), which consisted of 10.4 million to which Fannie and Freddie were exposed on June 30, 2008, 1.4 million insured or held by the FHA or the Veterans Administration, and 3.4 million self-denominated or other conventional Alt-A loans, for a total of 15.2

million. The total came to 31 million. This should be compared with Table 1.1, which combined subprime and Alt-A loans by entity exposed. With approximately 55 million mortgages in the United States on June 30, 2008, NTMs made up 57 percent of all U.S. mortgages outstanding.[2]

Pinto followed the same procedures for establishing the total exposure of government agencies to NTMs, concluding that on June 30, 2008, all government agencies as a group were exposed to 24 million NTMs (see Table 1.1), or 76 percent of all the NTMs outstanding. Of that 24 million, Fannie and Freddie had the greatest exposure—16.5 million loans, or 69 percent.[3]

These numbers are likely to be much higher than most observers of the mortgage markets have assumed, even six years after the financial crisis. The reasons for this discrepancy were noted in the previous chapter, and the consequences are covered extensively in chapter 10. Fannie and Freddie did not begin to fully disclose their exposure to NTMs until after they had been taken over by a government conservator in 2008. Given their size and the number of NTMs they held or had guaranteed, their failure to provide a true accounting had a profound effect on the severity of the financial crisis. Before the crisis, analysts, regulators, academic commentators, rating agencies, and even the Federal Reserve were seriously misled about the scope of the NTM problem, believing that it was much smaller, and that the number of traditional prime mortgages outstanding was much larger, than in fact they were. As a result, the markets were shocked by the number of mortgage defaults when they eventually began to appear in 2007 and 2008.

THE TRADITIONAL MORTGAGE

Specialists in mortgage underwriting have settled on three fundamental standards that are used to classify mortgages as prime or non-prime—the loan-to-value (LTV) ratio, the debt-to-income (DTI) ratio, and the borrower's credit record. The LTV ratio refers to the size of the loan in relation to the value of the home. For example, an $80,000 loan on a $100,000 home has an 80 percent LTV ratio. That means the buyer of the home was required to contribute the

$20,000 difference, called the down payment. With respect to home purchase loans, the LTV ratio and down payment are often used interchangeably, because they are just two sides of the same coin. For refinances, the relevant number is the homeowner's remaining equity after the mortgage is closed. The DTI ratio is the percentage of all the homebuyer's income that is consumed by his or her debts, also after the mortgage is closed, and is considered a good rule of thumb for determining whether a borrower has the financial capacity to meet the mortgage obligation in the future. The borrower's credit score refers to the borrower's record of meeting his or her financial obligations in the past. Since the mid-1990s, a credit score developed by the Fair Isaac Corporation (and thus known as the FICO score) has become the standard for measuring a borrower's willingness or propensity to pay.

In March 1992, Fannie Mae completed a statistically valid study (the Fannie Random Study) of approximately 26,000 randomly selected loans in its portfolio of loans acquired between 1988 and 1991.[4] The objective was to determine the borrower characteristics that were correlated with the presence or absence of serious delinquencies. The study showed that 94 percent of the loans had LTV ratios or equity that corresponded to at least a 10 percent investment in the home, and only 6 percent had LTV ratios of greater than 90 percent. Total DTI ratios were also low; 85 percent of borrowers had a total DTI ratio no higher than 38 percent. Credit records were excellent; although FICO scores were not in use at this point, more than 98 percent of the borrowers had no late mortgage payments in any year, and 99.5 percent had at most one late mortgage payment. Nonmortgage credit records were also excellent, with 85 percent having no more than two late payments. Of the 26,000 loans reviewed, only 175 loans had serious delinquencies (the usual precursor to default), or .68 percent. As noted earlier, even with these underwriting standards—which are decried today as an impossible hurdle for would-be homebuyers—the homeownership rate in the United States during these years hovered around 64 percent, just about where it is in 2014 after the experiment with the affordable-housing goals, the collapse of the great 1997–2007 housing bubble, the foreclosure of at least 5 million mortgages, and the financial crisis.

The Fannie Random Study is probably as accurate a description of traditional prime mortgages available anywhere at the time, and a good indication of what Fannie's mortgage exposure looked like prior to 1992. It's highly likely that Freddie's was the same. Of course, the GSEs were not exposed to all the mortgages in the United States, so the Random Study might have exaggerated the quality of all mortgages outstanding before 1992. However, as Thomas LaMalfa noted in 1989,[5] Fannie and Freddie were the standard-setters for the residential mortgage market, so it is unlikely that the rest of the market held prime mortgages that diverged very far from the GSEs' standards. Serious delinquencies on conventional loans, as reported by the Mortgage Bankers Association (MBA), averaged 1.1 percent over the period 1982–1991.[6] Because about 10 percent of the loans in this category were probably subprime, the serious delinquency rate on prime conventional loans was almost certainly below 1 percent, which also suggests that most other lenders were using the same underwriting standards as the GSEs.

THE PRIME MORTGAGE

The traditional mortgage was also a prime mortgage, which had a default rate of less than 1 percent under normal market conditions. The reason that prime loans perform better than NTMs—that is, have a lower rate of default than NTMs—is that prime loans conform to the more stringent underwriting standards outlined above.

To mortgage underwriting professionals, the three standards are known as the Three Cs of credit—collateral (LTV ratio or down payment), capacity (the DTI ratio), and character (the FICO score). Perhaps not altogether surprisingly, the borrower's character (that is, willingness or propensity to meet financial obligations) is the most sensitive of these standards; indeed, the discussion below shows that a mortgage cannot be a prime mortgage if the borrower's FICO score is 660 or less, but all three of the standards must be within a certain range before the mortgage will have a default rate of 1 percent or less in normal times and thus qualify as prime. Mortgages that fall outside that range would be considered non-prime or NTMs.

The predictive power of FICO scores and the significance of the

660 dividing line between prime and subprime loans were demonstrated in 1996 as part of a comprehensive study by the Federal Reserve.[7] Table 2.1, taken from that study, shows the results. When a borrower has a FICO score above 660 (the median FICO score in the United States is 720), the probability of default varies modestly with other factors, such as income and LTV ratio (the DTI ratio was not a part of this study). For example, the table sets an index of 1 for the likelihood of default for a loan that has a FICO score greater than 660, an LTV ratio lower than 81 percent (a down payment of 20 percent), and a borrower's income of any size. Then, varying these parameters, the table shows that the likelihood of default is 3.3 times greater—no matter what the borrower's income—if the LTV ratio is 81 percent or more (that is, the down payment is less than 20 percent) and the FICO score is more than 660. This is a substantial difference, attributable to the lower down payment. However, if the same loan (income of any size and LTV ratio greater than 81 percent) were made to a borrower with a FICO score of 621–660, the chances of a default are more than 15 times greater, and if the borrower's FICO score is less than 621, the chances of default are 47 times greater. This study, then, demonstrates the extraordinary sensitivity of the FICO score and the fact that there is a substantial difference between a FICO score greater than 660 and one 660 or below.

Five years later, perhaps relying on this data, U.S. bank regulators defined a subprime loan with reference to a FICO score of less than 660. In a 2001 ruling, the bank regulators declared that a loan was subprime if it was made to a borrower whose FICO credit score was 660 or less *or* whose DTI ratio was 50 percent or more after the mortgage loan was made.[8] The rule made clear that neither deficiency could be corrected by any other element of the loan, such as the size of the down payment:

The term "subprime" refers to the credit characteristics of individual borrowers. Subprime borrowers typically have weakened credit histories that include payment delinquencies, and possibly more severe problems such as charge-offs,

TABLE 2.1. Results of a 1996 Federal Reserve study of FICO scores

Indexed values
(1 = any income and LTV <81% and FICO >660)

Borrower income[a] (% of area median income[b])	Credit score[c]		
	Low (<621 FICO)	Medium (621–660 FICO)	High (>660 FICO)
All loans			
Less than 80	36.8	13.9	2.2
80 to 120	35.3	10.2	1.7
120 or more	31.1	8.9	1.5
All	33.9	10.3	1.5
Loan-to-value ratio less than 81 percent			
Less than 80	32.0	11.0	1.8
80 to 120	29.0	7.4	1.1
120 or more	22.0	6.7	0.7
All	26.9	7.9	1.0
Loan-to-value ratio 81 percent or more			
Less than 80	51.4	23.0	4.4
80 to 120	47.4	15.8	3.6
120 or more	46.7	12.9	2.8
All	47.6	15.3	3.3

Sources: Freddie Mac. Adapted from Robert B. Avery et al., "Credit Risk, Credit Scoring, and the Performance of Home Mortgages," *Federal Reserve Bulletin* (July 1996), http://www.federalreserve.gov/pubs/ bulletin/1996/796lead.pdf.

Note: The loans are for single-family owner-occupied properties and were purchased by Freddie Mac in the first six months of 1994. Index of foreclosure rate covers loans foreclosed by December 31, 1995; the index sets the average foreclosure rate equal to 1 for loans with borrower generic credit bureau scores of more than 660 and loan-to-value ratios of less than 81 percent.

[a]Borrower income is as of the time of loan origination.

[b]Area median income is the median family income of the property's MSA or, if location is not in an MSA, the median family income of the property's county.

[c]The credit score ranges correspond to generic credit bureau scores as follows: low = less than 621, medium = 621–660, and high = more than 660.

judgments, and bankruptcies. They may also display reduced repayment capacity as measured by credit scores, debt-to-income ratios, or other criteria that may encompass borrowers with incomplete credit histories. Subprime loans are loans to borrowers displaying one or more of these characteristics at the time of origination or purchase. Such loans have a higher risk of default than loans to prime borrowers. Generally, subprime borrowers will display a range of credit characteristics that may include one or more of the following:

- Two or more 30-day delinquencies in the last 12 months, or one or more 60-day delinquencies in the last 24 months;

- Judgment, foreclosure, repossession, or charge-off in the prior 24 months;

- Bankruptcy in the last 5 years;

- Relatively high default probability evidenced by, for example, *a credit bureau risk score (FICO) of 660 or below* (depending on the product/collateral), or other bureau or proprietary scores with an equivalent default probability likelihood; and/or

- *Debt service-to-income of 50% or greater,* or otherwise limited ability to cover family living expenses after deducting total monthly debt-service requirements from monthly income [emphasis added].[9]

Currently available data strongly supports the validity of this judgment, as well as the Federal Reserve's 1996 study. In March 2013, Freddie Mac released a dataset consisting of 15 million fixed-rate 30-year fully documented mortgages (the "Freddie dataset") that it had acquired between 1999 and 2011.[10] Fannie released a dataset several months later, but Fannie's data was less detailed, making it less useful for analysis than Freddie's. Nevertheless, because Fannie's and Freddie's acquisitions so closely paralleled one another, it is possible to estimate the composition of Fannie's exposures during the same time period. As large as it was, the Freddie dataset was incomplete, consisting of only 53 percent of the mortgages Freddie acquired during that thirteen-year period.[11] For some reason, Freddie omitted from its dataset loans such as adjustable-rate mortgages and the mortgages it acquired through special branded programs to comply with the affordable-housing goals. That would include, among others, an unknown number of subprime and Alt-A loans, non-amortizing mortgages, investor loans, and loans without full documentation. The result is that the loans Freddie disclosed are very likely the best loans available in the market during that period. Analyzing those loans permits us to demonstrate what factors will or will not produce a prime loan—that is, a loan with an incidence of default that is less than 1 percent in normal market conditions.

Table 2.2, prepared from the 1999 cohort of loans in the Freddie dataset, shows that the triad of underwriting standards that were part of a traditional home purchase mortgage—a FICO score above 660, an LTV ratio of no more than 90 percent (that is, a down payment of at least 10 percent), and a DTI ratio of no more than 38 percent—produced an incidence of default for home purchase loans of .55 percent in normal times. The 1999 cohort was chosen because that was the least stressful year in the dataset and the closest to the stable market that prevailed before 1992. It ends in 2007 because that was the last year before the onset of the worst part of the financial crisis. In each year after 1999, the housing bubble grew larger, and the quality of mortgages deteriorated further. The .55 percent default rate is what one would expect for a traditional prime mortgage in normal (not stressful) times, and it is clear from the data in the table that only by keeping all three elements of the triad within the stated limits is the lowest incidence of default achieved. If any one of the elements of the triad is outside the limits, the incidence of default increases, in some cases dramatically. It is important, in reviewing this table, to keep in mind that these are Freddie's best loans and do not include the loans they bought under specially branded programs in order to meet the affordable-housing goals. If those loans had been included, the default rates for the categories with elements outside the prime triad would be substantially higher. In addition, the default experience of these loans was improved somewhat by the growth of the housing bubble during the 1999–2007 period.

Among other things, Table 2.2 shows—with reference to actual market results—that the bank regulators' conclusion was correct: if the FICO score is 660 or less, the loan is a subprime loan, no matter

TABLE 2.2. Prime vs. non-prime default rates through 2007 on fully documented, Freddie Mac 30-year fixed-rate home purchase loans acquired in 1999

Loan type	Default rate (percentage)	Default rate as a multiple of prime default rate
A. **Prime** (>660 FICO, ≤90% LTV ratio, ≤38% DTI ratio)	0.55	1
B. **Non-prime** (missing one or more key elements of the prime loan triad)		
1. DTI ratio >38%, but prime-level down payments and FICOs	0.98	1.8
2. LTV ratio >90%, but prime-level FICOs and DTI ratios	2.24	4.1
3. Weighted average of all non-prime (number of loans missing one or more elements of the prime loan triad)	3.01	5.5
4. DTI ratio >38%, with non-prime down payments and/or FICOs	4.25	7.7
5. FICO <660, but prime-level down payments and DTI ratios	4.32	7.9
6. LTV ratio >90%, with non-prime FICOs and/or DTI ratios	5.26	9.6
7. FICO <660, with non-prime down payments and/or DTI ratios	7.00	12.7

Source: Freddie Mac dataset.

what the other elements of the triad are (see lines B.5 and B.7 in the table). The Freddie dataset also provides evidence, discussed in chapter 8, that the reduced underwriting standards the GSEs adopted in order to comply with the affordable-housing goals spread to the wider market in the period between 1999 and 2007. Recalling that the loans in the Freddie dataset were not all the loans Freddie acquired for compliance with affordable-housing goals, it is remarkable how far the market's underwriting standards had eroded as early as 1999. Among the loans Freddie disclosed, 16 percent had FICO scores of 660 or less, which would automatically score them as subprime according to the bank regulators and the Federal Reserve's 1996 study; 31 percent had DTI ratios above 38 percent; and another 30 percent had LTV ratios higher than 90 percent. If these deficiencies were present in the best mortgages Freddie made in 1999, one can only imagine how many NTMs were in the 47 percent of Freddie's 1999 cohort that were not disclosed. If we consider all the purchase loans in the dataset, rather than just the 1999 cohort, the number of NTMs are these: 626,724 (15 percent) were subprime because they had FICO scores less than 660; 1,631,386 (39 percent) had DTI ratios greater than 38 percent; and 1,066,485 (26 percent) had LTV ratios higher than 90 percent. And these, recall, were Freddie's best loans. At the very least, these deficiencies indicate that the degraded mortgage underwriting standards that the GSEs were compelled to adopt by the affordable-housing goals had not been confined to low-income borrowers. This issue is covered more fully in chapter 8.

It is worth noting that the Dodd-Frank Act tasked several agencies (the Federal Reserve, the Comptroller of the Currency, the Federal Deposit Insurance Corporation [FDIC], the SEC, the Federal Housing Finance Agency [FHFA], and the Department of Housing and Urban Development [HUD]) with the responsibility to develop a "qualified residential mortgage" (QRM)—that is, a mortgage of such quality that it would present a very low risk of default. To meet this standard, the agencies originally developed a mortgage with the same three underwriting constituents that had characterized the traditional prime mortgage: a substantial down payment on purchase money loans (20 percent), a DTI ratio after the mortgage of 36 percent, and a strong credit history (the agencies did not use the FICO score per se). However, succeeding events show that the lessons of the financial crisis had not been learned. The proposed rule was met with a sustained outcry from what might be called the "government mortgage complex"—realtors, banks, and community activists—who contended that the down payment and other provisions would deprive low-income borrowers and others of a chance to buy homes. Lawmakers who had voted for the QRM quickly reversed themselves in the face of this opposition and called on the agencies to repropose a more lenient rule.

In August 2013, accordingly, the agencies succumbed to this pressure and published a new proposal for the QRM. This one abandoned any reference to the traditional underwriting standards for a prime or low-risk loan and adopted as the standard a minimum mortgage standard that had been proposed in January 2013 by the Consumer Financial Protection Bureau. This standard did not require any particular down payment or credit record, and the agencies admitted in their reproposal that, by 2012, mortgages meeting this standard between 2005 and 2008 had experienced serious delinquency or default at a 23 percent rate.[12] The agencies also made their motivations clear when they noted that they were "concerned about the prospect of imposing further constraints on mortgage credit availability at this time, especially as such constraints might disproportionately affect groups that have historically been disadvantaged in the mortgage market, such as lower-income, minority, or first-time home buyers."[13] The rule was finalized in October 2014. In other words, the underlying ideas of the affordable-housing goals were going to be incorporated into the rules under Dodd-Frank, despite language in the act that had attempted to create a higher mortgage underwriting standard for at least some limited number of loans. Chapter 14 discusses how the failure to understand the lessons of the 2008 financial crisis will eventually bring about another.

Finally, the Freddie dataset shows that, as long as the FICO score exceeds 660, it is possible to create prime loans that have higher LTV ratios (i.e., lower down payments) and higher DTI ratios than shown in Table 2.2. For example, a loan with an LTV ratio as high as 95 percent can be a prime loan—with a rate of default no greater than 1 percent—if the borrower's FICO score is 720 (the median FICO score) or above, and his or her DTI ratio is no greater than 43 percent. But the basic point, and the dividing line between prime and subprime loans that will be used in this book, is that a FICO score of 660 and below denotes a subprime loan—a mortgage that would be considered an NTM.

THE NONTRADITIONAL MORTGAGE

There are two types of NTMs: subprime mortgages—those denominated as subprime and those made to borrowers with FICO scores of 660 or below—and Alt-A mortgages. As discussed above, a subprime mortgage is one made to a borrower who has a FICO score of 660 or less. An Alt-A loan, on the other hand, is considered a nontraditional loan because of deficiencies in the loan itself. For example, the loan might have a 3 percent down payment, no down payment, or inadequate or no documentation; it may be interest only, have a negative amortization feature, or be reset to a higher adjustable rate after a short "teaser" period; or the borrower might be an investor instead of the person who will occupy the home. All of these characteristics, among others, so substantially increase the likelihood of default that an Alt-A loan cannot be considered either a traditional mortgage or a prime mortgage. In Table 2.2, for example, a loan with an LTV ratio greater than 90 percent had a rate of default four times greater than a prime mortgage, even when the FICO score and DTI ratio were at prime levels. That's why, before 1992, subprime and Alt-A loans didn't meet GSE requirements and were considered NTMs.

With the validation of the prime mortgage triad, we now have a good definition of what a prime or traditional mortgage should look like, and this allows us to count up the number of loans in the financial system that did not meet this test in 2008. From this accounting we are able to show with some precision the relative importance of the contributions of the government and the private sector to the number of NTMs outstanding in the United States before the financial crisis produced a full-fledged panic in September 2008.

The affordable-housing requirements imposed on Fannie Mae and Freddie Mac, beginning in 1992, forced them to abandon their traditional focus on prime mortgages and to begin accepting NTMs. As the affordable-housing goals increased over time, these loans not only weakened the GSEs, eventually causing their insolvency, but spread NTMs to the rest of the market. By 2008, as noted earlier, 57 percent of all mortgages in the United States—31 million loans— were NTMs (see Table 1.1) with far higher rates of default than prime mortgages. These facts made the U.S. financial system extraordinarily vulnerable to the collapse of the housing bubble in 2007.

3

The Financial Crisis Inquiry Commission Report and Other Explanations for the Crisis

Why Conventional Explanations for the Crisis Are Inadequate

> It is not difficult to deprive the great majority of independent thought. But the minority who will retain an inclination to criticize must also be silenced. . . . Public criticism or even expressions of doubt must be suppressed because they tend to weaken public support.
>
> FRIEDRICH A. VON HAYEK, *The Road to Serfdom*

Dozens of books and countless articles and academic papers have been written about the financial crisis. This is as it should be. The crisis is seen today as a major event in the history of economics and finance. It will be the subject of discussion and debate—and will influence the actions of the government and U.S. voters—for years to come. However, none of the books and commentaries about the crisis has included or addressed what I believe is the central fact of that momentous event: on June 30, 2008, before the crisis began in earnest, there were at least 31 million nontraditional mortgages (NTMs)—57 percent of all mortgages—in the U.S. financial system. How this happened has never been explained, and in most cases the question is never even asked. In this chapter, I will first review the report of the Financial Crisis Inquiry Commission, from which I dissented, and then discuss the other major theories that have been advanced by government officials, commentators, scholars, and others as explanations for the crisis.

The ferocity of the left in defending Fannie Mae, Freddie Mac, and the government's housing policies before 2008 is sometimes shocking, especially when even Barney Frank has given up. It makes you wonder why this is so important to them. They have no data, no policy arguments, just a virulent denial that anything other than the private financial sector could possibly be responsible for the financial crisis.[1] Barry Ritholtz is one of these GSE defenders, and in November 2011 he wrote a piece for the *Washington Post* titled "What Caused the Financial Crisis? The Big Lie Goes Viral." It's as puzzling as it is pathetic that a rather dry policy argument—although important for future housing policy—would stimulate such a reaction, but Ritholtz is representative of several others when he invokes Goebbels to deny that government housing policy caused the financial crisis: "They are Winning. Thanks to endless repetition of the Big Lie. A Big Lie is so colossal that no one would believe that someone could have the impudence to distort the truth so infamously."[2]

What set off this absurd tirade was a statement by then New York mayor Michael Bloomberg, who stepped outside the left's approved range of opinion to suggest that the conventional view of the financial crisis was wrong. Here's Ritholtz again: "The Big Lie made a surprise appearance Tuesday when New York Mayor Michael Bloomberg, responding to a question about Occupy Wall Street, stunned observers by exonerating Wall Street: 'It was not the banks that created the mortgage crisis. It was, plain and simple, Congress who forced everybody to go and give mortgages to people who were on the cusp.'"[3]

The mayor may have overstated his case a bit, but it was heartening to see that an idea that has received very little attention in the media has at least gotten past the blocking and tackling of the *New York Times* and into the informed opinion of Michael Bloomberg. No wonder Ritholtz is worried. This leakage is a very bad sign for his side. Up to now, almost everyone with a media megaphone has been kept safely within the consensus view: that the financial crisis was caused by something other than government housing policy. Indeed, one reason for the deranged reaction to Bloomberg's anodyne statement may be the fear that people may actually become interested in the question. One way to prevent this might be to tell them it is just a Big Lie! Nothing to see here, folks; just move along.

The other frequently mentioned causes should be very familiar to readers—they are cited regularly in the media with little or no suggestion that they are only theories—but on close examination, which almost never occurs, they turn out to be deficient.

The story of the financial crisis is a prime illustration of why the study of history is often so contentious and why revisionist histories are so easy to construct. John F. Kennedy once related a story about World War I, in which Prince Bülow, the former German chancellor, asked his successor, "How did it all happen?" To which the reply, in the midst of the war, was, "Ah, if only one knew." The difficult task in history is to discern which, among a welter of possible causes, are the significant factors—the ones without which history would have been different. Using this standard, it is the thesis of this book that the 2008 financial crisis would not have occurred *but for* the housing policies of the U.S. government between 1992 and 2008. The basis for this conclusion is summarized in chapter 1. To support this proposition, however, a review of other theories about the causes of the crisis is necessary. There is some truth in all of them, but, as outlined below, none of them alone or in combination with others can fully explain why the crisis occurred.

THE REPORT OF THE FINANCIAL CRISIS
INQUIRY COMMISSION

Any discussion of the causes of the 2008 financial crisis would have to begin with the report of the Financial Crisis Inquiry Commission (FCIC), a ten-member group appointed by Congress in July 2009 to investigate the causes of the crisis and report its findings to Congress, the president, and the American people. I was a member of the FCIC, appointed by the then minority leader of the House of Representatives, John Boehner. Six of the members were appointed by the Democratic leaders in the House and Senate, and four were appointed by their Republican counterparts. The chair was Phil Angelides, a confidant of House Speaker Nancy Pelosi and a former Democratic candidate for governor of California. Angelides had a background in real estate development and had been the California state treasurer. The vice chair of the commission was Bill Thomas, a former Republican congressman from California who had been the chair of the House Ways and Means Committee when he served in Congress.

If the Democratic Congress really wanted a thorough or unbiased investigation of the financial crisis, it was a mistake to give one party a majority on the commission, at least without providing for an allocation of staff to the Republicans. Angelides, as the chair (apparently with the concurrence of Thomas), made no attempt to provide staff specifically to assist the Republican minority, and as far as I could tell, only one staff member out of almost eighty was assigned specifically to assist the Republicans on the commission, and none was assigned to represent the views of the Republican members in such vital activities as interviewing witnesses, conducting research, and drafting the report. This is not to say that the staff was biased. Many of the staff members I got to know were working hard to do a thorough and objective study, but they were led from the beginning to consider only one theory—that the crisis was caused by the risk-taking and greed of the private sector and could have been prevented by more energetic regulators with more regulatory control of the financial system.

For much of the commission's life, the executive director had been on loan from the Federal Reserve, which—along with other bank regulators—should have been a major target of the FCIC's investigation. The Federal Reserve was the closest thing we had at the time to a systemic regulator. The agency has always had exclusive regulatory jurisdiction over bank holding companies (companies that control banks) and since the enactment of the Gramm-Leach-Bliley Act in 1999 the Federal Reserve has had authority to oversee the entire regulated financial system; if any regulator missed excessive risk-taking by private-sector firms it was the Federal Reserve. It also had a huge and high-quality economics staff that should have been able to see the dangers in the housing system before anyone else—especially the development of the housing bubble. Although the Federal Reserve was mildly criticized in the FCIC's report, the reasons for its lapses were never explained. This absence of serious blame enabled Congress to reward the Federal Reserve—despite its obvious failures—with significant new powers in the Dodd-Frank Act.

Angelides controlled the writing and conclusions of the report; the Republican-appointed commissioners never had a voice in the direction of the investigation and were seldom informed about the work of the staff. If the only information I had about the causes of the financial crisis came from the media at the time and what the FCIC staff supplied to the commissioners, I probably would also have concluded, as the other commissioners did, that the government's housing policies and Fannie and Freddie had little or no role in the financial crisis. But fortunately I had access to several memoranda supplied to the FCIC by my AEI colleague Edward Pinto. These memoranda, described more fully below, contained well-documented information about the role of the affordable-housing goals in the deterioration of mortgage underwriting standards in the United States after 1992. Despite many efforts, I was unable to get the leadership of the commission to take this information seriously. If a Republican staff group had been appointed to participate in the interviews, research, and drafting process, the normal adversarial process would have ensured a more objective outcome of the commission's work; alternative explanations for the crisis might have been explored, and different conclusions—including the possibility that the financial crisis would not have occurred but for the government's housing policies—might have been drawn.

To be sure, there were partisan-based obstacles that a restructuring of the FCIC's staff might not have remedied. The Department of Housing and Urban Development (HUD) in the Bush administration had pursued the affordable-housing goals as aggressively as President Clinton's HUD, and it's entirely possible that partisan loyalties would have prevented a Republican staff and the other Republican commissioners from looking deeply into government housing policies. But with the limited information made available to them by the staff, the Republican commissioners never even had the chance.

Although the majority report was more than five hundred pages long, its analysis of the causes of the financial crisis added little if anything to the conventional views that were common in the media.[4] The majority concluded—very much in tune with the views of President Obama and the Democratic members of Congress—that the financial crisis could have been avoided through better regulation. "We conclude this financial crisis was avoidable" was the key finding of the majority report. "The crisis was the result of human action and inaction," it summarized, "not of Mother Nature or computer models gone haywire."

> The captains of finance and the public stewards of our financial system ignored warnings and failed to question, understand, and manage evolving risks within a system essential to the well-being of the American public. Theirs was a big miss, not a stumble. While the business cycle cannot be repealed, a crisis of this magnitude need not have occurred. To paraphrase Shakespeare, the fault lies not in the stars, but in us.[5]

In one sense, there is no arguing with this conclusion. There were, as there always are, multiple "failures of human action," by regulators, commercial banks, investment banks, mortgage originators, participants in the derivatives market, lenders, and rating agencies, among others. These were fulsomely detailed in the majority's report, usually supported by after-the-fact interviews of witnesses who were not put under oath, rather than through documents or data. Indeed, most of the report is based on statements made to the staff in more than seven hundred interviews. There was no adversarial process in the interviews that permitted verification of the accuracy of witness statements or their qualifications to make these statements. As far as I could tell from the witness interviews I was able to get, no one conducted any cross-examinations, and no one used any documents to question the witnesses' statements or otherwise test their veracity. The process simply validated the conventional view of the financial crisis that the media had already accepted and repeated. Witnesses testifying in these circumstances were unlikely to disagree with the consensus, and if they did their disagreement was never recorded in the majority report. Other than the few public hearings, the commissioners were never notified of who was being interviewed or given an opportunity to attend. Essential contextual details that would determine whether a particular interviewee had actual knowledge of facts, was qualified to express the opinion that was quoted, or was biased, were never provided to the members of the commission, who did not even see the vast majority of these quotes until they appeared in the report.

The errors that brought about the crisis, the report argued, could have been prevented by a more vigilant set of government regulators—with additional powers where their authority was deficient. This dovetailed precisely with the conclusions the Democratic Congress and the Obama administration wanted—fully supporting the enactment of the Dodd-Frank Act, which imposed heavy new regulation on virtually every part of the financial system. It is telling that Congress adopted the act in July 2010, six months *before* the FCIC's report was issued, a clear demonstration that the Democratic Congress knew well in advance exactly what this well-controlled commission would say.

As a diagnosis of the causes of the crisis, the majority report was seriously deficient. There is no question that, if regulators could have foreseen the crisis, they could have prevented it. But regulators are not omniscient; while they sometimes have better information than the general public, they have no special powers of foresight. Moreover, in this case the regulators did not have the facts they would have needed in order to decide that subprime mortgage lending should be reined in. The Federal Reserve had the *authority* to stop the activities of mortgage originators as well as banking organizations, and the Securities and Exchange Commission (SEC) could have intervened in the activities of the large Wall Street investment banks that also suffered major losses. But neither of them, as we will see, could have foretold from the information available to them that a massive financial collapse was looming in the immediate future. The fact that Fannie and Freddie had not fully disclosed the scope of their exposure to NTMs was never discovered by the commission, although that was one of the principal reasons that the regulators, as well as others, were shocked by the number of mortgage defaults that occurred when the housing bubble began to deflate.

Indeed, as discussed in chapter 10, a careful study of the period leading up to the crisis shows that, because of the GSEs' failure to disclose the full extent of their purchases of NTMs, literally no one, including the Federal Reserve with its vast data resources, had sufficient information about the number of NTMs in the financial system to recognize that an unprecedented torrent of mortgage defaults were inevitable when housing prices stopped growing. There were warnings—there always are, just as there are experts who contend that the warnings are wrong. To criticize regulators for failing to act, when no one, including the regulators, had the data that indicated a serious problem, is nothing more than 20/20 hindsight.

Nevertheless, quite apart from whether the regulators were really at fault, the FCIC majority concluded that the activities of the private sector were the *only* significant cause of the crisis. They blamed "dramatic failures of corporate governance and risk management . . . a combination of excessive borrowing, risky investments, and lack of transparency . . . a systemic breakdown in accountability and ethics . . . collapsing mortgage lending standards and the mortgage securitization pipeline . . . over-the-counter derivatives . . . [and] the failures of credit rating agencies."[6] But when it came to Fannie Mae and Freddie Mac, "these two entities contributed to the crisis, but were not a primary cause."[7] Yet Fannie and Freddie were the dominant players in the housing finance system and were subject to HUD regulations that required them to reduce their underwriting standards. They were almost literally elephants stomping around in the room. To fail to explore their role in detail reflects a willful blindness that was inconsistent with the commission's responsibility to the public. By keeping necessary information from the few commissioners who might have been willing to listen, and by failing to explore any alternative explanation for the crisis, the FCIC majority produced a narrative about the causes of the crisis that was useful only to those who saw the crisis as a chance to impose a "New New

Deal" (in Barney Frank's evocative phrase)—that is, a more stringent regulatory regime—on the U.S. financial system.[8]

One glaring example illustrates the bias of the FCIC majority. In March 2010, Edward Pinto provided the commission with a seventy-page, fully sourced memorandum, titled "Triggers of the Financial Crisis" (henceforth, the Triggers memo), that reported the number of NTMs in the financial system immediately before the financial crisis. In that memorandum, Pinto stated: "When the financial crisis hit in full force in 2008, approximately 26.7 million or 49% of the nation's 55 million outstanding single-family first mortgage loans had high risk characteristics, making them far more likely to default."[9] Pinto continued with the following:

> Over seventy percent of the 26.7 million high risk loans—19.25 million loans—were owned or guaranteed by (a) Fannie Mae and Freddie Mac (11.9 million), (b) the Federal Housing Administration and other federal agencies (4.8 million); (c) FHLB [Federal Home Loan Bank] investments in Alt-A and Subprime Private MBS [mortgage-backed securities] (0.3 million) or (d) banks and other lenders originating loans pursuant to Community Reinvestment Act (CRA) requirements and HUD's best practices program (2.2 million, net of CRA loans already accounted for in (a) and (b)).[10]

Pinto's numbers were increased in December 2011, after the SEC, in connection with a suit against top officers of Fannie and Freddie for failing to disclose the firms' exposure to NTMs, released non-prosecution agreements with both GSEs. These figures showed that Fannie and Freddie were exposed to an additional 1.76 million NTMs on June 30, 2008, increasing the actual number of NTMs outstanding to 28.46 million. Then, in March 2013, Freddie released its 15 million mortgage dataset, which indicated (after extrapolating from Freddie's numbers to establish Fannie's) that the GSEs had 3.5 million more NTMs even among their best loans. This brought the total number of NTMs that could be accounted for in 2008 to 31 million, of which 76 percent were on the books of government agencies or entities controlled or regulated by the government.

A few months later, after an interview by the FCIC staff, Pinto submitted another memorandum, this one titled "Government Housing Policies in the Lead-Up to the Financial Crisis: A Forensic Study," a 187-page fully footnoted analysis that outlined the development of the government's housing policies chronologically over thirty years.[11]

The astonishing statement in the Triggers memo that just before the 2008 financial crisis almost half of all the mortgages in the United States were NTMs and that 70 percent of those were held or guaranteed by government agencies like Fannie and Freddie should have alerted the FCIC to the existence of a valid alternative explanation for the crisis. Any objective investigation charged with telling Congress and the American people what caused the financial crisis would have taken a serious look at Pinto's data, combed carefully through his research, exposed his ideas to the members of the commission, taken Pinto's testimony in public or in private, and in discussions with Pinto tested the accuracy of his claim that the U.S. government's housing policies were responsible for the mortgage meltdown and the subsequent financial crisis. But this is not what happened. Although I sent copies of Pinto's Triggers memo to the other commissioners, Pinto's research, including his Forensic Study, was never formally made available by the chair or staff to the other members of the FCIC or even to the commissioners who were members of the subcommittee charged with considering the role of housing policy in the financial crisis. At my request, the staff interviewed Pinto; they heard him out, but the immediate response of the staff was not to explore the validity of his thesis but to challenge and refute it.

Ultimately, the FCIC's majority report dismissed Pinto's work in a few paragraphs, arguing that a loan with a FICO score of less than 660 should not be considered "subprime by characteristics" because, in effect, others were worse. The FCIC wrote in its majority report:

[A]s [our] review shows, the GSE loans classified as subprime or Alt-A in Pinto's analysis did not perform nearly as poorly as loans in non-agency subprime or Alt-A securities. These differences suggest that grouping all of these loans together is misleading. In direct contrast to Pinto's claim, GSE mortgages with some riskier characteristics such as high loan-to-value ratios are not at all equivalent to those mortgages in securitizations labeled subprime and Alt-A by issuers. The performance data assembled and analyzed by the FCIC show that non-GSE securitized loans experienced much higher rates of delinquency than did the GSE loans with similar characteristics.[12]

This statement was wrong in two respects. First, as shown in chapter 2, the Federal Reserve's 1996 study had shown that a loan to a borrower with a FICO score of 660 or less substantially raised the likelihood of default. Second, bank regulators had concluded in 2001 that a loan with a credit score of 660 or less was a subprime loan, no matter what other characteristics the mortgage might have had. In other words, to the bank regulators, a loan with a credit score of 660 or less *was* "subprime by characteristics." This had been explicitly laid out, with a citation, in Pinto's Triggers memo, which had apparently not been read by either the staff or the other members of the FCIC. The FCIC was either ignorant of these conclusions or disregarded them. Pinto did not. As shown earlier in Table 2.2, which was based on the Freddie dataset, this judgment was correct; loans in which the borrower's credit score was 660 or less, but which had prime-level down payments and debt-to-income (DTI) ratios, had almost eight times the incidence of default during normal times than loans with borrower FICO scores above 660.

Finally, the relevant question is not whether some subprime or Alt-A loans performed worse than others, but whether the performance of loans with high loan-to-value (LTV) ratios or low FICO scores performed badly enough that they should not have been acquired by Fannie and Freddie or allowed to spread to the rest of the housing market. The answer to that question should have been obvious, simply because Fannie and Freddie—two companies with gold-plated franchises and funding costs just shy of the U.S. Treasury—became insolvent under the weight of the NTMs they acquired. Relatively few of their loans were of the kind denominated as subprime or Alt-A by their originators. In fact, the number of such self-denominated subprime loans was, as Fannie had said, less than 1 percent of their exposure. For example, Table 3.1 shows that self-denominated subprime loans (in column 8)—those acquired from subprime lenders or denominated as such by originators—amounted to only $7.4 billion in a credit book of $2.8 trillion, far less than 1 percent.

But Fannie and Freddie were propelled to insolvency by the performance of two other kinds of NTMs, totaling almost $1 trillion, also disclosed in the credit profile: loans that Pinto called "subprime by characteristics"—that is, subprime because they had FICO scores of less than 660—and Alt-A loans with deficiencies such as high LTV ratios, negative amortization, interest only, and Alt-A for other reasons noted by Fannie itself. As shown in Table 3.1, the losses on these loans in 2009 were 81.3 percent of all of Fannie's losses in 2008 and 75 percent of losses in 2009.

In fact, the FCIC majority report failed to look seriously at any idea that was inconsistent with the narrative that the financial crisis was caused by the insufficiently regulated activities of the private sector. For example, although affordable-housing goals appear to have been the major reason that the GSEs acquired large numbers of NTMs, the majority report consistently downplayed the importance of HUD's administration of the goals and the effect of the goals on the composition of the GSEs' portfolios, suggesting incorrectly that the GSEs did not have to acquire NTMs in order to comply with the goals.[13] To reach this conclusion, the FCIC majority accepted uncritically the GSEs' claims that they did not require any significant number of NTMs in order to comply with the goals.[14] Data that Fannie Mae supplied to the FCIC—reproduced in chapter 7 as Table 7.1—showed this to be false. As outlined fully in chapter 7, the NTMs that the GSEs acquired as whole loans or as loans underlying private mortgage–backed securities (PMBS) were essential to the GSEs' effort to comply with the affordable-housing goals.

The FCIC majority's report further stated that "we also studied at length how the Department of Housing and Urban Development's (HUD's) affordable-housing goals for the GSEs affected their investment in risky mortgages. Based on the evidence and interviews with dozens of individuals involved in this subject area, we determined these goals *only contributed marginally* to Fannie's and Freddie's participation in those mortgages [emphasis added]."[15] To the contrary, as chapters 5 through 8 detail below, HUD relentlessly pressed the GSEs to meet the goals, and the GSEs' compliance eventually caused their insolvency and spread degraded mortgage underwriting standards to the wider market.

In a hearing before the FCIC in April 2010, Daniel Mudd, the last CEO of Fannie Mae before the firm was taken over by the government, left no doubt that Fannie had to go to great lengths for loans that would meet the affordable-housing goals:

> Fannie Mae's mission regulator, HUD, imposed ever-higher housing goals that were very difficult to meet during my tenure as CEO. The HUD goals greatly impacted Fannie Mae's business, as a great deal of time, resources, energy, and personnel were dedicated to finding ways to meet these goals. HUD increased the goals aggressively over time to the point where they exceeded the 50% mark, requiring Fannie Mae to place greater emphasis on purchasing loans in underserved areas. Fannie Mae had to devote a great deal of resources to running its business to satisfy HUD's goals and subgoals. This became particularly problematic when goal requirements grew to far exceed the proportion of eligible [mortgages] originated in the primary market.[16]

And somehow the FCIC's majority also managed to ignore this statement about the affordable-housing goals in Fannie Mae's 2006 10-K report:

> [W]e have made, and continue to make, significant adjustments to our mortgage loan sourcing and purchase strategies in an effort to meet HUD's increased housing goals and new subgoals. These strategies include entering into some

TABLE 3.1. Fannie Mae credit profile by key product features as of December 31, 2009

Credit characteristics of single-family conventional guaranty book of business

	Negative-amortizing loans	Interest-only loans	Loans with FICO <620[c]	Loans with FICO ≥620 and <660[c]	Loans with original LTV ratio >90%	Loans with FICO <620 and original LTV ratio >90%[c]	Alt-A loans	Subprime loans	Subtotal of key product features[a]	Overall book
				Categories not mutually exclusive[a]						
Unpaid principal balance ($ billions)[b]	13.7	183.2	109.3	230.4	262.6	24.0	248.3	7.4	837.8	2,796.5
Percentage of single-family conventional guaranty book	0.5	6.6	3.9	8.2	9.4	0.9	8.9	0.3	30.0	100.0
Average unpaid principal balance[b]	$131,732	$243,049	$123,981	$139,100	$143,557	$118,161	$166,966	$148,987	$152,277	$153,302
Serious delinquency rate	10.29%	20.17%	18.20%	13.01%	13.05%	27.96%	15.63%	30.68%	12.93%	5.38%
Origination years 2005–2007	60.3%	78.9%	55.2%	53.1%	53.4%	68.9%	73.4%	80.6%	58.8%	36.0%
Weighted average original loan-to-value ratio	71.3%	75.7%	76.6%	77.3%	97.2%	98.1%	73.0%	77.2%	79.6%	71.3%
Original loan-to-value ratio >90%	0.3%	9.2%	21.9%	20.7%	100.0%	100.0%	5.3%	6.8%	31.3%	9.4%
Weighted average mark-to-market loan-to-value ratio	99.0%	106.1%	81.9%	83.6%	103.4%	103.7%	91.6%	96.6%	90.5%	74.6%
Mark-to-market loan-to-value ratio >100% and ≤125%	14.3%	22.9%	14.2%	14.3%	29.9%	32.2%	15.2%	18.0%	18.2%	8.8%

Mark-to-market loan-to-value ratio >125%	34.2%	25.1%	7.8%	9.3%	14.1%	14.2%	17.3%	16.7%	12.7%	5.7%
Weighted average FICO[c]	705	724	588	641	698	592	717	622	686	730
FICO <620[c]	7.6%	1.3%	100.0%	—	9.1%	100.0%	0.7%	48.5%	13.1%	3.9%
Fixed-rate	0.2%	38.9%	92.7%	91.8%	94.0%	93.9%	72.1%	77.1%	80.8%	91.4%
Primary residence	69.2%	84.9%	96.7%	94.2%	97.1%	99.4%	77.3%	96.6%	89.5%	89.9%
Condo/Co-op	14.0%	16.5%	4.9%	6.6%	9.9%	6.1%	10.9%	4.4%	9.7%	9.4%
Credit enhanced[d]	73.3%	30.5%	32.4%	33.3%	87.3%	91.7%	33.3%	59.9%	41.5%	17.7%
Percentage of credit losses[e]										
2007	0.9	15.0	18.8	21.9	17.4	6.4	27.8	1.0	72.3	100.0
2008	2.9	34.2	11.8	17.4	21.3	5.4	45.6	2.0	81.3	100.0
2009	2.0	32.6	8.8	15.5	19.2	3.4	39.6	1.5	75.0	100.0
2009 Q1	1.8	34.2	10.7	16.0	22.5	4.9	39.2	2.0	77.7	100.0
2009 Q2	2.2	32.2	9.2	16.0	19.7	3.5	41.2	1.1	76.0	100.0
2009 Q3	1.8	31.8	8.6	15.3	18.9	3.2	39.1	1.6	74.4	100.0
2009 Q4	2.0	32.6	7.7	15.1	17.1	2.6	39.0	1.3	73.2	100.0

[a] Loans with multiple product features are included in all applicable categories. The subtotal is calculated by counting a loan only once even if it is included in multiple categories.

[b] Excludes non–Fannie Mae securities held in portfolio and those Alt-A and subprime wraps for which Fannie Mae does not have loan-level information. Fannie Mae had access to detailed loan-level information which constituted over 98% of its single-family conventional guaranty book of business as of December 31, 2009.

[c] FICO credit scores reported in the table are those provided by the sellers of the mortgage loans at time of delivery.

[d] Unpaid principal balance of all loans with credit enhancement as a percentage of unpaid principal balance of single-family conventional guaranty book of business for which Fannie Mae had access to loan-level information. Includes primary mortgage insurance, pool insurance, lender recourse, and other credit enhancement.

[e] Expressed as a percentage of credit losses for the single-family guaranty book of business. For information on total credit losses, refer to Fannie Mae's 2009 Form 10-K.

purchase and securitization transactions with *lower expected economic returns than our typical transactions. We have also relaxed some of our underwriting criteria to obtain goals-qualifying mortgage loans and increased our investments in higher-risk mortgage loan products that are more likely to serve the borrowers targeted by HUD's goals and subgoals, which could increase our credit losses* [emphasis added].[17]

It is clear from these statements alone that the commission majority ignored theories about the causes of the financial crisis that any objective investigation would have considered, while focusing solely on a narrative that advanced the political purposes of those in Congress and the administration who wanted to impose tighter regulation on the financial system. This was not the way an objective inquiry should have been carried out; unfortunately, the FCIC majority misused its mandate for political purposes.

Nor would it be accurate to say that the FCIC's majority report was the considered work of the members who voted for it. The commission's authorizing statute required that the commission report its findings on or before December 15, 2010. The original plan was for the commissioners to start seeing drafts of the report in April. No drafts were circulated until November, when chapters started to arrive in no particular order. The commissioners were then given an opportunity to submit comments in writing, but never had an opportunity to go over the wording as a group, to question the staff about the substance of what was written in the report, or to know whether their written comments were accepted. On December 15, commission members received a complete copy of the majority's report—almost nine hundred double-spaced pages—with a notice that the approval date was eight days later. During that period, we never met in person or in a telephone conference to go over the wording of the report. It is difficult to believe, in light of this process, that any member of the commission other than Angelides himself had read the report in full and approved it before its release.

When the report was finally issued, in January 2011, all four Republican-appointed members of the commission dissented, and I dissented separately with a statement that differed from the position taken by the other Republicans. Angelides had contracted for a commercial edition of the report that would be widely distributed in bookstores. That edition contained the majority report in full, but limited the dissents to 9,000 words for each dissenter. My 43,000-word dissent was seriously truncated in the commercial edition, but it was included in full in the official version of the report that was issued by the Government Printing Office. Nevertheless, most people who bought the commercial edition, available in bookstores all over the country, were not aware that the 9,000 words included at the back of the commercial edition were only a small portion of my complete dissent.[18]

I dissented from the report because I believed that the government's housing policies were the predominant cause of the financial crisis and that, without those policies, there would not have been a crisis. The private sector was involved, of course, but, as I argued in my dissent and as I show in this book, it was a minor factor compared to the role of the government's housing policies, and but for these policies the actions of the private sector alone would never by itself have caused the crisis.

OTHER EXPLANATIONS FOR THE CRISIS

The balance of this chapter reviews a number of other explanations for the financial crisis; these either have serious deficiencies—such as the absence of supporting data—or would not have been sufficient in themselves to cause the financial crisis unless U.S. government housing policies had already substantially reduced the quality of the mortgages in the U.S. financial system, and thus weakened many of the largest U.S. financial institutions.

Low interest rates and/or a flow of funds from abroad

The idea that the immense housing bubble that developed between 1997 and 2007 was the result of monetary policy is a story beloved of economists, who see a strong relationship between monetary policy, or the flow of funds from abroad, and the development of asset bubbles. In the case of monetary policy, the theory is that excessively low interest rates cause investors to bid up the prices of real assets, such as housing, in search of yield and as a hedge against inflation. In the case of a flow of funds from abroad, the theory is that economic growth in China and elsewhere, where savings rates are high but safe investments are few, caused investment funds to pour into the United States as a safe haven and found a home in housing investment.

It is certainly true that the collapse of the ten-year housing bubble was one of the primary causes of the unprecedented number of mortgage defaults that followed. These defaults in turn drove down housing prices and mortgage values, causing the weakness of financial institutions that turned into a full-fledged investor panic after the Lehman bankruptcy. These theories seem initially plausible. However, there isn't a great deal of data that actually tie low interest rates or a strong flow of funds from abroad to the 1997–2007 bubble. In addition, it isn't clear that the collapse of that bubble alone—without the weakness of the NTMs that filled it—accounts for the financial crisis.

Claims that low interest rates in the early 2000s or financial flows from abroad were responsible for the growth of the housing bubble are not adequate to explain its size. Figure 3.1, developed from data assembled by Robert Shiller, shows the modern history of housing

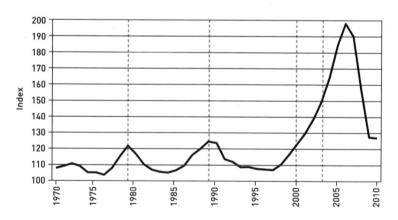

Source: Robert J. Shiller, http://www.irrationalexuberance.com/.

FIG. 3.1. Case-Shiller home price index, 1970–2010

bubbles in the United States in real (inflation-adjusted) terms. Among other things, the figure shows the extraordinary size of the bubble. The two vertical dotted lines on the left show the high points of the previous bubbles in 1979 and 1989; the vertical lines on the right show the size of the bubble in 2000 and 2003, which were important dates in analyzing whether the bubble was caused by low interest rates or fund flows from abroad.

The years before 2000 were marked by solid growth in the United States, especially in the stock markets during what has been called the dot-com bubble. Many economists argue that low interest rates or funds from abroad created the dot-com bubble, which ended in 2001. The usual narrative is that after the stock market losses in 2001 (because of the September 11 attacks) and 2002, the Federal Reserve cut interest rates in order to start a housing boom, create a wealth effect, and thus restart the economy. Any or all of this narrative could have been true, but the data do not support the idea that either strong fund flows from abroad or the Federal Reserve's monetary policy was responsible for most of the growth of the housing bubble. The dot-com boom was beginning to slow in 2000. If there were extraordinary amounts of funds flowing in from abroad that year, they were not visible in the longer-term rates. The ten-year note was in the 6 percent range at the beginning of the year and then fell into the 5 percent range after the deflation of the dot-com bubble and the resulting recession, staying there through 2001. For 2002 through 2007, the yield on the ten-year note was remarkably stable, averaging a bit over 4 percent. However, one would suppose that if funds were pouring in from abroad to fund investments in long-term assets such as mortgages, interest on the ten-year note would also have shown a decline during this period. Nevertheless, the FCIC report adopted the conventional idea that a lot of money was sloshing around looking for yield: "[W]ith yields low on other highly rated assets, investors hungered for Wall Street mortgage securities backed by higher-yield mortgages—those loans made to subprime borrowers, those with nontraditional features, those with limited or no documentation ("no-doc loans"), or those that failed in some other way to meet strong underwriting standards."[19] A 4 or 5 percent rate on a risk-free Treasury bond does not seem like a yield that would drive investors to risky mortgages, but that's the story the FCIC accepted.

As to monetary policy, there was no loosening of credit by the Federal Reserve in 2000 and 2001, but rates fell sharply from 2002 to 2004, rising again from 2005 to 2007.[20] From 2003 to 2005, according to the data, *real* interest rates were actually in negative territory when inflation is taken into account. There is some dispute among economists about whether these rates on three-month Treasury bills, which might be affected by the Federal Reserve easing, actually had an effect on mortgage rates. Alan Greenspan argues that during this period, lower Federal Reserve–induced interest rates were de-linked from long-term rates and so could not have affected home buying.[21] It is true, as Greenspan suggests, that the ten-year Treasury note hardly moved between 2002 and 2007, even though short-term rates were actually negative in real terms for the latter portion of that period.

Nevertheless, whether it was the flow of funds from abroad, a lot of money sloshing around in the market, or a lax monetary policy that supposedly built the 1997–2007 bubble, Figure 3.1 tells a different story. By the year 2000, before any monetary easing and when the ten-year note was in the 6 percent range, the housing bubble was already larger than any previous bubble. It had grown to that size, in other words, before any Federal Reserve effort to lower interest rates and when flows of funds from abroad were not having a noticeable effect on interest rates.

By the year 2003, according to Shiller's data, the bubble had grown to nearly *three times* the size of any previous bubble—again, before the Federal Reserve's policies had pushed short term interest rates into negative territory. To be sure, it may well be that interest rate policy accelerated the growth of the bubble *after* 2003, but clearly by that year the bubble's historic size was well established. The year 2003 is significant: John B. Taylor of Stanford University, who has written persuasively about the role of interest rates in the development of the housing bubble, has identified the years 2003–2005 as the years during which the Federal Reserve's monetary policy drove interest rates into negative territory and thus contributed to the development of the housing bubble.[22]

Accordingly, while there is a lively debate among economists about whether the 1997–2007 housing bubble was caused by low interest rates or fund flows from abroad, the bubble's extraordinary size seems to have had a significant boost from *something*—I would argue it was government housing policy—before low interest rates or a flow of funds from abroad could have had any effect. This issue is discussed fully in chapter 9.

In any event, the outcome of that debate is not material to the second question outlined above—does the collapse of a bubble, alone, account for the financial crisis? One of the arguments against the idea that government housing policy was the cause of the crisis is that other developed countries had large housing bubbles at the same time that the U.S. bubble was growing and that some of them might have been larger than the U.S. bubble. This suggests, say the proponents of this view, that the existence of Fannie and Freddie or U.S. housing policies in general could not have been a cause of the crisis. This argument assumes that the collapse of the housing bubble, with nothing more, caused the crisis. However, as also discussed in chapter 9, only in the United States did the collapse of the housing bubble have a devastating effect on housing prices and the condition of financial institutions. Elsewhere, the losses caused by mortgage defaults were in the low single digits, while in the United States the losses of Fannie and Freddie alone were 13 to 17 percent, and on PMBS much higher. The reason for this is simple: no other country had any significant number of subprime loans in its mortgage financing system, bringing the issue back to the role of housing policies. In chapter 9, I argue that U.S. government housing policies built the bubble, and the poor quality of U.S. mortgages—the result of those policies—created the devastating losses to homeowners and the U.S. financial system when the bubble deflated. Whatever the cause of the U.S. bubble, if it had not been seeded with an unprecedented number of NTMs, a financial crisis would likely not have occurred when the bubble collapsed.

Deregulation and risk-taking

This explanation for the crisis relies on the idea that, at some time in the recent past, financial deregulation allowed banks and other financial institutions to take excessive risks. This was Obama's explanation for the financial crisis in the presidential debates; it has consistently attracted the support of many on the left who have always distrusted capitalism and appealed to some on the right who were frightened by the chaos they saw after Lehman's bankruptcy.[23] As an explanation for the crisis it is deficient simply because there has been no significant and relevant deregulation of financial institutions in the last thirty years.

Gramm-Leach-Bliley and the "repeal" of Glass-Steagall

The most frequently cited culprit behind the financial crisis is the so-called repeal of the Glass-Steagall Act of 1933 by the Gramm-Leach-Bliley Act of 1999. However, Glass-Steagall as a whole was never repealed. The relevant portion of Glass-Steagall contains two separate prohibitions. One forbids banks to underwrite or deal in securities, and the other forbids affiliations between banks and firms that underwrite and deal in securities. Only the affiliation prohibitions of the act were repealed by the Gramm-Leach-Bliley Act; the prohibition on bank underwriting and dealing in securities still governs bank activities.

The repeal of the affiliation provisions, however, had no role in the financial crisis.[24] There is no evidence that any bank or bank holding company (that is, a firm that owns a bank) got into trouble because of an affiliation with a securities firm. The losses that banks and bank holding companies suffered in the financial crisis were the result of what had always been standard banking activity. Even under Glass-Steagall, banks and bank holding companies were permitted to invest in—and thus to buy and sell—mortgages and mortgage-backed securities (MBS), which were regarded by regulators as simply another way for banks to hold loans, a traditional banking asset. Loans and securities representing loans are a bank's stock in trade, as oil is to Exxon Mobil. Accordingly, the fact that banks suffered losses by investing in mortgages or MBS, or even private mortgage-backed securities (PMBS) backed by NTMs, had nothing to do with the repeal of the affiliation provisions of Glass-Steagall; banks and bank holding companies were only doing what these institutions had always been permitted to do under Glass-Steagall.[25]

Accordingly, it would be accurate to conclude that the enactment of Gramm-Leach-Bliley—to the extent that it allowed insured banks to affiliate through bank holding companies with securities firms—did not result in major losses to the banks. On the contrary, it seems clear that the banks got into trouble by doing exactly the things we expect them to do—make loans and hold and trade normal and traditional financial assets such as mortgages and mortgage-backed securities. There is one other possibility. Did the repeal by the Gramm-Leach-Bliley Act of the affiliation provisions in Glass-Steagall enable investment banks to establish relationships with commercial banks that led to the weakened financial condition of the Wall Street investment banks Merrill Lynch, Goldman Sachs, and Morgan Stanley and to the bankruptcy of Lehman Brothers? Hardly. Each of these investment banking firms had a subsidiary bank—something that would not have been possible before the repeal of the affiliation provisions of Glass-Steagall—but these bank affiliates were far too small to cause any serious losses to their massive parents, as shown in Table 3.2.

Given the huge disparities between the size of each major investment bank and the size of its depository institution subsidiary,

TABLE 3.2. Comparing the size of investment banks to the size of their insured subsidiary banks

	Investment bank assets (2008) ($ billions)	Subsidiary bank's assets ($ billions)
Goldman Sachs	800	25.0
Morgan Stanley	660	38.5
Merrill Lynch	670	35.0
Lehman Brothers	600	4.5

Sources: Goldman Sachs: Federal Reserve Board, "Order Approving Formation of Bank Holding Companies," The Goldman Sachs Group, Inc., September 21, 2009, p. 1. Morgan Stanley: Federal Reserve Board, "Order Approving Formation of Bank Holding Companies," Morgan Stanley, Inc., September 21, 2009, p. 1. Merrill Lynch: iBanknet, Merrill Lynch Bank & Trust Co., FSB, October 22, 2009; available at http://www.ibanknet.com/scripts/callreports/getbank.aspx?ibnid=usa_2577494. Lehman Brothers: Investigative Reporting Workshop, Woodlands Commercial Bank, available at http://www.ibanknet.com/scripts/callreports/getbank.aspx?ibnid=usa_3376461.

it is completely implausible that the insured bank subsidiary could cause any serious financial problem for the parent or significantly enhance the financial problems that the parent company had created for itself through its own operations.

Investment banks, insured deposits, and the discount window

Some commentators have asserted that the repeal of the affiliation provisions of Glass-Steagall permitted investment banks to gain access to bank deposits insured by the FDIC or gain access to the Federal Reserve's discount window. Neither assertion is true. First, only banks—entities specially chartered as such by the federal or state governments—can issue insured deposits. Investment banks, bank holding companies, and securities firms are all ordinary corporations, not banks, and cannot issue insured deposits. So the mere affiliation with a bank does not give investment banks or bank holding companies access to FDIC insured deposits. The only way that an insured bank can provide insured funds to an affiliate is through a loan,[26] and bank regulations restrict any such loan to 10 percent of the bank's capital (about 1 percent of the bank's assets) and 20 percent of the bank's capital to all affiliates as a group. Moreover, the loan must be on the same terms that a bank would lend to an unaffiliated third party and must be collateralized by U.S. government securities. These restrictions make affiliate lending unattractive. Accordingly, despite statements appearing in the media from time to time that investment banks could get access to insured deposits because they were affiliated with banks, these statements are incorrect if they are taken to mean that investment banks have unrestricted access to insured deposits through their insured bank subsidiaries.

The same is true of access to the Federal Reserve's discount window, which normally only banks—and not affiliates of banks—can access.[27] Investment banks, bank holding companies, and other bank affiliates cannot use the discount window as a matter of right, simply because they are affiliated with a bank. However, during the periods of the most severe illiquidity in the financial crisis, the Federal Reserve used a special provision of the Federal Reserve Act to open the discount window to primary dealers and to other specialized financial institutions that needed liquidity. This had nothing to do with whether these organizations were affiliated with banks. A bank can, of course, borrow from the discount window and lend the funds to an affiliate, but again the loan would be subject to the limitations outlined above, which would severely restrict the size of any such loan.

SEC "deregulation"

There has also been a lot of misinformation about the purported SEC "deregulation" of investment banks in the early 2000s. Under the Gramm-Leach-Bliley Act, the SEC was authorized to become the prudential regulator—a regulator that controls the risk-taking of a financial institution—for the major U.S. investment banks. This provision enabled the investment banks to continue to do business in the European Union (EU), which had decreed that no foreign financial institution could operate in the EU unless it had a home-country prudential regulator. Utilizing this authority, the five major U.S. investment banks—Goldman Sachs, Morgan Stanley, Merrill Lynch, Lehman Brothers, and Bear Stearns—all signed up for prudential regulation by the SEC.

After the onset of the financial crisis, a widely cited 2008 article in the *New York Times* by reporter Stephen Labaton incorrectly reported that in 2004 the SEC had loosened the capital requirements for the major investment banks, allowing them to take on much more leverage than had previously been permitted.[28] In reality, what the SEC had done in 2004 was to change the way the net capital of the broker-dealers—the subsidiaries of the investment banks—would be calculated. This had no effect on the capital of the parent companies and no major effect on the required capitalization of the broker-dealers.[29] Nevertheless, the Labaton mistake was then cited in numerous press and other reports as a reason that the large investment banks had increased their leverage before the financial crisis, suffering severe losses as a result.

Later investigations by the Government Accountability Office (GAO) showed that the five major investment banks cited above had not appreciably increased their leverage over its level in 1998, before they had signed up for SEC regulation.[30] Labaton's error achieved widespread currency because, as scholar Andrew Lo has pointed out, it was accepted as true and repeated by many well-known scholars who should have been more skeptical.[31] This demonstrates, as Lo observed, that a lot of misinformation about the financial crisis is floating around, even in respected news sources, and should be carefully examined before it is accepted. In my view, the idea that deregulation was a cause of the financial crisis is certainly in this category.

Nevertheless, the government rescue of Bear Stearns and the bankruptcy of Lehman, both in 2008, raised questions about whether investment banks should have been more strictly regulated. This was one of the arguments advanced by the FCIC majority report. Yet it is not a case of deregulation—these firms had never been subject to prudential regulation until the early 2000s, when they agreed to prudential regulation by the SEC—but rather a question of whether the financial crisis would have occurred if the SEC, as the regulator of the investment banks, had imposed stricter prudential regulation than it did. In this case, however, the argument is seriously weakened by the fact that, although insured commercial banks and savings and loans were regulated far more strictly than investment banks, three large ones—Wachovia, Washington Mutual, and IndyMac—failed in the financial crisis, along with about five hundred smaller banks. This suggests, of course, that the degree of regulation was not a decisive factor in whether or not a financial institution failed.

The question here is always whether these assertions about the need for additional regulation are realistic or merely a way to dispose of a problem by saying someone should have done something about it. The SEC probably had the authority to rein in the activities of the investment banks in the mortgage business, but there is no reason to believe that the SEC would have been able to foresee a problem that virtually no one else—including the Federal Reserve, with its vast data resources and huge staff of economists—foresaw at the time. Moreover, while the bubble was growing and the investment banks were buying and securitizing large numbers of subprime loans, the homeownership rate in the United States was growing significantly with few delinquencies and defaults. The reasons for this were dis-

THE FCIC REPORT AND OTHER EXPLANATIONS ■ 67

cussed earlier. If the SEC or any other regulator had attempted to stop the acquisition and securitization of subprime loans, it would have drawn strong opposition in Congress. Because bubbles suppress defaults, a courageous regulator who had both the data and the prescience to see what was coming would not have been able to show a critical Congress that the build-up of NTMs in the financial system was causing any appreciable increase in mortgage losses.

Riegle-Neal and the Basel risk-based capital rules

The only other major legislation in the last thirty years that could possibly be considered as significant deregulation of the banking sector was the Riegle-Neal Interstate Banking and Branching Efficiency Act of 1994, which lifted prior restrictions on mergers and acquisitions among banks and bank holding companies across state lines. This act set off a period of major merger and acquisition activity, and more than anything else has accounted for the large size of the major banks today. However, if anything, the Riegle-Neal Act made the large commercial banks more stable by enabling them to diversify geographically, and there was nothing in the act that enabled them to engage in any more risky activities than they had been permitted to pursue in the past. However, the Riegle-Neal Act did enable community activists to pressure banks seeking merger approvals for commitments on the amount of lending they would do under the Community Reinvestment Act (CRA). In that sense, the relaxed rules on interstate bank mergers might have contributed to the weakness of the banks that made these commitments, and to the growth of NTMs, but this result was caused not by deregulation but by the stricter CRA regulations that the Clinton administration adopted in 1995 and possibly by the Federal Reserve's willingness to hold up merger approvals until the banks involved had agreed to the demands of community activists for commitments on future CRA-based lending. This issue is discussed more fully in chapter 5.

Ironically, government regulatory action intended to tighten international rules that govern bank capital requirements wound up providing incentives for banks to increase their investments in risky mortgage assets and thus their risk-taking. Known as the Basel risk-based capital rules, these regulations were introduced in the 1980s and significantly revised in the mid-2000s. The Basel Accords, an agreement among bank regulators in developed countries, attempted to align the amount of bank capital with the risks that banks were assuming. For example, under Basel I, the first iteration of these rules, the regulators treated corporate loans as the most risky element of bank lending. Accordingly, a bank had to hold 8 percent capital ($8) for every $100 of its outstanding corporate loans. However, the Basel rules decreed lower capital requirements for mortgages (4 percent, or $4, for every $100 in residential mortgages) and lower requirements still for PMBS (1.6 percent or $1.60 for every $100 of AAA-rated PMBS). The incentives created by these capital discounts actually herded banks into mortgage investments, and even more so into PMBS, which turned out in 2007 and 2008 to be very bad investments indeed. When the Basel rules went into effect, no one would have thought, least of all the regulators who imposed the risk-based capital requirements, that these rules would actually increase bank risks rather than reduce them. This surprising result shows that regulation isn't always an unalloyed good, especially when it reduces bank diversification by encouraging all banks to hold the same types of assets.

A general point about regulation is appropriate here. The Basel capital rules debacle is only one example of how regulation can have adverse consequences. Alan Greenspan has argued that regulation increases moral hazard by giving investors and creditors the idea that the regulator is watching out for and reducing excessive risk-taking. Much of the time, as has been demonstrated most forcefully in the financial crisis, the regulators do not understand what is going on within large financial institutions even when—as is true for the largest banks—they have examiners embedded on the bank's premises. In addition, what happened with the Basel rules is just one example of the tendency of regulation to reduce diversification among regulated firms. Consciously or not, regulators often conclude that there is one right way to do things or that the only way they can properly supervise a firm is to have all regulated entities adhere to the same standards. The Basel capital accords are an example. This reduces diversification, which—as in genetics—is probably the only effective method for dealing with unforeseeable risks to a firm or a species. Finally, in addition to compliance costs, regulation inevitably suppresses risk-taking and change, imposing costs through a burdensome approval process on efforts by regulated firms to strike out into new areas of activity. Regulators do not like new activities because they create risks to the firm that could result in losses for which the regulators will be blamed. The conventional narrative of the financial crisis—that it could have been prevented by better regulation—is a perfect example of what regulators fear. Still, as absurd as it is, regulators tend to get more powers as a result of their failures. The Dodd-Frank Act is only the most recent example of this Washington phenomenon.

The FDIC Improvement Act

Far from being loosened, bank regulation was substantially *tightened* in 1991 with the enactment of the Federal Deposit Insurance Corporation Improvement Act (FDICIA) in the wake of the collapse of the savings and loan (S&L) industry—and the additional failure of 1,600 banks—at the end of the 1980s.[32] Among other things, the FDICIA required regulators to intervene when banks failed to meet required capital standards (a process known as "prompt corrective action"), annual on-site inspections, and bank disclosure of the fair market value of their assets; it also imposed limits on compensation and loans to officers and directors and provided for personal fines on directors and officers of up to $1 million per day for violations of bank regulations. At the time it was passed, it was hailed in Congress as legislation that would make bank crises a thing of the past, but of course FDICIA—the most stringent bank regulation since the adoption of deposit insurance—failed to prevent the 2008 financial crisis.

The failure to improve the regulation of Fannie and Freddie

Although financial regulation has a poor record of success, there is one case where it is necessary—where a firm, like a bank, enjoys the backing of the government through insured deposits or otherwise. This was also true of the GSEs, which were seen in the financial markets as backed by the government. Under these circumstances, they were stellar examples of moral hazard—where a firm seen as government-backed or -insured is able to avoid significant scrutiny of its risk-taking behavior because its creditors believe any losses on their loans will be picked up by the government. In cases of moral hazard, then, the phenomenon of market discipline—where creditors fear losses and watch risk-taking carefully—is severely limited or nonexistent. The GSEs had a regulator, the Office of Federal Housing Enterprises Oversight (OFHEO), an office within HUD, but its authority was woefully weak. Not only was it outclassed by the staff resources and political power of the GSEs, but it also lacked the usual authority of a financial regulator. For example, it did not have the power to adjust the capital requirements of Fannie and Freddie to account for the risks they were taking.

So if there was one case of regulatory failure that contributed to the financial crisis, it was the failure of Congress, until it was too late, to adopt one of many efforts by the Bush administration to increase the regulation of Fannie Mae and Freddie Mac. There were several false starts, even with a Republican House of Representatives, but the Democrats were solidly against it, led by Barney Frank (D-Mass.), a strong supporter of the GSEs and the affordable-housing goals.[33] Finally, in 2005 the Senate Banking Committee (also controlled by the Republicans at that point) adopted a bill that provided for a new regulator of the GSEs, with the power to increase their capital and reduce the size of the mortgage portfolios they held. At the time, most people who looked at the GSEs thought that their portfolios of mortgages represented their greatest risk—the same kind of interest-rate risk that took down the savings and loan industry in the 1980s. Few critics, including me at that point, realized the size of the credit risk they were assuming in order to comply with the affordable-housing goals. But reducing their portfolios and their interest-rate risk was highly controversial. The bill never reached the Senate floor because it could garner no significant Democratic support, and sixty votes were necessary under the cloture rules to bring up a bill for debate. One of those Democrats was Barack Obama.

In 2008, legislation was finally passed that provided the new and more powerful regulator that Fannie and Freddie required. That this happened is much to the credit of Barney Frank, who had become the chair of the House Financial Services Committee after the Democrats' takeover of the House in 2006. Working with Treasury Secretary Hank Paulson, Frank brought the House along to support a bill that provided for a tougher regulator than the House Republicans were able to push through over Frank's opposition in 2003. His reasons for this about-face are reasonably clear. In the process, he and the Democrats succeeded in lowering the LMI target in affordable housing from 100 percent of median income to 80 percent and established a "slush fund" for support of community activists. Still, the act provided for a new and more powerful regulator, the Federal Housing Finance Agency (FHFA), with more authority than existing law if the GSEs had to be taken over by the government. Of course, even under the dubious assumption that the new regulator could or would have stopped the GSEs' compliance with the affordable-housing goals, it was years too late; the GSEs had already become exposed to 16.5 million NTMs, enough to drive them into insolvency when these loans began to default.

The failure to adequately regulate "shadow banks"

All the large Wall Street investment banks—Bear Stearns, Lehman Brothers, Merrill Lynch, Goldman Sachs, and Morgan Stanley—encountered serious difficulty, and in some cases failure, because they held PMBS that not only declined substantially in value in the mortgage meltdown but also could not be used for collateralized borrowing. This situation gave rise to a view that these institutions were "shadow banks," carrying out bank-like functions but without the safeguards of deposit insurance, the prudential regulation required for commercial banks, or discount-window access that is made available by the Federal Reserve to commercial banks. The implication is that it was the absence of these government benefits—and especially prudential regulation—that resulted in the failure of the investment banks. Unsurprisingly, this view is prevalent among bank regulators,[34] as the following excerpt from a 2012 speech by Ben Bernanke demonstrates:

> Although the shadow banking system taken as a whole performs traditional banking functions, including credit in-
> ·termediation and maturity transformation, unlike banks,
> it cannot rely on the protections afforded by deposit insur-
> ance and access to the Federal Reserve's discount window to
> ensure stability. Shadow banking depends instead upon an
> alternative set of contractual and regulatory protections—
> for example, the posting of collateral in short-term borrow-
> ing transactions. . . . During the financial crisis, however
> these types of measures failed to stave off a classic and self-
> reinforcing panic that took hold of the shadow banking sys-
> tem and ultimately spread across the financial system more
> broadly.[35]

This view would be more persuasive if there were a major difference between what happened to insured and fully regulated commercial banks and savings and loans and what happened to investment banks in the financial crisis. But a significant difference is not apparent. Although two investment banks—Bear Stearns and Lehman Brothers—failed in the financial crisis, at least three large and insured banks or S&Ls—Wachovia, Washington Mutual, and IndyMac—failed or had to be rescued by forced merger or other government intervention. A fourth commercial bank, Citigroup, is often said to have been rescued, but it is not clear that the bank would have failed absent the support it was given.[36] This record of failure on the part of heavily regulated commercial banks casts serious doubt on the claim that if investment banks had been regulated like commercial banks—or had been able to offer insured deposits and had access to the Federal Reserve's discount window—they would not have encountered financial difficulties. The fact is that losses from the mortgage meltdown were devastating to commercial banks and investment banks alike—and for the same reasons—and it does not appear that the availability of deposit insurance or the discount window or more intrusive prudential regulation would have made any significant difference. Certainly, the availability of lending by the Federal Reserve made a difference in the financial crisis, but during the post-Lehman liquidity panic the Federal Reserve used its special lending authority under section 13(3) of the Federal Reserve Act to provide liquidity to many non-bank financial institutions, substantially diminishing the strength of the argument that the discount window is a unique and necessary attribute of banks. In addition, as noted earlier, banks are reluctant to use the discount window because they fear it signals to the market that they are in trouble.

Finally, as also noted above, the FDICIA, adopted in 1991, required bank and S&L regulators to take "prompt corrective action" as bank capital began to decline, tightening regulations and restricting risk-taking so that a bank would be closed down before it created losses to the deposit insurance fund. However, the FDIC has been unable to implement this requirement effectively. Bert Ely, a Washington, D.C., accountant and expert in bank regulation, has calculated that the FDIC's deposit insurance fund has lost an average of approximately 24 percent on the assets on each failing bank between 2007 and 2014.[37]

In any event, it is very difficult to contend that the investment banks did anything substantially different from the commercial banks in the years leading up to the crisis. Both of them got into trouble by doing the same thing—holding large amounts of PMBS that lost their value when the great 1997–2007 housing price bubble deflated. Under these circumstances, it is difficult to escape the conclusion that the concerns of bank regulators about "shadow banks" is more about turf than about public welfare or the health of the financial system. Since the 1980s, the securities industry—which is what the bank regulators are referring to when they express concern about "shadow banks"—has outcompeted the banking industry for the financing of corporations and state and local governments. The competition isn't really close; the securities markets in recent years have provided three times more financing than banks for business corporations and local governments, and, as shown in Figure 3.2, the gap is continuing to widen.[38]

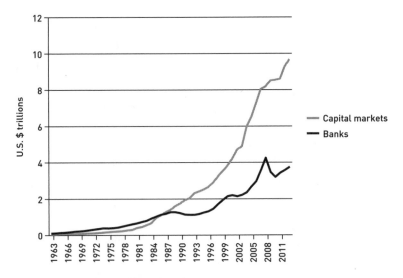

Source: Federal Reserve Flow of Funds.

FIG. 3.2. Comparing bank loans and fixed-income securities as sources of credit for business and state and local governments

Given this increasing competitive lag, it is little wonder that the bank regulators are eager to take control of the securities industry, but it would be a disastrous result for the U.S. economy if they were to succeed.

Credit default swaps

Some observers have also cited as "deregulation" the enactment of the Commodity Futures Modernization Act of 2000, which specifically forbade the Commodity Futures Trading Commission to regulate derivatives such as interest rate and currency swaps and credit default swaps (CDS). This, of course, was not deregulation; these financial instruments had never been regulated. Whether regulation of the derivatives market would have prevented the financial crisis is another question; the record of regulators is not exemplary. However, as the following discussion shows, CDS had no substantial role in the financial crisis, so regulating that market would not have prevented the crisis.

The government rescue of Bear Stearns in March 2008 with $29 billion in financial assistance from the Federal Reserve marked the first time that a financial institution other than an insured bank had been rescued with a direct government cash infusion. This unprecedented transaction prompted a lot of questions, especially about why Treasury Secretary Hank Paulson and Federal Reserve Chair Ben Bernanke thought it necessary to take this extraordinary step. The answer from the government was that the Treasury and the Federal Reserve were concerned about "interconnections" among financial institutions; if Bear Stearns went into bankruptcy, other large financial institutions would be brought down. When asked exactly how that would occur, government officials described credit default swaps, implying that these instruments created interconnections between financial institutions that would cause the failure of one to inflict unsustainable losses on others. An example of this view is the obscure and misleading explanation that Timothy Geithner, then the president of the New York Federal Reserve, gave to Congress in 2009: "The sudden discovery by Bear's derivatives counterparties that important financial positions they had put in place to protect themselves from financial risk were no longer operative would have triggered substantial further dislocation in markets."[39] Geithner undoubtedly knew that this was wrong, but his congressional listeners and the media did not. The simple fact, as explained below, is that the failure of a CDS player like Bear would have had no significant effect on its counterparties. CDS are a kind of financial insurance; they pay off in the event of a defined loss. If we think about them in this way, we can see why the failure of Bear Stearns would not, of itself, cause losses to Bear's CDS counterparties. If a homeowner has fire insurance on his house, he suffers no loss if his insurance company fails when his house has not suffered a fire loss; he simply goes out into the market and buys new insurance. That is exactly what the counterparties of Bear Stearns would have done. Having suffered no insurable loss, they simply needed to find a new CDS counterparty to supplant Bear.

However, the misleading idea that CDS foster dangerous interconnections has had a long shelf life, even among sophisticated observers of the market. In his book *The End of Wall Street*, Roger Lowenstein wrote: "In the eyes of each individual firm, risk was reduced [by CDS]. But systemic vulnerability—the danger that a failing firm could bring down a host of others—slowly and steadily accreted."[40] This statement reflects a regrettable misunderstanding about how CDS work. The failure of one firm would never "bring down a host of others" unless, like the homeowner in the fire insurance example, they had all suffered CDS-covered losses just before Bear failed, and had not had time to go out into the market to buy replacement coverage.

The best evidence that one failing firm will not topple many others is what happened after Lehman Brothers' bankruptcy. The firm was a major player in the CDS market, yet its failure brought down no one. And if Lehman didn't, we can be sure that Bear Stearns—at least 30 percent smaller—would not have had a systemic effect either if it had been allowed to fail.

Most of the adverse commentary about CDS and their alleged role in the financial crisis asserts that a failure of one participant will have or did have an adverse effect on the rest of the market because, like mountain climbers, all market participants are roped together through CDS; the fall of one can imperil all. This image is powerful but highly misleading, and does not reflect how the CDS market works or how the CDS market responded in the financial crisis to the collapse of a major CDS player like Lehman Brothers. When Lehman declared bankruptcy in September 2008, it became clear that the dangerous "interconnections" supposedly created by CDS were more imagined than real. In bankruptcy, Lehman could not, of course, meet its obligations on a large CDS portfolio, and to the extent that Lehman owed money on CDS contracts at the time of its bankruptcy these obligations were canceled by the bankruptcy trustee. In addition, the firms that had written protection (the CDS term for insurance) on Lehman's debt were required to make good on their obligations to the counterparties who had paid for protection against Lehman's default. Nevertheless, there were no serious repercussions of the Lehman bankruptcy as a result of these "interconnections" with other financial institutions. All the protection written on Lehman's debt was settled among the buyers and sellers in an auction process five weeks later, through the exchange of a little over $5 billion among hundreds of counterparties. Those who had purchased protection from Lehman, and would now not be paid, submitted their claims to the Lehman bankruptcy trustee, again without any financial institution having been dragged into insolvency by this loss. This should not be surprising. Recall the fire insurance analogy: if the insurer becomes insolvent, as Lehman did, there is no loss to the homeowner unless the house suffers a fire immediately before the insurer's failure. Because there were few additional failures in the market around the time of Lehman's bankruptcy, the firms that had bought loss protection from Lehman simply canceled their contracts and went out into the market to buy new protection against the same loss on which Lehman had written protection. This makes it more than a little doubtful that the failure of Bear Stearns, had it been allowed to occur, would have caused the financial catastrophe that the Treasury and the Federal Reserve had posited.

Still, CDS were part of the reason for the failure of AIG. One of its subsidiaries, AIG Financial Products (AIGFP) had sold protection on PMBS backed by subprime mortgages, and its obligations were guaranteed by AIG. As these securities lost value in 2007 and 2008, AIG was obligated to supply cash collateral to the firms that had purchased CDS protection through AIGFP. That's the way the CDS system works; cash collateral moves back and forth between counterparties as the underlying insured obligation weakens or strengthens. Because AIG could not come up with the cash collateral, by September 2008 it was on the verge of a default. At that point, the Federal Reserve came forward with an even larger financial rescue package than it provided for Bear Stearns. Once again the government described its action as necessitated by the dangers of CDS, encouraging the media and others to draw the same mistaken inference that Roger Lowenstein had drawn: that CDS were a dangerous financial product and perhaps even a cause of the financial crisis.

For example, an article in the *New York Times* on May 17, 2013, referred to unregulated derivatives as "an essential cause of the 2008 financial crisis."[41] The article went on to describe derivatives trading as something that occurred, as though furtively, in Wall Street's "shadows." Another popular formulation was the dramatic statement that derivatives trading almost brought the world's financial system "to its knees."[42] Then there is Warren Buffett's statement that CDS are "financial weapons of mass destruction." It later turned out that Buffett was a major user of these "weapons" and even sold CDS protection without hedging the risk—exactly what, with other errors, took down AIG. They were weapons of mass destruction, he explained in testimony to the FCIC, in the hands of those who didn't know how to use them.[43] Statements like these were made or repeated routinely in the media, although there was little or no evidence that derivatives, and particularly CDS, actually created any dangerous "interconnections" or were "an essential cause" of the crisis. None of these writers or government officials seemed to understand that CDS do not create new risks; they simply transfer risk between counterparties. In AIG's case, if the firm had actually been allowed to fail, all the counterparties that had relied on it for protection against losses on securities that they held would then have been required to go out into the market—as noted in the fire insurance example above—to buy new protection. This might have cost them somewhat more, given the state of the market at the time, but it would not have caused their failure. Some news articles suggested that some of AIG's counterparties would have failed because AIG was no longer able to meet its obligations, but that is highly implausible. It did not happen when Lehman failed and there is no reason to believe that it would have happened if AIG had been allowed to fail. CDS are contingent obligations. Before an obligation is fixed, there must be a "credit event"— an actual default by a party whose failure is insured against, known as the "reference entity." A credit event is like the fire in the fire insurance example. In the absence of that, AIG's counterparties would simply have bought substitute protection. This was entirely possible, because the CDS market continued to function throughout the financial crisis.

Anyway, AIG did not fail because it was required to pay off on CDS obligations. It failed because it didn't have the cash to meet the *collateral obligations* that accrued when the PMBS its subsidiary had insured lost value. Thus, the media fantasies about the Fed rescuing AIG in order to save Goldman Sachs or Deutsche Bank are absurd.

AIG had not failed to respond to a credit event; it had only failed to supply the cash collateral it owed to its counterparties. It didn't even fail, many will be surprised to know, solely because of its collateral requirements in the CDS market. An equally important element in its failure was a securities lending business that AIG carried on for many of its life insurance subsidiaries. This is described in a paper by Hester Peirce, a scholar at the Mercatus Center of George Mason University.[44] In a securities lending business, the lender receives cash collateral from firms that borrow the securities for such purposes as short-selling or options trading. Ordinarily, cash collateral is conservatively invested so that it can be retrieved quickly if needed, but AIG used the cash to invest in highly illiquid PMBS backed by subprime loans, in effect doubling down on the unhedged risks that AIGFP had already taken. When the market for PMBS began to decline, the borrowers returned the securities they had borrowed and wanted the return of their cash collateral. The return of this cash, of course, was impossible; AIG had invested it in securities that could not be sold for anything close to their original value. When AIG was bailed out by the Federal Reserve, almost as much of the cash AIG received was used to return the cash collateral it owed in the securities lending business as was used to meet the cash collateral it owed on its CDS obligations.

As it turned out, AIG was the only firm that encountered serious financial difficulties because of CDS. It came close to failure—apart from its securities lending problems—because AIGFP had written only protection—one side of the CDS transaction—and did not hedge its risks; that is, in order to increase its profitability, the subsidiary wrote insurance but did not hedge these risks by acquiring offsetting assets, as almost all other participants in the CDS market regularly did. If it had, it would have received cash from its counterparty that might have been sufficient to meet AIG's cash collateral obligations for its CDS obligations. Banning or heavily regulating CDS because of the errors of one firm would be as foolish as banning or heavily regulating lending because one bank made bad loans, yet since then AIG has been the poster child—really the only example—cited as a reason for regulating the CDS market.

CDS were a matter of particular interest for the FCIC because Brooksley Born, a member of the commission and a former chair of the Commodity Futures Trading Commission, had drawn wide praise on the left for her efforts in the late 1990s to regulate derivatives and particularly CDS. *Frontline*, a PBS program, had hailed her "failed campaign to regulate the secretive, multitrillion-dollar derivatives market."[45] Born had given the FCIC staff a list of twenty-three detailed requests for data about the derivatives market, past controversies, Lehman's and AIG's failures, and many other issues and had much to say in meetings about the dangers of unregulated derivatives, but the commission was never able to establish that any firm other than AIG was hurt by the use of derivatives. Despite a diligent search, the FCIC never uncovered evidence that unregulated derivatives, and particularly credit default swaps, were a significant contributor to the financial crisis. The most that could validly be said was that the derivatives market was not "transparent." Nevertheless, the FCIC majority stated in its report that derivatives, and particularly CDS, "amplified" the losses in the financial crisis "by allowing multiple bets on the same securities."[46]

This is a familiar charge, and has a certain surface plausibility, but it can be easily refuted by anyone who understands how CDS actually work. "Amplification" might be said to occur in three areas: first, through what are called "synthetic" collateralized debt obligations (CDOs), where derivatives are used to mimic how a "real" CDO would function; second, through the failure of a firm to meet its obligation on a debt when a creditor has bought CDS protection against the loss; and, third, when a party buys protection against a loss in which it has no direct interest—like betting that your neighbor's house will burn down.

In the first case, an investor may want exposure to a particular risk—say, the AAA tranche of a real CDO—but none is available in the market. So an investor would enter a "synthetic" CDS with a bank, selling the bank protection against the possibility of losses on the CDO; the CDS premium paid by the bank for protection would be the same as the yield the investor would have received from the shares in the CDO. If the CDO were to suffer losses, the investor—having written protection—would pay the bank. How has this transaction magnified the risk in the market? If the CDO doesn't fail, the bank is the loser, and the investor the winner. If it does fail, it's the reverse. The actual risk in the market nets to zero—one party loses, and one party gains. There is only one real loss—the loss on the mortgages underlying the CDO; everything else is simply a transfer of that loss from one party to another.

The same thing is true in the ordinary CDS transaction. Let's assume that bank A makes a $10 million loan to IBM, but wants protection against a possible loss. So A buys protection from B and agrees to pay B a premium. B then hedges its risk with C and D, in which each takes a share of B's obligation to A in exchange for a share of the premium that A is paying to B. Does this amplify the risk in the market? Of course not; it spreads the risk, but doesn't change its size. To be sure, there are more parties now sharing some of the risk that IBM will not meet its obligation, but the risk is not "amplified" or enlarged; it is spread so that there is more capital to cover it. The risk entered the market with A's loan to IBM; it doesn't get larger or smaller because it has been moved elsewhere through a series of CDS. If bank C or D should fail, B has not suffered any loss unless, just before that failure, IBM should also fail. But in the ordinary case, if C should fail, then B would immediately go back into the market and buy substitute protection. This could be more or less costly, depending on the market's view at that point of the risk of an IBM default.

With regard to the objection that the parties are just "betting"—they don't have any real interest in the referenced CDO, just as a person doesn't have any interest in his neighbor's house. Although public policy might forbid buying insurance on a neighbor's house (which might create unwanted incentives), in the context of a market in financial instruments, the relevant considerations are different. Betting, or speculation, is the essence of how markets work. For example, short-selling is widely practiced in the equity markets. The short seller, by definition, doesn't have any interest in the stock he's selling; he is speculating—betting—that the price will fall, so he borrows the stock, sells it, and then, if he's right, buys it back at a lower price later. Because a market is made up of buys and sells, the short sale itself tends to lower the price; the more investors think the price of the stock is too high, the more short-selling and the closer the price comes to what the market as a whole thinks the stock is worth. This process is known as price discovery and is the basic function of markets. In the examples involving the CDO and IBM, the betting or speculation in the CDS market by those buying or selling protection reflects the market's effort at price discovery for both the CDO and IBM. The more such speculation occurs, the more likely that the market's evaluation is correct at any point in time.

The argument that derivatives contributed to the financial crisis has little validity and appears to rest entirely on the fact that a single firm—AIG—suffered losses because of improper risk-taking by a subsidiary. In fact, there was authoritative support that the CDS market performed well during and after the financial crisis. On March 9, 2009, the Senior Supervisors Group, representing the senior financial supervisors in the seven countries with the most developed financial systems, reported on how the derivatives market functioned during the financial crisis. They noted at the outset that there had been an unprecedented twelve "credit events" in the second half of 2008. As noted above, a credit event triggers an obligation to pay under the terms of a CDS. The senior supervisors concluded that "overall, the review confirmed the effectiveness of the existing auction-based settlement mechanism. Surveyed participants reported that the recent credit events were managed in an orderly fashion, with no major operational disruptions or liquidity problems."[47]

Fitch Ratings also reported in August 2009, after surveying market participants, that the CDS market continued to function throughout the crisis:

The CDS market generally remained open throughout the crisis particularly for indices and single-name CDS contracts, and this has enabled market participants to hedge or

take on credit exposures. . . . In-house research by Fitch So-
lutions also indicates that contrary to assumptions made by
many models that liquidity declines across the board in times
of stress, liquidity for a certain range of asset classes may actually have improved during the crisis.[48]

With one exception, all the other objections to unregulated derivatives trading appear to be based on misunderstandings about
how CDS work. The exception is the lack of transparency in an over-
the-counter market. Normally, this lack of transparency adds costs
for those who use the market, largely because price discovery is im-
peded without immediate disclosure of transaction prices. However,
even that could be changed without regulation by better disclosure
and, where possible, the use of exchanges for trading CDS. The true
problem in 2008 was that neither relevant government officials or the
media seemed to understand how CDS work and used them to justify
bailouts of Bear Stearns and AIG that probably were not necessary.
Although better disclosure about positions and prices would have
been sufficient, the Dodd-Frank solution was substantial additional
regulation, which will drive up costs and reduce the value of CDS for
the important function of risk management.

Failures of risk management in banks
and other financial institutions

Claims that there was a general failure of risk management in financial institutions or excessive leverage or risk-taking are part of
what might be called a "hindsight narrative." This approach was a
favorite in the FCIC report. With hindsight, it is easy to condemn
managers for failing to see the dangers of the housing bubble or the
underpricing of risk that now looks so clear. The fact is, however,
as noted previously, that virtually everyone—regulators, investors,
rating agencies, analysts, housing experts, and the management of
financial institutions—failed to see the crisis coming. A transcript
of a discussion among the members of the Federal Reserve's Board
of Governors on August 7, 2007, reported in the *New York Times*

in January 2013, makes clear that the Federal Reserve was also in the dark about the scope of the subprime mortgage problem only a few months before the rescue of Bear Stearns.[49] Under these circumstances, it does not seem reasonable to blame the risk managers at financial institutions when even the Federal Reserve, with its enormous data resources and huge staff of economists, did not see the mortgage meltdown coming and did not grasp the seriousness of the situation in the housing market. It is also inherently implausible that risk managers at virtually every financial institution would all fail simultaneously to see something that was in fact foreseeable.

As discussed fully in chapter 10, information about the risks in the U.S. financial system, particularly the number of NTMs outstanding, was unavailable or inadequate before the crisis—and only came to light well afterward. Before writing my dissent from the FCIC majority report, I scoured the Internet to determine whether *anyone* was aware of the enormous number of NTMs in the financial system before 2008. I did another study while writing this book. I could find no published material by analysts, economists, academics, or anyone else in which the number of outstanding NTMs—now estimated to be at least 31 million—was recognized. Small wonder that risk managers in financial institutions failed to recognize the problem. It is possible that if risk managers knew that there were 31 million NTMs in the financial system in 2007, rather than one-quarter of that number as the Federal Reserve believed at the time, the risks of investing in PMBS backed by NTMs would have been clear. This information, however, was not available. Risk managers can only manage risks that they can identify.

The paucity of information was caused in large part by the fact that Fannie and Freddie did not disclose that they were holding large numbers of NTMs, and the firms that routinely aggregated the data published by Fannie and Freddie did not look behind the numbers the banks and GSEs supplied. Housing finance specialists had been brought up to believe that Fannie and Freddie only made prime mortgages, so their data on mortgages the GSEs acquired were always put into the prime category unless the GSEs stated otherwise.

In December 2011, the SEC sued three top officers of Fannie and Freddie who were in office just before the two firms were taken over by the government. Unlike the actions of their predecessors, who were equally guilty, the actions of these officers had not yet been barred by the statute of limitations. The SEC's claim was that both firms had failed adequately to disclose in their SEC filings or their communications with investors the extent of their exposure to risky NTMs. For years, in order to comply with the quotas established by HUD for the affordable-housing goals, Fannie and Freddie had been acquiring large numbers of NTMs but had continued to claim that their exposure to subprime mortgages was less than 1 percent. The fact that the GSEs were by far the largest buyers of these NTMs could account for the lack of information available to risk managers, regulators, analysts, and even such key market information sources as the rating agencies. Many other reasons for the lack of information or a failure to perceive the risks in the mortgage market as the financial crisis approached are recounted in chapter 10.

It's possible that the GSEs were following HUD's lead in downplaying their exposure to subprime loans. In chapter 4, we will discuss a HUD statement to the effect that, if the GSEs could become "comfortable with subprime lending," this would erase the line between prime and subprime loans. Eliminating underwriting standards that create a distinction between prime and subprime mortgages has long been an objective of the left, which would prefer a mortgage financing system that does not make the distinctions between borrowers that are inherent in the traditional mortgage underwriting system. Instead, as the left has shown again and again, they would prefer a system in which the only question is whether the borrower can repay a mortgage at the time it is closed. They believe that the borrower's history of meeting credit obligations should be irrelevant. The GSEs' refusal to recognize a distinction between mortgages that are prime or subprime by characteristics was a step down this road. On the other hand, both GSEs had a venal reason for denying that they were exposed to subprime loans: the information could have adversely affected their stock prices.

Securitization

Securitization, as it is done today for mortgages, was used in the 1920s but fell into disuse. The system was revived by Ginnie Mae in the 1970s to distribute FHA-insured loans, and it was adopted by Freddie Mac in the 1970s and by Fannie Mae in the 1980s. When Fannie and Freddie or other government-backed agencies use it, the system is simple: the sponsor collects a pool of mortgages from many originators or lenders. The pool then issues securities backed by the principal and interest paid on the mortgages in the pool, which is passed through to the security holders in proportion to their ownership percentages. In a government-backed securitization, the government agency takes the credit risk by guaranteeing that the principal and interest will be a certain amount; the investor in the securities takes the interest rate risk—the risk that the mortgages will prepay or that market interest rates will rise, reducing the value of the securities.

Private mortgage-backed securities are considerably more complicated because there is no guarantee of the credit risk. Instead, the PMBS securitization system relies on a senior/subordinate structure to create credit support for the senior securities. As principal and interest flow in, the senior securities, usually the AAA and AA tranches, are paid first, and the subordinated securities are paid last. In other words, the subordinated securities (those rated lower than AAA) take the losses if mortgages in the pool begin to default and the funds that are supposed to come into the pool are diminished. Each tranche is rated separately—from AAA at the top to an unrated equity portion at the bottom—by one or more rating agencies. Because its risk of loss is lowest, the AAA tranche at the top receives the lowest yield, and the equity portion at the bottom receives the highest yield because its risk is greatest. The thicker the subordinated level or levels in the tranching structure, the more security there is for the top AAA and AA tranches, which usually constitute between 85 to 90 percent of all the securities issued. In that case, the assumption is that the losses on the underlying mortgages are unlikely to be greater than 10 to 15 percent. If that assessment is correct, the senior securities should suffer no losses, all of which would be borne by the subordinate tranches.

The private securitization structure as just outlined has been pejoratively described as an "originate-to-distribute" system and has been blamed by some—including the FCIC—for the financial crisis. To the proponents of this view, securitization fosters risk because no one, from the originator of the loan to the securitizer that assembles the pool and sells the MBS, has any "skin in the game." The flaw in this argument is that there is a buyer at the end of the chain who has skin in the game and *is* concerned about risk; the only reason that the process begins with the origination of a risky loan is that the buyer at the end has signaled that it believes the risk-adjusted yield makes the security a good investment. What drives the securitization process is not—as the critics seem to assume—the origination of a loan; instead, the driving force is the *demand*, the desire of the final investor to acquire the mortgage or a security backed by a pool of mortgages.

That's why it is so important to an understanding of the financial crisis to know that 76 percent of the NTMs outstanding in 2008 were on the books of government agencies; that single fact shows where the demand for those mortgages came from. The NTMs that defaulted in 2007 and 2008 wouldn't have been originated in the first place without the government's desire to acquire them.

In reality, the private securitization system is simply another version of the familiar supply chain, in which the originator of a part of an end product sends it to an intermediate or final assembler. Supply chains operate in the same way, whether they involve the growing and marketing of lettuce or the manufacturing of an automobile. Each participant in the chain has no "skin in the game" other than its reputation for quality, backed by the possibility that it may be liable for the failure of what it has supplied to perform as advertised. The securitization of mortgages is no different. Indeed, as we have seen all through 2013 and 2014, the GSEs "put back" to banks and other originators loans that the GSEs contended were not of the quality the sellers had warranted. Apparently, if we are to believe these put backs were legitimate, the originators had skin in the game after all.

It might of course be true that the buyer of a mortgage-backed security was deluded or not fully informed about the risk, but that is a different question. In the case of the 76 percent of the NTMs that were on the books of government agencies, the agencies were unlikely to be deluded buyers. The GSEs and FHA had been specializing in taking mortgage risk for generations; they were as sophisticated about the subject as any buyer in the market. The idea that originators came up with NTMs or other low-quality loans, turned them into PMBS, and foisted them on the GSEs, or that banks saw the GSEs as a place to dump their bad loans, is absurd. "Belgian dentists"—the classic unsophisticated buyers—were perhaps so unsophisticated that they did not understand the risks of NTMs, but that is a distraction; sales to them or to other unsophisticated buyers were unfortunate, but they were irrelevant as causes of the financial crisis. What caused the financial crisis was the demand by the GSEs and other buyers around the world for exposure to NTMs. The GSEs wanted that exposure because of the affordable-housing goals; the others wanted it because they wanted higher returns without—they thought—commensurate risks. The U.S. financial institutions that got into trouble because they held AAA-rated PMBS appear to have done so because they thought those instruments were virtually risk free. But that's not an inherent fault of securitization; as I've noted previously, it can be attributed at least in part to insufficient information about the number of NTMs that were outstanding or other conditions in the market, a subject covered fully in chapter 10.

There is nothing about securitization per se that caused NTM buyers to regret their purchases. Every seller in the chain promises every buyer that the mortgages in the pool are of a certain quality. If they are not, the buyer has a right against the seller in the usual course, just like any supply chain. The fact that the seller is out of business when the buyer comes looking for redress is not an inherent problem in securitization either, but one of the costs of doing business that has to be addressed by the buyer before a transaction is completed. It's a cumbersome process, to be sure, but it is not an inherent problem with securitization. The same process works in virtually every other supply chain.

Ultimately, securitization is only a means of financing—a way for an investor's desire for a certain product to be satisfied and a way for a seller to be paid for an obligation previously assumed. For decades, without serious incident, securitization has been used to finance car loans, credit card loans, and jumbo mortgages that were not eligible for acquisition by Fannie Mae and Freddie Mac. The problem was not securitization itself; instead, investors (including particularly Fannie and Freddie) wanted the weak and high-risk loans that happened to be financed through securitization.[50]

Collateralized debt obligations

Although significant losses occurred to the holders of AAA-rated PMBS in the financial crisis, what happened to the AAA-rated tranches of CDOs was of a different order. In a sense, securitization in general has been blamed for losses that were largely attributable to CDOs, which were only a relatively small portion of the PMBS issued in 2005 and 2006—the years in which the PMBS of the lowest quality were issued. Most CDOs were composed of a pool of the lower and more risky tranches—say, the BBB-rated tranches—of PMBS pools already outstanding. As such, they were inherently more likely to suffer losses than the PMBS pools from which they were derived. However, if the subordinated portion of the CDO was thick enough—that is, if the lower-rated tranches were a larger proportion of the total CDO pool—it was theoretically possible to create a AAA layer that would not be likely to suffer losses even in a serious housing market downturn. Nonetheless, we had a serious housing market downturn in 2007 and 2008, and CDOs suffered what can only be called horrific losses. Obviously, the risk of loss on these instruments was not correctly assessed. With hindsight, the subordinated tranches should have been much thicker.

In May 2012, Larry Cordell, Yilin Huang, and Meredith Williams—three economists at the Federal Reserve Bank of Philadelphia—published a paper principally devoted to a detailed study of what happened to CDOs in the financial crisis.[51] According to the Cordell paper, a total of 727 CDO pools were issued between 1999 and 2007, with a total value of $641 billion.[52] This total included $201 billion that were synthetic CDOs made up primarily of credit default swaps that imitated real CDOs.[53] Almost two-thirds of the CDOs were issued in 2006 and 2007.[54] The paper estimated that the write-downs taken by the holders of these instruments will eventually total $420 billion, or 65 percent of $641 billion of total issuance.[55] This can be compared with impairment losses of 4.4 percent estimated by Moody's for AAA-rated PMBS tranches based on first lien subprime loans, as shown in Table 3.3.

Because of accounting rules, write-downs do not necessarily correspond to actual cash losses. As we will see, for reasons discussed in chapter 12, the accounting losses flowing from the use of mark-to-market accounting were probably a great deal larger than the actual cash losses. Indeed, some investors eventually made billions of dollars in profits by acquiring PMBS that the bankrupt Lehman estate had written down and sold off at distress prices.[56]

The Cordell paper puts the total amount of PMBS issued between 1998 and 2007 at $5.8 trillion, so CDOs accounted for about 11 percent of the PMBS issued during that period. A substantial portion of these CDOs ($342 billion) were made up of securities from PMBS that were rated A or better, and $299 billion were composed of what are called mezzanine-level (BBB or lower) securities and were thus inherently riskier. In addition, there were forty-eight offerings of what were called CDOs-squared—that is, CDOs made up of securities issued by other CDOs and based on the lower tranches of these original CDOs.[57] The paper makes the important point that the AAA-rated tranches of the mezzanine CDOs and CDOs-squared had levels of subordination behind them that were roughly equivalent to AAA-rated PMBS, although the risks were many times greater.[58] The authors explain that this was the result of a gross underestimation of the risks of CDOs, but do not address why the firms that held these securities—and the rating agencies that established the required subordination levels—failed to understand the severity of these risks. As a result, it is clear that major losses would have occurred to the holders of the AAA-rated tranches even in a modest turndown in the market. As the authors note: "As for the dealers at the center of [single-family mortgage] CDO issuance, our results

TABLE 3.3. Material impairments for 2005–2007 vintage U.S. RMBS/HEL backed by subprime first lien mortgages (as of year-end 2009)

Original rating	By number of tranches			By dollar volume (U.S. $ millions)		
	Impaired	Rated	% Impaired	Impaired	Rated	% Impaired
Aaa	433	5,303	8.2	36,618	840,240	4.4
Aa	1,665	2,941	56.6	49,846	95,666	52.1
A	2,341	2,973	78.7	37,798	49,778	75.9
Baa	2,838	3,003	94.5	33,549	35,132	95.5
Ba	903	917	98.5	9,098	9,156	99.4
B	2	2	100.0	19	19	100.0
Total	**8,182**	**15,139**	**54.0**	**166,928**	**1,029,992**	**16.2**

Source: Moody's Investors Service, "Default & Loss Rates of Structured Finance Securities: 1993–2009," p. 13, exhibit 19.

support the hypothesis that most were not fully aware of the risks in the CDOs, since the dealers that underwrote the worst-performing CDOs (Morgan Stanley, Citicorp, Bear Stearns, and UBS) all suffered large and debilitating losses from the 'super-senior' AAA bonds of the CDOs they underwrote and held."[59]

It is important to note that CDOs did not increase the losses in the financial system that arose out of the widespread distribution of PMBS based on NTMs. Those losses were what they were; the CDOs simply moved the losses in the higher-risk tranches (say, BBB) from the original holders to the new holders of the CDOs. Even the synthetic CDOs, which were based on credit default swaps as discussed earlier, did not increase the risks created by the securitization of NTMs; again, they simply moved the risk from one group to another. However, although CDOs did not multiply the losses, they did contribute to the financial crisis. This occurred because the AAA or super-senior-rated CDOs were frequently retained by many of the dealers in PMBS and CDOs, and this concentrated the losses in, and weakened, many of the major financial institutions in the United States and abroad. Ironically, if these securities had been sold, their decline in value would have been absorbed by much more capital than was available in the largest financial institutions. The amount of the losses on CDOs estimated by the Cordell paper, $420 billion, could easily have been absorbed by the multi-trillion-dollar global market. Still, if government housing policies had not built the bubble and caused the dispersion of NTMs throughout the economy, it is highly unlikely that CDOs would have ever come into existence, let alone become a sought-after investment.

There is some irony here. While the conventional narrative of the financial crisis blames the large (Wall Street) financial institutions for selling what they "must have known" were low-quality PMBS to customers around the world, the really significant losses in the financial crisis came from the CDOs that these firms *retained*. Why the major dealers were unaware of the risks these securities involved remains something of a mystery. The Cordell paper notes that a study by Lehman in 2005 (another irony) concluded that the ratings of the CDOs had assumed a continuation of 5 percent to 8 percent home price appreciation during their outstanding life.[60] This rate of appreciation, of course, was and proved to be unsustainable. When the housing bubble stopped growing, the losses began to show up and wiped out the lower-rated tranches of the PMBS on which the CDOs and CDOs-squared were based.

This is one of the areas where the lack of information about the holdings of the GSEs might have had an effect on risk management in the private sector. Based on the historical record and the failure of Fannie and Freddie to reveal the scope of their NTM holdings, it was plausible that the number of NTMs outstanding was seen as relatively small, leading private risk managers to believe that, even if the growth in housing prices leveled off, the decline in housing values—and thus the mortgage losses—would also be relatively small. But when the vast number of NTMs that the GSEs had acquired or securitized began to default, and housing prices began their 30- to 40-percent decline, these losses were of a size almost no one had expected. The same factors might have affected the models of the rating agencies, discussed below.

Credit rating agencies

One of the simplest explanations for the financial crisis is the claim that the rating agencies, either because of incompetence or venality, gave ratings to PMBS backed by NTMs that could not be rationally justified. If they had done their work better, runs the argument, there would not have been a financial crisis, because AAA-rated PMBS, CDOs, and CDO-squared securities would not have been issued because they could not have been sold. Based on the Cordell paper and the Moody's table (Table 3.3), where the rating agencies really failed was in giving AAA ratings to the top tranches of CDOs and CDOs-squared. Their ratings of normal PMBS based on subprime loans were roughly on target, making allowance for the unprecedented conditions in the market, with impairments of the AAA tranches at only 4.4 percent. Why they failed so seriously in their CDO ratings is another mystery, much like why so many banks retained the AAA-rated CDOs that were also disastrous investments. However, in the case of the rating agencies, this could be accounted for by the fact that the mortgage market was far different in the 2000s from what the rating agencies' models expected; the information available in the market had been distorted by the housing bubble and seriously truncated by the failure of the GSEs to disclose their true exposures to NTMs. These issues are discussed in detail in chapter 10.

The FCIC's review of the rating agencies was cursory and heavily weighted toward the idea that their objectivity was impaired by an insurmountable conflict of interest: they were paid by the financial institutions that were seeking the ratings.[61] That approach certainly has some surface plausibility, but there are many lingering questions. Conflicts of interest of this kind are common throughout our economy—companies pay their independent auditors, we rely on doctors to tell us the truth about whether surgery is necessary, and newspapers that take pride in their tough investigative reporting survive on advertising by business firms they are supposed to investigate—but we live with these conflicts because we have not found better ways to get the services we need. In addition, the objectivity or validity of the ratings that the agencies give to individual issuers and individual securities has seldom been challenged, even though the agencies are paid by the issuers. Why is it that the rating agencies became incompetent or venal when they rated pools of CDOs but not the debt of individual corporate issuers or pools of credit cards or car loans? Certainly government, although possibly more objective, lacks the incentive to do these tasks well or to improve them over time. At least rating agencies, auditors, doctors, and news outlets have to worry about their reputations because they are not monopoly providers.

But some critics assert, with reason, that rating agencies are different. They have functioned for many years under an informal government license, designated by the SEC as Nationally Recognized Statistical Rating Organizations (NRSROs). Many observers believe that this designation gave them enough market power to reduce their concern for their own reputations and exploit their government-conferred positions for profit. This is clearly a serious problem, but the SEC has now opened the process for becoming a NRSRO, and over time new entries should result in a more competitive market and hence more concern about reputation.

Perhaps what happened to the rating agencies is simply another iteration of what happened to the banks and other financial institutions that retained the disastrously overrated CDOs. It is the same problem that afflicted the corporate risk managers and the regulators who failed to recognize the risks that were building up in the housing finance market: key information about the composition of the market was not available because most observers of the housing market believed the GSEs only acquired prime loans and the GSEs had failed to disclose that the affordable-housing goals had changed the nature of their business.

The rating agencies may be particularly susceptible to this problem. They do their work through statistics; they do not examine individual mortgages. In rating PMBS, they were given a pool of several thousand mortgages and a tape or disk that describes the characteristics of those mortgages as a group—how many mortgages have down payments and in what size; how many have FICO scores below 660; how many have DTI ratios greater than 38 percent; how many are from Iowa, California, New Hampshire, or Minnesota; and dozens of other slices of information through the data. Geographical diversification was extremely important to ratings. Throughout the history of the mortgage market, serious downturns in prices had occurred only locally, never on a national basis. A widely diversified pool meant that the anticipated local losses, if any, were compensated by the continued housing price growth in other areas. However, the rating agencies were never asked to rate GSE MBS or those issued by Ginnie Mae. These were regarded as government-guaranteed, and no rating was considered necessary. As a result, the rating agencies had no idea that the GSEs were acquiring large numbers of NTMs, a fact that—if known—would have substantially affected their models of the financial system.

Using data it has about the market, the rating agency calculates the likelihood that a given number of mortgages in a PMBS pool will default and the likely losses given that number of defaults. To make such an estimate, they look at data from the past, including the rates of default for similar mortgages in California, say, or Minnesota. These data are built into the agencies' models. In the past, there were local market downturns, but modern times had not seen a nationwide housing price collapse comparable to what occurred in 2007 and 2008. A decline in housing values of 30 to 40 percent throughout the country was completely ahistorical; there had never been anything like it apart from the Great Depression. Housing market veterans could recall declines of 3 or 4 percent, and even these were only local. So, statistically, the geographical diversification was expected to provide some protection to the AAA-rated tranches against loss. However, because of the GSEs' failure to disclose their exposure to NTMs, the number of NTMs outstanding in 2007 and 2008 was much larger than had ever been true before—a fact that was unknown to the rating agencies and thus not plugged into their models. If it had been known at the time that more than half of all mortgages in the United States were NTMs, that fact alone might have suggested to the rating agencies that the market was far riskier than even the most overheated markets of the past. In other words, the failure of the rating agencies—especially with respect to CDOs— is likely to have occurred for reasons far more complex than the fact that they earned a lot of money for their ratings or benefited from an implicit government license.

Predatory lending

The FCIC's majority report also blames predatory lending for the large build-up of subprime and other high-risk mortgages in the financial system. There is little evidence to support this claim. In predatory lending, unscrupulous lenders take advantage of unwitting borrowers. This undoubtedly occurred, but it also appears that many people who received high-risk loans were predatory *borrowers*, or engaged in mortgage fraud, because they took advantage of low mortgage underwriting standards to benefit from mortgages they knew they could not pay unless rising housing prices enabled them to sell or refinance.

The FCIC was never able to shed any light on the extent to which predatory lending occurred. Substantial portions of the majority's report describe abusive activities by some lenders and mortgage brokers, but without giving any data on how widespread such practices were. This information would be essential if the prevalence of predatory lending is to be causally connected to an event as serious as the financial crisis. Furthermore, the majority's report fails to acknowledge that the biggest buyers of NTMs were government agencies or private companies complying with government requirements like the affordable-housing goals or the CRA. Although the notion that the crisis was caused in some substantial way by predatory lending is a popular idea on the left, the FCIC was unable to find any empirical data to support it, despite my frequent requests.

Thomas Sowell, as usual, summarized well the attitude on the left:

[T]he concept of "predatory lenders" has become widely applied loosely to all kinds of other situations and institutions whose only common denominator is that critics don't like them or don't understand them. . . . Many in politics have acted as if predatory lenders are what caused the housing crisis—a view especially common among those who themselves had a major role in bringing on the crisis.[62]

"Perfect storm" theories

With all the possible causes bouncing around in the ideas market, the easiest way to account for the financial crisis is to say, as so many speakers and writers have done since the crisis, that "everyone was at fault" or (the all-time favorite cliché) "there is plenty of blame to go around." Statements like these, apart from being meaningless, cannot be proved wrong; there is no question that virtually everyone made mistakes in one way or another leading up to the events of 2008.

But there are some interesting "perfect storm" theories postulating that the financial crisis would not have occurred at all if a series of events—some causes and some effects—had not happened at the same time. One example of this approach is the dissent of the other three other Republican members of the FCIC, Keith Hennessey,

Douglas Holtz-Eakin, and Bill Thomas. Their dissent argues that "ten causes, global and domestic, are essential to explaining the financial crisis."[63] These ten causes are as follows:

1. A credit bubble
2. A housing bubble
3. NTMs
4. Errors of credit rating agencies magnified by securitization
5. Concentrated, correlated risk in financial institutions
6. Leverage and liquidity risk
7. Risk of contagion
8. Common shock
9. Financial shock and investor panic
10. The financial crisis causes economic crisis

The statement that these ten items are essential to explaining the crisis makes their dissent a classic perfect storm analysis, especially because they made clear that all the elements had to occur together in order for the crisis to occur.

Another of these perfect storm theories was advanced by Alan Blinder of Princeton University and a former vice chair of the Federal Reserve. In his book *After the Music Stopped*, he notes, accurately, after reviewing the FCIC report and many other works, that the American people have never been given an explanation of why there was a financial crisis.[64] "Did anyone get the license number of that truck?" is the way he expresses the bewilderment of the American people. But then he names "seven villains" of the crisis:

1. A housing bubble
2. Excessive leverage
3. Lax financial regulation
4. Disgraceful banking practices
5. Unregulated securities and derivatives that were built on these mortgages
6. The abysmal performance of the statistical rating agencies
7. The perverse compensation systems in many financial institutions

Blinder's perfect storm has several points in common with the perfect storm imagined by Hennessey, Holtz-Eakin, and Thomas, and that in itself is an important point, highlighting one of the problems of perfect storm theories: it's hard to know when to stop listing causes. The more causes listed, the less we learn, and the less the theory can serve as a guide for policy makers in the future. In that sense, they are something of a cop-out, like saying "there is plenty of blame to go around." Moreover, and perhaps more important, perfect storms, almost by definition, are rare. If a financial crisis will occur in the future only when all the elements in these perfect storms come together at the same time again, there is little to worry about— the chances that they will all be present concurrently are vanishingly small.

Nevertheless, in one respect the two perfect storm analyses are the same. Neither gives any special role to government housing policy. Both explanations, like the FCIC's own narrative, are focused almost entirely on the errors of the private sector. Given the fact that a "mortgage meltdown" among NTMs preceded the crisis, that more than half of all mortgages in the United States were NTMs, and that more than three-quarters of those NTMs were on the books of government agencies and entities operating under government regulatory control, the elephant in the room was hiding in plain sight.

4

A Short History of
Housing Finance in the U.S.

How and Why Housing Finance
Was Substantially Changed in 1992

Lenders will respond to the most conservative standards unless
[Fannie and Freddie] are aggressive and convincing in their
efforts to expand historically narrow underwriting.

GALE CINCOTTA, testimony before the U.S. Senate
Committee on Banking, Housing, and Urban Affairs, 1991

The housing policies that were the major contributing cause of the financial crisis were the culmination of years of increasing government involvement in housing. Beginning in the Depression era, the government's role increased gradually until its policies—which initially sought to stabilize and rationalize the housing market—turned into a politically potent expression of social policy. This chapter is a short summary of how this occurred.

In the last forty years, enlightened government policy has reduced or eliminated regulation in many areas of the U.S. economy, with great benefits for consumers in the cost and quality of services. Some examples, among many others, are air travel, trucking, telecommunications, and securities trading. But this has not happened in financial services or housing. Instead, every time the government's policies have failed, its role in housing sector finance has grown. The financial crisis was simply the last—and greatest—of the government's debacles. And of course it came about because Congress and two presidents wanted to help low-income families to buy homes. This was a worthy goal, but it took a system that had the potential to function on its own and cut away its conceptual foundations, culminating in the Federal Housing Enterprises Financial Safety and Soundness Act of 1992 (the GSE Act) and the affordable-housing goals. "Only George Orwell," wrote Michael Cembalest of JPMorgan Chase, "could have named a bill that was so fundamentally contradicted by its purpose and consequence."[1]

THE FEDERAL HOUSING ADMINISTRATION

After the speculative boom of the late 1920s, in which mortgages with loan-to-value (LTV) ratios of 100 percent were not uncommon,[2] the Great Depression produced excessively conservative lending policies by the banks that had been the primary sources of housing finance. At the time, there were no national markets for mortgages, many local and regional differences in mortgage terms, very low LTV ratios of 50 to 60 percent, and a homeownership rate of less than 44 percent. Mortgages tended to be relatively short-term, with bullet payments at the end. If a mortgage could not be refinanced at the end of its term—and many in the Depression could not be—it was foreclosed. The U.S. government's direct involvement in housing finance began in 1934 with the creation of the Federal Housing Administration (FHA), which had the authority to insure mortgages for up to 100 percent of the loan amount. By providing a government guarantee, the FHA was intended to overcome the reluctance of banks and others to make long-term mortgage loans. Over time, the FHA had a major role in standardizing mortgage terms, increasing acceptable LTV ratios to approximately 80 percent, and encouraging the development of mortgages that amortized over multiyear periods. In 1934, FHA-insured loans had a maximum LTV ratio of 80 percent and a maximum loan term of twenty years. A 1936 FHA underwriting manual shows that, in addition, FHA underwriters wanted to see a good or excellent credit record and a relatively low debt-to-income ratio that took into account the borrower's residual income (remaining income after taxes, household costs, and outstanding debts).[3]

Because of these strict underwriting standards, the FHA's record for the next twenty years—through the Great Depression, World War II, and the postwar housing boom—was exemplary: defaults on FHA mortgages remained well under 1 percent.

However, when the U.S. economy went into recession in 1957, Congress—to stimulate housing demand—reduced the FHA's down payment requirement to 3 percent in steps between 1957 and 1961. This was not the first time that Congress had used underwriting standards for purposes other than ensuring the quality of mortgages or the safety and soundness of financial institutions. But in this case, Congress had made a major change in the conditions under which a mortgage would be granted. An important line had been crossed.

The results are clear in Figure 4.1. By the late 1960s, foreclosures were sixteen times higher for FHA mortgages than they had been in 1953. The chart also shows that conventional mortgage foreclosures remained relatively stable, primarily because the average LTV ratio of conventional loans at the time was much lower than for FHA mortgages. Between 1959 and 1967, the average LTV ratios of outstanding FHA loans ranged between 91 and 92.9 percent, while the LTV ratios of outstanding conventional loans ranged between 71.1 and 76.1 percent.[4] Nevertheless, although conventional mortgages were about two-thirds of all U.S. mortgages in the 1960s, the homeownership rate in the United States was approximately 64 percent, where it remained for the next thirty years.

The difference in foreclosure rates between the conventional and FHA markets is thus attributable to the fact that FHA underwriting standards could be easily manipulated by Congress—which was seeking to boost the housing market in the recessions of the late 1950s and early 1960s—while banks and the savings and loan associations described below continued to be regulated in the interests of safety and soundness. Under the control of Congress, which had always set its underwriting and lending limits, the FHA became a largely low-income lender, providing loans to borrowers who could not meet conventional underwriting standards. Beginning in 1993, the FHA was gradually shunted aside by Fannie and Freddie, which

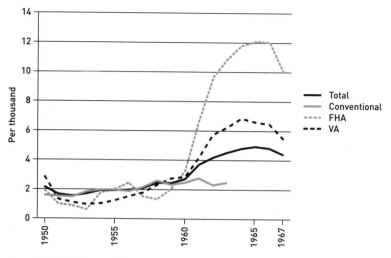

Source: John P. Herzog and James Earley, *Home Mortgage Delinquency and Foreclosure* (Cambridge, Mass.: National Bureau of Economic Research, 1970), 26, www.nber.org /chapter/c3294.pdf.

FIG. 4.1. Postwar foreclosure rates

were often looking for the same loans as the FHA in order to meet their affordable-housing requirements. As this book is being written, Congress is faced with the FHA's insolvency and trying to figure out how to stop the losses. Unfortunately, these are the result of a policy that Congress and presidents cherish—providing low-cost mortgages to people who don't have down payments, good credit, or steady employment. Stopping losses that add to the deficit and are ultimately borne by the taxpayers means that the government must get control of the costs of what is essentially a social policy.

FEDERAL SAVINGS AND LOAN ASSOCIATIONS

During the Depression, in addition to FHA and Fannie Mae, Congress also created the federal insurance structure for a system of federal savings and loan associations (S&Ls), financial institutions that were able to offer government-insured deposits and were limited to making investments in real estate—primarily residential mortgage loans. People would deposit their money safely in an insured S&L, and in turn the S&L would finance homes. It seemed like a good idea at the time, but ultimately the system was another example of a poorly designed government program. Insured S&Ls were regulated by the Federal Home Loan Bank Board (Bank Board), established in 1932. Before and after World War II, the conventional market constituted about two-thirds of the housing finance market. This market was also stable, with defaults under 1 percent, primarily because the Bank Board kept LTV ratios at 60 percent (that is, down payments of 40 percent) in the 1930s and no more than 80 percent in the postwar period.[5] Limiting the business of S&Ls to long-term residential loans, however, placed them in an untenable position. The principal risk of depository institutions like banks and S&Ls is the mismatch between short-term liabilities (often deposits that can be withdrawn on demand) and their long-term assets (loans and mortgages). This creates two additional kinds of risk; first, that depositors will seek to withdraw funds that have already been lent to borrowers, and, second, that the yield on the firm's assets (such as mortgages and other loans) will be less than the cost of its deposits and other liabilities.

Commercial banks can address both problems in part by making short-term commercial or consumer loans, or loans at variable interest rates, but S&Ls were expected to use their deposits to make 30-year fixed-rate mortgages. Congress may have thought that the risks to S&Ls inherent in lending at fixed rates for lengthy periods of time could be overcome by the Federal Reserve's Regulation Q. Beginning in 1934, Reg Q, as it was known, capped the rates that depository institutions were allowed to pay on their deposits. As long as inflation remained low and savers had few alternatives for their funds other than banks and S&L deposits, the cap on deposit interest rates worked to keep deposit and mortgage interest rates low, lending a temporary appearance of stability to both the S&L business model and the mortgage markets. The joke during this period was that S&L officers and owners were in the 3-6-3 business: borrow at 3 percent, lend at 6 percent, and be on the first tee at 3 p.m. It even got better. In 1966, in order to give S&Ls an advantage over banks in competing for deposits—and thus to give a financial preference to housing— the Federal Reserve adjusted the Reg Q cap so that S&Ls could pay one-quarter point more than banks for their deposits. The result was rapid growth in the S&L industry, which quadrupled in size between 1966 and 1979.

But while the Federal Reserve could control the rates that S&Ls could pay on deposits, it could not control general market interest rates, which responded to large international economic forces. The high interest rates associated with the inflationary period of the 1970s were fatal to the S&L business model. Once interest rates rose above the Reg Q caps, deposits flowed out of S&Ls and banks and were not replenished with new deposits as investors sought higher returns elsewhere. In these conditions, the Reg Q limitation on deposit rates became a serious problem for banks and S&Ls; they had trouble holding on to existing deposits and attracting new ones. But removing the limitations on deposit rates would exacerbate the mismatch between the yield on the low-interest 30-year mortgages that had been made by the S&Ls and the cost of new deposits. As market interest rates rose and fell, the funds available for housing became unstable, rising when rates fell and drying up when market rates rose. Although some observers of the post–World War II period recall it as a stable period for banks and S&Ls, it was in fact a time of unusual housing market volatility, with frequent severe recessions and long periods where there was no money available for housing at any price.[6]

The rise of money market mutual funds (MMFs) in the 1970s finally made Reg Q unworkable. Retail depositors now had a place to put their money when interest rates rose above the Reg Q caps, and they responded with enthusiasm. MMFs aggregated the funds of their shareholders to lend into the wholesale capital markets, receiving higher rates than Reg Q allowed and threatening the deposit bases of both banks and S&Ls. Because S&Ls made 30-year fixed-rate loans, they were more seriously damaged by this process than banks, although 1,600 small banks also failed during this period. By the time Congress finally authorized the removal of deposit interest rate caps in the Monetary Control Act of 1980, the S&L industry was in irremediable trouble. They were holding low-interest 30-year mortgages but were now exposed to the much higher market rates necessary to attract and hold deposits. Large portions of the industry became insolvent. The losses far exceeded the amount in the S&L insurance fund, and the taxpayers eventually had to absorb a loss estimated at approximately $150 billion. It is important to recognize that the only U.S. industry that has ever wholly collapsed was created, regulated, and insured by the government. The collapse of the S&Ls opened a door for Fannie Mae and Freddie Mac. Before, many mortgages went to the balance sheets of S&Ls; now they were available for acquisition by the government-sponsored enterprises (GSEs).

THE GOVERNMENT-SPONSORED ENTERPRISES
FANNIE MAE AND FREDDIE MAC

Although FHA insurance could overcome the reluctance of lenders to make mortgage loans, it could not provide them with the necessary liquidity. That role fell to Fannie Mae, formally called the Federal National Mortgage Association, which was originally chartered in 1938 to buy mortgages that had been FHA insured. By purchasing these loans, Fannie Mae provided banks and other mortgage originators with the necessary funds to make more mortgages and thus finance the growth of both homeownership and the U.S. housing industry. Between the Depression era and the years immediately after World War II, Fannie Mae's role in the housing finance market did not significantly change. During this period, it continued to be limited to acquiring FHA- and VA-insured loans, and Congress saw Fannie's purpose primarily as supplementing the financing available from banks and S&Ls when Reg Q–related disintermediation caused these depository institutions to falter. The larger conventional (uninsured) market was mostly served by banks and S&Ls, and there was no significant secondary market for these conventional mortgage lenders. This placed a limit on their mortgage lending, because it was not easy to sell existing conventional mortgages in a depository institution's portfolio.

This began to change in 1968. In that year, in the midst of the costly Vietnam War, President Johnson and his advisers were looking for ways to cut budgeted spending on domestic matters, and Fannie was a prime candidate. In the years before the technology of securitization was fully developed, Fannie's buying and selling of government-insured mortgages added to the deficit. If the enterprise could be removed from the government's budget and still perform the same role, it would be a win-win. Thus, as with so many government decisions, Fannie Mae was "privatized" for budgetary reasons. But this privatization, which began in 1968, was not complete; Fannie became a congressionally chartered private company with public shareholders. This removed Fannie from the federal budget, but the Johnson administration took steps to ensure that many of Fannie's benefits as a government agency were retained by the shareholder-owned company. Almost certainly, the officials who devised the privatization idea knew that Fannie could not continue to buy mortgages if it had to raise funds like an ordinary corporation. Its capitalization and earning power would not have enabled it to attain AAA status, and without the low-interest rates that a AAA rating would confer, it would not be possible for it to carry on a profitable business of buying and selling mortgages.

Thus, it was no accident that Fannie's privatization legislation included many continuing ties to the government—including, among many others, a congressional charter, a Treasury line of credit, exemption from the securities laws, and a government "mission" to establish and maintain a liquid secondary market in mortgages. These were signals to the capital markets that Fannie retained at least an implicit government backing, putting it in the category of a quasi-public/private company known as a government-sponsored enterprise. Officials in the Johnson administration were confident that Fannie, as a GSE, would be seen as government-backed.[7] Although Treasury Departments ever since have bravely asserted that Fannie and Freddie were not and would not be backed by the government, the markets never believed it. To be sure, the Treasury did not tell foreign central banks—avid buyers of GSE securities—that GSE securities were not backed by the U.S. government, and the FDIC encouraged banks to buy GSE securities, which were not subject to the usual limits on asset concentration because they were seen even within the government as essentially riskless.

Status as a GSE was exceedingly valuable. It enabled Fannie to raise funds at rates that were substantially lower than any private firms and only slightly higher than the Treasury itself. Furthermore, because its assets were government-insured mortgages, it was reasonable to believe that Fannie presented few risks. In 1970, Congress also chartered an identical GSE, the Federal Home Loan Mortgage Corporation, or Freddie Mac, specifically to provide liquidity to the S&L industry in the way that Fannie was providing liquidity to banks. However, Freddie Mac was not the most important element in the new law.[8] For the first time, both Fannie and the newly organized Freddie Mac were authorized to buy conventional mortgages—that is, mortgages not guaranteed by a government agency. This was a major turning point, and it is questionable whether Congress understood the importance of this step at the time. Fannie and Freddie were now companies with public shareholders and a different set of responsibilities and loyalties, interested in both profit and market share, and with access to the vast conventional market where it was possible to take substantial credit risks and make substantial profits.

Although not immediately obvious, it was at this point that the government essentially lost control of the GSEs. Although control could, of course, be reasserted through legislation, the GSEs could now build constituencies that would protect them against government encroachment. All that was necessary was for the two GSEs to provide support for housing finance; that made them valuable allies of banks, S&Ls, homebuilders, realtors, and others. Fannie and Freddie accomplished this easily, simply by creating the first active secondary market for conventional mortgages. This allowed banks and S&Ls to increase their mortgage activities without filling their balance sheets with mortgage assets. It also assisted realtors and homebuilders to sell homes by providing the necessary purchase funds. The foundations of what might be called the "government mortgage complex"—consisting of banks, realtors, and community activists—had been laid. Even today, Congress will face substantial opposition from these powerful interests if it seeks to eliminate either the GSEs or a significant government role in housing finance.

Still, the high-interest-rate environment of the inflationary 1970s and the deep recession of 1981–1983 took a toll. Fannie Mae—in effect a huge portfolio lender—encountered the same problem that ul-timately caused the collapse of the S&L industry, a mismatch between its fixed-rate long-term assets and the rising cost of its funds. Fan-nie was better able to survive than the S&Ls, in part because market participants considered all of its liabilities to be government-backed while only the S&Ls' deposits had this support. As a 1986 Depart-ment of Housing and Urban Development (HUD) report observed,

> FNMA [Federal National Mortgage Association] survived because (1) except for one brief period, FNMA continued to borrow at favorable rates due to its agency status and per-ceived Federal guarantee; (2) FNMA was able to spread the accounting recognition of its economic losses over time and pursue a strategy of generating accounting income to offset the operational losses from its portfolio; (3) its very low cap-ital/asset ratio allowed FNMA to grow out of its problems more easily than a private corporation could have; and (4) interest rates declined during the early 1980s soon enough to enable FNMA to continue without ever incurring a negative accounting net worth.[9]

Hidden in this anodyne description is the fact that Fannie sub-stantially reduced its mortgage underwriting standards, taking on subprime loans that would pay up-front fees. These saved Fannie from losses and possible insolvency, but they also produced higher rates of foreclosure later in the 1980s, similar to the higher default rates produced by the affordable-housing goals in the 1990s.[10] By the time the losses began to show up in the mid-1980s, interest rates had declined sufficiently so that Fannie was out of danger.

Writing in 1985, at a time when foreclosures were the highest they had been in thirty years, William R. Thomas, Freddie's execu-tive vice president for operations, described conditions that should be familiar to anyone who went through the 1997–2007 bubble, the 2007 mortgage meltdown, and the 2008 financial crisis: "In many market areas, skyrocketing house prices in the 1970s decreased the likelihood of mortgage default and tended to reduce the losses associated with individual foreclosures. Consequently, the risks that a borrower would default and that the collateral would be inadequate to cover the loan balance and foreclosure costs were not major concerns." But all this changed in the 1980s, when flat housing prices and new mortgage instruments with more borrower risk than fixed-rate mortgages "led to an increased incidence of mortgage default and a growing loss per default."[11]

In reaction to the losses piling up through foreclosures, the GSEs, lenders, mortgage insurers, and mortgage investors sought to improve and tighten mortgage underwriting standards, relying in part on the fact that the GSEs' congressional charters enjoined them to acquire only loans that would be acceptable to "private institutional investors." To the GSEs, this language meant loans of high quality—that is, prime loans—with low probabilities of delinquency or default. In general, the GSEs followed this guidance until 1992, establishing conservative underwriting standards that resulted in very low rates of delinquencies and defaults.

As outlined by Thomas, better-quality mortgages required more attention to two factors—the LTV ratio and the debt-to-income (DTI) ratio. At this point, FICO credit scores had not become available, so mortgage lenders and investors relied on credit histories supplied by credit agencies, the size of the borrower's down payment, and the borrower's other credit obligations in relation to income. According to Thomas, standards were also tightened in the secondary market "for loans with low downpayments, reflecting their greater potential risk. Fannie Mae has increased the required income a borrower needs to qualify for these loans. For loans with less than 10 percent downpayments, a borrower's monthly housing expenses cannot exceed 25 percent of gross monthly income, and housing expenses plus installment debt cannot exceed 33 percent."[12] These and other steps sharply reduced defaults. An internal Fannie study of the incidence of default in 30-year fixed-rate mortgages for loans with LTV ratios greater than 90 percent showed a decline in defaults from 20.4 percent in 1981 to 2.6 percent in 1986.[13]

The tighter standards prevailed through the balance of the 1980s. Fannie's Random Study, discussed in detail in chapter 2, showed that a triad consisting of a down payment of at least 10 percent (i.e., an LTV ratio of no more than 90 percent), a DTI ratio no higher than 38 percent, and a strong credit record was the foundation of a traditional prime mortgage, which in the case of the Fannie Random Study had a serious delinquency or default rate of .68 percent. There is no indication that Fannie's underwriting standards significantly differed from those of banks, S&Ls, and other mortgage lenders, yet the homeownership rate in the United States in the early 1990s did not significantly decline from 64 percent, the rate it had maintained since the mid-1960s.

One of the key contributions of Fannie and Freddie in creating a national market was the development of uniform standards for mortgage credit. As noted above, the congressional charters of both GSEs required that they purchase only mortgages "of such quality, type, and class as to meet, generally, the purchase standards imposed by private institutional investors,"[14] and through the 1970s the GSEs had maintained underwriting standards that generally produced prime loans. By the early 1980s, the operations of both the FHA and the GSEs had created the beginnings of a national market in mortgages. Terms had been standardized, and the technology of securitization had been sufficiently developed so that it was possible for many kinds of institutional investors—insurance companies, pension funds and mutual funds, as well as banks and other depositories—to hold the credit risk of conventional mortgages. Fannie and Freddie, with the implicit backing of the U.S. government, provided an important bridge between mortgage originators and the ultimate investors by placing their guarantee on securities that were backed by pools of mortgages (mortgage-backed securities, or MBS). This eliminated much of the credit risk for those investors who wanted government-backed credit and were not concerned about low yields.

THE CHOICE BETWEEN PRIVATIZATION AND SUBPRIME LENDING

In the early 1980s, various crosscurrents developed that significantly affected the future of the GSEs. The most pressing was the desire of the Reagan administration to achieve their privatization. The period of near-insolvency in the early 1980s was taken by the Reagan White House and HUD as a warning that the GSEs could one day become a serious cost to the taxpayers. The two companies were operating with the taxpayers' checkbook but without any regulation. Although regulation would be a fallback position if necessary, the priority of the Reagan White House was privatization. Fannie's management was reluctant to privatize but under administration pressure had begun serious planning for this purpose. By 1986, it had gone far enough to have developed a tentative structure in which the firm would be divided in two parts, one to retain its diminishing government role, and the other to be a fully privatized organization that would be free to pursue activities that would "improve the efficiency of the housing finance markets."[15] In approving Fannie's issuance of real estate mortgage investment conduits (REMICs) in 1987, HUD Secretary Samuel Pierce tied the decision to a demand that Fannie begin serious work with HUD toward developing privatization legislation.[16]

A second factor was the substantial growth in Fannie's conduit or securitization role. Freddie entered this business in 1976; Fannie joined in 1982.[17] By 1986–1987, Fannie and Freddie were doing $150 billion in securitization business.[18] The advent of securitization was particularly significant for Fannie and Freddie because in securitizations investors take the interest-rate risk—the risk that market interest rates would rise substantially above the interest rate paid on the mortgages. This would cause the value of mortgages to decline, and mortgage-backed securities along with them. Interest-rate risk was what had pushed many S&Ls and Fannie into insolvency during the high-interest and inflationary environment of the early and mid-1980s. Since Congress had been persuaded by the realtors and others that 30-year fixed-rate mortgages were good for home buyers, the interest-rate risk inherent in holding these long-term mortgages would always haunt the GSEs. If a larger portion of the GSEs' business could be done through securitization, rather than holding mortgages in their portfolios, their prospects for the future could be much brighter than they might have expected when Fannie's management began planning for privatization.

Finally, during this period the GSEs' underwriting standards began to receive unfavorable attention from community activists, who argued that these standards were keeping low-income borrowers from buying homes. A 1985 *New York Times* article noted that Fannie had announced that it was tightening its underwriting standards and referred to this, "at first glance," as "a particularly cruel blow to lower-income buyers and their dreams of home ownership."[19] According to the article, the new restrictions included a provision that borrowers who were offering less than a 10 percent down payment could not have fixed monthly expenses (such as taxes, insurance, and mortgage payments) that exceeded 25 percent of income or a DTI ratio that exceeded 33 percent.

In 1989, HUD created an Advisory Commission on Regulatory Barriers to Affordable Housing, and the commission's report, issued in 1991 and titled "Not in My Backyard: Removing Barriers to Affordable Housing," noted that "the market influence of Freddie Mac and Fannie Mae extends well beyond the number of loans they buy or securitize; their underwriting standards for primary loans are widely adopted and amount to national underwriting standards for a substantial fraction of all mortgage credit."[20] This remark would prove accurate when the affordable-housing goals required the GSEs to reduce their underwriting standards. A finer point was put on this in 1991 hearings before the Senate Banking Committee, where Gale Cincotta, one of the leaders of the effort to establish affordable-housing goals for the GSEs, noted that "lenders will respond to the most conservative standards unless [Fannie and Freddie] are aggressive and convincing in their efforts to expand historically narrow underwriting."[21] It was becoming clear that if the GSEs remained government-backed firms, they were soon going to have to back off their insistence on acquiring only prime mortgages.

David Maxwell, who retired as Fannie's chair in 1990, had managed the firm through the rough waters of the early 1980s, the development of the conduit business, and the late-1980s return to profitability. Now he was confronted with pressures for privatization from the Reagan administration. As part of his effort to assess Fannie's choices, he retained James A. Johnson, a well-known Democratic political operative, as a financial consultant. Johnson, who eventually succeeded Maxwell as Fannie's chair in 1991, opposed privatization, believing that Fannie's franchise—implicit government backing and a central role in the U.S. housing finance market— was too valuable to give up. Well in tune with Washington politics, Johnson apparently realized that a coalition was forming in Washington in reaction to the tighter underwriting standards that Fannie and Freddie had adopted. He also realized that the GSEs' franchise would not be safely out of danger until their activities were linked to a goal that drew strong support in Congress. According to Gretchen Morgenson and Joshua Rosner in *Reckless Endangerment*, Johnson concluded that Fannie's franchise could be preserved against challenge in the future if the firm, instead of being seen as an opponent of loose underwriting standards, were to become a source of financing for low-income borrowers.[22] As Timothy Howard, the chief financial officer of Fannie for a time in the mid-2000s, confirmed in his book, *The Mortgage Wars*, Johnson "understood that leadership in affordable housing was essential to maintaining our congressional support."[23] Not waiting to be pushed by political forces that were building within the Democratic Party, Johnson jumped, announcing in 1991 a $10 billion commitment to make affordable-housing loans under a program called Opening Doors.[24]

To publicize the Opening Doors program, by 1991 Fannie Mae was already advertising its willingness to adopt "flexible" underwriting standards in order to increase homeownership for low-to-moderate-income families. In 1992, when Congress adopted legislation that required the GSEs to meet affordable-housing requirements, Fannie was already there. It completed its $10 billion commitment in 1993, sixteen months ahead of schedule, and in 1994 announced a dramatic "$1 trillion commitment" to provide financing for 10 million low-to-moderate-income families. The Fannie Mae press release on the program had a modest heading: "Fannie Mae Chairman Commits Company to 'Transform the Housing Finance System.'" In many respects, Johnson did just that. The press release notes, "This initiative encompasses one of the most far-reaching commitments ever made by the company: to eliminate any final 'no' in the mortgage application process."[25] Given that Fannie was the standard-setter for the market in 1994, the catastrophic events of 2008 were dimly foreseeable even then. As Morgenson and Rosner observe, "While Johnson and his crew knew the risks among such loans . . . they also recognized that meeting the affordable housing goals would give Fannie Mae enormous political cover for its growth plans."[26]

"A MORAL CRUSADE FOR JUSTICE"

The pressure for reducing underwriting standards continued to build in 1991 and 1992, when two highly controversial studies suggested that there was racial discrimination in mortgage lending, adding a moral dimension to what had originally been seen solely as an economic issue. The first study, released by the Federal Reserve Board in 1991 and based on data reported under the Home Mortgage Disclosure Act, suggested that discrimination was pervasive. A *New York Times* headline for a story on the report read, "Racial Gap Detailed on Mortgages," and the news article that followed began: "The most comprehensive report on mortgage lending nationwide ever issued by the Government shows that even within the same income group whites are nearly twice as likely as blacks to get loans."[27] This was followed in October 1992 by a Federal Reserve Bank of Boston study that was seen as clinching the case. This study reported that black and Hispanic "minorities were two to three times as likely to be denied mortgage loans as whites. In fact, high-income minorities in Boston were more likely to be turned down than low-income whites."[28] This study, issued in the last feverish days of the 1992 presidential election campaign, produced many expressions of outrage, with few bothering to look at its deficiencies. The president of the Boston Federal Reserve at the time, Richard Syron, who would later lead Freddie Mac just before it was taken over by the government, concluded that "I don't think you need a lot more studies."[29] Later reviews of the Boston study, however, found many data errors and a failure to take important underwriting factors into account.[30]

By that time, it didn't really matter. "The incorrect Fed Study on racial discrimination in bank lending," John Allison pointed out, "turned subprime lending to minorities into a moral crusade for justice."[31] The possibility of racial discrimination was only one factor that added momentum to an idea whose time had come. The central point was eventually articulated in the Senate committee report that accompanied the legislation, the ironically named Federal Housing Enterprises Financial Safety and Soundness Act (the GSE Act):[32]

> In return for the public benefits they receive, Congress has mandated in the GSEs' Charter Acts that the GSEs carry out public purposes not required of other private sector entities in the housing finance industry. These statutory mandates obligate the GSEs to work to ensure that everyone in the nation has a reasonable opportunity to enjoy access to mortgage financing benefits resulting from the activities of these enterprises.[33]

Fannie and Freddie were not the targets here; the target was the perceived inequity that a government program was benefiting only those individuals and families who had the credit standing and the financial resources to qualify for a prime mortgage. The community activists had made this point and had won the day. This is the central reason why any government-backed housing program will eventually result in significant taxpayer losses and even a potential financial crisis. The desire to benefit all its citizens is in the nature of democratic government; whether it is through spending or through reducing underwriting standards for mortgages, that impulse will eventually prevail if the government is in charge. In early 2008, for example, Congress increased the conforming loan limits of the GSEs and the FHA so that homebuyers in expensive areas like San Francisco would have access to government-backed mortgages. The new top limit was $729,000, enough to buy a million-dollar home. It was apparently not considered fair to exclude people who are buying million-dollar homes from the benefits of government subsidy programs.

In 1992, however, Congress wanted to help only low- and moderate-income (LMI) homebuyers and had been persuaded that, while the GSEs enjoyed substantial government benefits, they were doing little to help LMI borrowers buy homes. (Low income is usually defined as 80 percent of area median income [AMI] and moderate income as 100 percent of AMI.) The principal vehicle pushed by community activists for attaining this objective was what was called the "affordable-housing goals." It was a rather blunt instrument—a quota system requiring that a certain percentage of the loans Fannie and Freddie acquired each year must have been made to borrowers who were at or below the median income in the communities where they lived.

Under the chairmanship of Henry Gonzales, the House Banking Committee had delegated the drafting of the affordable-housing provisions to activist groups for low-income housing. As Alan J. Fishbein, a former HUD official, described it, "The National Low Income Housing Coalition convened a 'working group' of major affordable-housing stakeholders, including ACORN [Association of Community Organizations for Reform Now] and Consumers Union, along with the major community development intermediaries. . . . Gonzales informally deputized the working group of housing advocates to develop workable provisions that would also be broadly acceptable to Fannie Mae and Freddie Mac."[34]

Initially, the GSE Act established an "interim" base goal of 30 percent for the two-year period beginning January 1, 1993. Under this requirement, 30 percent of the GSEs' mortgage purchases had to be affordable-housing loans, defined as loans to borrowers at or below the median income in the area where they lived (the AMI).[35] Furthermore, the act created a "special affordable" base goal to meet the "unaddressed needs of, and affordable to, low-income families in low-income areas and very low-income families." This category was defined as follows: "(i) 45 percent [of the special affordable goal] shall be mortgages of low-income families who live in census tracts in which the median income does not exceed 80 percent of the area median income; and (ii) 55 percent shall be mortgages of very low income families," which were later defined as 60 percent of AMI.[36] Finally, the act provided for what became known as the "underserved areas" base goal, referring to geographical areas that were both minority and low income. The GSEs were directed to "(A) assist primary lenders to make housing credit available in areas with low-income and minority families; and (B) assist insured depository institutions to meet their obligations under the Community Reinvestment Act [CRA] of 1977."[37] (See below and chapter 5 for a further discussion of the CRA and its effect on the growth of LMI mortgage credit.)

With the drafting help of the community activists, the GSE Act made clear that the real objective of the affordable-housing goals was to reduce or eliminate the traditional underwriting standards that produced prime loans. The HUD secretary was authorized to establish the affordable-housing goals, which could be adjusted in the future. Among the factors the secretary was to consider were national housing needs and "the ability of the enterprises [Fannie and Freddie] to lead the industry in making mortgage credit available for low- and moderate-income families." As we will see, the idea that the GSEs were to "lead the industry," which seems at first a fairly anodyne assignment, acquired great importance in the future as HUD interpreted the phrase to mean that the GSEs should not merely be ahead of the industry, but should pull the industry in the direction of providing greater mortgage credit for LMI homebuyers. Note that the purpose of the GSE Act was not, as many have said, to increase homeownership; although it certainly accomplished that purpose, it was explicitly designed to increase mortgage credit for LMI families by reducing or eliminating traditional underwriting practices.

Congress signaled this last objective by directing Fannie and Freddie to examine the following:

1. The extent to which the underwriting guidelines prevent or inhibit the purchase or securitization of mortgages for houses in mixed-use, urban center, and predominantly minority neighborhoods and for housing for low- and moderate-income families;

2. The standards employed by private mortgage insurers and the extent to which such standards inhibit the purchase and securitization by the enterprises of mortgages described in paragraph (1); and

3. The implications of implementing underwriting standards that—

(A) establish a down payment requirement for mortgagors of 5 percent or less;*

(B) allow the use of cash on hand as a source of down payments; and

(C) approve borrowers who have a credit history of delinquencies if the borrower can demonstrate a satisfactory credit history for at least the 12-month period ending on the date of the application for the mortgage.[38]

Each of these ideas represented a significant departure from good underwriting practices as understood at the time.

No studies by Fannie or Freddie in response to this congressional directive have come to light, but HUD understood the signal; it was to treat affordable-housing goals as a mechanism for reducing traditional mortgage underwriting standards. HUD ultimately became very explicit about this objective. In 2000, for example, in raising the affordable-housing goals to 50 percent and increasing the base goals, HUD suggested that if, as a result of the affordable-housing goals, the GSEs began to acquire more subprime loans, the traditional line between prime and subprime mortgages could be erased:

Because the GSEs have a funding advantage over other market participants, they have the ability to underprice their competitors and increase their market share. This advantage, as has been the case in the prime market, could allow the GSEs to eventually play a significant role in the subprime market. As the GSEs become more comfortable with

*The "or less" was important. At the time, 5 percent was the minimum down payment permitted by the GSEs and was usually accompanied by stringent credit record requirements, such as a DTI requirement of 33 percent or less after the loan was closed.

subprime lending, the line between what today is considered a subprime loan versus a prime loan will likely deteriorate, making expansion by the GSEs look more like an increase in the prime market. *Since . . . one could define a prime loan as one that the GSEs will purchase, the difference between the prime and subprime markets will become less clear* [emphasis added].[39]

As stated earlier, it has always been an objective of the left to eliminate underwriting standards that make a distinction between prime and subprime; in 2000, the idea that the GSEs could be used to erase that distinction was advanced by HUD as further support for raising the LMI goal to 50 percent.

In addition to outlining the affordable-housing goals themselves, the congressional reports accompanying the act contained a number of provisions signaling that what Congress had in mind was more than simply a reduction in underwriting standards; it also wanted to effect a comprehensive change in the GSEs, moving them from a focus on profit and mortgage market liquidity to something more like the administrators of a social program. As the Senate Committee report said at the time, "The purpose of goals is to facilitate the development in both Fannie Mae and Freddie Mac of an ongoing business effort that will be fully integrated in their products, cultures and day-to-day operations to service the mortgage finance needs of low-and-moderate-income persons, racial minorities and inner-city residents." This, too, was effective; no one can read the internal communications of the Fannie Mae staff without recognizing that they were devoted to the fulfillment of what they called their housing "mission"—an increase in the credit available to LMI and very-low-income and minority borrowers.

Sixteen years after the adoption of the GSE Act, the reduction in mortgage underwriting standards that Congress was after culminated in a meltdown of the U.S. housing finance system and a financial crisis. Yet this lesson has not been learned. As discussed in chapter 14, despite the destructive effect of the affordable-housing goals and other government policies that were intended to loosen underwriting standards, there is still substantial support on the left for eliminating underwriting standards entirely.[40]

THE COMMUNITY REINVESTMENT ACT

It might be said that the affordable-housing goals were enacted because the CRA had been a failure from the perspective of community activists. Although enacted in 1977, by the early 1990s it had yet to achieve the objectives of its sponsors. As initially written, the act directed government-insured banks and S&Ls to make credit available in their service areas to low-income borrowers and minorities, but it left open whether the normal credit standards for lending were to be applied. As long as banks applied those normal standards, it was inevitable that low-income and minority groups would receive fewer loans than middle- or upper-income borrowers; low-income borrowers often do not have the credit standing or the financial resources to be seen as sound credit risks.

Soon after entering office in 1993, in the wake of heavy news coverage of reports about racial bias in mortgage lending, President Clinton moved to amend the regulations under the CRA, turning it into an informal quota system. There was no minimum number of loans that a bank or S&L was required to make, but an examiner could give the institution an unsatisfactory grade if the number of its loans to the low-income and minority portions of its service area were deemed insufficient or below its peers. Low income was defined as 80 percent of the median income in the community. An unsatisfactory grade was a serious matter under the new regulations: it could mean that the institution would be denied various necessary regulatory approvals, including approvals for mergers or acquisitions. The new informal quota and the severity of the enforcement mechanism remade the CRA as a powerful vehicle for inducing banks and S&Ls to make loans they would not otherwise have made, but because of the absence of reliable data, it is not possible to compare it—other than in spirit—to the affordable-housing goals.

By 1995, CRA regulations explicitly required that banks and S&Ls be evaluated on their use of "innovative or flexible lending practices in a safe and sound manner to address the credit needs of low- or moderate-income individuals or geographies."[41] The terms "innovative" and "flexible," code words for reduced underwriting standards, appear again and again in the affordable-housing literature, used in this case by the FDIC, but used also by other bank regulators, and particularly by HUD. Banks and S&Ls would get "outstanding" CRA ratings if examiners found extensive use of innovative and flexible underwriting, which meant making loans that did not conform to traditional underwriting standards—in other words, nontraditional mortgages (NTMs). For reasons outlined in chapter 5, the CRA seems to have had most of its effect in connection with mergers and acquisitions by large banks. Its effects elsewhere have been hard to measure because only very few banks publish information on their CRA lending or their experience with CRA loans.

Part II of this book will describe how the affordable-housing goals and other programs based on the same ideas fared in practice after 1992.

PART

II

Government Housing Policies Take Effect

The affordable housing goals, HUD's central role,
the decline in underwriting standards, and the
spread of loosened standards to the wider market

5

HUD's Central Role

How HUD Used the Affordable-Housing Goals to Reduce Underwriting Standards

Our homeownership strategy will not cost the taxpayers one extra cent. It will not require legislation. It will not add more Federal programs or grow the Federal bureaucracy.

PRESIDENT BILL CLINTON, "Remarks on the
National Homeownership Strategy," June 5, 1995

Although Fannie Mae and Freddie Mac have taken most of the blame for misguided mortgage lending that ultimately led to their insolvency, they were only the tip of the spear. The moving force behind the government's effort to loosen underwriting standards was the Department of Housing and Urban Development (HUD) in both the Clinton and George W. Bush administrations. This chapter outlines the various government programs, in addition to affordable-housing goals—most of them initiated by HUD—that played a major role in the growth of nontraditional mortgages (NTMs), the financial decline of the government-sponsored enterprises (GSEs), and ultimately the financial crisis.

Imagine you're Daniel Mudd. It's 2004, and you've just succeeded Franklin Raines, who resigned as chair of Fannie Mae in the wake of an accounting scandal. You are now the head of a company that has always had its way with Washington. Among other things, it had a superb Washington network, a well-advertised connection to the

American dream of homeownership, a stable of compliant academics willing to support its positions for generous fees, and an ability to stir up a hornets' nest of grassroots opposition to any proposals in Congress that would tax or regulate it, not to mention its well-deserved reputation for destroying the Washington careers of those who opposed it.[1] But you find that, rather than first prize, you've been handed a hot potato. You gather your top staff, and this is what you tell them: "We are in a zero tolerance regulatory environment . . . we are losing friends, and our competitors are multiplying . . . Freddie Mac is back, and better . . . the market is turning against us . . . our mission costs [that is, the affordable-housing goals] are rising to heights that may well be unreachable . . . revenues are off, risks are up . . . opportunity wanes. . . . So what the hell do we do now?"[2]

How did this happen? How is it that a firm with a gold-plated franchise, a license to dominate the $8 trillion U.S. housing market in 2004, and the ability to fund its activities at a cost just shy of the Treasury itself could possibly be facing the problems outlined by Mudd? The answer is the affordable-housing goals and other government programs. As we will see, they changed the nature of the mortgage market by forcing a reduction in underwriting standards, built an enormous ten-year bubble, encouraged the entry of more nimble competitors who could exploit the new NTM market niches, forced Fannie's management to focus on its "mission" rather than its business, and added costs and ultimately losses to its bottom line. Four years later, Fannie was insolvent and had been taken over by a government conservatorship. James Johnson's plan to solidify Fannie's franchise had backfired; Fannie had become a tool of larger forces and lost control of its political risk.

This is all the more remarkable because of the behavior of the GSEs—and particularly Fannie Mae—through the 1990s and well into the 2000s. They regularly threatened and intimidated their would-be opponents and retaliated where they could against their critics. It took a British scholar, Oonagh McDonald, to write the first thorough account of their extraordinary use of political power in Washington:

The Government Sponsored Enterprises spent millions of dollars on lobbying, using every means possible to attack the politicians who sought to limit their power, and rewarding many Congressional members of the banking and financial services committees, which were responsible for the way in which Fannie and Freddie operated, by sponsoring housing projects for affordable-housing in their constituencies. . . . They exploited the weakness of their regulator and engaged in dubious accounting practices, whilst amassing huge fortunes for their top executives. All the time, they proclaimed their commitment to affordable housing and were aided and abetted in their activities by Presidents and politicians alike.[3]

With the adoption of the the GSE Act, three major vehicles were available for implementing the U.S. government's efforts to increase mortgage credit for low-income and minority borrowers: the affordable-housing goals, covering Fannie Mae and Freddie Mac; mortgage insurance through the Federal Housing Administration (FHA); and the Community Reinvestment Act (CRA). Of these, the affordable-housing goals became by far the most effective and the most consequential. Although Fannie and Freddie have been criticized for their contributions to the mortgage meltdown and ultimately the financial crisis, the record shows that they were forced to the edge, and over it, by HUD, implementing what it saw as the congressional purpose in the language of the GSE Act and the policies of both the Clinton and George W. Bush administrations.

By 2008, the housing market of 1990—dominated by prime mortgages—had been replaced by a market in which prime loans were a minority of the mortgage loans outstanding. The stability that had briefly returned to the market as inflation cooled in the late 1980s was replaced by a massive housing price bubble. Although there were many contributing factors, the 1997–2007 housing bubble would not have reached its dizzying heights or lasted as long, nor would the financial crisis of 2008 have ensued, but for the role played by the housing policies of the U.S. government between 1992 and 2008.

As a result of these policies, by the middle of 2008, as noted earlier, there were approximately 31 million NTMs in the U.S. financial system—more than half of all mortgages outstanding—with an aggregate value of more than $5 trillion. Of these NTMs, as shown in Table 1.1, at least 76 percent were on the books of government agencies such as Fannie, Freddie, and the FHA, or banks and savings and loan (S&L) institutions, holding loans they were required to make under the CRA, with the remainder—24 percent—on the books of the private sector. These were unprecedented numbers for NTMs, far higher than at any time in the past, and they demonstrate without question that the U.S. government had created most of the demand for these weak and ultimately destructive loans. The losses associated with the delinquency and default of these mortgages fully account for the weakness and disruption of the financial system that has become known as the mortgage meltdown and the financial crisis.

THE AFFORDABLE-HOUSING GOALS:
NEVER GOOD ENOUGH

The initial goal in the GSE Act—ensuring that 30 percent of loans acquired by Fannie and Freddie be made to low- and moderate-income (LMI) borrowers—was not difficult for the GSEs to meet; they were already at 34 percent, including multifamily housing, when the goals were established in 1992, and the original special affordable and underserved base goals were also relatively modest until the first HUD increases went into effect in 1996. The affordable-housing goals in that and subsequent years are set out in Table 5.1, which was prepared by the GSEs' regulator, the Federal Housing Finance Agency (FHFA); it shows the years in which the goals went into effect, rather than the years in which they were established. The table does not include the purchase money subgoals—the requirement that goals credit would be given only for mortgages that were used to purchase a house, not for refinancing—that were adopted in 2004. This new subgoal, as discussed below, substantially increased the goals pressure on Fannie and Freddie. As the three base goals were increased in and after 1996, however, it became more and more difficult for the

TABLE 5.1. Gradual increases in affordable-housing goals, 1996–2008, and GSEs' largely successful compliance

	1996	1997	1998	1999	2000	2001	2002	2003	2004	2005	2006	2007	2008
Low- and moderate-income goal (%)	**40**	**42**	**42**	**42**	**42**	**50**	**50**	**50**	**50**	**52**	**53**	**55**	**56**
Fannie actual (%)	45	45	44	46	50	51	52	52	53	55	57	56	54
Freddie actual (%)	41	43	43	46	50	53	50	51	52	54	56	56	51
Special affordable goal (%)	**12**	**14**	**14**	**14**	**14**	**20**	**20**	**20**	**20**	**22**	**23**	**25**	**27**
Fannie actual (%)	15	17	15	18	19	22	21	21	24	24	28	27	26
Freddie actual (%)	14	15	16	18	21	23	20	21	23	26	26	26	23
Underserved areas goal (%)	**21**	**24**	**24**	**24**	**24**	**31**	**31**	**31**	**31**	**37**	**38**	**38**	**39**
Fannie actual (%)	25	29	27	27	31	33	33	32	32	41	43	43	39
Freddie actual (%)	28	26	26	27	29	32	31	33	34	43	44	43	38

Adapted from: "The Housing Goals of Fannie Mae and Freddie Mac in the Context of the Mortgage Market: 1996–2009," FHFA Mortgage Market Note 10-2, February 1, 2010, http://www.fhfa.gov/webfiles/15408/Housing%20Goals%201996-2009%2002-01.pdf.

GSEs to maintain the underwriting standards that had made them the avatars of prime loans.

"The main objective of the housing goals is to encourage Fannie Mae and Freddie Mac to introduce new affordable lending programs in underserved areas," HUD wrote in an April 2002 review of the goals' effect in the period between 1993 and 2000.[4] HUD's data showed that in those years, home purchase loans that qualified for the LMI base goal had increased from 34.4 percent of the overall conventional conforming market in 1992 to 44.8 percent in 2000; very-low-income loans had increased from 8.7 percent to 14.7 percent; special affordable loans had increased from 10.4 percent to 17.1 percent; and loans in underserved areas had increased from 22.2 percent to 27.1 percent. These were substantial gains, but according to HUD they were not good enough: "The GSEs account for a significant share of the total (government as well as conventional conforming) market for home purchase loans," the report continued, "but their market share for each of the affordable lending categories is less than their share of the overall market."[5] In other words, HUD believed that the GSEs' share of the affordable-housing market should match their share of the overall conventional conforming market, although there was no reason to believe that the LMI market—a market that by definition was below median income—could produce enough mortgages of investment quality to allow the GSEs to maintain their underwriting standards.

This finding helps explain the increases in the affordable-housing goals that then HUD Secretary Andrew Cuomo ordered in 2000, which were to go into effect in 2001. As shown in Table 5.1, in 2001 the LMI base goal was increased to 50 percent, the special affordable goal to 20 percent, and the underserved areas goal to 31 percent. "The Department," HUD stated in its commentary on the new rule, "estimates that the two GSEs' mortgage purchases accounted for 55 percent of the total ... conventional, conforming mortgage market during 1998. In contrast, GSE purchases comprised only 44 percent of the low-and-moderate income mortgage market ... 46 percent of the underserved areas market and ... 33 percent of the special affordable market."[6]

LEADING THE MARKET

Accordingly, despite the risks that were inherent in lending to borrowers with weak credit standing and limited financial resources, HUD was pressing ahead with a theory that, by requiring Fannie and Freddie to "lead the market," Congress wanted the GSEs to have at least the same share of the LMI market as they had of the overall conventional conforming market. "HUD concludes," the commentary continued, "that due to their dominant role in the market, their ability to influence the types of loans that lenders will originate, their utilization of state-of-the-art technology, and their financial strength, the GSEs have the ability to lead the market in affordable lending and to reach out to those markets that have traditionally not received the benefits of an active secondary market."[7] This was a very aggressive interpretation of the idea that the GSEs should "lead the market." It implied not merely that they should be ahead of the market but that they should be pulling the market in the direction of more LMI lending. As it turned out, the requirement that they increase their share of the affordable-housing market was not only a significant burden for the GSEs, but also led them into lending policies that degraded their own mortgage underwriting standards as well as those of the rest of the mortgage lending community.

Four years later, during the Bush administration, HUD still wasn't satisfied with the GSEs' performance in the affordable-housing area. Although the GSEs' purchases under the affordable-housing goals were much closer to matching their percentage of the overall conventional conforming market, the homeownership rate among the targeted groups was not rising commensurately with the rate among higher-income groups. "Increasing homeownership is a national priority," HUD stated in support of its new regulation, "The past average performance of the GSEs in the home purchase market has been below market levels. . . . the GSEs must apply greater efforts to increasing homeownership for low- and moderate-income families, families living in underserved areas, and very-low-income families and low-income families living in low-income areas."[8]

Thus, HUD's next big step was to address the home purchase

issue directly, adding home purchase subgoals to the existing base goals and allowing affordable-housing goals credit only for mortgages that were used to purchase homes, not to refinance existing homes: "The Department's purpose," said HUD in a November 2004 statement accompanying its final rule, "is to encourage the GSEs to facilitate greater financing and homeownership opportunities for families and neighborhoods targeted by the Housing Goals. The final rule establishes levels of the Housing Goals that will bring the GSEs to a position of market leadership in a range of foreseeable economic circumstances related to the future course of interest rates and consequent fluctuations in origination rates on home purchase and refinance mortgages—both multifamily and single-family."[9] The new subgoals were to go into effect beginning in 2005 and would be stepped up along with the base goals through 2008. For some reason, the FHFA did not include these important subgoals in Table 5.1.

The new goals appear to have been a bridge too far. HUD seemed unaware of, or at least unsympathetic to, the problem of finding creditworthy borrowers in low-income or minority communities. Not only were the GSEs required to find borrowers there—at the same rate they were found in the market as a whole—but the borrowers now had to be buyers of homes and not just existing LMI homeowners who were refinancing. Although the purpose of the affordable-housing goals was to make the GSEs stretch to reach the goals, HUD had both increased the quota and substantially narrowed the kinds of loans that would qualify. Because of this, the quality of the loans acquired by the GSEs deteriorated even further between 2005 and 2007 than they had in the past.

One of the best academic works studying the causes of the financial crisis was *Guaranteed to Fail: Fannie Mae, Freddie Mac, and the Debacle of Mortgage Finance* by four professors at New York University's Stern School of Business, but even they missed the significance of the 2004 changes in the affordable-housing goals. Requiring subgoals that gave credit only for loans that were used to buy homes—rather than just loans that represented refinancing—was a material new burden, and communications within and outside the GSEs, before and after the new requirements were instituted, confirm this. In their book, the authors are searching for a reason that the quality of the GSEs' loan acquisitions deteriorated so significantly between 2004 and 2007. They write that although there were significant increases in the goals in between 1996 and 2008, "the largest increases took place in 1996 and 2001 . . . the target increases in 2005, 2006 and 2007 were more modest, yet that is when most of the increase in riskiness took place."[10] The implication is that some other motive was involved. However, the fundamental change in the burden that HUD instituted in 2004 accounts fully for the sharp deterioration in mortgage quality that the authors saw in the GSEs' data between 2005 and 2007.

Apart from the home purchase requirement, it is important to note in Table 5.1 that Fannie and Freddie met the base goals almost every year, but for the most part did not exceed the goals by significant amounts. This calls into question one of the most common explanations for the GSEs' insolvency—an explanation adopted by the Financial Crisis Inquiry Commission (FCIC)[11] and others—that the GSEs bought large numbers of subprime mortgages for market share or because these loans were highly profitable. If that were true, Fannie and Freddie would have exceeded the goals by wide margins. That they cleared these hurdles with little to spare in most years— and missed them occasionally—is strong evidence that they were dragged along by HUD's relentless pressure. Beginning in the Clinton administration and continuing through the Bush administration, HUD deliberately used the affordable-housing goals to force the GSEs deeper into NTM markets. HUD, therefore, had a central role in the deterioration in mortgage underwriting standards and thus in the financial crisis itself.

As their loosened underwriting standards spread to the larger conventional conforming market, the GSEs contributed to an unprecedented housing price bubble. As shown in Figure 5.1, the relationship between this bubble and the growth in the GSEs' affordable-housing goals purchases is remarkably close. The 1993 starting point was chosen because before 1993, 30 percent of the mortgages that the GSEs acquired met the goals. HUD policy and actions were directed

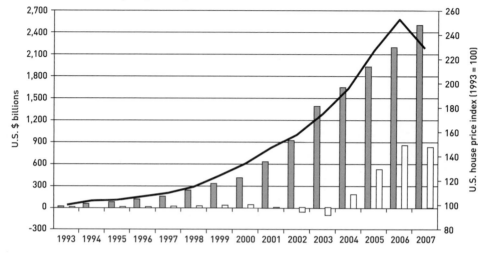

■ Cumulative GSE affordable-housing volume above 30% historic baseline[a]
☐ Cumulative self-denominated subprime volume above 1992 baseline of 9% of total originations[b]
━ U.S. house prices (1993 = 100)[c]

Sources: [a]HUD. [b]*Inside Mortgage Finance.* [c]S&P/Case-Shiller U.S. Index.
Compiled by Edward Pinto.

FIG. 5.1. GSE affordable-housing purchases and self-denominated subprime production in relation to U.S. house prices

at increasing the GSEs' goal performance above this baseline. Similarly, the baseline for self-denominated subprime loans—those acquired from subprime lenders—was 9 percent.

HUD DENIES ITS ROLE IN THE CRISIS

In light of this record, it is astonishing that HUD would attempt to deny its role in the insolvency of Fannie and Freddie. Yet, in a January 2010 report titled "Report to Congress on the Root Causes of the Foreclosure Crisis," HUD declared that

the serious financial troubles of the GSEs that led to their being placed into conservatorship by the Federal government provides [*sic*] strong testament to the fact that the GSEs were indeed overexposed to unduly risky mortgage investments.

However, *the evidence suggests that the GSEs' decisions to purchase or guarantee nonprime loans was [sic] motivated more by efforts to chase market share and profits than by the need to satisfy federal regulators* [emphasis added].[12]

Then, in testimony before the House Financial Services Committee on April 14, 2010, HUD Secretary Shaun Donovan said of the GSEs:

Seeing their market share decline [between 2004 and 2006] as a result of [a] change of demand, the GSEs made the decision to widen their focus from safer prime loans and begin chasing the non-prime market, loosening long-standing underwriting and risk management standards along the way. This would be a fateful decision that not only proved disastrous for the companies themselves—but ultimately also for the American taxpayer.[13]

Both of these statements were the standard explanation of the left, intended to exculpate the government for the mortgage meltdown and the financial crisis: because of the GSEs' desire to maintain their profits, market share, or both, they had gone over the edge (the FCIC majority report, without any evidence, added other reasons: "in order to meet stock market analysts' and investors' expectations for growth, to regain market share, and to ensure generous compensation for their executives and employees"[14]).

Finger-pointing in Washington is endemic when problems occur, and agencies and individuals are constantly trying to find scapegoats for their own bad decisions and incompetent performance, but HUD's effort to blame Fannie and Freddie for the decline in their underwriting standards sets a new record for evading responsibility. Contrast Donovan's 2010 statement quoted above with this statement by HUD in 2000, when it was significantly increasing the affordable-housing goals:

Lower-income and minority families have made major gains in access to the mortgage market in the 1990s. A variety of reasons have accounted for these gains, including improved housing affordability, enhanced enforcement of the Community Reinvestment Act, *more flexible mortgage underwriting,* and stepped-up enforcement of the Fair Housing Act. *But most industry observers believe that one factor behind these gains has been the improved performance of Fannie Mae and Freddie Mac under HUD's affordable lending goals. HUD's recent increases in the goals for 2001–03 will encourage the GSEs to further step up their support for affordable lending* [emphasis added].[15]

To be sure, HUD was far from innocent in the Bush administration. Its tone was equally aggressive in 2004, when it both raised the affordable-housing goals and added the purchase money subgoals:

Millions of Americans with less than perfect credit or who cannot meet some of the tougher underwriting requirements of the prime market for reasons such as inadequate income documentation, limited downpayment or cash reserves, or the desire to take more cash out in a refinancing than conventional loans allow, rely on subprime lenders for access to mortgage financing. *If the GSEs reach deeper into the subprime market, more borrowers will benefit from the advantages that greater stability and standardization create* [emphasis added].[16]

And, finally, consider this statement in a 2005 report commissioned by HUD:

More liberal mortgage financing has contributed to the increase in demand for housing. During the 1990s, lenders have been *encouraged by HUD and banking regulators* to increase lending to low-income and minority households. The Community Reinvestment Act (CRA), Home Mortgage Disclosure Act (HMDA), government-sponsored enterprises (GSE) housing goals and fair lending laws have strongly encouraged mortgage brokers and lenders to market to low-income and minority borrowers. *Sometimes these borrowers are higher risk, with blemished credit histories and high debt or simply little savings for a down payment. Lenders have responded with low down payment loan products and automated underwriting, which has allowed them to more carefully determine the risk of the loan* [emphasis added].[17]

Despite HUD's unseemly effort to deny its own role in fostering the growth of subprime and other high-risk mortgage lending, there is strong—indeed irrefutable—evidence that, beginning in the early 1990s, the department led an ultimately successful effort to lower underwriting standards in every area of the mortgage market where HUD had or could exert influence. With support in congressional legislation, HUD's policy was launched in the Clinton administration and extended almost to the end of the Bush administration. It involved the FHA, which was under HUD's direct control; Fannie Mae and Freddie Mac, which were subject to HUD's affordable-housing regulations; a program called the Best Practices Initiative, which applied mostly to the mortgage banking industry; and another program, begun at the request of President Clinton, called the National Homeownership Strategy, which seems to have applied to the entire housing industry. In addition, although not subject to HUD's jurisdiction, the new, tighter CRA regulations that became effective in 1995 gave community groups new leverage to obtain commitments for substantial amounts of CRA-qualifying mortgages when banks were applying for merger approvals.[18]

HUD'S BEST PRACTICES INITIATIVE

In 1994, HUD began to enlist other members of the mortgage financing community in an effort to reduce underwriting standards. In that year, the Mortgage Bankers Association (MBA)—a group of mortgage financing firms not otherwise regulated by the federal government and not subject to HUD's legal authority—agreed to join a HUD program called the Best Practices Initiative, described as follows by HUD:

> Since 1994, HUD has signed Fair Lending Best Practices (FLBP) Agreements with lenders across the nation that are individually tailored to public-private partnerships that are considered on the leading edge. The Agreements not only offer an opportunity to increase low-income and minority lending but they incorporate fair housing and equal opportunity principles into mortgage lending standards. These banks and mortgage lenders, as represented by Countrywide Home Loans, Inc., serve as industry leaders in their communities by demonstrating a commitment to affirmatively further fair lending.[19]

The circumstances surrounding these agreements are somewhat obscure, but at least one contemporary account suggests that the MBA signed on to this program to avoid having its members subjected to the CRA, which at that time, as now, applied only to government-insured banks and S&Ls.

> A group of lenders not subject to CRA—and more directly under HUD's purview—are the nation's mortgage banks. In mid-September [1994], the Mortgage Bankers Association of America—whose membership includes many bank-owned mortgage companies, signed a three-year master best-practices agreement with HUD. The agreement consisted of two parts: MBA's agreement to work on fair-lending issues in consultation with HUD and a model best-practices agreement that individual mortgage banks could use to devise their own agreements with HUD. The first such agreement, signed by Countrywide Funding Corp., the nation's largest mortgage bank, is summarized [below]. Many have seen the MBA agreement as a preemptive strike against congressional murmurings that mortgage banks should be pulled under the umbrella of the CRA.[20]

As the first member of the MBA to sign, Countrywide probably realized that there were political advantages in being seen as assisting low-income mortgage borrowers, and it became one of a relatively small group of subprime lenders who were to prosper enormously as Fannie and Freddie began to look for sources of the subprime loans that would enable them to meet the affordable-housing goals. By 1998, there were 117 MBA signatories to HUD's Best Practices Agreements, which HUD described as commitments to exceed "the responsibilities under the Fair Housing Act. . . . [The signatories] also assent to making loans of any size so that all borrowers may be served and to provide information on all loan programs for which an applicant qualifies." HUD concluded that "[t]he results of the initiative are promising. As lenders discover new, untapped markets, their minority and low-income loans applications and originations have risen. Consequently, the homeownership rate for low-income and minority groups has increased throughout the nation."[21]

Countrywide was by far the most important participant in this HUD initiative. Under the program it made a series of multibillion-dollar commitments, culminating in a "trillion dollar commitment" to lend to minority and low-income families, which in part it fulfilled by selling subprime and other NTMs to Fannie and Freddie. Countrywide's loose underwriting standards—it is now the poster child for irresponsible lending—brought it to the brink of insolvency in 2007. But only a few months before its rescue in 2008 by Bank of America, the firm reported that it had made $789 billion in mortgage loans toward its trillion-dollar commitment.[22]

THE NATIONAL HOMEOWNERSHIP STRATEGY

It turned out that 1995 was a significant year for the erosion of mortgage underwriting standards. That year, the Clinton administration increased the LMI base goal from the 30 percent level specified in the GSE Act to 40 percent in 1996 and to 42 percent for each of the succeeding four years; the administration also substantially increased the base goals for the special affordable and underserved areas and finalized new CRA regulations that imposed informal quotas for low-income and minority lending on banks and S&Ls. In addition, in 1995 HUD issued a Clinton administration policy statement titled "The National Homeownership Strategy: Partners in the American Dream." Prepared by HUD "in response to a request from President Clinton," the strategy paper began, "The purpose of the National Homeownership Strategy is to achieve an all-time high level of homeownership in America within the next 6 years through an unprecedented collaboration of public and private housing industry organizations."[23]

According to HUD, which had already done considerable work in lining up "supporters" of the strategy before the announcement, "Industry representatives agreed to the formation of working groups to help develop the National Homeownership Strategy," which was explicitly intended to increase homeownership by reducing down payments: "*Lending institutions, secondary market investors, mortgage insurers, and other members of the partnership should work collaboratively to reduce homebuyer downpayment requirements. Mortgage financing with high loan-to-value ratios should generally be associated with enhanced homebuyer counseling and, where available, supplemental sources of downpayment assistance* [emphasis added]."[24]

As described in a HUD summary, the purpose of the strategy was to make financing "more available, affordable, and flexible." The term "flexible," as noted earlier, was and still is a code word for loosened underwriting. The HUD statement continued:

> The inability (either real or perceived) of many younger families to qualify for a mortgage is widely recognized as a very serious barrier to homeownership. The National Homeownership Strategy commits both government and the mortgage industry to a number of initiatives designed to:
>
> > Cut transaction costs through streamlined regulations and technological and procedural efficiencies.

Reduce downpayment requirements and interest costs by making terms more flexible, providing subsidies to low- and moderate-income families, and creating incentives to save for homeownership.

Increase the availability of alternative financing products in housing markets throughout the country [emphasis added].[25]

Reductions in down payments, the area on which HUD particularly concentrated in pursuing its affordable-housing goals and the National Homeownership Strategy, are especially important in weakening underwriting standards and contributing to a housing bubble. Table 5.2, based on a large sample of loans from the 1990s, shows the way low down payments enhance mortgage risks. For example, when a loan with a relatively low FICO score below 620 is combined with various levels of down payment, the risk of default multiplies as the down payment grows smaller. It is almost five times greater when the down payment is less than 30 percent, eleven times greater when the down payment is less than 20 percent, and twenty times greater when the down payment is less than 10 percent.

Low down payments are particularly important in supporting

TABLE 5.2. High LTV ratios enhance the risk of low FICO scores

| FICO score | Risk of default | | | | Relation of column 5 to column 3 |
	≤70% LTV ratio	71–80% LTV ratio	81–90% LTV ratio	91–95% LTV ratio	
< 620	1.0	4.8	11.0	20.0	4.2 times greater
620–679	0.5	2.3	5.3	9.4	4.1 times greater
680–720	0.2	1.0	2.3	4.1	4.1 times greater
>720	0.1	0.4	0.9	1.6	4.0 times greater

Adapted from: Charles D. Anderson, Dennis R. Capozza, and Robert Van Order, "Deconstructing the Subprime Debacle Using New Indices of Underwriting Quality and Economic Conditions: A First Look" (University Financial Associates, July 2008), p. 4, http://www.ufanet.com/DeconstructingSubprimeJuly2008.pdf.

the growth of a housing bubble. A buyer who has $10,000 for a down payment could afford a $100,000 home when underwriting standards generally required a 10 percent down payment. But if the down payment required is only 5 percent—as it soon became under government pressures on the market—the buyer could afford a $200,000 home. Thus, in a low down payment environment there is increased bidding for larger and more expensive houses, which was a factor in building the massive U.S. housing bubble that developed between 1997 and 2007.

COMPETITION BETWEEN THE GSES AND THE FHA

In a 2000 report, the Fannie Mae Foundation noted that "FHA loans constituted the largest share of Countrywide's [subprime lending] activity, until Fannie Mae and Freddie Mac began accepting loans with higher LTVs [that is, lower down payments] and greater underwriting flexibilities."[26] This should surprise no one. HUD's management of the affordable-housing goals placed Fannie and Freddie in direct competition with the FHA, an agency within HUD itself, overseen by the same HUD assistant secretary who was responsible for setting the goals. Fannie treated it as a conflict of interest at HUD, but there is a strong case that this competition is exactly what HUD and Congress wanted. It is important to recall the context in which the GSE Act was enacted in 1992. In 1990, Congress had enacted the Federal Credit Reform Act (FCRA).[27] One of its purposes was to capture in the government's budget the risks to the government associated with loan guarantees and insurance, and in effect it placed a loose budgetary limit on FHA guarantees, which would become on-budget costs. For those in Congress and at HUD who favored increased mortgage lending to low-income borrowers and underserved communities, this consequence of the FCRA may have been troubling. What had previously been a cost-free way to extend support to groups who were not otherwise eligible for conventional mortgages—which generally required a 10 to 20 percent down payment and the indicia of willingness and ability to pay—could now be potentially restricted. Requiring the GSEs to take up the mantle of affordable housing would have looked at the time like a solution, since Fannie and Freddie had unlimited access to funds in the private markets and were off-budget entities.

From this perspective, it would make sense for Congress and HUD to place the GSEs and FHA in competition, just as it made sense to put Fannie and Freddie into competition with each other for affordable loans. With all three entities competing for the same kinds of loans, and with HUD's control of both the FHA's lending standards and the GSEs' affordable-housing requirements, underwriting requirements would inevitably be reduced. HUD's explicit and frequently expressed interest in reducing mortgage underwriting standards as a means of making mortgage credit available to low-income borrowers provides ample evidence of HUD's motives for creating this competition. Indeed, if it was not part of HUD's overall plan, it would have been a surprising oversight.

The Federal Housing Administration was created to encourage banks to make long-term mortgage credit available to people who could not meet the standards at the time for a bank-originated conventional loan. Initially, the loans it insured had a maximum LTV ratio of 80 percent. That would be seen as a tough standard today, and, as described earlier, congressional intervention moved it to 97 percent in 1961.[28] With its maximum LTV ratio remaining at 97 percent, FHA maintained average FICO scores for its borrowers just below 660 from 1996 to 2006. During this period, the average FICO score for a conventional (that is, nongovernmental) subprime borrower was somewhat lower.[29]

In several instances before and after the affordable-housing goals were imposed on Fannie and Freddie, the FHA appears to have tried to get out ahead of the GSEs or to offer them competition. For example, a major increase in the proportion of the FHA's loans with LTV ratios equal to or greater than 97 percent occurred in 1991, when the FHA's percentage of such loans suddenly rose from 4.4 percent to 17.1 percent.[30] That was the year before Congress imposed the affordable-housing goals on Fannie and Freddie and in effect directed them to consider down payments of 5 percent or less.

It appears that Fannie Mae deliberately targeted FHA borrowers with Fannie's Community Home Buyer Program (CHBP). Freddie was probably doing the same, but the data are not available. In an internal memorandum prepared in 1993, Fannie's Credit Policy group compared Fannie's then-proposed CHBP program to the FHA's requirements under its 1-to-4 family loan program (Section 203[b]) and showed that most of Fannie's requirements were competitive or better.[31] In 1993, shortly after Fannie and Freddie were introduced as competitors, the FHA began to increase its percentage of loans with low down payments. This had the predictable effect on its delinquency rates, as shown in Figure 5.2.

In 1999—just before the affordable-housing goals for Fannie and Freddie were to be raised again—the FHA almost doubled its originations of loans with LTV ratios equal to or greater than 97 percent, going from 23 percent in 1998 to 44 percent in 1999.[32] It also offered additional concessions on underwriting standards, including no minimum FICO score for applicants. The following is from a Quicken ad in January 2000, which is likely to have been based on an FHA program as it existed in 1999:

- *Borrowers can purchase with a minimum down payment.* Without FHA insurance, many families can't afford the homes they want because down payments are a major roadblock. FHA down payments range from 1.25% to 3% of the sale price and are significantly lower than the minimum that many lenders require for conventional or sub-prime loans.

- *With FHA loans, borrowers need as little as 3% of the "total funds" required.* In addition to the funds needed for the down payment, borrowers also have to pay closing costs, prepaid fees for insurance and interest, as well as escrow fees which include mortgage insurance, hazard insurance, and months worth of property taxes. A FHA-insured home loan can be structured so borrowers don't pay more than 3% of the total out-of-pocket funds, including the down payment.

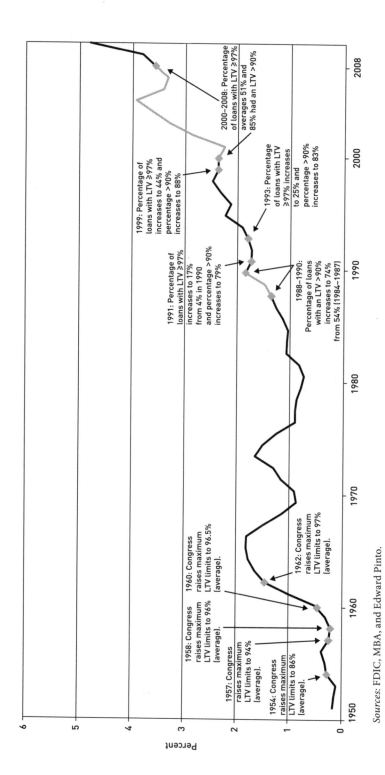

Sources: FDIC, MBA, and Edward Pinto.

FIG. 5.2. Impact of the FHA's increasing LTVs on annual foreclosure starts as a percentage of insured loans

- *The combined total of out-of-pocket funds can be a gift or loan from family members.* FHA allows homebuyers to use gifts from family members and nonprofit groups to cover their down payment and additional closing costs and fees. In fact, even a 100% gift or a personal loan from a relative is acceptable.

- *FHA's credit requirements are flexible.* Compared to credit requirements established by many lenders for other types of home loans, FHA focuses only on a borrower's last 12–24 month credit history. In addition, there is no minimum FICO score—mortgage bankers look at each application on a case-by-case basis. It is also perfectly acceptable for people with NO established credit to receive a loan with this program.

- *FHA permits borrowers to have a higher debt-to-income ratio than most insurers typically allow.* Conventional home loans allow borrowers to have 36% of their gross income attributed to their new monthly mortgage payment combined with existing debt. FHA program allows borrowers to carry 41%, and in some circumstances, even more [emphasis in the original].[33]

The elimination of any required FICO score in order to get an FHA-insured loan was a major concession, considering the effect of low FICO scores on the rate of delinquencies and defaults. Indeed, by 2000, the FHA had increased the percentage of its loans with FICO scores below 660 from 42 percent in 1994 to 71 percent.[34] Since the FHA is a government agency, its actions cannot be explained by a profit motive or a desire to please analysts or investors. Instead, it seems likely that the FHA reduced its lending standards as part of a HUD policy to induce the same action by Fannie and Freddie.

Despite these reductions in its underwriting standards, the FHA's market share in relation to the GSEs declined as the affordable-housing goals forced the GSEs deeper into the subprime and Alt-A market, especially after 2004, when the home purchase subgoals

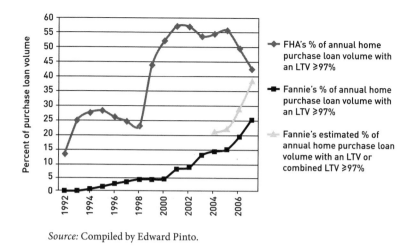

FIG. 5.3. Fannie's competition with the FHA: Ultra-high LTV (≥97%) lending by Fannie and the FHA

were introduced. According to Government Accountability Office data, in 1996, the FHA's market share among lower-income borrowers was 26 percent, while the GSEs' share was 23.8 percent. By 2005, the FHA's share was 9.8 percent, while the GSEs' share was 31.9 percent.[35] The result of Fannie's competition with the FHA in high LTV lending is shown in Figure 5.3, which compares the respective shares of the FHA and Fannie in the category of loans with LTV ratios equal to or greater than 97 percent, including Fannie loans with a combined LTV ratio equal to or greater than 97 percent.

Whether it was a conscious policy of HUD or not, competition between the GSEs and the FHA ensued immediately after the GSEs were given their affordable-housing mission in 1992. The effect was to drive down underwriting standards, which HUD had repeatedly described as its goal.

THE COMMUNITY REINVESTMENT ACT

The Community Reinvestment Act,[36] which operated outside HUD's jurisdiction, is the last of the government housing policies that made significant contributions to the financial crisis. The exact size of that contribution is a bit conjectural, however, because the CRA—unlike almost any other government program outside of national security —is kept hidden from scholars, taxpayers, Congress, and even the government agency that is supposed to keep tabs on it. Remarkably, of all the thousands of banks that have CRA obligations, only a handful have been known to disclose the dollar amount of the CRA loans they have made and the concomitant delinquency rates and charge-offs. Indeed, banks are not even required to disclose the number of their CRA loans to the Federal Reserve, which keeps the records on CRA lending. What the Federal Reserve receives is data on "high-cost loans" as defined under the Homeowners Protection Act (HOPA) and reported under the Home Mortgage Disclosure Act (HMDA)—loans with interest rates at least 3 percent higher than Treasury rates for equivalent maturities. From this, using data about the assessment areas of the banks, the Federal Reserve is supposed to compute the loans that would qualify under CRA. It is not even clear that the data on CRA lending exists anywhere, because it is not reported on regular bank call reports and examiners score bank CRA compliance in four broad categories: outstanding, satisfactory, needs to improve, and substantial noncompliance. These ratings are made public, but the data that underlie them, if any, are not.

Why the data on CRA compliance are so limited is probably a consequence of their political implications. If banks were required to report the facts about their CRA loans, it would likely become apparent that CRA-based mortgage lending is unprofitable and that banks are cross-subsidizing their mandatory CRA lending with higher costs for the mortgages they make to non-CRA borrowers. It is wryly amusing to attend a congressional hearing and listen to lawmakers who are CRA supporters worrying aloud that their constituents might have to pay 25 basis points more for a mortgage that is not guaranteed by the federal government, when they have no qualms about imposing costs on lenders through the CRA that are likely to increase mortgage rates for their constituents who are ordinary prime borrowers by considerably more than 25 basis points.

The CRA, which is applicable only to federally insured depository institutions, was originally adopted in 1977. Its purpose in part was to "require each appropriate Federal financial supervisory agency to use its authority when examining financial institutions to encourage such institutions to help meet the credit needs of the local communities in which they are chartered, consistent with the safe and sound operations of such institutions." The enforcement provisions of the act authorized bank regulators to withhold approvals for such transactions as mergers and acquisitions and branch network expansion if the applying bank did not have at least a satisfactory CRA rating.

Because the act in its initial form only required banks to reach out to the communities they served, and allowed them to maintain their lending standards, the CRA did not have a substantial effect on subprime lending in the years after its enactment. However, as noted earlier, in 1995 the Clinton administration tightened the regulations under the act, requiring banks and S&Ls to acquire or make "innovative" and "flexible" mortgages so as to ensure that all prospective borrowers in the communities they served would have access to mortgage and small business credit. In this sense, CRA requirements and the GSEs' affordable-housing goals are cut from the same cloth. In effect, banks were put to a choice between making loans they otherwise would not make for safety and soundness reasons and the very real possibility that they would be unable to obtain the regulatory approvals they needed for growth. Faced with this choice, banks most probably treated CRA loans as another cost of doing business. In that case, it is a hidden subsidy for low-income borrowers, paid for largely by the middle class. The secrecy surrounding the program is an effort to obscure that feature. Later, we will see that the GSEs were also cross-subsidizing the loans they acquired to meet the affordable-housing goals.

There are two distinct applications of the CRA. The first, and the one with the broadest applicability, is a requirement that all insured banks and S&Ls make CRA loans in their respective communities, known as their assessment areas. When the act is defended, it is almost always discussed in terms of this category—loans in bank assessment areas. Banks privately complain that they are required by the regulators to make imprudent loans to comply with the CRA. One example is the following statement by a local community bank in a report to its shareholders:

> Under the umbrella of the Community Reinvestment Act (CRA), a tremendous amount of pressure was put on banks by the regulatory authorities to make loans, especially mortgage loans, to low income borrowers and neighborhoods. The regulators were very heavy handed regarding this issue. I will not dwell on it here but they required [redacted name] to change its mortgage lending practices to meet certain CRA goals, even though we argued the changes were risky and imprudent.[37]

On the other hand, the regulators defend the act and their actions under it, and particularly deny that the CRA had a role in reducing mortgage underwriting standards. The most frequently cited defense of CRA practices is a speech by former Federal Reserve governor Randall Kroszner on December 3, 2008, in which he said, in pertinent part, based on a Federal Reserve study:

> Only 6 percent of all the *higher-priced loans* [those that were considered CRA loans because they bore high interest rates associated with their riskier character] were extended by *CRA-covered lenders to lower-income borrowers or neighborhoods in their CRA assessment areas*, the local geographies that are the primary focus for CRA evaluation purposes. This result undermines the assertion by critics of the potential for a substantial role for the CRA in the subprime crisis [emphasis added].[38]

If we unpack Kroszner's statement a bit, we see that he is arguing that CRA loans are only a small portion of outstanding subprime loans; in other words, CRA did not add materially to the subprime losses in the financial crisis. Two points in this statement require elaboration. First, it assumes that all CRA loans are high-priced loans. This is incorrect. In 2000, as required by the Gramm-Leach-Bliley Act, the Federal Reserve itself surveyed banks on this question, with the following result: "[A]bout 40 percent of respondents report that their CRA-related home purchase and refinance loans have lower prices than other home purchase and refinance loans. Only about 10 percent of the respondents report higher prices for CRA-related loans."[39] This was confirmed in an undated Fannie Mae response to a question at a meeting with the Urban Institute. Referring to CRA loans, Fannie noted: "In many instances, lenders consciously originated these [CRA] loans with features outside of the Fannie Mae and Freddie Mac underwriting guidelines and they cannot be sold to the secondary market because these loans are originated with below market interest rates and/or have high loan to value ratios but no mortgage insurance."[40] Many banks, then, in order to be sure of obtaining the necessary number of loans to attain a satisfactory CRA rating, subsidize the loans by making them at lower interest rates than their risk characteristics would warrant. Thus, a statement that only 6 percent of higher-priced loans were extended as CRA loans is somewhat misleading. It is likely that CRA loans are a much larger portion of all subprime loans, but their number is unknown for this and the other reasons explained earlier.

Kroszner also said in this speech that CRA loans did not perform any worse than other subprime loans, but this statement is difficult to interpret. The performance range of subprime loans is very wide and depends substantially on elements like FICO scores and down payments. Some subprime loans undoubtedly had high default rates. Few academic papers have evaluated whether the CRA promotes risky lending. However, in a National Bureau of Economic Research study published in December 2012, four economists studied the lending practices of banks around the time of their CRA examinations and concluded that the CRA did induce these banks to make riskier loans. In comparison with banks that were not preparing for CRA examinations, these banks were found to have made 5 percent more loans, and the loans they made defaulted about 15 percent more often.[41] This should not be an earthshaking conclusion—it should be obvious to anyone that the CRA was intended to induce banks to make loans they would not otherwise make—but the politics surrounding the act and the paucity of information about CRA loans provided by banks and the government have reduced academic interest in the subject. In any event, Kroszner's statement that CRA loans performed no worse than other subprime loans cannot be substantiated without data on the subprime loans he was using for comparison.

THE CRA-BASED CLAIMS OF THE NATIONAL COMMUNITY REINVESTMENT COALITION

The CRA's role in the financial crisis could be found to be significant in another way, if the data were available. In 1994 the Riegle-Neal Interstate Banking and Branching Efficiency Act for the first time allowed banks to merge across state lines under federal law (as distinct from interstate compacts). Under these circumstances, the enforcement provisions of the CRA, which required regulators to withhold approvals of applications for banks that did not have satisfactory CRA ratings, became particularly relevant for large banks that applied to the Federal Reserve for merger approvals. In a 2007 speech, Federal Reserve Chair Ben Bernanke stated that after the enactment of the Riegle-Neal legislation, "as public scrutiny of bank merger and acquisition activity escalated, advocacy groups increasingly used the public comment process to protest bank applications on CRA grounds. In instances of highly contested applications, the Federal Reserve Board and other agencies held public meetings to allow the public and the applicants to comment on the lending records of the banks in question. In response to these new pressures, banks began to devote more resources to their CRA programs."[42] This benign description, although accurate as far as it goes, does not fully describe the effect of the law and the application process on bank lending practices.

In 2007, the umbrella organization for many low-income or community advocacy groups, the National Community Reinvestment Coalition (NCRC), published a report titled "CRA Commitments" that recounted the substantial success of its members in using the leverage provided by the bank application process to obtain trillions of dollars in CRA lending commitments from banks that had applied to federal regulators for merger approvals. The opening section of the report states:

> *Since the passage of CRA in 1977, lenders and community organizations have signed over 446 CRA agreements totaling more than $4.5 trillion in reinvestment dollars flowing to minority and lower income neighborhoods* [emphasis in original].
>
> Lenders and community groups will often sign these agreements when a lender has submitted an application to merge with another institution or expand its services. Lenders must seek the approval of federal regulators for their plans to merge or change their services. The four federal financial institution regulatory agencies will scrutinize the CRA records of lenders *and will assess the likely future community reinvestment performance of lenders. The application process, therefore, provides an incentive for lenders to sign CRA agreements with community groups that will improve their CRA performance. Recognizing the important role of collaboration between lenders and community groups, the federal agencies have established mechanisms in their application procedures that encourage dialogue and cooperation among the parties in preserving and strengthening community reinvestment* [emphasis added].[43]

A footnote to this statement reports:

> The Federal Reserve Board will grant an extension of the public comment period during its merger application process upon a joint request by a bank and community group. In its commentary to Regulation Y, the Board indicates that this procedure was added to facilitate discussions between banks and community groups regarding programs that help serve the convenience and needs of the community. In its *Corporate Manual*, the Office of the Comptroller of the Currency

states that it will not offer the expedited application process to a lender that does not intend to honor a CRA agreement made by the institution that it is acquiring.[44]

In its report, the NCRC listed all 446 commitments and includes a summary list of year-by-year commitments (Table 5.3). The size of these commitments, which far outstrip the CRA loans made in assessment areas, suggests the potential significance of the CRA as a

TABLE 5.3. The NCRC's list of bank CRA commitments by year and total dollars of commitment[a]

Year	Annual dollars (millions)	Total dollars (millions)	Year	Annual dollars (millions)	Total dollars (millions)
2007	12,500	4,566,480	1991	2,443	8,811
2006	258,000	4,553,980	1990	1,614	6,378
2005	100,276	4,298,980	1989	2,260	4,764
2004	1,631,140	4,195,704	1988	1,248	2,504
2003	711,669	2,564,564	1987	357	1,256
2002	152,859	1,852,895	1986	516	899
2001	414,184	1,700,036	1985	73	382
2000	13,681	1,285,852	1984	219	309
1999	103,036	1,272,171	1983	1	90
1998	812,160	1,169,135	1982	6	89
1997	221,345	356,975	1981	5	83
1996	49,678	135,630	1980	13	78
1995	26,590	85,952	1979	15	65
1994	6,128	59,362	1978	0	50
1993	10,716	53,234	1977	50	50
1992	33,708	42,518			

Adapted from: National Community Reinvestment Coalition, "CRA Commitments" (September 2007), p. 8, http://www.community-wealth.org/_pdfs/articles-publications/cdfis /report-silver-brown.pdf.
[a]Dollar amount is cumulative from bottom to top.

cause of the financial crisis. The FCIC majority was not willing even to consider the significance of the NCRC's numbers. In connection with its only hearing on the housing issue, and before any research had been done on the NCRC statements, the FCIC published a staff report absolving the CRA of any responsibility for the financial crisis.[45]

To understand the CRA's role in the financial crisis, the relevant statistic is the $4.5 trillion in bank CRA lending commitments that the NCRC cited in its 2007 report. One important question is whether the bank regulators cooperated with community groups by withholding approvals of applications for mergers and acquisitions until an agreement or commitment for CRA lending satisfactory to the community groups had been arranged. It is not difficult to imagine that the regulators did not want to invite the criticism from Congress that would have followed their failure to assist community groups in reaching agreements with and getting commitments from banks that had applied for these approvals. In statements connected with mergers it has approved, the Federal Reserve has said that commitments by the bank participants about future CRA lending have no influence on the approval process. A Federal Reserve official also told the FCIC's staff that the agency did not consider these commitments in connection with merger applications. The FCIC did not attempt to verify this statement, but accepted it at face value from a Federal Reserve staff official, and there is no way of knowing whether that official was referring to substantive effects on an application or just a delay in the processing of the application until the community groups were satisfied. Nevertheless, there remains no explanation for why banks have been making these enormous commitments in connection with mergers and other expansion requests, but not at other times.

The largest of the CRA commitments, which totaled well over $4 trillion in the aggregate, were made in connection with mergers or acquisitions by four banks—Bank of America, JPMorgan Chase, Citibank, and Wells Fargo or their predecessors. Press releases by these banks in the years after the commitments were made indicate that substantial portions of the commitments were fulfilled. Edward Pinto has calculated, based on these announcements, that a total of at least $1.6 trillion in single family loans were actually made.[46] Pinto estimates that approximately 2.24 million loans, totaling $312 billion, were still outstanding in June 2008 and were not counted in any other category in Table 1.1.[47] However, we don't know how many commitments were actually fulfilled, where the rest of the loans are today, or what their delinquency and default rates may be. If they are still outstanding on the books of the largest banks, that would substantially increase the percentage of NTMs outstanding that would be attributable to government policies.

The delinquency rates on CRA loans are difficult to determine because, as noted above, they are not reported by banks in sufficient numbers to generalize. However, in the past few years, Bank of America has been reporting the performance of CRA loans in its annual report to the Securities and Exchange Commission (SEC) on Form 10-K. For example, the bank's 10-K report for 2009 contained the following statement: "At December 31, 2009, our CRA portfolio comprised 6 percent of the total residential mortgage balances, but comprised 17 percent of nonperforming residential mortgage loans. This portfolio also comprised 20 percent of residential net charge-offs during 2009." Similar statements were made for subsequent years. This figure could be an approximation for the delinquency rate on the merger-related CRA loans of the four banks that merged with Bank of America, but without definitive information on the actual number of loans made and the banks' current holdings, it is impossible to make this estimate with any confidence. In addition, we do not know how Countrywide loans were counted in the data from Bank of America. Further investigation of this issue is necessary—including research on the role of the Fed and other bank regulators—in order to determine why these huge commitments were made and what effect, if any, merger-related commitments might have had on the number of NTMs in the U.S. financial system before the financial crisis.

HUD'S "REVOLUTION IN AFFORDABLE LENDING"

By 2004, even though it was still dissatisfied with homeownership levels among low-income and minority borrowers, HUD believed it had achieved a "revolution":

Over the past ten years, there has been a "revolution in affordable lending" that has extended homeownership opportunities to historically underserved households. Fannie Mae
and Freddie Mac have been a substantial part of this "revolution in affordable lending." *During the mid-to-late 1990s, they
added flexibility to their underwriting guidelines, introduced
new low-downpayment products,* and worked to expand the
use of automated underwriting in evaluating the creditwor-
thiness of loan applicants. HMDA data suggest that the industry and GSE initiatives are increasing the flow of credit
to underserved borrowers. *Between 1993 and 2003, conventional loans to low income and minority families increased at
much faster rates than loans to upper-income and nonminor-
ity families* [emphasis added].[48]

The "revolution" turned out to be a monumental policy error. It
was a great experiment, and was perhaps entered with the view—
expressed in the preceding statement—that new technology like
automated underwriting would assure a safe result. But by now it
should be clear that loosening underwriting standards does not lead
to a stable mortgage financing system. The only path to a stable system is through prime mortgages. It is important to recognize that,
in addition to the taxpayers who ultimately had to foot the bill, the
groups most hurt by policies that favor reduced underwriting standards were—as Barney Frank admitted in 2010—the millions of
homeowners who were encouraged and enabled to purchase homes
that they could not afford to keep.

The affordable-housing goals, the CRA, the FHA, the Best Practices Initiative, and the National Homeownership Strategy, operating together between 1995 and 2008, spread NTMs throughout the
financial system, degraded underwriting standards, built an enormous and unprecedented housing bubble, and ultimately precipitated a massive mortgage meltdown. The result, as outlined in the
next chapter, was a financial crisis.

The great irony here is that when the affordable-housing goals
were adopted by Congress, homes in the U.S. were among the most

affordable in the world. In 1989, nearly 90 percent of U.S. housing markets were considered affordable, with homes costing only three times more than annual family incomes. However, by 2005, after the affordable-housing goals had worked their "revolution," less than 33 percent of U.S. markets were deemed affordable under this standard, and 20 markets were deemed severely unaffordable.[49]

In June 2008, just before the crisis fully gripped the nation, there was a moment of recognition that HUD's policies were at fault, when the fact that many families would lose their homes was connected to the affordable-housing goals. An article in the *Washington Post* captured that moment:

> In 2004, as regulators warned that subprime lenders were saddling borrowers with mortgages they could not afford, the U.S. Department of Housing and Urban Development helped fuel more of that risky lending. . . . Eager to put more low-income and minority families into their own homes, the agency required that two government-chartered mortgage finance firms purchase far more "affordable" loans made to those borrowers. HUD stuck with an outdated policy that allowed Freddie Mac and Fannie Mae to count billions of dollars they invested in subprime loans as a public good that would foster affordable housing.
>
> Today, 3 million to 4 million families are expected to lose their homes to foreclosure because they cannot afford their high-interest subprime loans. Lower-income and minority homebuyers—those who were supposed to benefit from HUD's actions—are falling into default at a rate at least three times that of other borrowers.[50]

Several former HUD officials were cited in the article to the effect that they had made a mistake or that things had not worked out as they'd hoped. But this recognition was fleeting. After the failure of Lehman Brothers in September 2008 and the resulting financial crisis, HUD's role in the weakening of underwriting standards, the loss of homes, and ultimately the financial crisis, disappeared from the

Washington consensus and from the mainstream media. It was replaced by a narrative that insufficiently regulated commercial banks, investment banks, shadow banks, rating agencies, mortgage brokers, and a myriad other private-sector actors were the responsible parties. This later analysis protected the government and absolved both political parties of responsibility for a financial disaster. But the stubborn fact remains that the government's housing policies added enormous numbers of NTMs to the nation's mortgage market, so many that it seems likely the financial crisis would never have occurred but for this serious policy error.

In the next chapter, we will see how the affordable-housing goals distorted the GSEs' mortgage purchases and drove them deeper into the NTM market.

6

The Decline in Underwriting Standards

How the Affordable-Housing Goals Forced an Increase in Nontraditional Mortgages

Our mission goals are really like CRA on steroids.

BARRY ZIGAS, Fannie Mae Senior Vice President,
November 16, 2000

Christina Natale, as the *New York Times* reported on November 8, 2008, seemed to be exactly the kind of person the affordable-housing goals were intended to help. The divorced mother of two had a steady job as an administrative assistant and took home almost $2,000 per month. She had recently sold her grandfather's house and used the proceeds for a $185,000 down payment (almost 50 percent) on a $385,000 three-bedroom townhouse on Staten Island. Her loan had been approved, and the broker seemed unconcerned. The trouble was, her monthly payment was only $100 short of her monthly take-home pay.[1] Why did she do it? "It made me feel good," she told the *Times* reporter. Why didn't the broker stop her or the bank turn down the loan? Probably because it had already been approved by Fannie or Freddie. And why didn't one of the GSEs turn her down? Because Natale's loan probably helped one of them meet its 2006 purchase money subgoal under the affordable-housing goals.

As discussed in chapter 4, before the adoption of the Federal Housing Enterprises Financial Safety and Soundness Act (the GSE

Act) in 1992 and the imposition of the affordable-housing goals, the GSEs followed conservative underwriting practices. Mortgage defaults were usually well under 1 percent, and the homeownership rate in the United States hovered around 64 percent, where it had been for almost thirty years. High-risk lending was confined primarily to the FHA (an agency controlled by the Department of Housing and Urban Development [HUD]) and to specialized subprime lenders. What caused these conservative standards to decline? The Financial Crisis Inquiry Commission (FCIC) and many private commentators blamed the irresponsibility of the private sector and Wall Street, as did Ben Bernanke.[2] However, there is no difficulty finding the source of this decline in the GSE Act and HUD's statements and policies during the 1990s and 2000s, both of which made clear that reducing underwriting standards was the underlying purpose of the affordable-housing goals. By the early 1990s, Fannie and Freddie had come to dominate the housing finance market. When they were compelled to reduce their underwriting standards, the lower standards—intended to assist low-income and minority borrowers— inevitably spread to the wider market.

JAMES JOHNSON AND THE FIRST "TRILLION DOLLAR COMMITMENT"

Under the direction of its chair, James Johnson, Fannie Mae had seen the political value of lending to low-income borrowers. In 1991, even before the enactment of the GSE Act, Fannie had made a $10 billion pledge of support for low-income housing, adapting a vehicle for reduced underwriting standards called the Community Home Buyer Program (CHBP).[3] By accepting "variances" from its regular underwriting requirements, the company could acquire mortgages that previously had not met its standards, but the effect of these variances proved to be an early warning of what was to come. In 1993 alone, the percentage of Fannie's business volume with loans that had loan-to-value (LTV) ratios over 90 percent had almost tripled, from 6.85 percent to 18.77 percent.[4] A report to Fannie's Credit Policy Committee in 1995 pointed out that "[p]erformance of the standard high-LTV community lending product is more than 50 percent worse than a control group for 1993."[5] The volume of this product had increased from $604 million in 1991 to $7.4 billion in 1994, but "CHBP loans with LTVs [greater than] 90 percent have significantly higher delinquency rates than their control groups." Thus, even before the affordable-housing goals were fully in effect, Fannie had begun to experience the costs associated with nontraditional mortgages (NTMs).

But Johnson pushed ahead. In 1994, Fannie made its first "Trillion Dollar Commitment," promising to spend this dramatic sum over ten years in support of low-income housing. Because the affordable-housing goals were already in force, this promise was making a virtue of necessity. But it reflected Johnson's view, again correct, that Fannie's franchise would be bulletproof in Congress if it committed itself to financing homes for low-income and minority borrowers. A 1997 article in the *New York Times* reported, "Mr. Johnson has won widespread admiration from advocacy groups for working to expand home ownership among low-income people and others left out of the housing market."[6] "We all understood," said Tim Howard, later to become Fannie's chief financial officer, "that accomplishing the goals of the Trillion Dollar Commitment would require an easing of our credit standards, specifically for loans with lower downpayments . . . and loans to borrowers with less than perfect credit."[7]

The year 1995 was pivotal in setting the pattern for the GSEs' later development. In that year, HUD ruled that Fannie and Freddie could get affordable-housing goals credit for buying private mortgage–backed securities (PMBS) that were backed by loans to low- and moderate-income (LMI) borrowers.[8] This ruling provided an opportunity for subprime lenders or securitization sponsors to create pools of subprime mortgages that were likely to be rich in loans that met the affordable-housing goals. These were then sold either directly or through Wall Street underwriters to Fannie and Freddie, which became by far the largest buyers of these high-risk PMBS. Between 1997 and 2007, Fannie and Freddie bought more than $700 billion in subprime PMBS—about 30 percent of all PMBS issued during that period—and an additional $154 billion in Alt-A PMBS, about 12.5 percent of the total issued.[9] As will be shown later, these

PMBS pools were bought not for profit or for market share, but to meet the affordable-housing goal quotas. By creating a large market for PMBS backed by NTMs, Fannie and Freddie enabled Wall Street firms—which had previously focused primarily on securitizing prime jumbo loans—to get their start in the business of issuing and underwriting PMBS backed by NTMs.

Also in 1995, HUD raised the LMI goal to 40 percent for 1996 and to 42 percent for subsequent years. The GSEs' baseline for LMI loan purchases was about 30 percent; that is, in the ordinary course of business, without any special intervention, about 30 percent of the loans they bought would have been made to borrowers below the median income where they lived.[10] Accordingly, the LMI goal that went into effect in 1996 was an increase of about 35 percent. HUD also increased the special affordable and underserved areas base goals. The baseline for the special affordable goal—which covered low- and very-low-income borrowers (80 percent and 60 percent of area median income, or AMI)—had been about 7 percent; that goal was raised to 12 percent, an increase of about 71 percent. This would be the pattern for the future; HUD would make small percentage increases in the LMI base goal but large increases in the special affordable and underserved areas base goals, driving the GSEs deeper into riskier territory to find loans to low- or very-low-income borrowers (80 percent and 60 percent of AMI, respectively) and to borrowers in "underserved areas," which were principally Hispanic or African American communities. As early as November 1995, Fannie's staff had reported that loans with a 97 percent loan-to-value (LTV) ratio—that is, a 3 percent down payment—were showing significant rates of serious delinquency that exceeded Fannie's expected rates by 26 percent in origination year 1992, 93 percent in 1993, and 57 percent in 1994.[11]

In the thirteen-year period from 1995 through 2007, Countrywide Financial Corporation became the largest supplier of loans to the GSEs. It was the largest supplier in eight of those years and second in five, accounting for 29 percent of Fannie's purchases and 16 percent of Freddie's.[12] This should not be surprising; according to HUD, "Subprime lending grew rapidly in the 1990s. Between 1993 and 1998, subprime lending increased 760 percent for home purchases and 890 percent for refinance mortgages; during the same period, the prime market grew 38 percent and almost 3 percent, respectively."[13] Countrywide, through its sales to Fannie and Freddie, became the undisputed leader in subprime lending. Angelo Mozilo, the chair of Countrywide, formerly just another subprime lender, became a national figure, making speeches around the country about the virtues of subprime lending. Many other subprime lenders also made fortunes selling subprime loans to Fannie and Freddie. As a harbinger of things to come, however, according to a 1995 report of Fannie's credit policy committee, Countrywide's loans performed 30 percent more poorly than a control group.[14] Significantly, that did not reduce Fannie's interest in Countrywide's production.

In 1996, a major Federal Reserve study showed that reductions in underwriting standards of the kind HUD was pressing on the GSEs could result in high levels of default, especially when high LTV ratios are combined with low median incomes and low FICO scores (see the discussion in chapter 2 and Table 2.1). The study showed that a loan to a borrower with a credit score of less than 621 and a down payment of less than 20 percent, whose income was less than 80 percent of median income—the very borrowers who were targeted by the special affordable base goal—would have over *51 times* the foreclosure rate of a borrower of any income level who had a credit score of 660 or more and a down payment of 20 percent.[15]

HUD ignored these findings and kept the pressure on Fannie and Freddie. In 1997, it commissioned the Urban Institute to study the GSEs' credit guidelines. The resulting report commented favorably on the reduction in underwriting standards that the GSEs had undertaken to meet the affordable-housing goals: "Almost all informants said their opinion of the GSEs had changed for the better since both Fannie and Freddie had made substantive alterations to their guidelines and developed new affordable loan products with more flexible underwriting guidelines." Nevertheless, the report criticized the GSEs for failing to do enough to assist low-income borrowers, even suggesting that they might be discriminating against minorities. "Informants did express concerns about some of the GSEs' practices. The GSEs' guidelines, designed to identify creditworthy applicants, are more likely to disqualify borrowers with low incomes, limited wealth, and poor credit histories; applicants with these characteristics are disproportionately minorities."[16] This idea, that the GSEs were not really trying, was echoed in HUD's commentary on the major affordable-housing goals increase in 2000: "A large percentage of the lower-income loans purchased by the enterprises have relatively high down payments, which raises questions about whether the GSEs are adequately meeting the mortgage credit needs of lower-income families who do not have sufficient cash to make a high down payment."[17] After the Urban Institute report, the share of subprime loans (including both self-denominated subprime and loans to borrowers with FICO scores less than 660) guaranteed or acquired by Fannie and Freddie and insured by the FHA increased from 51 percent to 65 percent.[18]

"CRA ON STEROIDS"

A major step to increase the affordable-housing goals was taken after Andrew Cuomo replaced Henry Cisneros as HUD secretary in 1997. A HUD press release on July 29, 1999, announced a plan "to require the nation's two largest housing finance companies [Fannie and Freddie] to buy $2.4 trillion in mortgages over the next 10 years to provide affordable housing for about 28.1 million low- and moderate-income families." Without specifics about how this plan would be carried out, the release promised that the affordable-housing goals would be substantially raised and that "[u]nder the higher goals, Fannie Mae and Freddie Mac will buy an additional $488.3 billion in mortgages that will be used to provide affordable housing for 7 million more low- and moderate-income families over the next 10 years . . . over and above the $1.9 trillion in mortgages for 21.1 million families that would have been generated if the current goals had been retained."[19]

When the new affordable-housing goals were finally announced, just before the 2000 election, they contained dramatic increases and drove Fannie and Freddie into a new and far more challenging era. As Barry Zigas, then a senior vice president at Fannie, told a housing group, "Our mission goals are really like CRA on steroids."[20] The basic goal, an LMI requirement of 42 percent, was raised to 50 percent, a substantial increase in itself, but the special affordable base goal was raised from 14 to 20 percent, and the underserved areas goal was raised from 24 to 31 percent. As a result, 75 percent of the increase in goals was concentrated in the underserved and low- and very-low-income categories, where the risks were the greatest.[21] In a December 2000 memorandum, a Fannie staffer noted that the line between prime and subprime was disappearing: "[A]s Fannie Mae and Freddie Mac are expanding approvals through automated underwriting, the distinction between prime and subprime is increasingly difficult to articulate."[22] This observation recalls the HUD statement, made in connection with the 2000 affordable-housing goal increase, that "[a]s the GSEs become more comfortable with subprime lending, the line between what today is considered a subprime loan versus a prime loan will likely deteriorate, making expansion by the GSEs look more like an increase in the prime market." This idea, as noted earlier, was consistent with the left's effort to erase the distinction between prime and subprime mortgages, and from the Fannie staffer's comment it appears that HUD's strategy was working.

The substantial increase in the affordable-housing goals in 2000 was also based on HUD's interpretation of the congressional directive in the GSE Act:

To fulfill the intent of [the GSE Act], the GSEs should lead the industry in ensuring that access to mortgage credit is made available for very low-, low- and moderate-income families and residents of underserved areas. HUD recognizes that, to lead the mortgage industry over time, *the GSEs will have to stretch to reach certain goals and close the gap between the secondary mortgage market and the primary mortgage market* [that is, reach parity in loan purchases between the LMI market and the regular market]. *This approach is consistent with Congress' recognition that "the enterprises will need to stretch their efforts to achieve" the goals* [emphasis added].[23]

These new and more stringent affordable-housing goal requirements immediately stimulated strong interest at Fannie and Freddie in CRA loans, substantial portions of which were likely to be goals-qualifying. Fannie's Vice Chair Jamie Gorelick told an American Bankers Association conference on October 30, 2000, just after HUD announced the latest increase in the affordable-housing goals for the GSEs:

Your CRA business is very important to us. Since 1997, we have done nearly $7 billion in specially targeted CRA business—all with depositories like yours. But that is just the beginning. Before the decade is over, Fannie Mae is committed to finance over $20 billion in specially targeted CRA business and over $500 billion in CRA business altogether. . . .

We want your CRA loans because they help us meet our housing goals. . . . [W]e will buy them from your portfolios, or package them into securities. . . . We will also purchase CRA mortgages you make right at the point of origination. . . . You can originate CRA loans for our purchase with one of our CRA-friendly products, like our 3 percent down Fannie 97. Or we have special community lending products with flexible underwriting and special financing. . . . Our approach is "CRA your way" [emphasis added].[24]

The 50 percent level in the new HUD regulations, together with the increases in the other base goals, was a turning point. Fannie and Freddie had to stretch to reach the previous goals, but 50 percent—coupled with the new special affordable and underserved base goals—was a major challenge. As Daniel Mudd, Fannie's chair before it was taken over by the government, told the FCIC,

Fannie Mae's mission regulator, HUD, imposed ever-higher housing goals that were very difficult to meet during my tenure as CEO [2005–2008]. The HUD goals greatly impacted Fannie Mae's business, as a great deal of time, resources, energy, and personnel were dedicated to finding ways to meet these goals. HUD increased the goals aggressively over time to the point where they exceeded the 50% mark, requiring Fannie Mae to place greater emphasis on purchasing loans in underserved areas. Fannie Mae had to devote a great deal of resources to running its business to satisfy HUD's goals and subgoals.[25]

Mudd's point can be illustrated with simple arithmetic. At the 50 percent level, for every mortgage acquired that was not goal-qualifying, Fannie and Freddie had to acquire a goal-qualifying loan. Although about 30 percent of prime loans were likely to be goal-qualifying in any event (because they were made to borrowers at or below the applicable area median income [AMI]), most prime loans were not. Subprime and other NTM loans were goals-rich, but not every such loan was goals-qualifying. Accordingly, in order to meet a 50 percent goal, let alone the higher goals established after 2000, the GSEs had to purchase ever-larger amounts of goals-rich NTMs in order to acquire sufficient quantities of goals-qualifying loans. To the extent that an NTM did not meet the technical require-ments of the goals,[26] it would go into the denominator of the fraction that determined what percentage of the GSEs' acquisitions received goals credit, but not into the numerator. In that case, each NTM ac-quired that did not meet the goals displaced a less risky prime loan. In effect, once the 50 percent level was put in place, Fannie and Fred-die were in the business of supporting affordable housing rather than assisting middle-class homeownership. The revolution was complete. As Kevin Villani, a former chief economist for Freddie, observed, "Politicians may note that it was not their 'intent' that these strate-gies result in losses. But losses were inevitable."[27]

THE ADOPTION OF PURCHASE MONEY SUBGOALS

The last increase in the affordable-housing goals occurred in 2004, when the Bush administration's HUD raised the LMI goal to 52 per-cent for 2005, 53 percent for 2006, 55 percent for 2007, and 56 percent for 2008. Again, the percentage increases in the special affordable and underserved categories outstripped the general LMI goal, putting added pressure on Fannie and Freddie to acquire even more risky NTMs. The special affordable goal increased from 20 percent to 27 percent over the period, an increase of about 33 percent, and the underserved goal increased from 31 percent to 39 percent.

But none of these increases was as consequential as the purchase money subgoals that HUD added to every base goal category. These required the GSEs to more directly affect homeownership by allowing affordable-housing goals credit only for loans intended for the purchase of a home, as opposed to a refinancing. As the rule moved toward its final form, the GSEs and many commentators argued that instituting the purchase money subgoals would force Fannie and Freddie to further loosen the standards they had been using to acquire subprime loans, but HUD was confident that the GSEs could overcome the obstacles.

> The experience of Fannie Mae and Freddie Mac in the subprime market indicates that they have the expertise and experience to develop technologies and new products that allow them to enter new markets in a prudent manner. Given the innovativeness of Fannie Mae and Freddie Mac, other strategies will be available as well. In fact, a wide variety of quantitative and qualitative indicators suggest that the GSEs have the expertise, resources and financial strength to improve their affordable lending performance enough to lead the home purchase market for special affordable, low- and moderate-income, and underserved areas loans. The recent improvement in the affordable lending performance of the GSEs, and particularly Fannie Mae, further demonstrates the GSEs' capacity to lead the home purchase market.[28]

Fannie had anticipated this added pressure, arguing to HUD without avail in March 2003 that "[h]igher goals force us deeper into FHA and subprime."[29] According to HUD data, as a result of the affordable-housing goals, Fannie Mae's acquisitions of goal-qualifying purchase money mortgages (which were primarily NTMs) increased for low- and very-low-income (special affordable) borrowers from 6.2 percent of their acquisitions in 1992 to 12.6 percent in 2007; for underserved areas from 18.3 percent in 1992 to 23.6 percent in 2007; and for less-than-median-income borrowers (which includes the other two categories) from 29.2 percent in 1992 to 42.1 percent in 2007.[30] By 2004, Fannie and Freddie were sufficiently in need of subprime loans to meet the affordable-housing goals that their CEOs went before a meeting of mortgage bankers to ask for more subprime loan production: "The top executives of Freddie Mac and Fannie Mae [Richard Syron and Franklin Raines] made no bones about their interest in buying loans made to borrowers formerly considered the province of nonprime and other niche lenders," reported *Mortgage Banking* on December 1, 2004. "Raines told mortgage bankers in San Francisco that . . . *we have to push products and opportunities to people who have lesser credit quality*" [emphasis added].[31] At this point, Fannie and Freddie were using every available resource to meet the goals, including subprime loans, Alt-A loans, and the purchase of PMBS backed by these NTMs.

Just how desperate Fannie and Freddie were to meet their affordable-housing quotas is revealed by two events that became public in 2005. As reported in the *American Banker* on May 13, 2005,

A House Financial Services Committee report shared with lawmakers Thursday accused Fannie Mae and Freddie Mac of engaging over several years in a series of dubious transactions to meet their affordable-housing goals. . . . The report cited several large transactions entered into by Fannie under which sellers were allowed to repurchase loans without recourse. For example, it said that in September 2003, Fannie bought the option to buy up to $12 billion of multifamily mortgage loans from Washington Mutual, Inc., for a fee of $2 million, the report said. Under the agreement, the GSE permitted WaMu to repurchase the loans. . . . This was the largest multifamily transaction ever undertaken by Fannie Mae and was critical for Fannie Mae to reach the affordable-housing goals, the report said.[32]

Another description of this kind of transaction—this one involving Freddie Mac—is contained in Washington Mutual's Form 10-K, dated December 31, 2003:

> The Company received $100 million in nonrefundable fees [from Freddie Mac] to induce the Company to swap approximately $6 billion of multi-family loans for 100% of the beneficial interest in those loans in the form of mortgage-backed securities issued by Freddie Mac. Since the Company has the unilateral right to collapse the securities after one year, the Company has effectively retained control over the loans. . . . This transaction was undertaken by Freddie Mac in order to facilitate fulfilling its 2003 affordable housing goals as set by the Department of Housing and Urban Development.

In other words, Fannie and Freddie were both paying holders of mortgages to "rent" them the loans they needed to satisfy the affordable-housing goals. After the end of the year, Washington Mutual could repurchase the loans. There can be little doubt, then, that as early as 2003 Fannie and Freddie were under so much pressure to find the subprime or other loans they needed to meet their affordable-housing obligations that they were willing to pay substantial sums to deceive HUD by window-dressing their goals reports.

THE POLITICAL ROOTS OF GSE COMPLIANCE

Why such desperation? It is important to recall Fannie Chair James Johnson's original perception that Fannie's franchise would be impossible to challenge if the firm were associated in Congress with assisting low-income housing. From that time forward, the first rule of Fannie's management and employees was to preserve the franchise. That objective had become all the more compelling in 2003, when the Bush administration was beginning to propose tougher regulation of Fannie and Freddie to a Republican Congress, and some of the more zealous free marketeers (like me) were suggesting that Fannie and Freddie be privatized.[33] A failure to meet any significant portion of the affordable-housing goals would have given more ammunition to the administration and the Republicans in Congress, increasing the chances that tougher regulatory legislation, perhaps even privatization, would be enacted. To fend this off, the GSEs needed solid Democratic support in Congress, and that support depended crucially on whether Fannie and Freddie were continuing and even increasing their support of affordable housing.

On June 24, 2004, seventy-six House Democrats, led by Nancy Pelosi (D-Calif.) and Barney Frank (D-Mass.), delivered the necessary support through a letter to President Bush, showing at the same time how much their support was linked to the affordable-housing goals. "We write as members of the House of Representatives who continually press the GSEs to do more in affordable housing," the letter began.

> Until recently, we have been disappointed that the administration has not been more supportive of our efforts to press the GSEs to do more. We have been concerned that the administration's legislative proposal regarding the GSEs would weaken affordable-housing performance by the GSEs, *by emphasizing safety and soundness*. While the GSEs' affordable housing mission is not in any way incompatible with their safety and soundness, an exclusive focus on safety and soundness is likely to come, in practice, at the expense of affordable housing [emphasis added].[34]

Other pressures were also developing. In late 2003 and 2004, Countrywide and other subprime lenders for the first time became effective distributors of their own NTMs through the creation and sale of PMBS. This was troubling to Fannie for two reasons. First, as noted earlier, Countrywide had been Fannie's largest supplier of subprime mortgages, which were necessary for the GSEs to meet their affordable-housing quotas; the fact that Countrywide could now securitize mortgages it formerly sold to Fannie meant that Fannie would have greater difficulty finding subprime mortgages that were goals-eligible. Second, if Countrywide and others were able to securitize substantial numbers of subprime loans, including many that were goals-eligible, it raised questions about whether the GSEs were actually necessary for the support of affordable housing. Perhaps it would be better and more effective to have dynamic private-sector firms like Countrywide spearhead this effort. It's easy to see in this light why Fannie and Freddie would be concerned about falling short of the affordable-housing goals and losing their leadership position in support of low-income lending. If Fannie or Freddie failed to meet the current goals, the Republicans would be able to argue that the Democrats' demand for more low-income lending was unrealistic and could not be achieved, and anyway private-sector subprime lenders were doing a better job than the GSEs. This would have given the Republicans an open field for stricter regulation of the GSEs or even privatization. Further growth of PMBS backed by NTMs in 2005 and 2006 caused great concern among Fannie's top officers about what they called Fannie's "relevance." This was code for what they feared would be the loss of political support among congressional Democrats if the GSEs failed to lead the industry in low-income and minority lending. All of these factors, clearly foreseeable in the future, probably accounted for the GSEs' desperation as the end of 2003 approached and they had not yet met their affordable-housing goals for the year.

GSE COMPLIANCE WITH THE
AFFORDABLE-HOUSING GOALS OVER TIME

The data on the GSEs' acquisition of NTMs and PMBS backed by NTMs in the early 1990s is sketchy or not available. Although none of the data is complete, the information below is what can be assembled from various sources. The best data covers home purchase loans (that is, loans to buy a home, not loans to refinance an existing home) with high LTV ratios. The next best is data, beginning in 1997, on self-denominated subprime loans and those loans that are classified as subprime because the borrower's FICO score was less than 660. Finally, limited data on Alt-A loans is available from 2002 forward and consists only of Alt-A and self-denominated Alt-A loans acquired by Fannie and Freddie through acquiring PMBS.[35]

From the beginning of its administration of the affordable-housing goals, HUD had concluded that the down payment requirement in a traditional mortgage was the most important barrier to homeownership for LMI and minority borrowers. In the 1995 National Homeownership Strategy, for example, HUD listed cutting transaction costs, reducing down payments and mortgage costs, and increasing the availability of financing as the three key changes they would press on the private sector. "For many potential homebuyers," HUD told its private-sector "partners," "the lack of cash available to accumulate the required downpayment and closing costs is the major impediment to purchasing a home. Other households do not have sufficient available income to make the monthly payments on mortgages financed at market interest rates for standard loan terms. Financing strategies, fueled by the creativity and resources of the private and public sectors, should address both of these financial barriers to homeownership."[36] Clearly, HUD wanted concessions on both down payments and interest rates.

HUD's policy of reducing down payments was highly successful with the GSEs. Between 1992 and 2007, Fannie's percentage of home purchase loans with LTV ratios greater than 90 percent increased from 15 percent to 35 percent, and Freddie's percentage increased from 13 percent to 29 percent.[37] These figures compare to only 9 percent of purchase loans in Fannie's 1992 Random Study. Indeed, over the period that HUD was administering the affordable-housing goals, down payments fell precipitously. In 1992, neither Fannie nor Freddie had any loans with down payments less than 5 percent, but by 2007, 26 percent of Fannie's loans and 19 percent of Freddie's had down payments at this level.[38] Table 6.1 summarizes the gradual increase in the LTV ratios of loans acquired by the GSEs as a means of meeting the affordable-housing goals.

As large as these numbers are, the actual percentage of high LTV mortgages in the financial system was probably much larger. For one thing, this data covers only home purchase loans; the mortgages that the GSEs acquired in refinances are not included. In addition, data from HUD often did not include information on second mortgages, which substantially increase LTV ratios and thus substantially reduce loan quality. This is a particularly troubling element of the reporting by both HUD and the FHFA during this period. A mortgage reported as having an LTV ratio of 80 percent could have a second mortgage of 20 percent that was unreported—often called a "silent second"—so that the mortgage was essentially a zero-down-payment loan. Thirty-year mortgages with no down payment are very risky, and when combined with low credit scores they have extremely high levels of default. This stands to reason, because the buyer has virtually no investment in the home. In a report issued by the FHFA in September 2010, the agency noted that "loans with LTV ratios at origination of 80 percent or 90 percent tend to have higher delinquency rates than loans with slightly higher LTV ratios in several origination years. That observation is consistent with the existence of

TABLE 6.1. Fannie and Freddie's acquisition of loans
with LTV ratios higher than 95 percent

	1999	2000	2001	2002	2003	2004	2005	2006	2007
Fannie Mae									
All home purchases (%)	4.1	4.3	7.1	7.7	11.5	12.9	14.8	19.4	25.9
Low and moderate income (%)	7.1	7.4	12.7	12.7	19.3	21.7	23.4	31.0	40.7
Underserved areas (%)	6.9	7.2	12.4	12.4	18.9	21.0	22.9	28.5	37.1
Special affordable (%)	7.2	8.4	15.7	14.7	22.9	25.3	30.9	39.6	50.9
Freddie Mac									
All home purchases (%)	5.1	5.9	5.3	7.9	10.3	6.5	8.0	9.8	19.3
Low and moderate income (%)	6.2	10.1	10.7	8.5	12.7	9.0	13.2	15.0	33.2
Underserved areas (%)	5.6	9.4	10.1	7.5	12.2	8.5	12.8	14.2	29.3
Special affordable (%)	7.2	12.6	15.5	9.7	15.4	11.5	18.2	20.3	39.4

Source: HUD Office of Policy Development and Research.
   Adapted from: Edward J. Pinto, "Government Housing Policies in the Lead-Up to the Financial Crisis: A Forensic Study," draft manuscript, February 5, 2011, Chart 29, http://www.aei.org/publication/government-housing-policies-in-the-lead-up-to-the-financial-crisis-a-forensic-study.

second liens that are not captured in the LTV ratio."[39] In other words, it appears that many loans with 80 percent LTV ratios actually had silent seconds and were defaulting at rates that were not consistent with 20 percent down payments, but the FHFA did not have the data to verify this. The FHFA drew essentially the same conclusion in its reports for 2008 and 2009 but apparently did not attempt to stop the practice.

The growth of silent seconds was yet another adverse result of the efforts by Fannie and Freddie to compete for NTMs. The GSEs were required by their congressional charters to have mortgage insurance whenever the LTV ratio of a loan was higher than 80 percent. In order to reduce the cost of their loans, the GSEs turned a blind eye to second mortgages that might be as high as 20 percent of the total loan, thus evading the need for mortgage insurance and reducing the down payment in effect to zero. The GSEs reported these loans as 80 percent LTV mortgages, knowing that in reality large numbers of them were zero-down-payment loans and far riskier than the loans reported. Although there is no data that fully capture this phenomenon, it is one more reason why the numbers of prime loans outstanding was smaller—and the number of NTMs larger—than data aggregators reported in the years before the mortgage meltdown.

The competitive effect of what the GSEs were doing should be clear. Imagine how difficult it would be for a lender to require a 20 percent down payment when others were offering no-down-payment loans that were still eligible for the favorable interest rates that the GSEs were offering. As a consequence, the loosening of the GSEs' underwriting standards spread to the wider market, a subject covered in chapter 8. The consequences for policy analysis and risk management were also unfavorable. Looking at the raw numbers, and not knowing that many loans with 80 percent LTV ratios were actually far riskier than they looked, would have misled risk managers, academics, and others who study the housing finance markets.

That the affordable-housing goals were the reason Fannie increased its high LTV lending is clearly described in a Fannie presentation to HUD Assistant Secretary Albert Trevino on January 10, 2003: "Analyses of the market demonstrate the greatest barrier to home ownership for most renters are [sic] related to wealth—the lack of money for a downpayment . . . our low-downpayment lending—negligible until 1994—has grown considerably. It is a key part of our strategy to serve low-income and minority borrowers."[40]

Growth in the GSEs' acquisitions of subprime loans—loans with FICO scores below 660—reveals a similar pattern. Between 1997 and 2007, Fannie acquired $969 billion and Freddie acquired $553 billion in subprime loans to borrowers whose FICO scores were less than 660, for a total of $1.52 trillion.[41] In addition, the GSEs acquired $707 billion self-denominated subprime loans in PMBS during the same period, for a total of $2.2 trillion.[42] To be sure, the GSEs applied modest risk-based pricing to these riskier loans, but, as we will see, it was insufficient to cover the full extent of the risks, especially the risk under stress conditions. This was also clear from the FHFA's analysis of loans acquired by the GSEs in 2007 and 2008. The FHFA noted that the GSEs regularly cross-subsidized the loans they were required to buy in order to comply with the affordable-housing goals.[43] Once again, this meant that borrowers with good credit and substantial down payments were paying more for their mortgages so that the GSEs could compete for and acquire NTMs with lower guarantee fees than their riskiness would generally require.

For much of this period, Fannie filed Form 10-K reports with the Securities and Exchange Commission (SEC), in which it disclosed in tables at the back of the report that about 16 percent of the mortgages to which it was exposed (either held in portfolio or guaranteed in a securitized pool) had FICO scores of 660 or less—the definition of a subprime loan, according to the bank regulators. But the text portion of the filings in many cases stated that Fannie's exposure to subprime loans was substantially smaller. For example, in its 2006 Form 10-K (which was filed late in 2007), Fannie stated: "We estimate that, as of June 30, 2007, subprime mortgage loans or structured Fannie Mae MBS backed by subprime mortgage loans represented approximately 0.2% of our single-family mortgage credit book of business. As of June 30, 2007, we had invested in private-label securities [i.e., PMBS] backed by subprime mortgage loans totaling $47.2 billion, which represented approximately 2% of our single-family mortgage credit book of business."[44] At that point, Fannie's actual exposure to mortgages with FICO scores of 660 or less was approximately 17 percent.[45]

Between 2002 and 2007, the GSEs acquired a total of $773 billion in self-denominated Alt-A loans, including $154 billion in PMBS backed by Alt-A loans.[46] According to its 2009 credit profile, Fannie suffered an additional 28 percent of its losses in 2007 from loans that could be characterized as Alt-A because they had various deficiencies, such as negative amortization or low or no documentation, and 46 percent of its losses from these loans in 2008.[47]

Table 6.2 summarizes the GSEs' acquisitions of NTMs described above. The subprime PMBS acquired from 1997 to 2001 were estimated, using the percentages of PMBS purchases in subsequent years. Alt-A loans are understated because Fannie and Freddie used their various affordable-housing programs and individual lender variance programs to approve loans with Alt-A characteristics, but they generally did not classify these loans as Alt-A. There is an unknown number of additional loans that had higher debt ratios, loosened credit requirements, expanded seller contributions, and similar deficiencies that would be characterized as Alt-A, but there is insufficient information to identify the location of these loans, and they are not included. Because loans may have more than one NTM characteristic, they may appear in more than one category. Totals are not adjusted to take this into account.

Nevertheless, the table shows that the GSEs were acquiring PMBS backed by subprime loans, whole subprime loans, and high LTV ratio loans in the 1990s, well before any substantial activity involving these NTMs had begun on Wall Street. This is important because, as we shall see in the next chapter, the supporters of the GSEs on the left (including the FCIC) have asserted, without evidence, that Fannie and Freddie merely followed Wall Street into this business. Indeed, the FCIC did not even bother to look at the GSEs' acquisition of subprime loans or other NTMs before 2004.

When they were taken over as insolvent by the FHFA in 2008, Fannie Mae and Freddie Mac together were exposed—either through whole loans or through PMBS backed by NTMs—to 16.5 million

TABLE 6.2. What is known of Fannie and Freddie acquisitions of NTMs and PMBS based on NTMs between 1997 and 2007 ($ billions)

	1997	1998	1999	2000	2001	2002	2003	2004	2005	2006	2007	1997–2007
Subprime PMBS	3	18	18	11	16	38	82	180	169	110	62	707
Subprime loans	37	83	74	65	159	206	262	144	139	138	195	1,502
Alt-A PMBS	–	–	–	–	–	18	12	30	36	43	15	154
Alt-A loans	–	–	–	–	–	66	77	64	77	157	178	619
High LTV ratio loans	32	44	62	61	84	87	159	123	126	120	226	1,124
Total	72	145	154	137	259	415	592	541	547	568	676	4,106

Adapted from: Edward J. Pinto, "Government Housing Policies in the Lead-Up to the Financial Crisis: A Forensic Study," draft manuscript, February 5, 2011, Chart 52, http://www.aei.org/publication/government-housing-policies-in-the-lead-up-to-the-financial-crisis-a-forensic-study/.

NTMs, with a total unpaid principal balance of $2.5 trillion.[48] Other federal government agencies—the FHA, VA, the Federal Home Loan Banks, and the Rural Housing Service of the Department of Agriculture—accounted for an additional 5 million loans with an unpaid principal balance of $500 billion; the CRA and the various HUD programs outlined above accounted for 2.2 million additional loans with an unpaid principal balance of $300 billion.[49] The total federal government exposure to NTMs, therefore, was 24 million loans, with an unpaid principal balance of $3.4 trillion. As shown in Table 1.1, this was at least 76 percent of the 31 million NTMs outstanding on June 30, 2008. For reasons outlined earlier, the deficiencies in the available data make it difficult to be sure that all the NTMs in the financial system in June 2008 were identified and located. Later, we will see that the spread of the GSEs' reduced underwriting standards to the wider market reduced the quality of what were originally thought to be prime loans so that their delinquency rate exceeded the rate usually expected of prime loans.

The GSEs' willingness to accept large numbers of NTMs—and PMBS based on these loans—was a direct consequence of the affordable-housing goals. There was no way for Fannie and Freddie to meet the goals other than by seeking out borrowers with credit records that were far weaker than those that were reported in Fannie's 1992 Random Sample, and as the goals increased, the quality of the mortgages the GSEs acquired in order to meet the goals deteriorated further.

HUD pursued the policies underlying the affordable-housing goals throughout the balance of the Clinton administration and into the administration of George W. Bush. Ultimately these policies would lead to the mortgage meltdown in 2007, as vast numbers of mortgages with low or no down payments and other nontraditional features suffused the financial system. But in June 1995, the known dangers in HUD's policies were ignored. President Clinton would probably want to retract his 1995 statement, "Our homeownership strategy will not cost the taxpayers one extra cent. It will not require legislation. It will not add more Federal programs or grow the Federal bureaucracy,"[50] but he has not done so. George W. Bush has issued his retraction: "At the height of the housing boom," he said in his memoirs, "homeownership hit an all-time high of almost 70 percent. . . . I was pleased to see the ownership society grow. But the exuberance of the moment masked the underlying risk."[51]

One lesson here is that it can look for a long time as though the government's interference in the market will not cost the taxpayers anything. But when the costs embedded by the government's actions finally become apparent, they can be—as they were in 2008—colossal. Another lesson is that the government can accomplish a lot of its housing finance goals without direct spending; for example, it can reduce underwriting standards, as it did with the affordable-housing goals, or it can enlist the private sector to act in ways that run counter to normal market incentives, as it did with HUD's Best Practices Initiative and the National Homeownership Strategy. As we have all now learned, however, that does not mean that the taxpayers will not ultimately be faced with the costs.

In the next chapter, we will show that the affordable-housing goals— and not a desire for additional profits or market share—were the reason that the GSEs acquired large numbers of NTMs.

7

Force Fed

Why the Affordable-Housing Goals, and Not Market Share or Profit, Were the Sole Reason the GSEs Acquired Nontraditional Mortgages

The GSEs are increasing their business, in part, in response to higher affordable housing goals set by the U.S. Department of Housing and Urban Development (HUD) in its new rule established in October 2000. In the rule, HUD identifies subprime borrowers as a market that can help Fannie Mae and Freddie Mac meet their goals.

THE URBAN INSTITUTE, "Subprime Markets, The Role of GSEs, and Risk-Based Pricing," 2002

Up to this point, we have seen that the policy of the Department of Housing and Urban Development (HUD) was to reduce underwriting standards in order to make mortgage credit more readily available to low-income borrowers and that Fannie and Freddie not only took the affordable-housing goals seriously but were willing to go to extraordinary lengths to meet them. Nevertheless, it has become an accepted idea on the left[1]—including in the majority report of the Financial Crisis Inquiry Commission (FCIC)—that between 2004 and 2007 Fannie and Freddie bought large numbers of subprime and Alt-A loans for profit or to recover market share they had lost to subprime lenders such as Countrywide. This explanation helps to exculpate the government's housing policies and further implicate the profit motive as one of the causes of the crisis; it was repeated by

HUD Secretary Shaun Donovan in a statement to Congress in 2010 and is part of the narrative about the financial crisis that has been widely accepted and repeated in the media.[2] But it is contradicted by numerous documents in the contemporaneous written record. This chapter will show that the government-sponsored enterprises (GSEs) acquired large numbers of nontraditional mortgages (NTMs) and private mortgage–backed securities (PMBS) backed by NTMs solely to meet the affordable-housing goals, and not because they were fighting "Wall Street" or anyone else for market share or thought the NTMs they were acquiring would be profitable.

Tellingly, none of HUD's statements about its efforts to reduce underwriting standards managed to make it into the FCIC's majority report, which also ignored statements in the SEC filings of the GSEs about the importance of subprime mortgages for meeting the affordable-housing goals. Instead, the FCIC majority promoted the false idea that the GSEs' underwriting standards were reduced because of their desire to "follow Wall Street and other lenders in [the] rush for fool's gold" and that neither the NTMs nor PMBS based on NTMs were necessary to meet the affordable-housing goals.[3]

The discussion that follows shows, first, that subprime loans and other NTMs were essential for GSE compliance with the goals quotas established by HUD. It then shows that neither market share nor profit were reasons for the GSEs to acquire these risky loans.

THE "ELEPHANT UNDER THE CARPET"

The written record of the GSEs' activities is replete with statements by managers at Fannie Mae and Freddie Mac that NTMs and PMBS backed by NTMs were acquired in order to comply with the affordable-housing goals. For example, in 2004, Daniel Mudd told Fannie's top staff:

> We project extreme difficulty meeting our minority goals in 2005, and a progressive squeeze on HUD goals from 2006 on. . . . There is no easy work left here. It is clear to me that after a full year of managing the goals lending efforts—the primary market is simply not going to deliver us the business

it should. We meet monthly to review the numbers and the deals. We have studied FHA, new products, new channels, and alternative structures . . . and concluded that *there is only one place to change the market and acquire the business in sufficient size—subprime.* In 2005, we'll have to stop talking around that elephant under the carpet [emphasis added].[4]

That same year, Paul Weech, Fannie's director of market research and policy development, wrote in a memo to a colleague, "In 1998, 2002, and 2003 especially, the Company has had to pursue certain transactions as much for housing goals attainment as for the economics of the transaction."[5]

In a 2005 memorandum to CEO Daniel Mudd, Adolfo Marzol, Fannie's chief credit officer, noted that "large 2004 private label [PMBS] volumes were necessary to achieve challenging minority lending goals and housing goals."[6] In 2006, James Cotton, Freddie's vice president of single-family marketing, told the *American Banker* that "Freddie has decided to be more accepting of risk in pursuit of specific housing goals credit," and Patti Parsons, a director of product development at Fannie Mae, told the *American Banker* that the housing goals were "certainly an underpinning for our whole effort" to take additional risk.[7]

In the early 2000s, Fannie and Freddie bought large amounts of PMBS backed by NTMs because these securities were goals-rich. To facilitate this process, the aggregators and underwriters of these securities provided the GSEs with tapes or disks that contained loan level data that showed whether the underlying loans were goals-eligible. As the system became more sophisticated and efficient, 100 percent of the loans in some pools qualified for the affordable-housing goals.[8]

A Freddie Mac memo of August 2, 2005, referred to PMBS as essential for meeting the affordable-housing goals: "These assets are extremely goal rich and a key element in meeting our housing goals, especially sub-goals,"[9] and in September 2005, responding to a request from Fannie Mae, HUD provided a detailed memorandum describing how the GSEs could receive affordable-housing goals credit if they purchased only a portion of a PMBS issuance.[10] Also in 2005, in a presentation for HUD, Fannie reported that it "has limited options for meeting the 46% 2006 low and moderate income [purchase] goal. Subprime is Our Best Bet for Finding [these] Loans."[11] In an October 2005 presentation to HUD, Fannie described "undesirable tradeoffs necessary to meet the goals." These included:

> Having to compromise credit standards or waive credit enhancement requirements . . .
> Deal economics are well below target returns . . .
> Competition driving G-Fees [guarantee fees] to zero on some goals-rich deals . . .
> G-fees may not cover expected losses . . .
> Potential need to waive our responsible lending policies to get goals business.[12]

And in 2006, when the first difficulties in the subprime market began to emerge, and subprime mortgage originations began to wane, Fannie reported in its 2006 10-K that the problem of finding subprime mortgages was making it difficult to meet the affordable-housing goals: "[B]ecause subprime mortgages tended to meet many of the HUD goals and subgoals, recent disruption in the subprime market has further limited our ability to meet these goals."[13]

In February 2007, as the subprime market was deteriorating, Freddie announced that it would reduce its purchases of PMBS backed by subprime loans. The talking points that explained this move were prepared by Freddie's staff in question-and-answer form and included this passage:

> Q: Will these new standards affect your ability to meet the HUD affordable housing goals?
>
> A: Freddie Mac will continue to do everything that it can to meet its affordable housing goals. *However, the fact is that one of the ways we have been able to achieve the HUD-mandated goals is through the purchase of asset-backed securities. . . .*

To achieve this success, we have imposed additional burdens on the dealer community to create tailored bonds for our investments. By further reducing the universe of loans we are willing to allow to back the bonds we invest in, we further complicate the process and reduce the economic incentive for the capital markets to support our policies *so the additional requirements we are adopting could materially reduce our ability to invest in private label securities and as such hurt our ability to meet the goals* [emphasis added].[14]

Furthermore, in financial statements it released quarterly through 2007, Freddie also made clear that reducing its purchases of subprime loans would have an adverse effect on its ability to meet its affordable-housing goals. For example, in the quarterly financial statement released for the period ended September 30, 2008, Freddie noted that its regulator had directed it to follow the "Interagency Guidance on Nontraditional Mortgage Product Risks." This is the bank regulator's ruling, which we've covered in chapter 2, establishing that a borrower's FICO score of 660 or less would designate a mortgage as subprime.[15] This ruling declared that any loan to a borrower with a FICO score of 660 or less was a subprime loan, no matter what the other terms of the loan might be. This should have created a serious problem for the GSEs in 2001, because they would then have had to admit at that time that they had been acquiring large numbers of subprime mortgages in order to comply with the affordable-housing goals. But it appears that until 2008 the Office of Federal Housing Enterprise Oversight (OFHEO), a HUD agency and the GSEs' regulator, did not require that the GSEs recognize this 2001 ruling. The connection between subprime loans and the affordable-housing goals was also made clear in Freddie's September 30, 2007, financial report, in which it explicitly linked its ability to acquire subprime loans with its ability to meet the affordable-housing goals:

Declining market conditions and regulatory changes during 2007 have made meeting our affordable housing goals and subgoals even more challenging than in previous years. The increased difficulty we are experiencing has been driven by a combination of factors, including the decreased affordability of single-family homes that began in 2005; deteriorating conditions in the mortgage credit markets, particularly with respect to *greatly reduced origination of subprime mortgages*; and increases in the levels of subgoals. *These factors make it substantially more difficult for us to meet all of the HUD goals and, especially, the home purchase subgoals for 2007 compared to previous years.* We anticipate that these market conditions will continue to affect our affordable housing activities in 2008 [emphasis added].[16]

In December 2007, Daniel Mudd told Brian Montgomery, the assistant secretary of housing, "One strategy that Fannie Mae has used in the past to meet the subgoals is the purchase of private label securities (PLS) [PMBS]. In 2006, purchases of PLS contributed significantly to subgoals performance, increasing our scores by nearly 2 percentage points on the low- and moderate-income subgoal and 80 basis points on our special affordable subgoal."[17]

Finally, the data in Table 7.1, which Fannie furnished to the FCIC, shows that all three categories of NTMs—subprime loans, Alt-A loans, and PMBS—fulfilled one or another part of the affordable-housing goals for the years and in the percentages shown. (Bold numbers were in the original and show where the particular category exceeded the applicable goal.) The table, which was also ignored by the FCIC, shows, significantly, that the gradual increase in Fannie's purchases of these NTMs closely followed the gradual escalation of the affordable-housing goals between 1996 and 2008.

In 2010, Freddie Mac provided a similar table (Table 7.2) to the staff of the FCIC, and this was also ignored in the FCIC's majority report.[18] Tables 7.1 and 7.2 also show that ordinary subprime loans, Alt-A loans, and PMBS backed by subprime loans were not always sufficient to meet the affordable-housing goals (except the under-served base goal). For this reason, Fannie and Freddie developed special categories of loans in which the firm waived even its looser

TABLE 7.1. Nontraditional mortgages and
the affordable-housing goals

	Low- and moderate-income base goal (%)		Special affordable base goal (%)		Underserved base goal (%)	
	Actual[a]	Goal	Actual[a]	Goal	Actual[a]	Goal
Credit score <660 originations						
1996	38.08	40	**12.31**	12	**32.10**	21
1997	38.04	42	12.35	14	**33.03**	24
1998	37.72	42	11.76	14	**29.37**	24
1999	40.36	42	**14.04**	14	**30.87**	24
2000	**43.69**	42	**17.83**	14	**35.79**	24
2001	45.98	50	17.90	20	**34.91**	31
2002	49.66	50	**20.09**	20	**37.29**	31
2003	49.18	50	19.38	20	**34.12**	31
2004	**52.71**	50	**22.14**	20	**37.54**	31
2005	**54.39**	52	**24.21**	22	**44.38**	37
2006	**56.34**	53	**25.85**	23	**46.34**	38
2007	**55.47**	55	24.76	25	**46.45**	38
2008	55.24	56	25.50	27	**45.39**	39
Alt-A originations						
1999	**48.83**	42	**24.17**	14	**37.41**	24
2000	40.61	42	**18.74**	14	**41.03**	24
2001	39.05	50	16.41	20	**40.66**	31
2002	42.77	50	18.13	20	**40.08**	31
2003	42.42	50	16.81	20	**37.34**	31
2004	44.13	50	18.56	20	**40.08**	31
2005	43.12	52	18.57	22	**45.36**	37
2006	40.43	53	18.09	23	**46.40**	38
2007	39.02	55	17.29	25	**50.29**	38
2008	42.37	56	18.52	27	**42.10**	39

Adapted from: Table FM-FCIC-N_00007, which was submitted by Fannie Mae to the FCIC.
It was not used in the FCIC majority report.
Note: Bold figures indicate that a category exceeded its goal.
[a]Percent of unit financed that qualified for base goals.

TABLE 7.1 (continued)

	Low- and moderate-income base goal (%)		Special affordable base goal (%)		Underserved base goal (%)	
	Actual[a]	Goal	Actual[a]	Goal	Actual[a]	Goal
PLS backed by subprime						
2003	51.43	50	19.57	20	47.09	31
2004[b]						
2005	50.95	52	19.86	22	61.13	37
2006	60.63	53	23.51	23	60.12	38
2007	52.96	55	19.21	25	54.55	38
2008	51.42	56	17.68	27	64.45	39

[b]Not included in housing goals scoring in 2004.

underwriting requirements in order to supplement what it was getting from higher-quality NTMs. The two principal categories used by Fannie were My Community Mortgage (MCM) and Expanded Approval (EA) loans. In many cases, these two categories enabled Fannie to meet the goals, but at the cost of much higher delinquency rates than occurred among the NTMs they usually acquired. As the goals increased, Fannie had to acquire larger numbers of loans in these categories. As shown in Table 7.3, which was prepared by Fannie and submitted to the FCIC, these larger numbers of low-quality loans also exhibited increasing delinquency rates as the years went on. This table and its data were also ignored by the FCIC.

As we have seen, HUD itself—despite its record of increasing the affordable-housing goals—has tried to avoid responsibility for its actions by claiming that Fannie and Freddie acquired NTMs to compete for market share with Wall Street or to profit from acquiring risky mortgages. The FCIC joined this chorus, as did many on the left. No significant evidence exists for either of these contentions, and none has ever been presented, but in light of the substantial coverage these claims have received in the media they deserve to be examined.

TABLE 7.2. Goal- and subgoal-qualifying rates for PMBS purchases by Freddie Mac

	Low Mod eligible adjusted units	Low Mod qualified adjusted units	Low Mod goal-qualifying rates [%]	Special affordable eligible adjusted units	Special affordable qualified adjusted units	Special affordable goal-qualifying rates [%]	Underserved eligible adjusted units	Underserved qualified adjusted units	Underserved goal-qualifying rates [%]
Goal-qualifying rates for PLS purchase, 2003–2006									
2003	213,915.28	103,991.24	48.61	213,915.28	43,737.61	20.45	214,033.38	96,543.92	45.11
2004	587,329.78	314,673.60	53.58	587,329.78	129,815.20	22.10	585,734.20	280,441.64	47.88
2005	976,123.83	456,497.60	46.77	976,123.83	187,814.66	19.24	976,245.60	563,186.57	57.69
2006	722,139.68	366,117.73	50.70	722,139.68	143,699.09	19.90	745,525.65	405,396.85	54.38
Subgoal-qualifying rates for PLS purchases, 2005–2006									
2005	320,607.28	187,447.94	58.47	320,607.28	74,828.02	23.34	320,618.76	174,275.70	54.36
2006	168,360.71	142,235.13	84.48	168,360.71	57,281.87	34.02	168,331.18	95,938.16	56.99

Source: Freddie Mac.

TABLE 7.3. Higher-risk loans produced
higher delinquency rates at Fannie Mae

EA/MCMa and housing goals	Loan count	Serious delinquency rate
2004 and prior	115,686	17.59%
2005	56,822	22.35%
2006	110,539	25.19%
2007	224, 513	29.70%

Adapted from: Table FM-FCIC-2_00001215, which was among data that Fannie Mae
submitted to the FCIC. It was not used in the majority report of the FCIC.
aEA, Expanded Approval loans; MCM, My Community Mortgage loans.

WERE THE GSES SEEKING TO RECOVER MARKET SHARE?

The discussion above shows beyond question that Fannie and Freddie bought the NTMs and PMBS backed by NTMs in order to meet the affordable-housing goals. However, the FCIC majority and many commentators on the left, with no data, have stated with certainty since the financial crisis that these acquisitions—and the decline in underwriting standards they reflected—were actually done for other reasons.

The FCIC and others hoping to exculpate the government's housing policies from responsibility for the financial crisis must explain why two companies like Fannie Mae and Freddie Mac would destroy their franchises by acquiring low-quality and risky PMBS and NTMs. Figure 7.1, which has been used by protectors of HUD and the GSEs in several different forms, offers one possible but misleading explanation. It shows that for a period of about three years, the private-sector issuers of PMBS had a larger share of the mortgage securitization market than the GSEs. A chart like this was used by the FCIC to argue that Fannie and Freddie reduced their underwriting standards during these years in order to recover the market share they had lost to the private sector. Recall, as noted in chapter 5, that HUD Secretary Donovan also adopted this argument, telling Congress: "The GSEs made the decision to widen their focus from safer prime loans and

begin chasing the non-prime market, loosening long-standing underwriting and risk management standards along the way," and the
FCIC followed suit by claiming that the GSEs "relaxed their underwriting standards to purchase or guarantee riskier loans and related
securities" to meet investors' expectations for growth and to regain
market share.[19]

This is nothing more than wishful thinking. There is no documentary or other evidence to support it, and neither HUD nor the
FCIC bothered to present any. There was certainly considerable debate at Fannie about whether and how the firm could get into the
securitization of subprime mortgages. As explained earlier, there
was great concern at Fannie about remaining "relevant," by which
Fannie's management meant demonstrating to the Democrats in
Congress that Fannie was meeting the credit needs of low-income
borrowers. Those at Fannie who wanted the firm to get into the
business of securitizing subprime loans meant that Fannie should
buy whole subprime loans for the purpose of securitizing them, not
just for the purpose of meeting the affordable-housing goals. In any
event, Table 5.1—the FHFA table that shows the GSEs' compliance
with the affordable-housing quotas—demonstrates that neither Fannie nor Freddie took any action to compete with the issuers of PMBS
by increasing their purchases of subprime loans above the levels required by the affordable-housing goals. The numbers in Table 5.1 include the GSEs' purchases of PMBS backed by subprime and other
NTMs. Obviously, the mere loss of market share between 2004 and
2007 is not evidence that the GSEs took action to regain it, that they
had the capabilities to do so, or that they did so by further reducing their underwriting standards as HUD and the FCIC majority
claimed. Indeed, Table 7.1 shows that PMBS (called PLS in the table)
only satisfied one goal—the underserved base goal—every year.

Still, those who want to deny the government's responsibility for
the mortgage meltdown and the financial crisis make another and
somewhat inconsistent claim about the implications of Figure 7.1—
that it shows the GSEs were not leading the market when the worst
abuses and the worst mortgages were made and securitized. At that

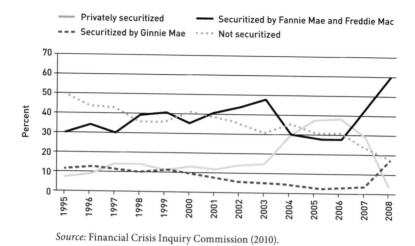

Source: Financial Crisis Inquiry Commission (2010).

FIG. 7.1. Shares of total residential mortgage originations

point, the argument runs, "Wall Street" was in charge, and Fannie and Freddie were merely followers.

However, the data again show that both these explanations are false. As shown in Table 6.2, in chapter 6, the GSEs were acquiring NTMs long before they lost market share to the private sector, and they continued to acquire NTMs at an increased pace through the 2004–2007 period as their affordable-housing goals quotas increased. By 2002, when the PMBS market passed $100 billion for the first time, the GSEs had already acquired well over a trillion dollars in NTMs, and a substantial portion of these were the result of their purchases of PMBS backed by NTMs in the growing market.

Figure 7.1 is also misleading in several other ways. First, it covers only securitization, and not the purchases of whole mortgages, which are shown in Table 6.2. In addition, and this is the key point, the GSEs themselves were the largest purchasers of PMBS from the private-sector issuers. If we allocate to Fannie and Freddie the PMBS they were buying from the private-sector issuers, as in Figure 7.2, the picture looks considerably different.

Further evidence about which firms were first into the NTM market is provided by Fannie's 2002 Form 10-K. This report states that as of December 31, 2000, 14 percent of Fannie's conventional

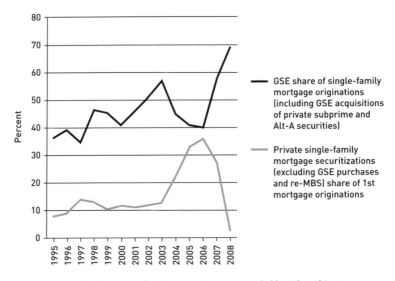

Source: Data from *Inside Mortgage Finance*, compiled by Edward Pinto.

FIG. 7.2. Securitization of NTMs with GSE purchases of PMBS allocated to GSEs

credit book (either in portfolio or guaranteed) had FICO scores below 660. Fannie did not identify these loans as subprime, but we know now that loans to borrowers with credit scores of 660 or below were subprime. Fannie's total conventional credit book at the end of 2000 was $1.3 trillion, so Fannie's total exposure to subprime loans (14 percent of $1.3 trillion) was $182 billion at the end of that year.[20] Note that at this time the *entire amount* of subprime PMBS issued in 2000 was only $56 billion, including the $11 billion sold to the GSEs.[21] Moreover, if we look only at acquisitions, we see that in 2000 Fannie and Freddie acquired $100 billion in self-denominated subprime loans and $65 billion in subprime loans based on FICO scores, three times the total issuances of PMBS backed by NTMs in that year.[22] Of course, these numbers do not include low down payment loans or other loans that would be classified as Alt-A and included as NTMs. Finally, Fannie reported in 2002 that as its credit book grew from $1.3 trillion in 2000 to $1.5 trillion in 2001 and $1.6 trillion in 2002, the percentages of loans it was acquiring in each of those years that had FICO scores of 660 or less were 18 percent in 2000 and 2001 and 17 percent in 2002. In other words, Fannie was continuing to add subprime loans to its growing credit book, well before the private issuers of subprime PMBS had reached $100 billion in issuances.[23]

Even if the GSEs had decided in 2004 to start acquiring large numbers of NTMs, as suggested by the FCIC, it would not be true to say that they were competing with Wall Street for market share. Although Wall Street firms might have been the underwriters for the PMBS that were offered during these years, they were not large issuers of these securities. If the GSEs were competing with any group for market share, it was with lenders like Countrywide, which had either figured out how to offer PMBS themselves or assembled the pools of NTMs for which Wall Street firms acted as distributors or underwriters.

According to *Inside Mortgage Finance*, only one Wall Street firm was among the top five issuers of subprime PMBS in 2004. The leader that year was Ameriquest Mortgage ($55 billion), followed by Countrywide Financial ($41 billion), Lehman Brothers ($27 billion), GMAC-RFC Holding Company ($26 billion), and New Century ($22 billion). Other than Lehman, Wall Street firms were scattered through the list of the top twenty-five issuers, but they were not significant players as a group.[24]

In 2005, the biggest year for subprime PMBS issuances, the five leaders were the same, although New Century had moved into fourth place, ahead of GMAC-RFC. The total for all subprime PMBS issuance was $508 billion.[25] In 2006, Lehman had dropped out of the top five, and Countrywide had taken over the leadership among the issuers with $39 billion in subprime issuances, followed by New Century ($34 billion), Option One ($31 billion), Fremont ($30 billion), and Washington Mutual ($29 billion). The total for the year for all issuers was $483 billion.[26]

By the middle of 2007, the PMBS market had declined to such a degree that the market share numbers were meaningless. However, in that year the GSEs acquired $62 billion in subprime PMBS, which was slightly more than 25 percent of the $219 billion market total.

Before leaving this point, we should take note of what happened when the PMBS market collapsed in mid-2007. Because of their dependence on PMBS for the goals-rich loans they contained, one would expect to see the GSEs' share of the much-reduced PMBS market increase substantially as others left the market; that is exactly what we see in both Figures 7.1 and 7.2. Moreover, it would also be expected that in the absence of sufficient PMBS to meet their need for goals-rich loans, the GSEs would have to increase their acquisition of NTMs in whole loan form. Again, that is exactly what we see in Table 6.2, which shows substantial increases over previous years in the GSEs' acquisition of subprime loans ($195 billion), Alt-A loans ($178 billion), and loans with a high loan-to-value (LTV) ratio ($226 billion). Thus, the numbers in Table 6.2 are consistent with the view that the principal driver of the GSEs' acquisition of NTMs was not competition with Wall Street or anyone else—the private sector had virtually dropped from sight in the market at that point—but the GSEs' need to comply with the affordable-housing goals.

There is also very strong financially based evidence that, from 2004 to 2006, Fannie either never tried or was never financially able to compete for market share with Countrywide and other subprime lenders. Set out in Table 7.4 are Fannie's key financial data, published by the Office of Federal Housing Enterprise Oversight (OFHEO), its former regulator, in early 2008.

Table 7.4 shows that Fannie's average guarantee fee *increased* during the period from 2003 to 2007. If Fannie had wanted to compete with the private issuers for subprime and other loans, there was only one way to do it—by reducing its guarantee fees to make the firm a less costly distribution channel for any originator that wanted to sell its loans. The fact that Fannie does not appear to have done so is strong evidence that it never seriously tried to compete for market share with Countrywide and the other subprime issuers. The financial summary also suggests that by 2004 or 2005 Fannie had very little flexibility to compete by lowering its guarantee fees. Its net income and its return on equity were all declining quickly during this period, and a cut in its guarantee fees would have hastened this decline.

Nevertheless, some defenders of the government's policies argue that the GSEs only began to acquire risky PMBS backed by NTMs

TABLE 7.4. Fannie Mae financial highlights

Earnings performance	2003	2004	2005	2006	2007
Net income ($ billions)	8.1	5.0	6.3	4.1	−2.1
Net interest income ($ billions)	19.5	18.1	11.5	6.8	4.6
Guarantee fees ($ billions)	3.4	3.8	4.0	4.3	5.1
Net interest margin (%)	2.12	1.86	1.31	0.85	0.57
Average guarantee fee (basis points)	21.9	21.8	22.3	22.2	23.7
Return on common equity (%)	27.6	16.6	19.5	11.3	−8.3
Dividend payout ratio (%)	20.8	42.1	17.2	32.4	N/M[a]

Source: Fannie Mae. Adapted from Office of Federal Housing Enterprise Oversight, "Mortgage Markets and the Enterprises in 2007," July 2008, revised February 2009, pp. 33–34, http://www.fhfa.gov/webfiles/1164/MME2007revised.pdf.
[a]N/M = Not meaningful.

after Wall Street had already entered the business and were realizing vast profits. The FCIC majority saw it as following Wall Street "in a search for fool's gold" and asserted that the GSEs did not need either NTMs or PMBS based on NTMs in order to meet their affordable-housing goals. In their book *All the Devils Are Here*, Bethany McLean and Joe Nocera depict Fannie's management as agonizing over whether to enter the subprime market to compete with the private sector.[27] The impression they leave is that Fannie began to buy subprime mortgages or PMBS backed by NTMs only reluctantly. This has been another favorite theme on the left, also adopted by the FCIC majority. But this narrative is upside down, and reflects a lack of knowledge about the pressures faced by the GSEs. There was certainly a debate within Fannie about whether the firm should compete with the private sector by acquiring and securitizing subprime mortgages (see chapter 6 for a discussion of the reasons for this—involving the need for continuing support by the Democrats in Congress). But there was no debate about whether they had to buy subprime loans and other NTMs in order to meet the affordable-housing goals. Fannie had been doing that—as shown in Table 6.2—since the early 1990s, when they first became subject to the goals.

Thus, there is no question that the GSEs were deep into NTMs well before the private sector began to securitize these loans in sizable amounts through PMBS. Fannie and Freddie were also the largest individual purchasers of subprime PMBS from 2002 to 2006, when the market was strongest, acquiring 30 percent of the total issuances, or $579 billion.[28] Indeed, it would be more accurate to say that the willingness of the GSEs to buy NTMs—beginning shortly after the imposition of the affordable-housing goals in 1992—created a huge market for NTMs that subprime lenders had never enjoyed before. Because of the goals, NTM lenders like Countrywide grew into powerful firms that could eventually issue their own PMBS rather than selling to the GSEs.

Finally, to make its assertion that the GSEs did not need either NTMs or PMBS based on NTMs in order to meet the affordable-housing goals, the FCIC majority had to ignore a great deal of evidence to the contrary, including an undeniable written record and the many statements by GSE officials quoted above about the importance of NTMs for meeting the goals. After all, the GSEs' acquisitions were not small numbers. The FCIC majority reported that these "purchases represented 10.5% of non-GSE subprime mortgage-backed securities in 2001, with the share rising to 40% in 2004, and falling back to 28% by 2008."[29] Forty percent of the NTM-backed PMBS market in 2004 was about $160 billion, or approximately 1.2 million mortgages. Despite all the evidence provided both in this chapter and in chapter 6, the FCIC majority argued that, in any event, the PMBS backed by NTMs were not necessary to meet the goals:

> Using data provided by Fannie Mae and Freddie Mac, the FCIC examined how single-family, multifamily, and securities purchases contributed to meeting the affordable housing goals. In 2003 and 2004, Fannie Mae's single- and multifamily purchases alone met each of the goals; in other words, the enterprise would have met its obligations without buying subprime or Alt-A mortgage–backed securities. . . . In 2005, the goals were increased above 50%; but even then, single- and multifamily purchases alone met the overall goals. Securities purchases did, in several cases, help Fannie meet its

subgoals. . . . In 2005, Fannie missed one of these subgoals and would have missed a second without the securities purchases; in 2006, the securities purchases helped Fannie meet those two subgoals.[30]

However, if we look back at the table furnished to the FCIC by Fannie Mae, reproduced above as Table 7.1, we can see that PMBS (called "PLS backed by subprime" in the table) and NTMs in general were very helpful in meeting the goals—especially the underserved goal—in every year, including the years 2003 to 2008. Taking 2003 as an example, the table shows that, of the PMBS acquired by Fannie in that year, 51.43 percent were helpful in meeting the "Low- and moderate-income [LMI]" base goal, 19.57 percent were helpful in meeting the "Special affordable" base goal, and 47.09 percent were helpful in meeting the "Underserved" base goal. There is every reason to believe that these goals would not have been met in 2003 or any other year without the contribution by NTMs and the NTM-backed PMBS Fannie had acquired in those years. Similarly, Table 7.2, supplied to the FCIC by Freddie, shows that PMBS ("PLS") were very important for Freddie's goal and subgoal qualifications.

Given these facts, it would be more accurate to say that the private securitizers, who later became important in the PMBS market for the years 2004 to 2006, followed the GSEs into a market the GSEs had created through their huge purchases. As a matter of simple chronology, that is in fact what happened.

In its 2005 Form 10-K (which, as restated and filed in May 2007, covered both 2005 and 2006), Fannie claimed that it lost market share between 2004 and 2006 because it refused to buy the high-risk loans that were being securitized by subprime lenders and Wall Street:

[I]n recent years, an increasing proportion of single-family mortgage loan originations has consisted of non-traditional mortgages such as interest-only mortgages, negative-amortizing mortgages and subprime mortgages, while demand for traditional 30-year fixed-rate mortgages . . . has decreased. *We did not participate in large amounts of these non-tra-*

ditional mortgages in 2004, 2005 and 2006 because we determined that the pricing of these mortgages often offered insufficient compensation for the additional credit risk associated with these mortgages. *These trends and our decision not to participate in large amounts of these non-traditional mortgages contributed to a significant loss in our share of new single-family mortgage-related securities issuances to private-label issuers during this period, with our market share decreasing from 45.0% in 2003 to 29.2% in 2004, 23.5% in 2005 and 23.7% in 2006* [emphasis added].[31]

To some extent this is true, but only because the GSEs, as the largest customers for PMBS, were able to get the securitizers of PMBS to create special PMBS pools of mortgages that were still goals-rich but generally less risky than others being securitized. This highlights another issue that is often used by commentators on the left as if it somehow relieves the GSEs from responsibility for the mortgage meltdown and the financial crisis. McLean and Nocera, for example, observe that "after the crisis, Fannie and Freddie defenders would point out that in every mortgage category, from prime to Alt-A to subprime, the GSEs' loans defaulted at rates below the national average."[32] David Min, writing in February 2011 for the leftist Center for American Progress, notes that "mortgages originated for Fannie and Freddie securitization have performed far better than those originated for 'private-label' securitization—even when controlling for all other factors such as the fact that Fannie and Freddie did not securitize subprime loans. Overall, private-label mortgages that were packaged and securitized defaulted at more than six times the rate of those originated for Fannie and Freddie securitization."[33] The FCIC makes the same argument: "The Commission also probed the performance of the loans purchased or guaranteed by Fannie and Freddie. While they generated substantial losses, delinquency rates for GSE loans were substantially lower than loans securitized by other financial firms. For example, data compiled by the Commission for a subset of borrowers with similar credit scores—scores below 660— show that by the end of 2008, GSE mortgages were far less likely to be seriously delinquent than were non-GSE securitized mortgages: 6.2% versus 28.3%."[34]

These arguments are not persuasive. In particular, the numbers cited by the FCIC majority are far off the mark because they uncritically accepted Fannie Mae's numbers. There is no question that the NTMs acquired by the GSEs to meet the affordable-housing goals were of better quality than the loans that private-sector issuers were securitizing. Table 7.5 shows the delinquency rates by significant groups of all mortgages outstanding on June 30, 2008. The contrast in quality, based on delinquency rates, between these loans and the Fannie and Freddie prime loans in lines 9 and 10 is clear. The fact that the mortgages acquired by the GSEs were of better quality than those securitized by the private sector, however, misses the point; almost 11 million loans in the GSEs' credit books of business had delinquency rates between 13.8 and 17.3 percent and were bad enough to cause their insolvency.

The NTMs acquired by Fannie and Freddie were of better quality than the PMBS for several reasons. First, as Fannie pointed out in its 2005 Form 10-K, quoted above, they refused to take "large amounts" of these high-risk loans, although they did take relatively small numbers when that was required to meet their goals quotas. When it became difficult to find enough of the lower-risk NTMs on this basis, they resorted to PMBS backed by NTMs, rationalizing that those securities were rated AAA. Second, because of their GSE status, Fannie and Freddie had the lowest funding costs in the market and thus could outbid competitors for the "best of the worst." As HUD noted in 2000: "Because the GSEs have a funding advantage over other market participants, they have the ability to underprice their competitors and increase their market share."[35] Moreover, the loans they acquired were generally fixed-rate 15- and 30-year mortgages. By acquiring the NTM versions of these normally high-quality loans, they drove private issuers further out on the risk curve. This was somewhat ironic, because the GSEs were then compelled by the affordable-housing goals to buy securities based on packages of NTMs that they had refused to buy on a whole-loan basis. Finally, Fannie and Freddie were the biggest customers in the market

TABLE 7.5. Delinquency rates on nontraditional mortgages

Loan type	Estimated number of loans (millions)	Total delinquency[a] rate (%)
1. High rate subprime (including Fannie/ Freddie PMBS holdings)	6.7	45.0
2. Option Arm	1.1	30.5
3. Alt-A (including Fannie/Freddie/FHLBs PMBS holdings)	2.4	23.0
4. Fannie subprime/ Alt-A/nonprime	6.6	17.3
5. Freddie subprime/ Alt-A/nonprime	4.1	13.8
6. Government	4.8	13.5
Subtotal	**25.7**	
7. Non-agency jumbo prime	9.4	6.8
8. Non-agency conforming prime		5.6
9. Fannie prime	11.2	2.6
10. Freddie prime	8.7	2.0
Total	**55.0**	

Adapted from: Edward J. Pinto, "Government Housing Policies in the Lead-Up to the Financial Crisis: A Forensic Study," draft manuscript, February 5, 2011, Chart 53, http://www.aei.org/publication/government-housing-policies-in-the-lead-up-to-the -financial-crisis-a-forensic-study/.

Note: Information in the Fannie and Freddie datasets shows that there were 1.9 million Alt-A loans held by Fannie and 1.5 million Alt-A loans at Freddie for which the delinquency rates could not be determined, so they are not included in this table. The table also includes an estimated 1 million subprime loans (FICO <660) that were (i) not high rate and (ii) non-prime CRA and HUD Best Practices Initiative loans. Line 3 excludes loans owned or securitized by Fannie or Freddie. Lines 7 and 8 count jumbo prime and conforming prime together. Lines 9 and 10 exclude Fannie and Freddie subprime/Alt-A/nonprime and loans owned or securitized by Fannie and Freddie. The table does not include the delinquency rates for the 1.43 million NTMs that the SEC found in connection with its suit (discussed in chapter 3) against officers of Fannie and Freddie.

[a]30+ days and in foreclosure.

for PMBS, and for that reason alone could demand that the highest-quality NTMs available be included in the PMBS they would buy.

This discussion makes clear that the GSEs acquired large numbers of NTMs between the mid-1990s and 2007, but they did not do so to compete with Wall Street or subprime issuers like Countrywide. Instead, their motive was to meet the affordable-housing goals. When private securitizers realized that Fannie and Freddie were enormous and profitable customers, they expanded to meet the demand from the GSEs and others. Fannie and Freddie, accordingly, did not follow Wall Street or the subprime issuers into PMBS; instead, as the biggest customers for these securities, they provided the foundation for the development of that market. So the left's fantasy that perfidious Wall Street hawkers of subprime MBS lured innocent Fannie and Freddie into the risky subprime market is at best little more than a cherished urban myth. Because of the affordable-housing goals, Fannie and Freddie were already there when the private-sector PMBS issuers—not actually from Wall Street anyway—arrived on the scene in force.

DID THE GSES BUY NTMS FOR PROFIT?

This leaves one other possibility—that Fannie and Freddie were buying NTMs not for market share but because they were profitable investments. McLean and Nocera reported in their book that "the real reason Fannie was willing to finally move into riskier territory was the same reason Countrywide did: profits."[36] After the GSEs' insolvency and the financial crisis, as the government scurried away from the blame it deserved, many in Congress and elsewhere wondered why the GSEs had bought so many low-quality loans. HUD was ready with an explanation. In a report to Congress in January 2010, HUD said that "the GSEs' decisions to purchase or guarantee non-prime loans was [sic] motivated more by efforts to chase market share and profits than by the need to satisfy federal regulators." This became the standard excuse for those who wished to obscure the GSEs' role in the financial crisis and of course was adopted by the majority report of the Financial Crisis Inquiry Commission.[37]

This might have been plausible if the GSEs were "gambling for resurrection"—taking extraordinary financial risks to restore their profitability, as failing savings and loan (S&L) institutions had done in the 1980s. But the record shows that the GSEs saw these loans as unprofitable from the beginning and bought them only to meet the affordable-housing goals.

As shown in Table 5.1 and discussed earlier, Fannie and Freddie exceeded the affordable-housing goals almost every year, but not by significant margins. They simply kept pace with the increases in the goals as these requirements came into force. This pattern alone suggests that they did not increase their purchases because those loans were more profitable than others. If that had been their purpose, they would have substantially exceeded the goals, because their financial advantages (low financing costs and low capital requirements) allowed them to pay more for the mortgages they wanted than any of their competitors. The only year in which the GSEs exceeded the applicable affordable-housing goal by any significant amount was 2000. The reason for this is also clear. HUD announced in 1999 that the goals would be increased to 50 percent, but did not actually publish the new goals until nearly the end of 2000. The GSEs, however, had to assume that the new HUD goal would be made retroactive to 2000 when it was finally announced and thus made efforts in 2000 to meet a 50 percent goal that did not come into force until 2001.

By 2000, Fannie was effectively in competition with banks that were required to make mortgage loans under the Community Reinvestment Act (CRA) to roughly the same population of low-income borrowers targeted in HUD's affordable-housing goals. Rather than selling their CRA loans to Fannie and Freddie, however, banks and S&Ls were retaining the loans in their portfolios. In a presentation in November 2000, Barry Zigas, a senior vice president of Fannie, pointed out that "our own anecdotal evidence suggests that this increase [in banks' and S&Ls' holding loans in portfolio] is due in part to below-market CRA products."[38] In other words, as we saw earlier in Fannie's response to a question from the Urban Institute, banks and S&Ls subject to the CRA were making mortgage loans at below-market interest rates and with features that did not comply with

Fannie's statutory requirements, particularly the need for mortgage insurance on every loan with an LTV ratio over 80 percent. Thus, these loans could not be sold to Fannie even though many of them would have qualified for the goals. Not only that, if the banks and S&Ls that made these concessionary loans actually sold them to the GSEs they would have to recognize a loss, because the risks on these loans were considerably larger than their interest rates suggested. As long as the loans were performing and were held in the lender's portfolio, no loss would have to be recognized.

It is important to understand what was happening here. Fannie was now looking to the banks and S&Ls that were required to make low-income loans under the CRA as sources for the NTMs it needed to meet the goals, but many of those never entered the market so Fannie could acquire them. In effect, the banks and S&Ls, in order to meet their CRA requirements, had lowered their underwriting standards even below Fannie's standards. Simply as a result of supply and demand, all of the participants in this competition were required to pay higher prices for these increasingly risky mortgages than loans with similar likely default rates would otherwise be worth in the market. In effect, the banks and S&Ls were cross-subsidizing these mortgages. The FHFA reported in 2008 and 2009 that the GSEs had also engaged in cross-subsidization,[39] undoubtedly of NTMs they had to acquire to meet the affordable-housing goals. It goes without saying that loans that have to be cross-subsidized are not likely to be profitable loans.

In March 2003, as Fannie prepared for new increases in the affordable-housing goals, its staff prepared a presentation, perhaps for HUD or for policy defense in public forums. The apparent purpose of the presentation was to show that the goals should not be increased significantly in 2004, and it reported:

> In 2002, Fannie Mae exceeded all our goals for the 9th straight year. But it was probably the most challenging environment we've ever faced. Meeting the goals required heroic 4th quarter efforts on the part of many across the company. Vacations were cancelled. The midnight oil burned. More-

over, the challenge freaked out the business side of the house. Especially because the tenseness around meeting the goals meant that we considered not doing deals—not fulfilling our liquidity function—*and did deals at risks and prices we would not have otherwise done* [emphasis added].[40]

This doesn't sound like Fannie was buying profitable mortgages, and it is important to recall that this and all of the documents cited in this section were in the possession of the FCIC but were ignored.

In a June 2005 presentation titled "Costs and Benefits of Mission Activities," Fannie authors note that affordable-housing goal costs— which involved buying NTMs—had risen from $2.6 million in 2000 to $13.4 million in 2003. On a slide titled "Meeting Future HUD Goals Appear[s] Quite Daunting and Potentially Costly," they report that "based on 2003 experience where goal acquisition costs (relative to Fannie Mae model fees) cost between $65 per goals unit in the first quarter to $370 per unit in the fourth quarter, meeting the shortfall could cost the company $6.5–$36.5 million to purchase sufficient units." The presentation concludes: "Cost of mission activities— explicit and implicit—over the 2000–2004 period likely averaged approximately $200 million per year."[41]

As shown in chapter 6, Fannie and Freddie window-dressed their affordable-housing goals records for HUD by temporarily acquiring loans that would comply with the affordable-housing goals, while giving the seller the option to reacquire the loans at a later time. In 2005, we begin to see efforts by Fannie's staff to accomplish the same window-dressing in another way, that is, by delaying acquisitions of non-goal-eligible loans—which go into the denominator of the affordable-housing goals fraction—so Fannie can meet the affordable-housing goals in that year. In a presentation dated September 30, 2005, Zigas, the key Fannie official on affordable housing, outlined a "business deferral option." Under that initiative, Fannie would ask seven major lenders to defer until 2006 sending non-goal loans to Fannie for acquisition. This would reduce the denominator of the affordable-housing goal computation and thus bring Fannie nearer to goal compliance in the fourth quarter of 2005. The cost of the deferral alone was estimated at \$30–38 million, hardly something that would be necessary if Fannie were purchasing profitable assets.[42] If they were profitable, Fannie could just buy more of them.

In the same year, Fannie also began to calculate systematically the effect of goal-compliance on its profitability. In a presentation to HUD on October 31, 2005, titled "Update on Fannie Mae's Housing Goals Performance,"[43] Fannie noted several "Undesirable Trade-offs Necessary to Meet Goals." These included significant additional credit risk and negative returns ("Deal economics are well below target returns; some deals are producing negative returns," and "G-fees [guarantee fees] may not cover expected losses").

In May 2006, a staff memo to Fannie's single-family business credit committee revealed the serious credit and financial problems Fannie was facing when acquiring subprime mortgages to meet the affordable-housing goals. The memo describes the competitive landscape in which

> product enhancements from Freddie Mac, FHA, Alt-A and subprime lenders have all contributed to increased competition for goals rich loans. . . . On the issue of seller contributions [in which the seller of the home pays cash expenses for the buyer] even FHA has expanded their guidelines by allowing 6% contributions for LTVs up to 97% that can be used toward closing, prepaid expenses, discount points and other financing concessions.[44]

A sense of how difficult it became for the GSEs to meet the goals in the mid-2000s is given by a summary of the problem in a Fannie staff presentation on the 2007 housing plan: "Regular business misses goals by a significant amount. Execution of special initiatives required to meet the goals; will come down to the wire again."[45] The "special initiatives" were such special deals as MCM (My Community Mortgage), EA (Expanded Approval), and DU Boost (occasionally called DU Bump), all of which referred to special tweaks in Fannie's automated underwriting system (called Desktop Underwriter) so that it would accept loans and PMBS that would otherwise have been rejected.

Table 7.6 shows the costs of NTMs in terms of the guarantee-fee "gap." In order to determine whether a loan contributed to a return on equity, Fannie used a guarantee-fee pricing model that took into account credit risk as well as a number of other factors; a guarantee-fee "gap" was the difference between the guarantee fees required by the pricing model for a particular loan to contribute to a return on equity and a loan that did not. The original table in the Fannie Mae memo shows the results for three subprime products under consideration: a 30-year fixed-rate mortgage, a 5-year adjustable-rate mortgage, and 35- and 40-year fixed-rate mortgages. For simplicity, I will discuss only the 30-year fixed-rate product.

According to Table 7.6, the base product, the 30-year fixed-rate mortgage with a *zero* down payment, should be priced according to the model at a guarantee fee of 106 basis points. However, Fannie is actually buying loans like that at a price consistent with a guarantee fee of 37.5 basis points, producing a gap (or loss from the model) of 68.5 basis points. The reason the gap is so large is shown in the table: the anticipated default rate on that zero-down mortgage was *34 percent.*

TABLE 7.6. Fannie Mae took losses on higher-risk mortgages necessary to meet the affordable-housing goals

Individual enhancements	30-year fixed-rate mortgage		
	Model fee	Average default rate (%)	Gap
Base:[a] 100% loan-to-value ratio, 20% mortgage insurance	106	34	−68.50
Interest first	129	40	−91.50
Seller contribution	115	23	−77.50
Temporary buydown	118	37	−80.50
Zero down	106	34	−68.50
Manufactured housing	227	42	−189.50

Adapted from: Fannie Mae, "2007 Housing Goal Plan," provided to FCIC and numbered FM-FCIC_0172982, p. 8.
[a]Cost analysis for "base" My Community Mortgage enhancement—not layered.

From this report, it is clear that in order to meet the affordable-housing goals, Fannie had to pay up for goals-rich mortgages, taking a huge credit risk along the way. In no sense were these loans profitable; they were more like deferred losses, and when the losses came, both GSEs became insolvent. "Everybody understood that we were now buying loans that we would have previously rejected," said a former Fannie executive, "but our mandate was to stay relevant and to serve low-income borrowers. So that's what we did."[46]

In a 2005 presentation for HUD, when the housing market was still booming, Fannie reported a litany of complaints associated with meeting the goals:

> Having to compromise credit standards and reduce or waive credit enhancement requirements;
> Credit enhancement costs at desired levels are too high to win deals;
> Deal economics are well below target returns;
> Some deals are producing *negative* cash flows;
> Competition driving [guarantee] fees to zero on some goals-rich deals;
> Buying exotic product encourages continuation of risky lending.[47]

The underlying reasons for "below target returns" were reported in February 2007 in another document the FCIC received from Fannie, which noted that for 2006 the "cash flow cost" of meeting the housing goals was $140 million while the "opportunity cost" was $470 million.[48] Another Fannie report to HUD, dated April 11, 2007, notes the constituents of these costs: "The largest costs [of meeting the goals] are opportunity costs of foregone revenue. In 2006, opportunity cost was about $400 million, whereas the cash flow cost was about $134 million. If opportunity cost was $0, our shareholders would be indifferent to the deal. The cash flow cost is the implied out of pocket cost."[49]

By this time, "Alignment Meetings"—in which Fannie staff considered how they would meet the affordable-housing goals—were taking place almost monthly (according to the frequency with which presentations to Alignment Meetings occur in the documentary record). In an Alignment Meeting on June 22, 2007, about a "Housing Goals Forecast," three plans were considered for meeting the 2007 affordable-housing goals, even though half the year was already gone. One of the plans was forecast to result in opportunity costs of $767.7 million, while the other two plans resulted in opportunity costs of $817.1 million.[50] In a Forecast Meeting on July 27, 2007, a "Plan to Meet Base Goals" (which meant only the topline LMI goal and the special affordable and underserved base goals) placed the cost at $1.156 billion for 2007, apparently without considering the purchase money subgoals for each base goal.[51]

In a December 21, 2007, letter to Brian Montgomery, assistant secretary for Housing, Fannie CEO Daniel Mudd asked that, in light of the financial and economic conditions then prevailing in the country—particularly the absence of a PMBS market and the increasing number of mortgage delinquencies and defaults—HUD's affordable-housing goals for 2007 be declared "infeasible." He noted that HUD also has an obligation to "consider the financial condition of the enterprise when determining the feasibility of goals." Then he continued: "Fannie Mae submits that the company took all reasonable actions to meet the subgoals that were both financially prudent and likely to contribute to the achievement of the subgoals. . . . *In 2006, Fannie Mae relaxed certain underwriting standards and purchased some higher risk mortgage loan products in an effort to meet the housing goals.* The company continued to purchase higher risk loans into 2007, and believes these efforts to acquire goals-rich loans are partially responsible for increasing credit losses" (emphasis added).[52]

Finally, in a July 2009 report, the Federal Housing Finance Agency (FHFA, the GSEs' new regulator, which replaced OFHEO), noted that Fannie and Freddie both followed the practice of cross-subsidizing the subprime and Alt-A loans that they acquired:

> Although Fannie Mae and Freddie Mac consider model-driven estimates of cost in determining the single-family guarantee fees they charge, their pricing often subsidizes

their guarantees on some mortgages using higher returns they expect to earn on guarantees of other loans. In both 2007 and 2008, cross-subsidization in single-family guarantee fees charged by the Enterprises was evident across product types, credit score categories, and LTV ratio categories. In each case, there were cross-subsidies from mortgages that posed lower credit risk on average to loans that posed higher credit risk. The greatest estimated subsidies generally went to the highest-risk mortgages.[53]

The higher-risk mortgages were the ones most needed by Fannie and Freddie to meet the affordable-housing goals.

REPORTS TO THE SEC

In 2002, Fannie and Freddie agreed with Congressman Richard Baker, then one of the GSEs' few congressional critics, that they would voluntarily file financial reports with the SEC under the Securities Exchange Act of 1934. Fannie began to file in 2003, but Freddie—because it was attempting clear up accounting irregularities discovered in 2003—did not file its first report until 2008. These reports were discussed and cited in chapters 3 and 6 above, when I noted that Fannie did not fully disclose the size of its exposure to subprime loans. In August 2009, however, after it was taken over by the government, Fannie published a credit supplement to its second quarter 2009 Form 10-Q, reproduced here as Table 7.7. This supplement contained an accounting of Fannie's subprime and Alt-A credit exposure as of June 30, 2009, and is the closest we can come to Fannie's own estimate of the number of NTMs it was holding before the 2008 financial crisis began. An earlier credit profile, as of December 31, 2008, did not provide a total in dollars or percentages that NTMs represented in Fannie's credit book, and so it was not as useful as the August 2009 supplement. The August report identified the dollar amount of Fannie's credit book that had at least one of the NTM characteristics that Fannie called "key features." The 2008

TABLE 7.7. Fannie Mae credit profile by key product features as of June 30, 2009

Credit characteristics of single-family conventional mortgage credit book of business

	Categories not mutually exclusive[a]			
	Negative-amortizing loans	Interest-only loans	Loans with FICO <620[c]	Loans with FICO ⩾620 and <660[c]
Unpaid principal balance (billions)[b]	$15.4	$195.9	$115.6	$242.3
Share of single-family conventional credit book	0.6%	7.1%	4.2%	8.8%
Average unpaid principal balance	$137,513	$242,048	$125,165	$140,431
Serious delinquency rate	8.48%	15.09%	13.07%	9.13%
Origination years 2005–2007	61.3%	80.7%	55.8%	54.1%
Weighted average original loan-to-value ratio	71.2%	75.8%	76.7%	77.4%
Original loan-to-value ratio >90%	0.3%	9.3%	22.0%	20.9%
Weighted average mark-to-market loan-to-value ratio	97.5%	103.2%	80.4%	82.2%
Mark-to-market loan-to-value ratio >100% and ≤125%	15.6%	23.1%	13.4%	13.9%
Mark-to-market loan-to-value ratio >125%	33.0%	22.4%	6.6%	8.0%
Weighted average FICO[c]	702	724	588	641
FICO <620[c]	9.1%	1.3%	100.0%	0.0%
Fixed-rate	0.2%	39.6%	93.4%	92.2%
Primary residence	69.7%	84.7%	96.7%	94.3%
Condo/co-op	13.8%	16.5%	4.9%	6.6%
Credit enhanced[d]	74.4%	35.6%	33.5%	35.1%
Percentage of credit losses[e]				
2007	0.9	15.0	18.8	21.9
2008	2.9	34.2	11.8	17.4
2008 Q3	3.8	36.2	11.3	16.8
2008 Q4	2.2	33.1	11.5	17.2
2009 Q1	1.8	34.2	10.7	16.0
2009 Q2	2.2	32.2	9.2	16.0

Source: Fannie Mae.

[a]Loans with multiple product features are included in all applicable categories. The subtotal is calculated by counting a loan only once even if it is included in multiple categories.

[b]Excludes non–Fannie Mae securities held in portfolio and Alt-A and subprime wraps, for which Fannie Mae does not have loan-level information. Fannie Mae has access to detailed loan-level information on approximately 95% of its conventional single-family mortgage credit book of business. Certain data contained in this presentation are based upon information that Fannie Mae receives from third-party sources. Although Fannie Mae generally considers this information reliable, it does not guarantee that it is accurate or suitable for any particular purpose.

TABLE 7.7 (continued)

Categories not mutually exclusive[a]					
Loans with original LTV ratio >90%	Loans with FICO <620 and original LTV ratio >90%[c]	Alt-A loans	Subprime loans	Subtotal of key product features[a]	Overall book
$265.3	$25.4	$269.3	$7.9	$878.2	$2,744.2
9.7%	0.9%	9.8%	0.3%	32.0%	100.0%
$141,622	$118,569	$168,784	$149,958	$152,814	$150,966
9.66%	21.37%	11.91%	21.75%	9.36%	3.94%
56.8%	69.5%	73.3%	80.8%	60.6%	40.5%
97.2%	98.1%	72.9%	77.2%	79.3%	71.6%
100.0%	100.0%	5.4%	6.8%	30.2%	9.7%
101.9%	101.5%	89.0%	93.8%	88.6%	74.0%
29.8%	31.2%	14.8%	17.0%	17.7%	9.1%
13.2%	12.2%	15.3%	14.3%	11.4%	5.3%
695	592	718	623	686	727
9.6%	100.0%	0.7%	48.0%	13.2%	4.2%
94.2%	95.5%	72.2%	74.4%	80.9%	91.1%
97.2%	99.4%	77.3%	96.6%	89.3%	89.8%
9.9%	6.0%	10.9%	4.6%	9.7%	9.3%
91.0%	92.7%	38.9%	63.1%	43.9%	19.5%
Percentage of credit losses[e]					
17.4	6.4	27.8	1.0	72.3	100.0
21.3	5.4	45.6	2.0	81.3	100.0
21.5	5.4	47.6	2.1	82.4	100.0
23.1	5.2	43.2	2.0	81.0	100.0
22.5	6.5	39.2	2.0	77.7	100.0
19.7	5.7	41.2	1.1	76.0	100.0

[c]FICO credit scores reported in the table are those provided by the sellers of the mortgage loans at time of delivery.

[d]Unpaid principal balance of all loans with credit enhancement as a percentage of unpaid principal balance of single-family conventional mortgage credit book of business for which Fannie Mae has access to loan-level information. Includes primary mortgage insurance, pool insurance, lender recourse, and other credit enhancement.

[e]Expressed as a percentage of credit losses for the single-family mortgage credit book of business. For information on total credit losses, refer to Fannie Mae's 2009 Q2 Form 10-Q and 2008 Form 10-K.

supplement showed that Fannie's total credit book was $2.73 trillion on December 31, 2008, which is quite close to the $2.74 trillion in the December 2009 supplement (Table 3.1), indicating that there was not much change in the ensuing six months. Although the supplement was published by Fannie well before the FCIC issued its majority report, the FCIC's majority report does not mention it or the $878.2 billion in loans that Fannie identified as NTMs. Neither does the McLean and Nocera book, *All the Devils Are Here: The Hidden History of the Financial Crisis*, which was published in 2011, or any other books that purport to describe Fannie's role in the financial crisis.

The key features listed in the report included loans with borrower FICO scores less than 660 and less than 620 (which meant, as Fannie was implicitly admitting, that they were subprime) and loans with such well-known Alt-A-type deficiencies as interest-only or negative amortization. Other more common Alt-A deficiencies, such as low- or no-documentation loans, were not mentioned, although they might have been picked up in the Alt-A category. With these inclusions and exclusions, Fannie disclosed in this report that on June 30, 2009 (and probably June 30, 2008) it was exposed to NTMs with an aggregate unpaid principal balance of $878 billion. These loans had an average size of $153,000, so the total number of NTMs is 5.7 million loans, not including the loans backing the PMBS that Fannie had acquired.

Fannie's total book at that point included approximately 20 million loans. Fannie also disclosed its credit losses from these NTMs, which amounted to 72.3 percent of all its losses in 2007 and 81.3 percent of all its losses in 2008. Forty percent of the losses in 2007 and 29 percent of the losses in 2008 came from mortgages with borrower credit scores of 660 or less. Since Fannie's losses were $60 billion through the end of 2008, we can assume that Fannie suffered losses of approximately $49 billion from its exposure to NTMs at about the time it was placed in a conservatorship by its regulator. Because Fannie's net worth was $44 billion at the end of 2007, the losses on NTMs were more than enough to cause the insolvency of a financial institution with the huge leverage ratio that Fannie and Freddie were allowed by the GSE Act.

If any confirmation were needed that Fannie was not buying these NTMs for profit, it was made clear in the organization's 2006 Form 10-K:

[W]e have made, and continue to make, significant adjustments to our mortgage loan sourcing and purchase strategies in an effort to meet HUD's increased housing goals and new subgoals. These strategies include entering into some purchase and securitization transactions with *lower expected economic returns than our typical transactions.* We have also *relaxed some of our underwriting criteria to obtain goals-qualifying mortgage loans* and increased our investments in *higher-risk mortgage loan products* [i.e., PMBS] that are more likely to serve the borrowers targeted by HUD's goals and subgoals, *which could increase our credit losses* [emphasis added].[54]

This statement, in a public document available to any objective researcher, was ignored by the FCIC and either ignored or never found by the many writers on the left who expressed certainty that the affordable-housing goals had nothing to do with the GSEs' acquisition of NTMs.

Freddie Mac and the affordable-housing requirements

Things were not substantially different at Freddie Mac. After its takeover by the government, Freddie published a summary of its financial results, including roughly the same data that were in Fannie's December 2008 SEC filing. The summary showed that the unpaid principal balance of Freddie's credit book on December 31, 2008 (close to June 30, 2008) was $1.84 trillion, with an average of $143,500 per loan, for a total of 12.8 million loans.[55] Like Fannie's 2008 disclosure, Freddie limited the usefulness of this report by failing to disclose the total dollar amount or the percentages of its credit book that were attributable to NTMs. Without this information it is not possible to determine Freddie's total exposure to NTMs on June 30, 2008. In later reports, Freddie improved its disclosures somewhat by including more key features that would classify a loan as an NTM. According to the credit supplement that accompanied Freddie's 2009 financial results, for example, in 2008, 19 percent of its total portfolio were loans with FICO scores of less than 660, and 13 percent had original LTV ratios greater than 90 percent.

As discussed in chapter 2, the Freddie dataset released in 2013 was made up of Freddie's best mortgages—15 million 30-year fixed-rate fully documented loans. An analysis of those loans showed that a mortgage with a borrower's FICO score below 660, but a down payment of at least 90 percent and a debt-to-income (DTI) ratio of no more than 38 percent, had a default rate 7.9 times higher than a mortgage with the same terms but a FICO score above 660. Similarly, a loan with an LTV ratio of more than 90 percent, even if the borrower had a FICO score above 660 and a DTI ratio of less than 38 percent, still had a default rate 4.1 times greater than a mortgage with the same terms but a down payment of at least 10 percent. The default rates got much higher, even among these relatively good-quality loans, if a low FICO score was combined with another weak characteristic, such as an LTV ratio greater than 90 (see Table 2.2).

The dataset did not include either the loans Freddie acquired under special programs to comply with the affordable-housing goals or other risky loans, so it is likely that Freddie suffered much higher losses on those than on the mortgages in its dataset. In addition, Freddie suffered significant losses on the PMBS it acquired in order to comply with the affordable-housing goals. In its 2008 Form 10-K, Freddie reported that the delinquency rate on PMBS backed by subprime loans was 38 percent and for PMBS backed by Alt-A loans was 17 percent.[56] So even without adequate disclosure it was possible to see that most of Freddie's losses, like Fannie's, came from the NTMs in its credit book. Freddie's financial supplement for the fourth quarter of 2008 showed a net loss of $24 billion and net worth of –$31 billion. It is not possible to determine from Freddie's disclosures what percentage of this loss was attributable to its NTM exposure. However, if we assume that its losses were similar in percentage to Fannie's (81.3 percent), then Freddie's losses on NTMs in 2008 would amount to about $19.5 billion.

In a 2009 report to a committee of the board of directors, Freddie's management summarized several points that show the experience of Freddie was almost identical to Fannie's:

- Our housing goals compliance required little direct subsidy prior to 2003, but since then subsidies have averaged $200 million per year.

- Higher credit risk mortgages disproportionately tend to be goal-qualifying. Targeted affordable lending generally requires "accepting" substantially higher credit risk.

- We charge more for targeted (and baseline) affordable single-family loans, *but not enough to fully offset their higher incremental risk.*

- *Goal-qualifying single-family loans accounted for the disproportionate share of our 2008 realized losses* that was predicted by our models.

- In 2007 Freddie Mac failed two subgoals, but compliance was subsequently deemed infeasible by the regulator due to economic conditions. In 2008 Freddie Mac failed six goals and subgoals, five of which were deemed infeasible. No enforcement action was taken regarding the sixth missed goal because of our financial condition.

- Goal-qualifying loans tend to be higher risk. Lower household income correlates with various risk factors such as less wealth, less employment stability, higher loan-to-value ratios, or lower credit scores.

- Targeted affordable loans have much higher expected default probabilities. . . . *Over one-half of targeted affordable loans have higher expected default probabilities than the highest 5% of non-goal-qualifying loans* [emphasis added].[57]

The last point is highly significant, given the fact that Freddie did not disclose in its dataset the mortgages that it acquired to meet the affordable-housing goals. It suggests that the undisclosed loans have far worse incidences of default than those released. As argued throughout this book, that outcome should be expected, but the Freddie statement is implicit confirmation.

Accordingly, both market share and profitability must be excluded as reasons that Fannie and Freddie acquired PMBS backed by NTMs. The only remaining motive—and the valid one—was the effect of the affordable-housing goals imposed by HUD.

Many ideologues on the left were wrong when they concluded, without evidence, that the affordable-housing goals had no role in the financial crisis. But given the fact that all the evidence outlined above was available to the FCIC majority when they prepared the commission's report, they failed in their obligation to the public by suppressing information that contradicted the pre-determined conclusions of their report.

Force-feeding the affordable-housing goals to reduce the GSEs' underwriting standards was a major policy error by HUD in two successive administrations, and must be recognized as such if we are ever to understand the causes of the financial crisis and prevent a recurrence. Ultimately, the affordable-housing goals led to loosened mortgage underwriting standards, which started and extended the housing bubble, infused it with weak and high-risk NTMs, caused the insolvency of Fannie and Freddie, and—together with other elements of U.S. housing policy—was the principal cause of the financial crisis itself. Unfortunately, the fall of Fannie and Freddie—as troubling as it was for taxpayers—was only the prologue to the financial crisis of 2008, a far more serious event. The link between the GSEs and the financial crisis is both direct and indirect. The loans they sought in order to comply with the affordable-housing goals became delinquent and defaulted in unprecedented numbers, driving down housing values throughout the United States. But as the dominant players in the housing finance market, their declining underwriting standards degraded the quality of the mortgages that were originated in the wider market, as we will see in the next chapter.

8

Going Viral

Why and How Reduced Underwriting Standards Spread to the Wider Market

At the height of the housing boom, homeownership hit an all-time high of almost 70 percent. . . . I was pleased to see the ownership society grow. But the exuberance of the moment masked the underlying risk.

PRESIDENT GEORGE W. BUSH, *Decision Points*

The affordable-housing goals were intended to increase the mortgage credit available to low-income and minority borrowers, but it would be wrong to conclude that mortgage defaults by these borrowers alone were the principal cause of the financial crisis. The 31 million nontraditional mortgages (NTMs) outstanding in the U.S. market on June 30, 2008, were not solely mortgages acquired to comply with the goals. It is important to understand that the underwriting standards implemented by Fannie and Freddie in order to comply with the goals spread to the wider market, so that the unprecedented 30- to 40-percent decline in housing prices in 2007 and 2008 came not only from the loans that qualified for the goals but also from non-qualifying mortgages that were made under the same loosened underwriting standards that Fannie and Freddie were required to use in order to meet the goals.

Carl Richards was a financial planner and an author of books such as *The Behavior Gap: Simple Ways to Stop Doing Dumb Things with Money*. In 1999, having moved up through several jobs, he was a

Merrill Lynch financial adviser and a certified financial planner. He and his wife began looking for a $350,000 house in Las Vegas, a price he thought they could afford, but this search was unsuccessful. Then one day he spotted a house in a great neighborhood for $575,000. The owners wouldn't bargain. "[I]t just wasn't that kind of market," he said.

> We borrowed 100 percent of the purchase price. . . . I had perfect credit and a solid income that was growing. But even so, when the lender approved us at 100 percent, it was more than I had expected. I remember thinking something like "Wow. I guess if they're willing to lend it to us it must be O.K." I should have known better. No matter how well things are going, borrowing 100 percent of the purchase price of a home is not a good idea.[1]

Eventually, Richards lost his home in a short sale, which relieved him of both his first and second mortgages. None of this could have happened if prime mortgages were the predominant method of home finance, and his story thus illustrates how the degrading of mortgage standards by the government-sponsored enterprises (GSEs) spread to the wider market. The Richards' mortgage, at $575,000, was not eligible for acquisition by Fannie or Freddie. Moreover, if the underwriting standards had not been reduced between 1993 and 1999, Richards would not have been able to get what was probably a combined first and second mortgage so that in the end he made no down payment. That allowed him to spend more on the house, adding to the buying frenzy that built the bubble and left him with a larger monthly payment than he could afford when his business slowed and housing prices fell.

"Although the problem manifested itself first in the subprime sector," two economists of the National Economic Research Associates (NERA) wrote in 2009, "we now know that delinquencies and foreclosures of prime loans have also soared. Several factors contributed to the credit deterioration in the mortgage sector, including: 1) relatively lax underwriting standards in recent years; 2) increased indebtedness on the part of homeowners; 3) the combination . . . of the availability of cheap credit and increasing housing prices during the years 2000 to 2005; and 4) the increase in the use of non-traditional mortgage products."[2]

What the NERA authors did not realize, and what we can now demonstrate with the Freddie dataset first discussed in chapter 2, is that the "prime" loans they referred to had deteriorated in quality during the 1990s and 2000s; many were no longer the traditional prime mortgage, although they were the best mortgages in the market at the time. The reduced underwriting standards that Fannie and Freddie had adopted for low-income and minority borrowers had, through the pressure of competition in the mortgage market, spread to the wider market.

Chapter 5 covered in detail the various efforts of the Department of Housing and Urban Development (HUD) under two administrations to make mortgage credit available to low-income borrowers by reducing underwriting standards. Chapter 6 covered the decline in underwriting standards used by the GSEs as they struggled to meet the increasing affordable-housing goals, and chapter 7 showed that the goals were the sole reason the GSEs acquired NTMs—and the losses they incurred as a result. In this chapter, we will show how and why the low-quality loans that were induced by the various HUD programs led to a decline in underwriting standards throughout the housing market, not only in the sectors covered by Fannie and Freddie and not only in support of low-income housing.

Although HUD's various programs were intended to reduce underwriting standards for a limited number of low-income and minority borrowers, it was not possible to confine these reduced standards to particular groups. As noted earlier, a HUD advisory committee observed in 1991 that the GSEs' underwriting standards for primary loans "are widely adopted and amount to national underwriting standards for a substantial fraction of all mortgage credit."[3] In other words, even as early as 1991, the GSEs were setting the mortgage underwriting standards for the market as a whole; if their standards changed, so would market standards. This was the key insight of the community activists who pressed Congress for the affordable-housing goals in the late 1980s and early 1990s. They complained that there would be no change in underwriting standards until the GSEs became less concerned about the quality of the loans they bought. In this they were certainly right.

Mortgage lending is a competitive business. Once the two GSEs began to lower their traditional standards in the early 1990s, most lenders would have to do the same, even if their loans were not going to be sold to Fannie or Freddie. Potential homebuyers will go where they can get the best deal; even if they had a good credit record and could afford a traditional prime loan with a 10 to 20 percent down payment, the opportunity to make a smaller down payment or to get a loan that required no amortization might mean that they could buy a larger house for the same monthly payment. Thus, although HUD's intention in raising the affordable-housing goals was to reduce mortgage underwriting standards for low- and moderate-income (LMI) borrowers, the result was to change the standards for all borrowers. As HUD continued to increase the affordable-housing goals over time, mortgage underwriting standards throughout the market were commensurately loosened. As one academic study noted even before the financial crisis: "Over the past decade, most, if not all, the products offered to subprime borrowers have also been offered to prime borrowers."[4] By 2006, according to a study by the National Association of Realtors, 45 percent of first-time homebuyers and 19 percent of repeat buyers provided no down payment. The median first-time buyer provided a down payment of 2 percent.[5]

In 1997, Freddie Mac estimated that 10 to 30 percent of subprime borrowers could qualify for a prime loan. This statement was interpreted by the left as evidence that unscrupulous mortgage originators were tricking people into taking mortgages that were more expensive than the conventional prime mortgages for which they were eligible. This may have happened, of course, but it is more reasonable to believe that most of those borrowers were people who could have qualified for conforming loans but preferred interest-only loans or low down payments so they could afford a larger house or who wanted the opportunity to invest their down payment or principal payments in the stock market or their own businesses.

In a memorandum to the Freddie Mac board of directors in February 2007, Richard Syron, Freddie's chair, reported: "Throughout this decade, we have enjoyed very low credit losses (1–2 bp [basis points] on the portfolio). We expect that period has ended: our models project a significant increase in losses on new business, 7 bp. *Our originator-customers have been producing riskier loans;* and we have to buy riskier product to fulfill our HUD goals, at very low returns [emphasis added]."[6] In other words, what Freddie Mac was seeing was the gradual decline in underwriting standards in the whole market, a process set off by a combination of the affordable-housing goals and its own efforts to comply.

THE FREDDIE DATASET

In this chapter, in order to distinguish the mortgages in the Freddie dataset from NTMs, I use the term "non-prime" to refer to any loan in the dataset that does not meet one of the triad of key underwriting standards that were described in chapter 2 as the key elements for creating a prime loan. In the rest of the book, a "subprime" loan has been defined as any loan in which the borrower has a FICO credit score of 660 or less. This conforms to the bank regulators' 2001 ruling, also discussed in chapter 2. However, for the purposes of showing the deterioration of the best loans in the market between 1999 and 2007, it makes more sense to use a term that includes all the loans in the Freddie dataset that do not meet one or more of the traditional prime loan standards. Accordingly, in this chapter a non-prime loan will be any loan in the dataset that fails to meet at least one of the triad of underwriting standards that defined the traditional prime loan described in chapter 2. These standards included a down payment of 10 to 20 percent (a loan-to-value [LTV] ratio of no more than 90 percent); a record of meeting credit obligations (a FICO score over 660); and the financial capacity to do so (a debt-to-income [DTI] ratio of no more than 38 percent). Not all the mortgages in the Freddie dataset meet the prime loan standard—far from it—but the 1999 Freddie cohort in Table 2.2 is likely to be the closest to a traditional prime mortgage among the loans Freddie released, even though there had been some deterioration in standards between 1992 and 1999. In addition, because the refinance loans can have highly variable characteristics that distort comparisons, I will use only purchase money mortgages in the Freddie dataset for making loan quality comparisons between cohorts and periods.

Figure 8.1 displays the relative sizes of the government and private mortgage markets between 1990 and 2010. The government's share, principally Fannie and Freddie, was growing rapidly through the 1990s, while the private-sector share was largely stagnant. The private sector grew as fast as it did in the 2000s because the mortgages that private firms acquired as the bubble grew tended to be significantly larger in dollar terms and because Fannie and Freddie became the largest buyers of the private mortgage–backed securities (PMBS) backed by NTMs that the private sector was creating

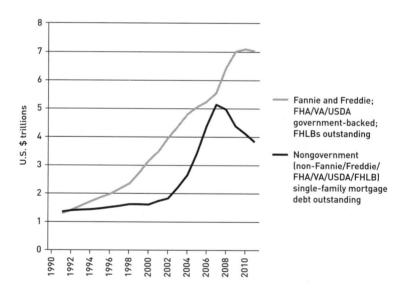

Sources: Fannie Mae and Freddie Mac financial statements, 1994–2010; Mortgage Debt Outstanding: Federal Reserve Board's Flow of Funds Accounts of the United States, Annual Flows and Outstandings, March 11, 2010.

Note: Freddie Mac and Fannie Mae adopted new accounting standards as of January 1, 2010. Calculations prior to this year are based on the net total of the Retained Mortgage Portfolio.

FIG. 8.1. Relative size of government and nongovernment mortgage assets

specifically for these two massive buyers. These securities, as discussed in chapter 7, were necessary to enable Fannie and Freddie to meet the ever-growing affordable-housing goals. Competition at the origination level caused looser mortgage underwriting standards—initially employed by the GSEs to meet the goals—to spread to the wider market. As the GSEs reduced their underwriting standards, the private sector was compelled to follow suit, simply because the riskier and lower-cost mortgages Fannie and Freddie were offering were more attractive to homebuyers.

To demonstrate the spread of the GSEs' reduced underwriting standards to the wider conventional market, we need a proxy for the mortgage market that does not include either the government's share or the mortgages that Fannie and Freddie were acquiring to comply with the affordable-housing goals. For that, the Freddie dataset, discussed in detail in chapter 2, may be the ideal data source for this purpose. These 15 million 30-year fixed-rate fully documented mortgages—53 percent of all the mortgages Freddie acquired between 1999 and 2011—are the best mortgages that Freddie bought during this period. In releasing the dataset, Freddie noted that it did not include any of the loans that it acquired under special programs to comply with the affordable-housing goals. Nor did Freddie include such riskier mortgages as those with adjustable rates.[7] So a subset of the 15 million fixed-rate 30-year fully documented loans would be the closest we can come to the terms of the traditional prime mortgage in the market during those years. It is also true that the loans Freddie acquired were likely to be the best loans in the market at the time they were acquired. As has been noted, Fannie and Freddie—because of their lower funding costs and higher leverage—could outbid any other buyer for the loans they wanted. Thus, if the data show that the quality of the loans Freddie acquired was declining between 1999 and 2008, that would be a strong indication that the quality of the best mortgages was also declining. Indeed, that is what we observe, as summarized in the tables and figures below. A large proportion of the best purchase money mortgages that Freddie acquired between 1999 and 2007 were no longer traditional prime mortgages, and, as shown in Figure 8.2, the deterioration in standards grew as

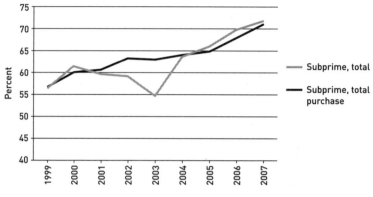

Source: Freddie Mac Single Family Loan-Level Dataset.

FIG. 8.2. Freddie Mac's non-prime purchase loans as a percent of all purchase loans and all non-prime loans as a percent of all loans acquired from 1999 to 2007

the years advanced. If Fannie and Freddie couldn't find prime mortgages among the home purchase loans coming into the market, it's likely that they didn't exist.

This does not necessarily mean, of course, that the loosened underwriting standards required by the affordable-housing goals caused this decline in mortgage quality between 1999 and 2007; correlation is not the same as causation. However, it is difficult to identify any factors in the market other than the GSEs that were being continuously pressed to reduce their underwritings standards, and because the GSEs had been the standard-setters for the mortgage market since at least the mid-1980s, it is highly likely that as they reduced their standards in response to HUD's demands, the rest of the market followed suit.

The deterioration between 1999 and 2007, despite the fact that it was a boom period, can be shown by comparing the default rates of the best home purchase mortgages in Table 2.2 (which includes the best purchase mortgages in the 1999 cohort), with the best home purchase mortgages in Table 8.1, which includes all home purchase mortgages acquired by Freddie between 1999 and 2007. This comparison also shows a deterioration even among the highest-quality mortgages in the market at that time. The 1999 cohort in Table 2.2 had a default rate of .55 percent, whereas the best mortgages in Table

8.1 had a default rate of 1.6 percent—almost three times as high—during the boom years between 1999 and 2007. Thus, deterioration in quality is shown to have occurred among the best loans being made in the market as a whole between 1999 and 2007.

Figure 8.3 slices the same Freddie data in another way, showing that the likely incidence of default for both the prime and non-prime purchase mortgages made in 1999 was considerably better than the incidence of default for the prime and non-prime mortgages in all of Freddie's best 2007 purchase mortgages.

Other indicators also show a deterioration in the quality of the mortgages Freddie Mac was acquiring between 1999 and 2007. Figure 8.4 shows the change in the DTI ratio on mortgages that Freddie required from 1999 through 2007. As noted earlier, the DTI ratio is

TABLE 8.1. Default experience with variations in underwriting standards used for purchase loans acquired by Freddie Mac between 1999 and 2007

Loan type[a]	Default rate (%)	Number of loans	Percent of loans	Index (prime = 1)
A. Prime (>660 FICO, ≤90% LTV ratio, ≤38% DTI ratio)	1.60	1,760,153	42	1.0
B. Non-prime (missing one or more key elements of a prime loan)	6.30	2,410,258	58	3.9
1. FICO <660, but prime-level down payments and DTI ratios	7.30	197,736	5	4.6
2. FICO <660, with non-prime down payments and/or DTI ratios	12.94	428,988	10	8.1
3. LTV ratio >90%, but prime-level FICOs and DTI ratios	4.57	439,836	11	2.9
4. LTV ratio >90%, with non-prime FICOs and/or DTI ratios	10.70	626,649	15	6.7
5. DTI ratio >38%, but prime-level down payments and FICOs	3.39	985,445	24	2.1
6. DTI ratio >38%, with non-prime down payments and/or FICOs	10.21	645,941	15	6.4

Source: Freddie Mac.
[a]Fully documented, 30-year fixed-rate home purchase loans acquired 1999–2007.

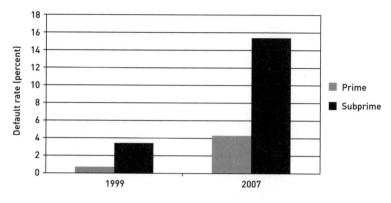

Source: Freddie Mac Single Family Loan-Level Dataset.

FIG. 8.3. Decline in quality of Freddie Mac's best loans, 1999–2007

an indicator of whether the borrower has the wherewithal to meet his or her payment obligations under the mortgage. A DTI ratio of 38 percent seems—in light of the default rate in the Freddie dataset—to be the limit for a prime loan. The chart shows that Freddie accepted higher and higher DTI ratios as the years went on.

Another example of the deterioration in mortgage quality is the growth in the combined LTV (CLTV) ratios of the mortgages

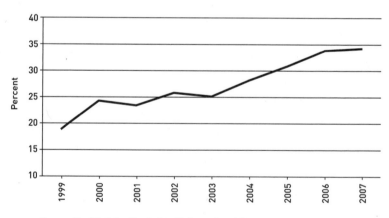

Source: Freddie Mac Single Family Loan-Level Dataset.

FIG. 8.4. Percent of single-family loans accepted by Freddie Mac from 1999 to 2007 with a debt-to-income ratio greater than 42 percent

that Freddie was accepting. A CLTV ratio, by definition, involves two mortgages—a first mortgage that is below the level at which the GSEs were required by statute to have mortgage insurance (i.e., an 80 percent LTV ratio) and a second mortgage that covers all or part of the difference between the first mortgage and a 100 percent LTV ratio. Fannie or Freddie would take the first mortgage but would avoid having to purchase (and charge for) mortgage insurance by turning a blind eye to the second. This would reduce the cost of the mortgage for a low-income borrower whose mortgage would help one of the GSEs to meet the affordable-housing goals. Obviously, there was deception in this practice; an 80 percent first mortgage with a 20 percent second mortgage is a mortgage with no down payment. It appears that by 2007 almost 40 percent of the mortgages Freddie was accepting had CLTV ratios over 90 percent, and 20 percent had what were effectively no down payments (Figure 8.5). Again, this development reflects the concessionary standards required by the affordable-housing goals that were being adopted in the market as a whole.

Despite these obvious dangers, HUD saw the erosion of down payment requirements as one of the keys to the success of its strategy

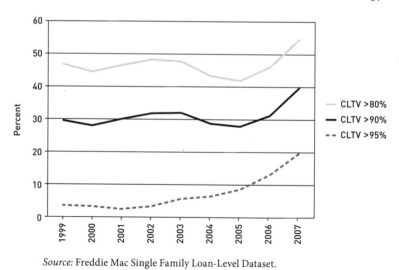

Source: Freddie Mac Single Family Loan-Level Dataset.

FIG. 8.5. Rise of CLTV mortgages in the Freddie Mac dataset between 1999 and 2007

to increase homeownership through the "partnership" it had established with the mortgage financing community under the National Homeownership Strategy: "The amount of borrower equity is an important factor in assessing mortgage loan quality. *However, many low-income families do not have access to sufficient funds for a downpayment. While members of the partnership have already made significant strides in reducing this barrier to home purchase, more must be done.* In 1989 only 7 percent of home mortgages were made with less than 10 percent downpayment. By August 1994, low downpayment mortgage loans had increased to 29 percent" (emphasis added).[8]

Even without the use of the Freddie dataset, it can be demonstrated that there was a significant decline in the size of the down payments (i.e., an increase in LTV ratios) associated with all mortgages after 1992, the year in which the affordable-housing goals were adopted. In 1989, for example, only one in 230 homebuyers bought a home with a down payment of 3 percent or less, but by 2003 one in seven buyers was providing a down payment at that level, and by 2007 the number was one in less than three. The gradual increase in LTV and CLTV ratios under HUD's policies is shown in Figure 8.6. Note the date (1992) when HUD began to have some influence over the down payments that the GSEs would accept.

Thus, what we see in the Freddie dataset and other data is a gradual deterioration in the quality of the best loans Freddie Mac made between 1999 and 2007, even though these were not the loans that Freddie acquired specifically to meet the affordable-housing goals. The picture is not pretty; the loose underwriting standards that the GSEs began to adopt in 1993 were bleeding over into the mortgage mainstream. It appears that HUD was correct when it predicted that eventually the GSEs' compliance with the affordable-housing goals would erase the difference between prime and subprime mortgages. In the figures above, we are seeing that happen before our eyes. The community activists of the late 1980s and early 1990s were also right to believe that getting the GSEs to abandon their strict underwriting standards was the key to unlocking mortgage credit for low-income homebuyers. What no one seemed to anticipate was that the effect would be a general deterioration in mortgage underwriting standards, a giant housing bubble, and, ultimately, a financial crisis.

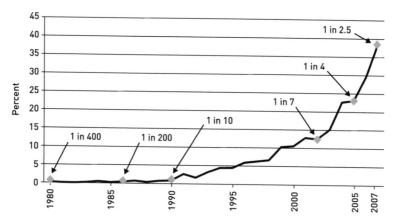

Source: FHA 2009 Actuarial Study; HUD's Office of Policy Development and Research—Profiles of GSE Mortgage Purchases in 1999 and 2000, in 2001–2004, and in 2005–2007; Fannie's 2007 10-K. Compiled by Edward Pinto.
Note: Fannie's percentage of home purchase loans with an LTV or CLTV ratio ≥97 percent used as the proxy for conventional loans.

FIG. 8.6. Percentage of home purchase volume with an LTV or CLTV of ≥97 percent

Before the enactment of the affordable-housing goals, Fannie had very few loans with down payments of as little as 3 percent, but almost immediately after the goals were put in place, that percentage began to grow as the firm sought weaker credits in order to comply with the goals. As the bubble grew, it became more difficult to find loans even among borrowers above the median income who were willing to offer down payments above 3 percent. As homes became more expensive, homebuyers at all levels of income began to seek low-down-payment mortgages in order to afford more expensive homes with the lowest possible monthly payment. Freddie was undoubtedly encountering the same conditions. DTI ratios also increased for the same reason as homebuyers took on more debt in order to buy bigger and more expensive homes. Figure 8.7 shows the gradual deterioration of the GSEs' down payment and DTI ratios after the enactment of the affordable-housing goals.

As the bubble continued to grow, fixed-rate mortgages declined as a percentage of Freddie's volume, and the default rate for both prime and non-prime loans rose in the Freddie dataset. However, the default rates on prime loans stayed within an acceptable range as

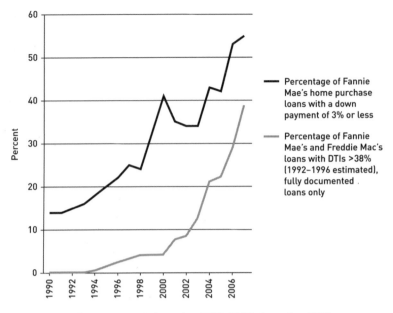

Sources: Down payment information: HUD; DTI information: CFPB.

FIG. 8.7. Deterioration in the down payments and DTI ratios, 1990–2006

the bubble flattened out during 2006, while the default rate on non-prime loans rose sharply (Figure 8.8).

Thus, while the reduction in mortgage underwriting standards adversely affected the exposures of Fannie and Freddie and ultimately caused their insolvency, it also spread to the conventional market as a whole with even more significant consequences. The default of unprecedented numbers of NTMs acquired by Fannie and Freddie would have been an important event—perhaps in itself large enough to cause a financial crisis—but the fact that the underwriting standards the GSEs used for meeting the affordable-housing goals had spread to the rest of the market made a financial crisis unavoidable.

This concludes the portion of the book that deals with the implementation of the affordable-housing goals and their contribution to the insolvency of Fannie and Freddie and the decline in underwriting standards. In the next Part, we'll look at contributions

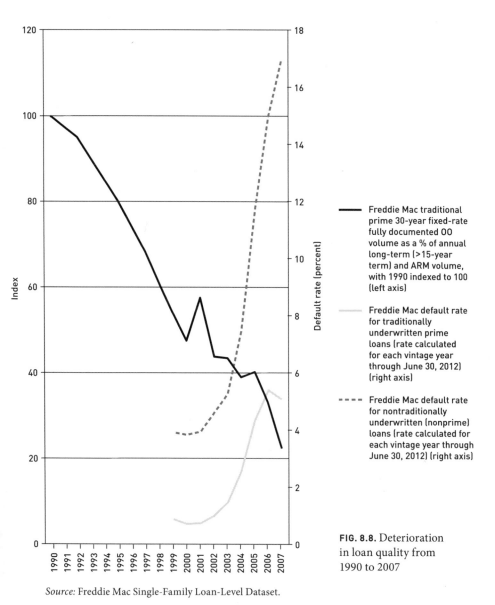

FIG. 8.8. Deterioration in loan quality from 1990 to 2007

Source: Freddie Mac Single-Family Loan-Level Dataset.

of various factors—the housing price bubble, mark-to-market accounting, the absence of reliable data, and the securities market's vulnerability to panic selling—that turned a mortgage meltdown into a financial crisis.

PART

III

The Financial Crisis
and Its Accelerants

The great housing price bubble, the paucity of accurate data,
how nontraditional mortgages precipitated a crisis,
and the effect of mark-to-market accounting

9

The Great Housing Price Bubble

How Loosened Underwriting Standards Stimulated Its Growth

> What could explain a bull market in a non-earning asset
> in a non-inflationary era? . . . Ample credit is the first answer.
>
> JAMES GRANT, *Mr. Market Miscalculates*, 2008

The housing price bubble that developed in the United States between 1997 and 2007 was truly extraordinary—nine times larger
than any previous bubble—and its deflation reduced home prices
nationally by an equally extraordinary 30 to 40 percent. This in turn
triggered the mortgage meltdown and ultimately the financial crisis.
There are inevitable questions about the bubble: What caused it, was
its deflation the principal cause of the financial crisis, and how could
U.S. government policy have been responsible if there were other
large housing bubbles in other developed countries at the same time?
These questions are addressed in this chapter.

In November 2004, an article in *Newsday* began with this:

Anthony James just didn't want to wait anymore. Interest
rates were low. Home prices would likely continue to rise.
It was time to buy, James thought. But there was a problem.
James and his wife, Tanya, didn't have the savings for a down
payment and would likely need two more years before they
could come up with it. Nonetheless, last September [2004],
the James family moved to its first home—a $285,000 three-

bedroom cape in Baldwin [Long Island, New York]. They financed the entire house, plus closing costs, in what is known as a 106 percent mortgage, at 6.9 percent. "There was so much action going on in the housing market, and we were tired of where we were staying," Anthony James, 38, said of their apartment in Brooklyn. The couple, and their two children, are thrilled with their decision, he said. But some experts call it a risky move. With no equity and a high mortgage, the family could see the value of the home sink below their loan amount. And if they lose their jobs . . . they could owe more than they could pay if the real estate market shifts. . . . "We didn't come out here to move," James said. "And if we had waited, we would have had a better down payment, but it would have been a higher price in the long run."[1]

There is no way to know whether you are in a bubble, and Anthony James had no better or worse information than anyone else. The bank that made him a 106 percent loan may have believed that it was protected by the continued rise of housing prices, but in any event it is likely to have sold the loan to Fannie Mae or Freddie Mac, which may have needed it to meet the affordable-housing goals. In fact, housing prices did continue to rise for almost three years after James bought. Maybe then he was able to refinance into a lower-cost loan, with a loan-to-value (LTV) ratio below 100 percent. Let's hope so. But the point is that he was able to place himself in a very precarious position because mortgage underwriting standards had deteriorated to the point where a 106 percent loan was acceptable. And 106 percent loans would inevitably build a bubble.

THE CAUSES OF BUBBLES

As James Grant said, ample credit is certainly the first answer to what might have caused a bubble, so it should not surprise anyone that Grant cited rapid growth in lending: "in the first quarter [of 2001], Fannie Mae, Freddie Mac and the Federal Home Loan Banks together expanded their book by $84.7 billion, or 12.7% annualized."[2] But credit has two facets—low interest rates and low collateral requirements. In their analyses of the great housing bubble, most economists have focused on the low interest rates that resulted from the Federal Reserve's accommodative monetary policy in the early 2000s. The idea, fairly conventional at this point, is that low interest rates encourage investment in assets of various kinds, and in this case the assets happened to be housing. Economists have been vigorously debating whether the Federal Reserve's monetary policy in the early 2000s caused the bubble by keeping interest rates too low for too long. Naturally enough, Ben Bernanke and Alan Greenspan have argued that the Federal Reserve was not at fault.[3] On the other hand, economist John B. Taylor, author of an eponymous rule for monetary policy, contends that the Federal Reserve's violation of this rule was the principal cause of the bubble.[4] Other theories blame huge inflows of funds from emerging markets or from countries that were recycling the dollars they received from trade surpluses with the United States. In chapter 3, I pointed out that the 1997–2007 housing bubble was already three times larger than the any bubble in modern U.S. history when the Federal Reserve's short-term interest rates became negative in 2003 and that before that time there was little evidence that funds from abroad were driving down U.S. rates.

The seemingly weak correlation between interest rates and the bubble suggests that we ought to look at collateral for the answer. Few analysts have focused on the extraordinarily high leverage that developed in the housing market beginning in the mid-1990s, which grew wider and more widespread in the 2000s. That leverage was supplied by mortgage lending with low down payments—in other words, lending on low collateral—the very policy that was promoted most forcefully by the Department of Housing and Urban Development (HUD) as part of its administration of the affordable-housing goals. It was also the key element of the National Homeownership Strategy, a major initiative of the Clinton administration that sought to enlist the private sector in reducing down payments, which HUD regarded as the principal obstacle to homeownership faced by low- and moderate-income (LMI) borrowers.

By definition, a low down payment for a home means high leverage; the amount of collateral put up by the borrower is small in relation to the size of the loan. Leverage enhances a bubble, and bubbles feed on themselves. If a potential home buyer has 10 percent for a down payment, she can buy a $100,000 home if the down payment is 10 percent; but if the down payment is reduced to 5 percent, she can buy a $200,000 home. So it's easy to see how reducing down payments could have increased competition for more expensive homes and thus fed the growth of the housing price bubble. Once begun, a bubble tends to obscure delinquencies and defaults, sending the wrong signals to potential investors. As house prices rise, homeowners get a kind of free equity in their homes that they didn't have to pay for. This enables them, if they are having trouble meeting their mortgage obligations, to refinance or sell the house. The added equity also provides an incentive to stay in the house by sacrificing elsewhere. As a result, we should see delinquencies and foreclosures fall as housing prices rise in a bubble, a phenomenon illustrated in Figure 9.1.

Because of these factors, housing price bubbles tend to be highly procyclical. As a bubble grows, it creates conditions that encourage further growth. The absence of defaults encourages lenders to believe that the risks are low, so they are willing to make 106 percent loans, as Anthony James's lender did. That much credit also induces more bidding for more expensive houses, again enlarging the bubble. In this sense, leverage is procyclical when a bubble is growing—it tends to increase the bubble's growth. That process is also helped, one might add, by the absurd persistence of support for the 30-year fixed-rate mortgage, especially among members of Congress. A lawmaker can in the same sentence criticize excessive leverage in the financial system and then pivot to fulsome praise for the 30-year mortgage. That mortgage is the very embodiment of leverage and itself contributed substantially to the growth of the bubble by keeping monthly payments low (because the 30-year loan amortizes principal slowly) and enabling homebuyers to make lower monthly payments for larger houses. The beneficiaries of this policy are realtors and homebuilders; lawmakers ought to keep this in mind when they consider the virtues of 30-year fixed-rate mortgages. The leverage inherent in a low down payment and a 30-year fixed-rate mortgage increases demand for larger and more expensive houses, driving up

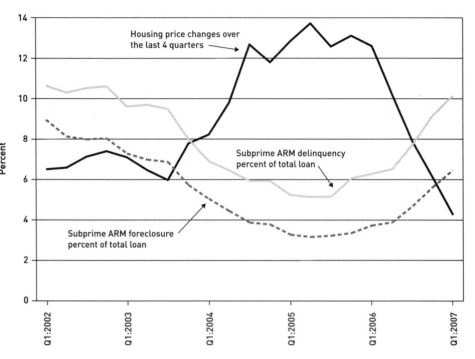

Housing price changes over
the last 4 quarters

Subprime ARM delinquency
percent of total loan

Subprime ARM foreclosure
percent of total loan

Adapted from: John B. Taylor, *Getting Off Track* (Hoover Institution Press, 2009), p. 12.

FIG. 9.1. Inverse relationship between house prices
and delinquencies and defaults

housing prices and also adding to the bubble. As HUD pressed on
with its policy of reducing down payments, in other words, it was
directly increasing the size of the bubble.

But leverage is procyclical in both directions; it is also procyclical
on the way down, when the bubble is deflating. Homeowners with
low down payments—that is, high leverage—are extraordinarily
vulnerable to loss if housing prices decline. For example, if a homeowner congratulates herself for getting a 3 percent down payment on
a $100,000 home, she will see the downside of her success when the
market turns and housing prices in her neighborhood fall. In that
case, a decline in housing prices of, say, only 5 percent means that the
homeowner has lost her down payment, cannot refinance without
providing more equity, and can't move elsewhere to find a better job
without paying the holder of the mortgage the difference between the

mortgage note and the selling price of the house. In that case, many borrowers would be inclined to simply walk away from the mortgage. And many have, despite the loss of credit standing. There has been a lot of focus on the high leverage of investment banks before the financial crisis, and how irresponsible it was for these firms to operate with so little capital, but there has been very little attention to the effects of HUD's low down payment policies on the well-being of homeowners and the effect of millions of underwater borrowers on the recovery from the recession. One explanation for the destructiveness of the bubble's deflation in the United States is the procyclicality of the high leverage that HUD and U.S. housing policy promoted before the bubble collapsed.

THE INSIDER AND THE MINSKY MODEL

Figure 9.2, based on Robert Shiller's data, shows the dramatic growth of the housing bubble in the United States. By mid-2007, home prices in the United States had increased substantially for ten years. The growth in real dollar terms had been almost 90 percent. There is good reason to believe that the 1997–2007 bubble grew larger and extended longer in time than previous bubbles because of the government's housing policies, which artificially increased the demand for housing by funneling more money into the housing market than would have been available if traditional underwriting standards had been maintained and the government had not promoted the growth of subprime lending.

That the 1997–2007 bubble lasted about twice as long as the prior housing bubbles is significant in itself. Mortgage quality declines as a housing bubble grows and originators try to structure mortgages that will allow buyers to meet monthly payments for more expensive homes; the fact that the most recent bubble was so long-lived was an important element in its ultimate destructiveness when it deflated.

Why did this bubble last so long? Housing bubbles deflate when delinquencies and defaults begin to appear in unusual numbers. Investors and creditors realize that the risks of a collapse are mounting. One by one, investors cash in and leave. Eventually, the bubble tops

Source: Robert J. Shiller, *Irrational Exuberance*, 2nd ed. (2006).

FIG. 9.2. The bubble according to Shiller—real housing prices for 120 years

out, those who are still in the game run for the doors, and a deflation in prices sets in. Generally, in the past, this process took three or four years. In the case of the most recent bubble, it took ten. The reason for this longevity is that one major participant in the market was not in it for profit and was not worried about the risks to itself or to those it was controlling. In the Minsky model, discussed in chapter 1, this was an insider who kept buying, injecting more and more money into the market. In the end, the insider never sold, which should not happen in the Minsky model. Instead, it held on to the assets as they fell in value because it was not in the game for the profits it could reap. This insider was the U.S. government pursuing a social policy—especially by making mortgage credit available to low- and moderate-income borrowers—and requiring the agencies and financial institutions it controlled or could influence through regulation to keep pumping money into housing long after the bubble, left to itself, would have deflated. As two scholars noted about this period, "The availability of housing finance and the relaxation of lending standards provided a flow of new buyers into the market that even rapid investment in new housing construction couldn't fully accommodate, so housing prices rose dramatically."[5]

THE UNIQUENESS OF THE 1997–2007 U.S. BUBBLE

Apart from what caused the housing bubble, was it simply the *collapse* of the bubble that caused the financial crisis? The United States has had housing bubbles in the past—most recently in the late 1970s and late 1980s—but when these bubbles deflated they caused only modest local downturns. In addition, and more significant, other developed countries also experienced housing bubbles in the 2000s, some even larger than the U.S. bubble, and this has led many scholars and others to question whether U.S. government housing policies could have been responsible for the bubble and the financial crisis. After all, runs the argument, other countries didn't have our housing policies—with the government-sponsored enterprises (GSEs) and other government involvement—yet they also had huge bubbles. How can that be explained? The answer is relatively simple. There were many causes for the enormous U.S. housing bubble, as outlined above, and it really doesn't matter if only some of them—or all of them—were contributors. The collapse of the U.S. bubble in 2007 and 2008 was destructive not just because it was so large, but principally because the mortgages that were inside were so weak. It is true that other countries had large housing bubbles in the 2000s, but when their bubbles deflated, the housing losses were small. This is clear in Table 9.1 prepared by Dwight Jaffee of the University of California at Berkeley, which shows that in other developed countries the losses associated with mortgage delinquencies and defaults when their bubbles deflated were far lower than the losses suffered in the United States when the 1997–2007 bubble deflated. Jaffee's data, then, suggests that not every bubble—even a large bubble—has the potential to cause a financial crisis when it deflates. The U.S. bubble was unique. It was as large as others, but far more destructive. The reason was that the U.S. bubble contained a far larger percentage of nontraditional mortgages (NTMs) than was true of other countries, where subprime loans are uncommon.

The underlying reasons for the outcomes in Jaffee's data were provided in testimony before the Senate Committee on Banking,

TABLE 9.1. Troubled Mortgages,
Western Europe and the United States

	≥ 3 month arrears (%)	Impaired or doubtful (%)	Foreclosures (%)	Year
Belgium	0.46	—	—	2009
Denmark	0.53	—	—	2009
France	—	0.93	—	2008
Ireland	3.32	—	—	2009
Italy	—	3.00	—	2008
Portugal	1.17	—	—	2009
Spain	—	3.04	0.24	2009
Sweden	—	1.00	—	2009
UK	2.44	—	0.19	2009
U.S.				
All loans	9.47	—	4.58	2009
Prime	6.73	—	3.31	2009
Subprime	25.26	—	15.58	2009

Source: European Mortgage Federation (2010) and Mortgage Bankers Association for U.S. Data.
Adapted from: Dwight M. Jaffee, "Reforming the U.S. Mortgage Market through Private Market Incentives," paper prepared for presentation at "Past, Present and Future of the Government Sponsored Enterprises," Federal Reserve Bank of St. Louis, November 17, 2010, Table 4.

Housing, and Urban Affairs in September 2010 by Dr. Michael Lea, director of the Corky McMillin Center for Real Estate at San Diego State University:

The default and foreclosure experience of the U.S. market has been far worse than in other countries. Serious default rates remain less than 3 percent in all other countries and less than 1 percent in Australia and Canada. Of the countries in this survey only Ireland, Spain and the UK have seen a significant increase in mortgage default during the crisis.

There are several factors responsible for this result. First subprime lending was rare or non-existent outside of the U.S. The only country with a significant subprime share was the UK (a peak of 8 percent of mortgages in 2006). Subprime accounted for 5 percent of mortgages in Canada, less than 2 percent in Australia and negligible proportions elsewhere. . . . [T]here was far less "risk layering" or offering limited documentation loans to subprime borrowers with little or no downpayment. There was little "no doc" lending. . . . [T]he proportion of loans with little or no downpayment was less than the U.S. and the decline in house prices in most countries was also less. . . . [L]oans in other developed countries are with recourse and lenders routinely do go after borrowers for deficiency judgments.[6]

This point can also be illustrated with data from Canada. Comparing the experiences of the United States and Canada can have some validity, because macroeconomic factors were roughly the same in the years 1993 through 2007, and both countries had sharp run-ups in housing prices. Yet Canada had nothing like the mortgage meltdown that was a major feature of the collapse of the U.S. bubble. A 2009 article published by the Federal Reserve Bank of Cleveland suggests that the amount of subprime lending in the United States was a major factor in the different experiences of the two countries:

[W]hile subprime lending also increased in Canada, the subprime market remains much smaller than in the US. The most cited estimate is that subprime lenders [in Canada] had a market share of roughly 5 percent in 2006—compared to 22 percent in the US. . . . The rapid growth of the subprime market provided an additional boost to demand in the US that is consistent with the more rapid house price appreciation in the US than in Canada. . . . While the expansion of subprime lending provided a temporary boost to housing price growth rates [in the United States], when prices stopped rising, the inability of some borrowers to refinance homes they could not afford led to a spike of delinquencies.[7]

All the foregoing data are significant for a proper analysis of the role of government policy and NTMs in the financial crisis. We can argue about the cause of the bubble—whether it was low mortgage down payments, 30-year mortgages, low interest rates, flows of funds from abroad, a half dozen other possibilities, or all of them in concert—but there is little doubt it wasn't just the size of the U.S. bubble that was important; it was the content. The enormous delinquency rates in the United States were not replicated elsewhere, primarily because other developed countries did not have the numbers of NTMs that were present in the U.S. financial system when the bubble deflated. These mortgage defaults were translated into huge housing price declines and from there—through the private mortgage-backed securities (PMBS) that banks and other financial institutions were holding—into actual or apparent financial weakness in particular firms. Accordingly, if the 1997–2007 housing bubble had not been seeded with an unprecedented number of NTMs, it is likely that the financial crisis would never have occurred. But that unprecedented number of NTMs was a result of a conscious government policy to ease credit and loosen loan terms. As HUD noted in 2005: "Aggressive mortgage financing can boost demand for housing, and that demand can drive up house prices. As interest rates fall and loan terms relax, borrowers have more buying power to raise the offer price on a home purchase."[8] Just so. But HUD never bothered to consider what effect its policies might have when those house prices came tumbling down. Indeed, as discussed in the next chapter, HUD may not even have known what damage it had done.

10

Flying Blind into a Storm

How the GSEs' Failure to Disclose Their Acquisition of Nontraditional Mortgages Magnified the Crisis

The greatest enemy of knowledge is not ignorance,
it is the illusion of knowledge.

STEPHEN HAWKING (attributed)

After the financial crisis and resigning as U.S. Treasury Secretary, Hank Paulson wrote in his memoir of the time that "the crisis in the financial markets that I had anticipated arrived in force on August 9, 2007. It came from an area we hadn't expected—housing—and the damage it caused was much deeper and much longer lasting than any of us could have imagined."[1] This chapter is about why the mortgage meltdown and the financial crisis were such a surprise to policymakers, and how things might have been different if they had been better informed about the risks building up in the mortgage market.

The event that took Paulson by surprise on August 9, 2007, was the announcement, discussed earlier, by a French bank, BNP Paribas, that it was suspending redemptions on three of its funds invested in U.S. subprime private mortgage-backed securities (PMBS). At this time and for more than a year afterward, Fannie Mae and Freddie Mac—by far the biggest players and the market leaders in U.S. mortgages—were still reporting that the only subprime loans they acquired were the relatively few they bought from subprime lenders, and Fannie routinely noted in its 10-K reports that its exposure to subprime loans was .2 percent,[2] or, occasionally, "less than 1 percent."[3] The balance of its subprime and other nontraditional mortgages (NTMs)—those that had FICO scores less than 660, low down payments, and other deficiencies—were reported to various industry data services as prime loans. Freddie Mac did the same. Accordingly, in August 2007, few if anyone outside the GSEs knew that the number of mortgages in the prime category was much lower than the available numbers showed; in fact, more than half of the mortgages outstanding in the years before the crisis were NTMs, which made the market substantially weaker and more prone to defaults than anyone understood at the time. Paulson's surprise was the first example of the adverse effect that would flow from the GSEs' failure to disclose their true exposure to NTMs. There would be many more.

"THE MARKET IS NOT OPERATING IN A NORMAL WAY"

Six months earlier, in March 2007, Federal Reserve Chair Ben Bernanke testified before the Joint Economic Committee of Congress on the economic outlook. He noted that economic growth had slowed since 2006, pointing to a "substantial correction" in the housing market as the culprit. Still, after describing a decline in sales of new homes and a substantial rise in delinquency rates on subprime mortgages, he concluded that "at this juncture, however, the impact on the broader economy and financial markets of the problems in the subprime market seems likely to be contained."[4]

In May, in a speech at the Chicago Federal Reserve Bank, Bernanke noted that "we have spent a bit of time evaluating the financial implications of the subprime issues, tried to assess the magnitude of losses, and tried to determine how concentrated they are. There is a sense that, although there is always a possibility for some kind of disruption . . . the financial system will absorb the losses from the subprime mortgage problems without serious problems."[5] He provided the Federal Reserve's best estimate that "about 7-1/2 million first-lien subprime mortgages are now outstanding."[6] This number, which is close to what most regulators and scholars were using right up to the time of the financial crisis in 2008, probably came from LoanPerformance, the most commonly used source for this data, although the

Federal Reserve might have had internal sources. As noted earlier, however, the figure consisted almost entirely of the self-denominated subprime loans reported by the GSEs and various subprime lenders, but it was less than a quarter of the NTMs then outstanding in the U.S. financial system (see Table 1.1).

Three months later, on August 7, 2007, with the capital markets looking even weaker, mortgage defaults continuing to rise, and a substantial number of bankruptcies among mortgage firms, the Federal Reserve's open market committee—perhaps influenced by the relatively small number of subprime loans they thought were outstanding—continued to see the problems in the housing field as a "correction," not even mentioning housing in its unanimous statement that the target Federal Reserve funds rate would stay at 5¼ percent.[7] Only two days later, in the wake of the BNP announcement, the spreads over the risk-free rate in all markets widened substantially. Investors were worried, but they didn't know why. In an emergency telephone conference call the next morning, Bernanke told his Open Market Committee colleagues that "the market is not operating in a normal way."[8]

HAPHAZARD DATA COLLECTION
AND THE ONCOMING TRAIN

But the market *was* behaving normally; the problem was that the Federal Reserve did not know what the market was seeing. It must seem strange to most readers that the top officials of our government—with access to the best information and the most sophisticated advice—could miss an oncoming train as big and destructive as the financial crisis of 2008. If they couldn't foresee—only a year in the future—a financial catastrophe that they now say threatened "the collapse of the global financial system," what could they ever be expected to foresee? This is a serious problem. Alan Greenspan, a former chairman of the Federal Reserve, has written a whole book, *The Map and the Territory*, about the failure of economic forecasters, including those at the Federal Reserve itself, to see the financial crisis coming. To address this shortcoming, Greenspan calls for a better understanding of the "animal spirits" that motivate market actors.[9] Regulators and government officials are not clairvoyant, and clearly the financial crisis was a big miss, but in this case it is possible that they and virtually everyone else who was a serious observer of the mortgage markets were blindsided by insufficient and incorrect data because of the GSEs' failure to report their acquisitions of NTMs accurately.

This situation never improved before the financial crisis. As late as August 2008, just one month before the failure of Lehman Brothers and the onset of the financial crisis, three widely respected Federal Reserve economists published a paper that estimated the total number of subprime loans then outstanding (see Table 10.1). "This market," they wrote, "is estimated to encompass 6.7 million loans with a total value of about $1.2 trillion,"[10] again, less than one-quarter of the total when one includes the loans that should be categorized as subprime or Alt-A because of their characteristics.

Nearly everyone agrees today that the financial crisis was initiated by a "mortgage meltdown" that began with the housing bubble's deflation in 2007. Very few, however, seem to have recognized, even today, the dimensions of the NTM problem before the bubble deflated. The majority report of the Financial Crisis Inquiry Commission (FCIC) notes that "there were warning signs." There always are, if one searches for them with the acuity of hindsight. However, as Michael Lewis showed so vividly in *The Big Short*, very few people in the financial world were actually willing to bet money—even at enormously favorable odds—that the bubble would burst with huge losses.[11] Most seem to have assumed that NTMs were present in the financial system, but not in unusually large numbers.

Even today, there are few references in the media to the number of NTMs that had accumulated in the U.S. financial system before the meltdown began. Yet this is by far the most important fact about the financial crisis. None of the other reasons generally advanced to explain the crisis—lack of regulation, poor risk management, Wall Street greed and compensation policies, systemic risk caused by

TABLE 10.1. Federal Reserve estimate of subprime loans outstanding in August 2008

	Number		Value		In foreclosure[a]	Average size[b]
	Total (millions)	Total (%)	Total ($ trillions)	Total (%)	(thousands)	($ thousands)
All loans	54.7	100	10.1	100	1,352	200
Subprime[c]	6.7	12	1.2	12	721	177
Fixed-rate	3.2	6	0.4	4	145	142
Adjustable-rate	3.2	6	0.7	7	543	218
Other	0.3	1	0.1	1	8	268
Prime and near-prime[c]	42.7	78	8.2	81	521	202
Fixed-rate	33.5	61	5.5	55	224	181
Adjustable-rate	7.7	14	2.5	24	266	331
Other	1.5	3	0.2	2	39	140
FHA/VA	5.3	10	0.7	7	111	140

Source: Calculations by Federal Reserve Board staff using Mortgage Bankers Association and First American LoanPerformance data.

Adapted from: Scott Frame, Andreas Lehnert, and Ned Prescott, "A Snapshot of Mortgage Conditions with an Emphasis on Subprime Mortgage Performance," August 27, 2008, p. 4, http://www.clevelandfed.org /our_region/community_development/pdf/mf_knowledge_snapshot-082708.pdf.

Notes: Reliable estimates of the size of the so-called "Alt-A" or near-prime sector are difficult to obtain, though they are probably concentrated in the adjustable-rate prime category. Outstanding "Alt-A" securities account for roughly 6 percent of mortgages; near-prime loans not securitized may account for up to an additional 4 percent of outstanding mortgages.

[a] "In foreclosure" refers to the inventory of loans in foreclosure. About half of loans that enter the foreclosure process proceed to final sale. Counts for subcategories (fixed-rate, adjustable-rate, other) do not add up to the category total because foreclosure counts are calculated from foreclosure rates for each subcategory and a separate foreclosure rate for that category.

[b] Average loan sizes are adjusted by approximately 12 percent to match total value with the outstanding mortgage debt reported from Table Z.1 of the Flow of Funds accounts.

[c] Subprime and Prime and near-prime include loans not classified as either fixed or variable rate.

credit default swaps, excessive liquidity, and easy credit—do so as plausibly as the failure of a large percentage of the 31 million or more NTMs that existed in the financial system in 2007 and 2008.

Most emblematic of this problem is Ben Bernanke's statement to Congress in March 2007 that the subprime mortgage problem was "contained" and the lack of alarm about subprime loans that showed so clearly in the transcript of the Federal Reserve's Open

Market Committee only two days before BNP Paribas suspended redemptions in three of its funds. The BNP event, more than any other, seemed to bring to the sudden attention of the financial community the fact that there was a serious problem in the mortgage market. It is certainly unlikely that Bernanke and the Open Market Committee would have been so complacent if they had known—as we know now—that more than half of all mortgages in the U.S. financial system were NTMs, with a high propensity to default when the great housing bubble stopped growing. But market participants were unprepared for the destructiveness of this bubble's collapse because of a chronic lack of information about the composition of the market. The deficiency of the Federal Reserve's data was particularly influential.

FANNIE AND FREDDIE AND THE INFORMATION GAP

Here is the nub of the problem. What had been reported to the market and collected by the Federal Reserve as data on the number and value of subprime loans outstanding was wrong. As noted in chapter 2, data collection and key definitions in the housing finance market are haphazard, but this was probably unknown to the Federal Reserve economists whose paper I cited above. They and many other authors thought that when they saw numbers for subprime loans, these loans were defined in the same way that they defined subprime loans. But this was not the case. LoanPerformance, for example, one of the major aggregators of data in the housing finance market, classified all the loans acquired by Fannie and Freddie as prime loans unless the loan was specifically designated as a subprime loan. And Fannie and Freddie, as discussed in chapter 2, recorded as subprime loans only those that they acquired from subprime lenders or were denominated as subprime by the seller. This created a gap between the information available to the market and the reality of what was actually in the market.

Accordingly, when the Federal Reserve staff counted up the subprime loans outstanding and provided this data to Bernanke and other members of the Board of Governors or the Open Market

Committee, the data grossly understated the number of loans in the financial system that actually met the definition that the Federal Reserve economists had assumed. Instead of 6.7 million, the actual number was probably closer to 18 million, and, including Alt-A loans and loans backing PMBS, at least 31 million. Most of the missing subprime loans were on the balance sheets of Fannie and Freddie, which were hiding the numbers of subprime loans they had acquired to meet the affordable-housing goals. No wonder that Bernanke thought the subprime loan problem was contained and that until August 2007 Bernanke and the Open Market Committee thought that what the market was experiencing was simply a correction.

In *The Map and the Territory*, Greenspan recounts that he was at first uncertain of the role that the GSEs played in the financial crisis, until their disclosures in 2009 revealed the true size of their exposure: "I recollect getting a call in late October 2008 from Henry Waxman, a senior House Democrat, inquiring whether I agreed with the position that the housing bubble's primary cause was the heavy demand by the GSEs for subprime mortgages and securities, as some House members had argued. [At this point, Greenspan was no longer chair of the Federal Reserve.] . . . I responded that I thought the GSEs did contribute to the crisis, but that their holdings of subprime securities did not seem sufficiently large to account for the size of the bubble. With the new disclosures [in 2009], it was obvious that Fannie and Freddie played a far more important role—perhaps even a key role—in the momentum that developed behind the housing bubble than many had theretofore recognized."[12] The FCIC, which reported in 2011, never caught on.

The Federal Reserve wasn't the only financial agency of the U.S. government to be surprised by the severity of the mortgage meltdown. Hank Paulson assumed, as did most high-level policy makers at the time, that if there were a financial crisis, it would originate with hedge funds. But hedge funds as an industry sailed through the financial crisis with minimal difficulties. Only eight days before the BNP announcement, in Beijing, according to Reuters, Paulson had said that "the repricing of credit risk was hitting financial markets, but subprime mortgage fallout remained largely contained due to the strongest global economy in decades. . . . [H]e did not see anything that caused him to reconsider his view that the economic damage from the housing correction was 'largely contained.'"[13]

PRIVATE SECTOR ALSO IN THE DARK

What was happening in the market, of course, naturally stimulated other investigations. In September 2007, for example, after the deflation of the bubble had begun, and various financial firms were beginning to encounter capital and liquidity difficulties, two Lehman Brothers analysts issued a highly detailed report titled "Who Owns Residential Credit Risk?"[14] In the tables associated with the report, they estimated the total unpaid principal balance of subprime and Alt-A mortgages outstanding at $2.4 trillion, less than half the actual number at the time. Based on this assessment, when they applied a stress scenario in which housing prices declined about 30 percent, they still found that "the aggregate losses in the residential mortgage market under the 'stressed' housing conditions could be about $240 billion, which is manageable, assuming it materializes over a five- to six-year horizon." In the end, of course, the losses were much larger, and were recognized under mark-to-market accounting (discussed in chapter 12) almost immediately, rather than over a five- to six-year period. But the failure of these two analysts to recognize the sheer size of the subprime and Alt-A market, even as late as 2007, is the important point.

It seems reasonably clear where the Lehman analysts went wrong. Under the "stressed" housing conditions they applied, they projected that the GSEs would suffer aggregate losses of $9.5 billion (net of mortgage insurance coverage) and that their guarantee fee income would be more than sufficient to cover these losses. The basis for this spectacularly low estimate had to be the GSEs' own estimate of the subprime mortgages they held, which of course was far below the actual number. In Fannie's credit profile for the second quarter of 2009, showing its exposures as of June 30, 2009, Fannie estimated that it had subprime loans with a value of $7.9 billion, but its exposures to mortgages with FICO scores of less than 660 totaled

$358 billion—about 45 times as much. Based on known capital losses and support from the Treasury to keep the GSEs solvent, the GSEs' credit losses alone would eventually total less than $260 billion (the Treasury's contributions plus the GSE capital that was wiped out)— more than twenty-six times the Lehman analysts' September 2007 estimate. The analysts could only make such a colossal error if they had not realized that 37 percent—or $1.65 trillion—of the GSEs' credit risk portfolio consisted of NTMs (see Table 1.1) or that these weak loans would account for about 75 percent of Fannie's credit losses over 2008–2010.[15] It is also instructive to compare the Lehman analysts' estimate that the 2006 vintage of subprime loans would suffer lifetime losses of 19 percent under "stressed" conditions to other analysts' later and more informed estimates. In early 2010, for example, Moody's made a similar estimate for the 2006 vintage and projected a 38 percent loss rate after the 30 percent decline in housing prices had actually occurred.[16]

Another example is a much more downbeat projection for the future of the U.S. housing market by BCA Research in September 2007. This analysis began, "We conclude that the housing downturn is not even at the halfway point yet in terms of duration. There is still plenty of downside for housing sales and starts, which will play out over the next 2–3 years. Perhaps more importantly, nominal home prices will experience the largest decline in the postwar period. Nationally, home prices have fallen by 3 1/2 %, but could fall another 10–15% before it is over."[17] Still, this analysis concluded that subprime and Alt-A mortgages accounted for about 20 percent of the U.S. market, well below half of the actual amount.[18]

The Lehman loss rate projection suggests that the analysts did not have an accurate estimate of the number of NTMs actually outstanding in 2006. The BCA projection—even as late as 2007—shows explicitly that the analysts did not have accurate data. Indeed, I have not found any studies in the period before the financial crisis in which anyone—scholar or financial analyst—actually seemed to know how many NTMs were in the financial system at the time. Even well after the BNP Paribas announcement, respected academic analysts of the housing market were still using subprime numbers drawn from the GSEs' self-serving conclusion that the only subprime mortgages they held were those they acquired from subprime lenders.[19]

The mortgage market is studied constantly by thousands of analysts, academics, regulators, traders, and investors. How could all these experts have missed something as important as the actual number of NTMs outstanding? One of the reasons could have been sheer bone-headed ignorance. Nobel Laureate Paul Krugman, for example, informed his *New York Times* readers on July 14, 2008, that Fannie and Freddie "didn't do any subprime lending, because they can't: the definition of a subprime loan is precisely a loan that doesn't meet the requirement, imposed by law, that Fannie and Freddie buy only mortgages issued to borrowers who made substantial down payments and carefully documented their income."[20]

Happily, most market participants were at least a step above this level of misplaced certitude and appear to have merely assumed in the bubble years that Fannie and Freddie continued to adhere to the same conservative underwriting policies they had previously pursued. Until Fannie and Freddie were required to meet the affordable-housing goals, they rarely acquired subprime or other low-quality mortgages. Indeed, the very definition of a traditional prime mortgage was a loan that Fannie and Freddie would buy.[21] Lower-quality loans were rejected and were ultimately insured by the Federal Housing Administration or made by a relatively small group of subprime originators and investors.

It was only after the financial crisis, when Edward Pinto began gathering the relevant data from various unrelated and disparate sources, that the total number of NTMs in the financial market became clear. As a result, all loss projections and assignments of responsibility before Pinto's work were bound to be faulty.

Although anyone who followed HUD's affordable-housing regulations and thought through their implications should have realized that Fannie and Freddie must have been shifting their buying activities to low-quality loans, few people had incentives to uncover this new buying pattern. Indeed, I was one of those who failed to see the significance of the affordable-housing goals. I had been holding conferences and writing about Fannie and Freddie for several years, beginning in 1999, and did not realize that meeting the affordable-housing goals required them to reduce their underwriting standards and take greater credit risks. I saw them taking substantial interest rate risks with the immense portfolios of mortgages they were accumulating, but none of the academics and housing policy experts I had been consulting even mentioned the possibility that they might be taking significant credit risks. I now believe that these experts, too, were unaware that the affordable-housing goals required that the GSEs substantially change their mortgage acquisition standards —although in retrospect it should have been obvious. Much to my subsequent embarrassment, I even organized conferences at the American Enterprise Institute to address the fact that the GSEs, despite their government subsidies, were not aggressively pursuing the affordable-housing goals.

In 2008, the GSEs' then regulator, the Office of Federal Housing Enterprise Oversight (OFHEO), reported to Congress on the GSEs' purchases of whole mortgages and PMBS from 1990 to the fourth quarter of 2007.[22] The report noted "a virtual collapse of the primary and secondary markets for subprime and nontraditional mortgages" but never managed to say how many NTMs the GSEs were actually exposed to.[23] In the extensive tables accompanying the report, the OFHEO showed the GSEs' purchases and exposure to both whole loans and PMBS, but did not differentiate between prime loans and NTMs or provide information about the GSEs' exposure to NTMs through the PMBS they had acquired. Whether the OFHEO, a subordinate agency within HUD, was tailoring its disclosures to minimize the differences between prime and subprime loans is a question for the future.

FINALLY THE TRUTH, BUT TOO LATE

When Fannie voluntarily began filing reports with the Securities and Exchange Commission (SEC) in 2003, it disclosed in tables at the back of its reports that 16 percent of its credit obligations on mortgages had FICO scores of 660 or less—as described earlier, the banking regulators' definition of a subprime loan. No one at the time seemed to pay much attention to this disclosure, however, even though two years had passed since the bank regulators had declared that a FICO score at that level would classify a loan as subprime. Fannie certainly did not point this out in its 2003 filing, and didn't abide by it either. Moreover, in its 2005 10-K (not filed with the SEC until May 2, 2007), when it was exposed to $311 billion in subprime loans, Fannie reported that "the percentage of our single-family mortgage credit book of business consisting of subprime mortgage loans or structured Fannie Mae MBS [mortgage-backed securities] backed by subprime mortgage loans was *not material* as of December 31, 2005" [emphasis added].[24] Finally, in the credit supplement to its 2008 10-K, Fannie included loans with FICO scores of 660 or below among the "key features" of its mortgage exposures, for the first time implying that loans with borrower FICO scores at that level were not considered prime loans.[25]

Fannie was able to avoid admitting to this fact for as long as it did because, as noted earlier, it defined subprime loans as loans it purchased from subprime lenders or loans that were specifically sold to it as subprime loans. Thus, in its 2007 10-K report, Fannie stated: "Subprime mortgage loans are typically originated by lenders specializing in these loans or by subprime divisions of large lenders, using processes unique to subprime loans. In reporting our subprime exposure, *we have classified mortgage loans as subprime if the mortgage loans are originated by one of these specialty lenders or a subprime division of a large lender*" [emphasis added].[26] The credit scores on these loans, and the riskiness associated with these credit scores, were not deemed relevant. Accordingly, as late as its 2007 10-K report, Fannie considered itself free to make the following statements, even though it is likely that at that point it held or guaranteed enough subprime loans to drive the company into insolvency if a substantial number of these loans were to default:

> Subprime mortgage loans, whether held in our portfolio or backing Fannie Mae MBS, represented *less than 1%* of our single-family business volume in each of 2007, 2006 and 2005 [emphasis added].[27]

> We estimate that subprime mortgage loans held in our port-
> folio or subprime mortgage loans backing Fannie Mae MBS
> ... represented approximately *0.3% of our single-family mort-*
> *gage credit book of business* as of December 31, 2007, com-
> pared with 0.2% and 0.1% as of December 31, 2006 and 2005,
> respectively [emphasis added].[28]

These statements could have lulled market participants and others—including the Lehman and BCA Research analysts and perhaps
the Federal Reserve, the rating agencies, and other analysts who
study the housing markets—into believing that Fannie and Freddie
did not hold or had not guaranteed substantial numbers of high-risk
loans and thus that there were many fewer such loans in the financial
system than in fact there were at the time.

Of course, in the early 2000s, apart from the bank regulators'
ruling, there was no generally understood definition of the term
"subprime," so Fannie and Freddie could define it as they liked; the
widespread but false assumption that the GSEs only made prime
loans was consistent with their public disclosures. So when lenders reported that they had sold loans to the GSEs, these loans were
automatically classified as prime loans by the data aggregators that
kept the market's records. These reports jibed with GSEs' records,
so the aggregators continued to follow industry practice by placing
virtually all the GSEs' loans in the "prime" category, except those
specifically denominated as subprime or Alt-A by the GSEs. Without
understanding the GSEs' peculiar and self-serving loan classification
methods, the recipients of information about the GSEs' mortgage
positions simply seemed to assume that all these mortgages were
prime loans, as they had always been in the past, and added them to
the number of prime loans outstanding. Accordingly, by 2008 there
were approximately 20 million more NTMs in the financial system—
and 20 million fewer prime loans—than most market participants
realized.

As a member of the FCIC, I had an opportunity to question the
few witnesses who came before the commission in public hearings.

Whenever appropriate, I asked analysts and market participants whether they knew that 25 million subprime and Alt-A mortgages—the number I was aware of at that point through Pinto's early work—were outstanding in the U.S. financial system before the financial crisis occurred. It was clear from their responses that none of the witnesses had any idea what that number was, and it appeared that none suspected that the number was large enough to substantially affect losses after the collapse of the bubble. Oddly, even though 25 million was a striking number, and I used it frequently when questioning witnesses in publicly televised hearings, I never received a question about it from anyone in the media, and the number never appeared in any mainstream media report about a public FCIC hearing. It is still a puzzle why no reporter was interested in where I'd gotten this number or whether any understood its significance for the causes of the financial crisis. The lack of curiosity in the media about what actually happened in the financial crisis is still, to this day, a mystery to me. It could have been based on sloth, stupidity, or ideological factors, but this failure was also a major contributing factor to the conventional view that the financial crisis was caused by insufficient regulation of the financial system. In theory, an independent media is supposed to question the government's efforts to avoid blame for events like the financial crisis; in this case the media was an enabler of the government's cover-up.

It was only on November 10, 2008, after Fannie had been taken over by the federal government, that the company admitted in its 10-Q report for the third quarter of 2008 that it had classified as subprime or Alt-A only those loans that it purchased from self-denominated subprime or Alt-A originators, and not loans that were subprime or Alt-A because of their risk characteristics. Even then Fannie was less than candid. After describing its classification criteria, Fannie stated, "However, we have other loans with some features that are similar to Alt-A and subprime loans that we have not classified as Alt-A or subprime because they do not meet our classification criteria."[29] Still, no one seemed curious enough about their classification criteria to ask them to explain what that sentence meant.

All this information was available to the FCIC, which was put on notice by Pinto's memoranda, but the FCIC leadership wasn't interested. An extensive and thorough staff study was made of misleading disclosure in private securitizations[30]—which in total had resulted in about one-quarter of all the NTM loans that were dragging down the economy—but no investigation at all of whether the GSEs had been truthful with investors about the degree of their NTM exposure or indeed candid with the FCIC itself when Fannie Mae informed the commission that its aggregate exposure to subprime mortgages amounted to 3 million loans. Alone among the financial regulatory agencies, the SEC took an interest in the truthfulness of the GSEs' disclosures. In December 2011, the SEC sued top officers of Fannie Mae and Freddie Mac for failing to adequately disclose the risky nature of their NTM exposures. Because the companies were now in effect owned by the taxpayers, they were not made defendants, but, as described in chapter 3, both Fannie and Freddie signed nonprosecution agreements with the SEC in which they admitted that they had recognized the inherent riskiness of some mortgages they had acquired, that they had kept track of these loans separately from others, and that they had never disclosed them as subprime or Alt-A.[31] At this writing, the suit is still pending.

It is almost incomprehensible that in a financial system as fully covered as this one by analysts, academics, financial media, government officials, regulators, and investors, something as large and potentially destructive as the presence of more than 32 million NTMs could have escaped notice. Clearly, one of the reasons for this is that Fannie Mae and Freddie Mac were very unusual critters. They were thought, correctly, to be backed by the U.S. government, so they presented little risk of loss to fixed-income investors. They were regulated for safety and soundness by the federal government, which might have lulled their public shareholders into believing that someone was keeping track of their risk-taking—another example, if we needed one, that regulation itself creates moral hazard. When they voluntarily began to disclose financial positions in filings with the SEC, their disclosures were initially insufficient and misleading. Until they were required by the affordable-housing goals to change their mortgage purchasing practices, they had always been conservative investors in mortgages, and they gave no indication in their public disclosures that the affordable-housing requirements were modifying their traditional business model. Finally, they dealt in U.S. mortgages that had once been famous around the world for their quality as investments.

COULD IT HAVE BEEN DIFFERENT?

All these factors allowed Fannie and Freddie to evade the usual scrutiny of the market until it was too late. Although their creditors were saved by the government, the millions of NTMs they had acquired were the basis for a mortgage meltdown that took virtually everyone by surprise—and was more destructive for that reason. If analysts, academics, or investors had understood the size of the NTM bomb that Fannie and Freddie were building, could things have been different? It is always treacherous to deal in counterfactuals and "what ifs," but perhaps if the GSEs had revealed the true quality of their exposures, the bubble would not have grown so big, because hedge funds and others would have begun earlier to use credit default swaps to sell the market short and thus dampen the building enthusiasm; the rating agencies might have recognized that a market with 31 million NTMs is a much riskier market than one with less than a quarter of that number; the Bush administration might have been able to move Congress for stronger regulation sooner; the affordable-housing goals might have been modified, or at least HUD might have moderated its pressure for tighter and broader affordable-housing goals; the banks and other financial institutions, recognizing the risk, might have shed some of their mortgage assets; and the chair of the Federal Reserve, or the director of their former regulator, OFHEO, with timely testimony to congressional committees, might have been able to alert Congress and the public to the danger of large numbers of NTMs accumulating in the financial system. That none of these things happened is largely attributable to the lack of rigor in the definitions of NTMs used in the housing finance market, HUD's effort to erase the line between prime and subprime mortgages, and the willingness of the managements of Fannie and Freddie to mislead investors about their true exposure to mortgage risk.

In the next chapter, we will see that the lack of information in the market, combined with the tendency of investors to withdraw from markets when they don't have the information they need, led to financial crisis.

11

31 Million Nontraditional Mortgages Precipitate a Crisis

Why Even Government-Backed Mortgage Securities Were Contributors

> You only find out who is swimming naked
> when the tide goes out.
>
> WARREN BUFFETT, Berkshire Hathaway
> chairman's letter, 2001

One question that should be asked about the financial crisis is how the defaults on the nontraditional mortgages (NTMs) acquired by the government-sponsored enterprises (GSEs) caused investor losses; after all, the GSEs were backed by the government, and the government made all their investors whole. So how did the GSEs' acquisition of NTMs—no matter how many they acquired—cause or even contribute to the financial crisis? This chapter will explain the relationship between the large number of NTMs the GSEs had acquired and the financial crisis that ensued when those mortgages began to default.

From what was discussed in the last chapter, it should now be understandable why the high levels of delinquency and default that became apparent to market participants and regulators in 2007 and 2008 were such a shock; we also know why there were so many NTMs in the financial system in those years and that at least three-quarters of these were on the books of government agencies—primarily Fannie Mae and Freddie Mac. What is not yet clear is how the NTMs that were largely on government books did so much damage to private financial institutions that a major financial crisis was the result. To begin to answer this question, it seems most appropriate to start with Ben Bernanke's description of the crisis in a speech at Morehouse College in April 2009:

> The credit boom began to unravel in early 2007 when problems surfaced with subprime mortgages—mortgages offered to less-creditworthy borrowers—and house prices in parts of the country began to fall. Mortgage delinquencies and defaults rose, and the downturn in house prices intensified, trends that continue today. Investors, stunned by losses on assets they had believed to be safe, began to pull back from a wide range of credit markets, and financial institutions—reeling from severe losses on mortgages and other loans—cut back their lending. The crisis deepened [in September 2008], when the failure or near-failure of several major financial firms caused many financial and credit markets to freeze up.[1]

Of course, this summary of the causes of the financial crisis is a bit like saying the cause of World War II was Germany's invasion of Poland; it misses a few of the preliminaries. Still, the summary makes clear that the precipitating cause of the financial crisis was a rapid decline in the value of one specific and widely held asset: U.S. residential mortgages. From the previous chapters, we know that the number of NTMs in the U.S. financial system was largely the result of U.S. government housing policy and that the overwhelming majority of these loans were held by Fannie and Freddie or other government agencies, but how exactly did mortgages that were on the government's books cause what Bernanke called "severe losses" for financial institutions in the United States and around the world?

We can assume, first, that the early mortgage defaults that began to show up in 2007 were occurring among NTMs. As shown by the Mortgage Bankers Association's National Delinquency Survey, prime mortgages did not suffer substantial losses at the outset of the mortgage meltdown, although, as the financial crisis turned into a severe recession and housing prices continued to fall, losses among prime mortgages began to rise to levels much higher than in the past.[2] We also know from the Freddie dataset that many mortgages considered "prime" in and after 1999 did not meet prime mortgage standards as outlined in chapter 2. Still, those losses were far lower than the losses on NTMs, which—as Table 7.5 shows—reached levels of delinquency between 13 and 45 percent because the loans involved were weaker as a class and larger in number than in any previous housing crisis. It was the number and not the dollar value of failing NTMs that mattered, because it was the number of delinquencies and defaults that caused the catastrophic housing price declines and fueled the financial crisis.

HOW RISING PRICES DISGUISED MORTGAGE WEAKNESS

When the housing bubble began to deflate in mid-2007, delinquency rates among NTMs increased substantially. Although these mortgages were weak and high risk, they had relatively low delinquency rates. That was a consequence of the bubble itself, which, as discussed earlier, inflated housing prices so that homes could be refinanced or sold with no loss in cases where borrowers could not meet their mortgage obligations. Rising housing prices—coupled with liberal appraisal rules—created a form of free equity in a home, allowing it to be easily refinanced, perhaps even at a lower interest rate. However, rising housing prices eventually reached the point where even easy credit terms could no longer keep the good times rolling, and at that point the bubble flattened and weak mortgages became exposed for what they were. As Warren Buffett suggested in the epigraph at the beginning of this chapter, when the tide goes out, the truth is exposed.

The role of the government's housing policy was crucial at this point. As discussed earlier, if the government had not been directing money into the mortgage markets, NTMs in the bubble would have begun to default relatively soon after they were originated. Following the Minsky model, however, the continuous inflow of government or government-backed funds kept the bubble growing—not only in size but over time—and this tended to suppress the significant delinquencies and defaults that had brought previous bubbles to an end in only three or four years. That explains why private mortgage–backed securities (PMBS) based on NTMs could become so numerous and so risky without triggering the delinquencies and defaults that had caused earlier bubbles to deflate within a shorter period. With few losses and time to continue originations, Countrywide and others were able to securitize subprime PMBS in increasingly large amounts, especially from 2002 to 2006, without causing the substantial increase in delinquencies that would ordinarily have alarmed investors and brought the bubble to a halt.

Indeed, the absence of large numbers of delinquencies had the opposite effect. As institutional investors in the United States and around the world saw housing prices rise in the United States without any significant losses even among subprime and other high-yielding loans, they were encouraged to buy AAA-rated PMBS based on NTMs that offered attractive yields with little apparent risk. As shown in Table 11.1, PMBS issuances backed by NTMs began to

TABLE 11.1. Issuance of PMBS and GSE purchases of PMBS, 1997–2007 ($ billions)

Year	Prime	Subprime	Alt-A	GSE purchases
1997	49.9	56.9	6.5	6.0
1998	97.3	75.8	21.2	31.4
1999	74.6	55.8	12.0	31.8
2000	53.5	52.4	16.4	18.8
2001	142.2	87.1	11.4	28.0
2002	171.5	122.7	53.5	66.9
2003	237.4	195.0	74.1	103.1
2004	233.4	362.5	158.6	211.7
2005	280.7	465.0	332.3	221.3
2006	219.0	448.6	365.7	180.0
2007	180.5	201.5	249.6	113.5

Sources: PMBS data from *Inside Mortgage Finance*, Non-Agency Issuance by Type; GSE Purchases of PMBS from the Office of Federal Housing Enterprise Oversight 2008 Report to Congress.

outstrip PMBS backed by prime loans in 2002 and continued to grow in relation to prime loans until the PMBS market fell apart in 2007. In other words, by encouraging the growth of the bubble, the government's housing policies increased the worldwide demand for PMBS based on NTMs. By 2008, according to Table 1.1, PMBS backed by NTMs and held by private-sector institutions and investors totaled 7.8 million loans, about 24 percent of all the NTMs outstanding.

DEFLATION OF THE BUBBLE AND THE FINANCIAL CRISIS

The best summary of how the deflation of the housing bubble led to the financial crisis was contained in the prepared testimony that FDIC chair Sheila Bair delivered to the Financial Crisis Inquiry Commission (FCIC) in a September 2, 2010, hearing:

Starting in mid 2007, global financial markets began to experience serious liquidity challenges related mainly to rising concerns about U.S. mortgage credit quality. As home prices fell, recently originated subprime and non-traditional mortgage loans began to default at record rates. These developments led to growing concerns about the value of financial positions in mortgage-backed securities and related derivative instruments held by major financial institutions in the U.S. and around the world. The difficulty in determining the value of mortgage-related assets and, therefore, the balance-sheet strength of large banks and non-bank financial institutions ultimately led these institutions to become wary of lending to one another, even on a short-term basis.[3]

All the important elements of what happened are present in this succinct statement. The liquidity and solvency challenges she mentioned were the result of the market's sudden concern—as housing prices began to fall—about the credit quality of NTMs. As delinquencies and defaults among NTMs began to occur at unprecedented and unexpected rates, it became difficult to determine the value of PMBS and thus the financial condition of the institutions that held them. Finally, as a consequence of all this uncertainty—especially after the failure of Lehman Brothers—financial institutions became wary of lending to one another. That phenomenon *was* the financial crisis. The following discussion will show how each of these steps operated to bring down the financial system.

The decline of housing prices

All mortgages are connected through home prices. The importance of loan-to-value (LTV) ratios tells us that there is a very strong relationship between home prices and mortgage quality. When home prices are rising, mortgages become stronger because the homeowner has more equity in the home. With more equity, the homeowner can weather deeper declines in house prices and still have an incentive keep the home. Conversely, when home prices fall, mortgages become weaker; there is a greater chance that a mortgage will default because the homeowner has less of a stake in the home; if the decline in home prices is the result of a general recessionary trend in the economy, the chances of job losses among homeowners increases; and if the homeowner defaults, the chances that the holder of the mortgage will recover the full amount of the loan are diminished. Thus, as the great housing bubble flattened out and began to deflate in early 2007, the likelihood of defaults increased, and mortgages grew weaker as investments.

But there is an even closer relationship between mortgage defaults and the value of homes that is a characteristic of mortgages not present with other assets. If a credit card holder defaults on his or her obligations, it has little effect on other credit card holders, but if a homeowner defaults on a mortgage, the resulting foreclosure has an adverse effect on the value of all homes in the vicinity and thus on the quality of all mortgages on those homes. This occurs through appraisals, which use prices on comparable homes to estimate the value of a home for purchase or refinancing, and through a general lowering of the quality of a neighborhood when there are abandoned and foreclosed homes in the area. Also, of course, the adverse effect comes through simple supply and demand. A foreclosed home is now available for sale, and the financial institution that holds the foreclosed property is usually willing to sell quickly and at an attractive price to keep the property from deteriorating further.

Thus, as home prices throughout the United States began to decline in early 2007, mortgage values also declined, and as the process continued more and more mortgages became delinquent and defaulted—beginning, of course, with NTMs, which were weak to begin with. This initiated a downward spiral, with falling housing prices causing an increase in the number of mortgage defaults, increasing mortgage defaults causing more foreclosures and abandoned homes, and backlogs of unsold and abandoned homes causing more housing price declines and more mortgage defaults. Note that this effect occurred even though most of the mortgages were held or guaranteed by the federal government. The government protected investors, but it did not protect homeowners or their neighbors against the consequences of many local foreclosures and the resulting decline in home prices.

Because at least 76 percent of the NTMs outstanding were held, insured, or guaranteed by government agencies, the defaults on these loans were likely to be geographically widespread and would thus have had the most substantial effect—through the recursive system described above—in weakening other outstanding mortgages and home values on a nationwide basis. This was the simple transmission mechanism through which the losses on mortgages in government-backed MBS increased the losses on the PMBS, which were held by banks and investors in the United States and around the world. The larger the number of defaults among the mortgages that were in GSE pools, the lower the value of the houses and the mortgages that backed the PMBS—and, of course, the failure of mortgages underlying the PMBS reflected back on and increased the delinquencies and defaults on mortgages and mortgage-backed securities held by the GSEs or other government agencies.

The vulnerability of PMBS to investor sentiment
The fact that the mortgages underlying the PMBS were held in securitized form was also an important element of the crisis. There are many reasons securitization is a popular way to finance mortgages.

MBS are attractive to investors because, as securities, they are far more liquid than whole mortgages and can be easily sold if an investor wants to rebalance a portfolio in response to events in the economy. Moreover, for roughly the same reason, it was also easier and could be very profitable to finance a portfolio of MBS with short-term loans that were likely to be substantially less costly than the long-term interest rates the mortgage holder was receiving on the MBS. The attractive features of MBS were enhanced in 2002, when the Basel risk-based capital regulations were modified to reduce to 1.6 percent the capital that banks were required to hold when they invested in highly rated MBS (GSE-backed MBS or AAA- or AA-rated PMBS). With this inducement, banks were encouraged—perhaps "herded" would be a better term—to make substantial investments in mortgages that began to lose substantial value in 2007.

However, some of the benefits of securitized mortgages are also detriments when certain mortgage market conditions prevail. If housing values are declining, losses on whole mortgages—because they are not actively traded—are recognized only slowly, if at all, in a bank's financial statements and are recognized even more slowly in the wider market. PMBS, on the other hand, are far more vulnerable to swings in sentiment, for several reasons. First, because PMBS pools differ substantially from one another, PMBS markets tend to be thin (with few buyers and sellers), exacerbating the problem of volatility. In addition, simply because they are bought and sold in public markets, PMBS values can be more quickly and adversely affected by negative information about the underlying mortgages than whole mortgages with the same terms. If investors believe that mortgages in general are declining in value, or if they learn of a substantial and unexpected number of defaults and delinquencies, they may abandon the market for all PMBS until more information is available, causing the general PMBS price level to fall sharply. Finally, the sources of short-term financing for PMBS may be adversely affected by the same lack of information, with short-term lenders withdrawing support—that is, refusing to roll over financing—until the facts are clarified. This seems to be exactly what happened in the PMBS market, as shown in Figure 1.4. Investors, uncertain about which pools were good and which not, simply left the market, causing all pools to lose value.

Record mortgages defaults
and solvency and liquidity challenges

The near-failure of Bear Stearns in March 2008 is an excellent example of how the unexpected collapse of the PMBS market could cause a substantial loss of liquidity for a financial institution and ultimately keep it from surviving the resulting loss in market confidence. The FCIC staff's review of the liquidity problems of Bear Stearns, in a Preliminary Investigative Report prepared for hearings in May 2010, showed that the loss of the PMBS market was the single event that was crippling for Bear, because it eliminated a major portion of the firm's liquidity pool, a substantial portion of which were AAA-rated PMBS. Bear used these AAA securities to borrow short-term funds, often overnight. According to the report, 97.4 percent of Bear's short-term funding was secured and only 2.6 percent unsecured. "As of January 11, 2008," the FCIC staff noted, "$45.9 billion of Bear Stearns' repo [repurchase agreement] collateral was composed of agency (Fannie and Freddie) mortgage-related securities, $23.7 billion was in non-agency securitized asset backed securities [i.e., PMBS], and $19 billion was in whole loans."[4] The agency MBS were unaffected by the collapse of the PMBS market and could still be used for funding, but the PMBS could not.

Thus, about 27 percent of Bear's readily available sources of funding, primarily through AAA-rated PMBS, became unusable for repurchase agreement financing when the PMBS market disappeared. The sudden loss of this source of liquidity put the firm in serious jeopardy; rumors swept the market about Bear's condition, and clients began withdrawing funds. Bear's officers told the FCIC that the firm was profitable in its first 2008 quarter—the quarter in which it failed; ironically, they also told the staff that they had in recent years moved all Bear's short-term funding from commercial paper to MBS because they believed that collateral-backed funding would be more stable. In the week beginning March 10, 2008, according to the FCIC staff report, Bear had over $18 billion in cash reserves, but by March 13 the liquidity pool had fallen to $2 billion.[5] It was clear that Bear—solvent and profitable or not—could not survive a run that was fueled by fear and uncertainty about its liquidity and solvency. Accordingly, the only way that the firm could avoid bankruptcy was through an acquisition by JPMorgan Chase, with an agreement by the Federal Reserve to assume the risk of a $29 billion pool of PMBS.

Financial institutions become wary of lending to one another

Bair also pointed to the relationship between the decline in the value of PMBS and "the balance-sheet strength" of financial institutions that held these assets. Adding to liquidity-based losses, balance sheet write-downs were another major mechanism for the transmission of loss. As discussed in the next chapter on fair-value (mark-to-market) accounting, securitized assets held by financial institutions are subject to accounting rules that require securities to be marked to market prices under certain circumstances. Since the market was no longer functioning, either there were no prices for many pools of PMBS, or, if prices existed, they were at distress levels. These rules, for reasons that have never been adequately explained, were not suspended by the SEC when the market stopped functioning. Thus, banks and other financial institutions that were holding securitized mortgages in the form of PMBS were subject to large *accounting* losses—but not necessarily cash losses—when investor sentiment turned against securitized mortgages and market values collapsed. Once large numbers of delinquencies and losses started showing up in the financial news, it was not necessary for cash losses to be realized before the PMBS lost substantial value. All that was necessary was that the market for these assets become seriously impaired. This is exactly what happened in the middle of 2007, which led immediately not only to severe adverse liquidity consequences for financial institutions that held PMBS but also to capital write-downs that made them *appear* unstable and possibly insolvent.

Mark-to-market capital losses, as it turned out, could be greater than the actual credit losses that resulted. As one Federal Reserve study put it,

> The financial turmoil . . . put downward pressure on prices of structured finance products across the whole spectrum of [asset-backed] securities, even those with only minimal ties to the riskiest underlying assets. . . . [I]n addition to discounts from higher expected credit risk, large mark-to-market discounts are generated by uncertainty about the quality of the underlying assets, by illiquidity, and by price volatility. . . . This illiquidity discount is the main reason why the mark-to-market discount here, and in most similar analyses, is larger than the expected credit default rates on underlying assets.[6]

In other words, the illiquidity discount associated with the uncertainties about the value of collateral could be substantially larger than the credit default spread because the spread reflects only anticipated credit losses.

As shown so dramatically in Figure 1.4, the collapse of the market for PMBS was a seminal event in the history of the financial crisis. Even though delinquencies had only just begun to show up in mortgage pools, the absence of a functioning market meant that PMBS simply could not be sold at anything but distress prices. The inability of financial institutions to liquidate their PMBS assets other than at distress values had dire consequences, especially under mark-to-market accounting rules. In effect, a whole class of assets—involving almost $2 trillion—came to be called "toxic assets" in the media and had to be written down substantially on the balance sheets of financial institutions around the world. Although this made financial institutions look weaker than they actually were, the PMBS they held, despite being unmarketable at that point, were in many cases still flowing cash at close to expected rates. Instead of a slow decline in value—which would have occurred if whole mortgages were held on bank balance sheets and gradually deteriorated in quality—the loss of marketability of these securities caused a crash in value.

The investor panic that began when unanticipated and unprecedented losses started to appear both among NTMs generally and in the PMBS mortgage pools now spread to financial institutions themselves; investors were no longer sure which of these institutions could survive severe mortgage-related losses, even though those losses had not yet materialized. This process was succinctly described in an analysis of fair-value or mark-to-market accounting in the financial crisis issued by the Institute of International Finance, an organization of the world's largest banks and financial firms:

> [O]ften-dramatic write-downs of *sound* assets required under the current implementation of fair-value accounting adversely affect market sentiment, in turn leading to further write-downs, margin calls and capital impacts in a downward spiral that may lead to large-scale fire-sales of assets, and destabilizing, pro-cyclical feedback effects. These damaging feedback effects worsen liquidity problems and contribute to the conversion of liquidity problems into solvency problems [emphasis in the original].[7]

COLLATERAL DAMAGE

In summary, then, these are the steps through which the government's housing policies transmitted losses to the largest financial institutions:

1. The 24 million NTMs acquired or guaranteed by government agencies were major contributors to the growth of the bubble and its extension in time.

2. The growth of the bubble suppressed the losses that would ordinarily have brought the development of NTM-backed PMBS to a halt and made these instruments look like good investments.

3. When the bubble finally burst, the unprecedented number of delinquencies and defaults among all NTMs—the majority of which were held or guaranteed by the government agencies— drove down housing prices.

4. Falling home prices produced losses on mortgages, whether they were in GSE-backed securities or PMBS.

5. Losses on mortgages caused investors to flee the PMBS market, reducing the liquidity of the financial institutions that held the PMBS.

6. Mark-to-market accounting required these institutions to write down the value of the PMBS they held, as well as their other mortgage-related assets, reducing their capital positions and raising further questions about their stability and solvency.

In this way, a poorly conceived and executed government housing policy brought ruin to private-sector financial institutions that were, in several senses, what might be called collateral damage. The next chapter, on mark-to-market accounting, will explain in greater detail how this collateral damage came about.

12

Fair-Value Accounting Scales Up the Crisis

How Mark-to-Market Accounting Made Financial Firms Look Weak or Unstable

> Fair value accounting dictates that financial institutions holding financial instruments available for sale (such as mortgage-backed securities) must mark those assets to market. That sounds reasonable. But what do we do when the already thin market for those assets freezes up and only a handful of transactions occur at extremely depressed prices?
>
> WILLIAM M. ISAAC, former chair of the Federal Deposit Insurance Corporation

In the previous two chapters, we saw the importance of information to the functioning of the market. Where it is missing it tends to produce panic. Investing or buying and selling are not for the fainthearted. In this chapter, which covers mark-to-market accounting, we will see that otherwise accurate information can be distorted by what are essentially government regulatory decisions about how it can be used.

When the French investment bank BNP Paribas announced that it would no longer allow investors to redeem their shares in BNP-sponsored investment funds, it noted that "the complete evaporation of liquidity in certain market segments of the U.S. securitization market has made it impossible to value certain assets fairly regardless of their quality or credit rating."[1] On that day, the LIBOR-OIS spread—a measure of risk in the money markets—jumped from 10 basis points, where it had been since at least the beginning of the year, to almost 100. It remained elevated all through the subsequent crisis, but at this early stage the high money market spread reflected little more than an inchoate fear, as though the market was being stalked by an unseen specter.

The first reaction of policy makers was to see the problem as one of liquidity. The Federal Reserve, seeing the market's nervousness as threatening a credit crunch rather than something more serious, and believing bank capital was adequate, cut interest rates in late August by a half point, and cut them again by another half point in mid-September. Indeed, as transcripts of the Board of Governors meetings show, the Federal Reserve did not take the threat of a mortgage melt-down seriously until the crisis was fully under way. Many academic critics have argued that the Federal Reserve was slow off the mark in recognizing that the problems in the market were solvency problems and not simply a shortage of liquidity. At this point, that judgment seems premature. As discussed in chapter 3, the losses on AAA- and AA-rated private mortgage–backed securities (PMBS) turned out to be far lower than had been feared—estimated by Moody's at about a 4.4 percent impairment. These were not the toxic assets they were said to be. Most of the losses came through CDOs that were retained by many of the financial intermediaries (i.e., lenders like commercial banks and investment banks) that had created them. There has never been an accurate reconstruction of how many losses fell on the intermediaries that retained and were seriously weakened by the CDOs and those that had been acquired by other financial institutions (not intermediaries but principally investors like hedge funds) which had acquired CDOs solely for investment or speculative purposes.

The distinction is important. The financial crisis was primarily the result of the apparent financial weakness of the largest commercial and investment banks in the United States and Europe. Their financial weakness and inability to lend to one another after the Lehman Brothers bankruptcy was what made the crisis so startling and frightening to participants in the financial markets. Because of mark-to-market accounting, which required all financial intermediaries to write down the value of their PMBS assets, including the CDOs, or sell them at distress prices, the losses they apparently suffered were likely to be far greater than the actual losses they would have suffered if the accounting treatment had been different—say, amortized cost or even discounted cash flow. In addition, if most of the real (non-accounting) losses were suffered by the investment community, an enormous capital pool, the financial crisis would have looked more like the collapse of the dot-com bubble in 2000 and 2001, when the losses were taken by investors rather than financial institutions; in that case, there was no financial crisis even though the paper losses were even greater than in the financial crisis. If the losses of the banks were primarily losses attributable to mark-to-market accounting, the financial crisis would look more like a panic than a solvency event that was the result of a collapse in mortgage values. On the other hand, if the intermediaries did take real losses, enough to endanger their highly leveraged capital positions, the financial crisis looks more like the solvency event that academic critics have posited. At this point, because of the distortions introduced by mark-to-market accounting and an insufficiency of relevant information, it is too early to tell. The losses that were to come as mortgages became delinquent and defaulted were certainly real, but their actual size and their effect on financial institutions and the economy were magnified by new accounting rules for financial institutions that had been adopted only a little over a decade before by the Financial Accounting Standards Board (FASB)—a small group of financial accounting experts to whom the Securities and Exchange Commission (SEC) had delegated the power to set U.S. accounting standards. As suggested above, the effect of these new rules was a major element of the financial crisis that has never been adequately explored.

THE GENESIS OF FAS 115

Despite its reputation as boring and formulaic, financial accounting is a highly conceptual activity. The configuration of a financial statement, for example, is determined by two fundamental but frequently unstated questions: what is the purpose of, and who is the audience for, a financial report? If its purpose is to inform investors, it is likely to focus on the income statement, which is the principal interest of equity investors. However, if its purpose is to inform creditors, the financial report is likely to focus on the balance sheet, which is of more interest to creditors. Bank holding companies—that is, companies that control banks—register their securities with the SEC, which sees its role as ensuring that equity investors—those who buy and sell shares in the securities markets—have the most accurate and fairly presented information concerning the firm's earnings. To the SEC, the market value of a firm's assets at any point in time is of lesser value. On the other hand, creditors (and bank regulators) are more interested in the long-term stability and solvency of financial institutions, so to them day-to-day changes in asset values are not as important as their long-term values. They prefer to focus on the balance sheet and what it says about an institution's ability to meet its financial obligations over time. Thus, in the 1990s a largely unobserved struggle broke out between bank regulators and the SEC about the use of fair-value accounting for banks and bank holding companies.

In November 1990, for example, the chair of the Federal Reserve, Alan Greenspan, wrote to Richard Breeden, the chair of the SEC, "Only about one-third, on average, of banks' assets have ready market values," Greenspan observed. "The adoption of market value accounting for a portion of the bank balance sheet, such as all or a substantial component of investment securities . . . could result in volatility in reported earnings and capital that is not indicative of the bank's true financial condition."[2] Indeed, as one academic study pointed out twenty years later, at a time of market stress, fair-value or mark-to-market accounting can have serious adverse effects on public confidence:

> From a supervisor's perspective, fair value can have a number of potentially negative impacts on capital when applied to long-term assets and most liabilities. Investors are also not immune to these effects. Under volatile market conditions, fair value can cause earnings and capital to appear and disap-

pear quarter over quarter. Fair value estimates can generate public uncertainty in the absence of market-derived prices or transparent modeling approaches. It has the potential to produce excess volatility that can result in pro-cyclical effects during both economic upswings and downswings. . . . [C]apital is expected to play a critical stabilizing role for a financial institution during a crisis. Yet, it is during periods of market stress that fair value can have its most detrimental impact on capital.[3]

The protests of bank regulators, which went on for several years, were to no avail. The SEC's institutional position—favoring the interests of investors—could not be changed. Having delegated to the FASB the authority to determine financial accounting standards, the SEC was in a position to dictate the outcome of the dispute. And it did. Accordingly, in 1993, the FASB adopted Financial Accounting Standard (FAS) 115, which applied a system of "fair value accounting" for "equity securities that have readily determinable fair values and for all investments in debt securities."[4] The inclusion of debt securities would have a major effect on financial institutions such as banks, bank holding companies, insurance companies, finance companies, pension funds, and others that held large amounts of debt securities. By "fair value," the rule generally meant the price that a seller would receive for selling the security into a market, so the fair-value accounting system is often called, more descriptively, "mark-to-market" accounting. Nevertheless, a concession was made to bank regulators: the FASB adopted what was called a mixed-measurement approach, allowing some assets to be valued at historical cost if they were intended to be held to maturity for the cash flows they produced.

Thus three categories of securities assets were established, each with a different method of determining and accounting for value:

1. Securities that the firm "has the positive intent and ability to hold to maturity are classified as *held-to-maturity securities* and reported at amortized cost."

2. Securities bought and held primarily for "selling in the near term are classified as *trading securities* and reported at fair value, with unrealized gains and losses included in earnings."

3. Securities not classified in either of the other two categories "are classified as *available for sale securities* and reported at fair value, with unrealized gains and losses excluded from earnings and reported in a separate component of shareholders' equity" [emphasis in the original].[5]

The FASB cited a mixture of accounting and policy reasons for adopting the fair-value system. As a matter of accounting consistency, it wanted to encourage more uniform reporting about securities assets among different industries—to make their results more comparable—and to prevent management's manipulation of financial reports. But in describing its policy reasons, it was surprisingly diffident: "Some believe," the FASB said, "that fair value information about debt securities is more relevant than amortized cost information in helping users and others assess the effect of current economic events on the enterprise."[6] As a rationale for overturning long-established rules of financial accounting for whole industries, this was hardly a ringing statement of purpose, but future events would call into question whether showing "the effect of current economic events on the enterprise" was really such a good idea. There had been some controversy about the rule within the FASB itself, but not about the overall salutary effect of the fair-value concept.[7] However, there was little indication in the FASB's commentary that the group had seriously considered the procyclicality effects that are built into the mark-to-market idea.

Procyclicality turned out to be the most problematic element of fair-value accounting, and its consequences became apparent almost as soon as the new rules were implemented. As it happens, in the mid-1990s, a developing U.S. housing boom was in its early stages, and it was soon to become a massive housing price bubble. Few observers have connected the housing bubble to the procyclicality inherent in fair-value accounting, but the connection is not hard to draw. As housing prices rose, mortgage defaults declined; borrowers who might otherwise have defaulted were able to refinance their homes with equity created by the rising home prices. Subprime mortgages, which paid higher fees and were charged higher interest rates than prime loans, seemed safer than anticipated, and the yields on a portfolio of MBS based on subprime mortgages were more profitable than a portfolio based on prime mortgages, even when defaults were taken into account. As required by mark-to-market accounting, the *unrealized* gains on the securities went directly to bottom-line earnings when held in a trading account. There seemed no limit to this growth as long as mortgage values kept rising. When the chair of Citigroup, Charles O. Prince, famously said in July 2007, "As long as the music is playing, you've got to get up and dance. We're still dancing," he was probably referring to this phenomenon. The unrealized gains on assets that Citi held in its trading account would continue to aid its bottom line as long as asset values grew in the bubble economy. As described in chapter 9, the mid-1990s housing boom—stimulated initially and pushed along by the government's housing policies—turned into a ten-year housing price bubble, the largest by far in U.S. history. It seems highly likely that the procyclicality built into mark-to-market accounting contributed to this phenomenon. As mortgage values rose, financial firms sought to acquire PMBS for their trading accounts, padding their earnings reports but also feeding the outsized bubble.

Not surprisingly, there was only limited interest in the problem of mark-to-market procyclicality while MBS values were rising. However, when the housing bubble flattened in late 2006 and began to deflate in 2007, procyclicality spread despair instead of joy. Unprecedented numbers of mortgages became delinquent or defaulted when borrowers could no longer refinance their loans, and fear spread through the markets that even the AAA-rated tranches of PMBS pools would suffer serious losses. Investor fear and overreaction to the sudden prospect of losses is a familiar pattern when markets reverse and start to decline, but it was exacerbated by the procyclicality of fair-value accounting. Now, assets in Citi's trading accounts caused unrealized losses and earnings declines rather than gains. Mr. Prince lost his job. In effect, mark-to-market accounting incorporates into the value of securities the effects of the illiquidity that always accompanies declining markets. This phenomenon was discussed in a July 2011 paper issued by the Financial Services Roundtable:

> Over the course of the crisis, financial services firms experienced significant fluctuations in the valuations of portions of their balance sheets which, to varying degrees took their toll on the accounting valuation of equity capital. . . . The reason is that when markets become illiquid, market prices for a period of time tend to be less, and potentially significantly less, than intrinsic value . . . which would prevail in a normal market in which buyers and sellers are not influenced by liquidity or other extraneous factors.
>
> Forced sales in distressed markets can lead to a spiraling-down effect in market prices. Declining prices can trigger additional downward pressure on market prices by precipitating margin calls and risk management policy forced sale requirements, as collateral values and risk grades fall.[8]

Although FAS 115 applied only to equity and fixed-income securities—not to whole mortgages or traditional bank loans—its procyclicality had a substantial adverse effect on both the earnings and the apparent financial condition of banks, which held much of their mortgage investments in the form of PMBS, when the housing and mortgage markets began to deteriorate in 2007. The fact that banks held their assets in securitized form—and were thus subject to mark-to-market accounting—was a direct result of the incentives created by the Basel risk-based capital regulations, an international agreement of bank regulators first adopted in the late 1980s under the auspices of the Bank for International Settlements in Basel, Switzerland. The Basel rules attempted to match the capital of banks to the risks associated with their assets, and established differential capital requirements for different kinds of assets. As described in chapter 3, corporate loans, for example, were considered the most risky, requiring banks to hold 8 percent of the amount of the loan as capital. Sovereign debt was considered the least risky asset, requiring no capital charge; mortgages were somewhere in between. Mortgages held as whole loans required a 4 percent risk-based capital charge, while MBS required only a 1.6 percent charge. This lower capital requirement created a strong incentive for banks to hold mortgages as MBS rather than as whole loans, and it accounts for the highly adverse effect of mark-to-market accounting on banks in particular when housing and mortgage values began to decline.

From the beginning, it was apparent that mark-to-market accounting could have significant effects on earnings and capital. In a rising market it would be advantageous to classify assets as held for trading purposes; unrealized increases in market value were then immediately recognized in earnings. Similarly, if a market were declining, it would be advantageous to classify assets as held to maturity, thus avoiding the recognition of unrealized losses. In order to prevent managements from using these factors to game the system, FAS 115 required that each security's category was to be established at the time it was acquired, and management's ability to move assets from one category to another was strictly limited. Securities originally categorized as held to maturity were still vulnerable to writedowns if their credit quality deteriorated. In that case, they were written down to market value if management determined that their decline in value was an "other than temporary impairment (known as OTTI)." This reduction in asset values would directly reduce the firm's capital. Many conservative banks and other financial institutions carried their securities assets in the middle category, as "held for sale." If the value of these assets rose or fell, it would not affect the all-important bottom line; instead, unrealized gains or losses would go to a special equity account called Other Comprehensive Income (OCI). That treatment would increase shareholders' equity if the asset had gained value, and would reduce it if the asset had lost value.

Accordingly, as the financial industry entered 2007, a substantial portion of the industry's assets was subject to the vicissitudes of the market. If the market for PMBS rose, banks and others would appear more profitable because the assets they held for trading were increasing in value; they also looked healthier because increases in the prices of the PMBS they held for sale were adding to the size of their shareholders' equity accounts. But when unprecedented numbers of mortgages became delinquent or defaulted in 2007, housing and mortgage values fell, and the procyclicality of mark-to-market accounting proved disastrous for financial institutions, seriously eroding their earnings and their capital positions.

This situation immediately raised an unanswerable philosophical question: is the day-to-day market's judgment about the value of mortgage-backed securities "reality" in the sense that it should be reflected in the financial statements of banks and other financial firms, or simply a temporary aberration that should be ignored? Although there were strong arguments on both sides at the time, later events have shown that the sharp write-downs in the assets and earnings of financial institutions during this period were temporary effects and not in any sense the reality with which the health of financial institutions should be judged. This judgment does not necessarily call all of fair-value accounting into question, but it does raise serious issues about whether mark-to-market accounting should have remained in force during what was undoubtedly a financial panic. As John Allison, former chair of BB&T Corporation, astutely commented, "One of the basic principles underlying accounting models is that businesses will be valued as going concerns. In other words, the assumption is that the business will continue to operate. Fair-value accounting is inconsistent with this concept, because it effectively assumes that the business's assets are being liquidated under stress."[9]

One other effect of procyclicality has not been widely noted. In a 2010 paper, two Federal Reserve economists commented on the effect that the decline in asset values had on liquidity:

In a financial system in which balance sheets are continuously marked to market, changes in asset prices show up immediately on them and have an instant impact on the net worth of all constituents of the financial system. The net worth of financial intermediaries is especially sensitive to fluctuations in asset prices given the highly leveraged nature of such intermediaries' balance sheets. Far from being passive, the evidence points to financial intermediaries adjusting their balance sheets actively and doing so in such a way that leverage is high during booms and low during busts. That is, leverage is procyclical.[10]

In other words, as asset prices rise and fall, financial intermediaries adjust their balance sheets accordingly. When asset values rise, intermediaries find that they have more equity than they expected; their leverage has declined. As a result, they borrow in order to increase their return on equity with additional assets. The opposite is true when asset values fall. In that case, their leverage has increased because their asset base has grown smaller while their liabilities have remained the same. In these circumstances, they reduce or stop lending, drying up liquidity. If we follow through this analysis, the decline in asset values as the bubble deflated led to a decline in liquidity, which in turn stressed intermediaries like commercial and investment banks. This stress was exacerbated by operating losses, which further reduced market confidence in the banks' financial health. The virtuous circle of rising asset prices turned into a death spiral for financial firms.

FAS 157 AND THE DETERMINATION OF MARKET VALUE

Well before the issue of procyclicality was forced to the forefront of public debate, there was a practical question about how exactly firms and auditors were to determine the value of fixed-income securities like PMBS, especially when there was no active trading market. For all its detail, FAS 115 had not dealt sufficiently with this issue. It was easy to mark to market if the asset was an equity security traded on a stock exchange, but many debt securities were traded over the counter in markets that were too thin to permit the determination of a reliable market price by simply looking at trades. Similarly, in some cases, especially when mortgage and housing values were falling during 2007 and 2008, the holders of securities were compelled to sell in order to raise badly needed cash and would take any price; how were these "distress" sales to be valued? Further clarification was necessary. In 2006, the FASB issued FAS 157, in which it attempted to resolve how fair value would be determined even if there was no active market.

The rule began with a definition of fair value as "the price that would be received to sell an asset . . . in an orderly transaction between market participants at the measurement date."[11] The target—the value of a specific asset—was obviously important because net earnings or the size of shareholders' equity were determined by how specific fixed-income securities were valued. Yet for lightly traded fixed-income securities, there were likely to be few if any "orderly transactions" involving the particular securities that a firm's management and its auditors were attempting to value. In the case of PMBS, the question was particularly acute, because there were thousands of issues, most with multiple tranches, each of them different from the others in terms of the collateral involved, the extent of collateral support for the higher tranches, and the yield. Even in an active market it would be difficult to find a transaction involving a willing buyer and seller in a security that was identical—or even similar—to the one that was being valued. So the task of marking to market was far more difficult than it would first appear and involved both a high degree of judgment and a large potential for error by either a firm's management or its auditors.

A complete summary of FAS 157 is beyond the scope of this book, but two of its important elements deserve attention. First, the rule established a "fair-value hierarchy" that gave the highest priority—called Level 1—to *"quoted prices* in *active markets* for *identical assets or liabilities."* I have italicized the key terms in order to emphasize how difficult it would be to meet this standard when pricing pools of PMBS. Level 2 included quoted prices for *"similar* assets or liabilities," or other indicia of value (called "inputs") that are "observable," such as interest rates and yield curves for securities with similar characteristics like credit risks, default rates, or loss severities.[12] Thus, Level

2 introduced a great number of complex variables that would tax the judgment of the officers of reporting companies and their auditors in normal times, but would be particularly difficult in the chaotic markets that developed as the mortgage meltdown proceeded in 2007. Level 3 in the hierarchy allowed "unobservable" inputs that, according to the rule, "shall be used to measure fair value to the extent that *observable* inputs are *not available*" (emphasis added).[13]

Language of this kind suggests that the rule contained a strong bias in favor of inputs that were "observable" in the market, and thus leaned heavily against the use of *unobservable* inputs that were permitted for evaluations under Level 3. This bias appears to have had a major effect on how MBS assets were valued when the mortgage meltdown and the financial crisis made the operation of the fair-value rules crucial to the perceived health of financial intermediaries in the United States and elsewhere.

MARK-TO-MARKET ACCOUNTING AND THE CRISIS

Although the chaotic portion of the financial crisis is usually said to have begun with the Lehman Brothers bankruptcy on September 15, 2008, for most financial firms it had been going on since August 2007, when BNP Paribas notified its clients that it was closing down redemptions from those of its funds that were invested in U.S. mortgages. During this period, financial firms had a substantial stake in appearing as safe, strong, and stable as possible. Many began to raise fresh capital, which diluted their existing shareholders and caused substantial declines in their stock prices. In most cases, the AAA-rated MBS that they held were still paying principal and interest as expected, and they could see no reason why these should be written down. Indeed, if they had been allowed to use a standard Level 3 measurement—discounted cash flow—many firms wouldn't have had to take significant write-downs at all. But Level 3, which was only usable when observable inputs were not available, was seldom approved by auditors as a valuation method. Demonstrating the absence of observable inputs was a high standard to meet, especially when auditors—conservative by nature and imbued with accounting's inherent preference for conservative reporting—were afraid of lawsuits based on the claim that they had allowed reporting companies to overstate the value of their assets. Given the wide variety of possibilities outlined in Level 2, there were always *some* observable inputs, enabling auditors to claim that the use of a Level 3 valuation was not permitted. As a result, companies had to begin writing down their PMBS assets to something that approximated the prices in the market. Over time, these included PMBS that were held to maturity, because the pools in which they were located had been downgraded by the rating agencies and the idea that they were only temporarily impaired could no longer be sustained.

The market was a mess. Since August 2007 the media had been reporting a steady stream of bad economic and financial news. The following is a sample of Bloomberg headlines for late 2007 and early 2008 that captures the atmosphere in which managements and auditors were struggling to establish fair values for MBS:

- August 9, 2007: "BNP Paribas Freezes Funds as Loan Losses Roil Markets"

- August 14, 2007: "Goldman and Investors to Put $3 Billion into Fund"

- August 15, 2007: "Countrywide Financial 'Risks Bankruptcy' "

- August 22, 2007: "H&R Block Taps Credit Line, Cites 'Unstable' Markets"

- August 22, 2007: "Lehman, Accredited, HSBC Shut Offices; Crisis Spreads"

- August 23, 2007: "Fed Lends $2 Billion to Banks to Ease Credit Woes"

- August 29, 2007: "Basis Yield Files Bankruptcy over Subprime Defaults"

- September 17, 2007: "NovaStar Can't Pay Dividend, Forfeits REIT Status"

- October 5, 2007: "Merrill in $5.5bn Sub-Prime Loss"

- October 24, 2007: "Merrill Lynch Reports Loss on $8.4 Billion Writedown"

- November 8, 2007: "Morgan Stanley Takes $3.7bn Hit"

- December 10, 2007: "UBS Posts Fresh $10bn Writedown"

- December 10, 2007: "MBIA Gets $1 Billion from Warburg Pincus, Sees Losses"

- December 10, 2007: "Bank of America to Liquidate $12 Billion Cash Fund"

- December 14, 2007: "Citigroup Rescues SIVs with $58 Billion Debt Bailout"

- January 15, 2008: "Citi Writes Down $18 Billion; Merrill Gets Infusion"

- January 22, 2008: "As Markets Implode, Fed Panics and Cuts 75bps"

- February 14, 2008: "UBS Confirms Sub-Prime $18.4 Billion Loss"

- March 3, 2008: "HSBC in $17bn Credit Crisis Loss"

- March 6, 2008: "Peloton Capital Hedge Fund Collapses"

- March 11, 2008: "Carlyle Fund Tries to Halt Liquidation"

- March 14, 2008: "JPMorgan and Fed Move to Bail Out Bear Stearns"

- April 1, 2008: "UBS Writes Down Another $19 Billion"

- April 1, 2008: "Deutsche Bank to Write Down $4B"[14]

Anxious and confused by reports of unprecedentedly high delin-quency rates and defaults—which were accompanied by announcements of massive write-downs and declining earnings or operating losses by banks and others—investors were leaving the PMBS market in droves. But things would get markedly worse.

RATINGS, MARKET PRICES, AND REALITY

In January 2006, Markit Group Ltd., a data vendor, launched the Markit ABX.HE index, based on credit default swaps (CDS) covering a specified basket of subprime MBS of differently rated credit qualities. This was the first index of its kind, and might have been subject to design problems on that account, but the index showed far greater potential losses than the reality it was supposed to be reflecting. As one academic paper describes it, "We find that prices for the AAA ABX.HE index CDS during the crisis were inconsistent with any reasonable assumption for mortgage default rates, and that these price changes are only weakly correlated with observed changes in the foreclosure performance of the underlying loans in the index, casting serious doubt on the suitability of these CDS as valuation benchmarks."[15] Yet, as Gary Gorton of Yale observes, "Once the ABX indices started to drift downward, accountants required market participants to use these indices for mark-to-market purposes."[16] Gorton argues that the ABX was an important trigger of the panic because, for the first time, it provided investors with information: "common knowledge that the situation of subprime borrowers was deteriorating quickly and that the value of subprime-related bonds and structures was going down. By 2007, the ABX indices had become the focal point of the crisis."[17]

This was more than simply an academic judgment after the fact. Gorton was pointing out that the index counted as an *observable input* for the purposes of FAS 157, and thus would not only imply a lower price for the AAA tranches of MBS than their actual experience would suggest but would also make it highly unlikely that a Level 3 valuation—one, for example, that used the cash flows to the AAA tranches—would be permitted by a firm's auditors. After all, FAS 157 said that Level 3 could not be used unless observable data were *not* available, and auditors were reluctant to open themselves to legal liability by moving a centimeter away from the written standard. It is hard to avoid the conclusion that the index added materially to the anxiety of investors and the doubts of those who might consider acquiring the MBS that were now balefully called "toxic assets" by the media. As Gorton notes, "The accounting rules put the accountants at the forefront of decision-making about the value of complex financial instruments. While the accounting outcome is basically negotiated, the rules put management at a bargaining disadvantage."[18]

Ratings downgrades also contributed to the MBS price declines that in turn led to write-downs by firms with substantial portfolios of private MBS. According to the majority report of the Financial Crisis Inquiry Commission (FCIC), as the number of delinquencies and defaults rose in 2007 and 2008, Moody's downgraded 73 percent of the MBS pools it had rated AAA in 2006.[19] This statistic was meant to be shocking, an indictment of Moody's for its prior carelessness, or worse, in issuing its ratings. However, a downgrade of an MBS pool is different from the downgrade of the debt of a single obligor. A rating is an estimate of the likelihood of default. In a pool of thousands of loans, there will definitely be some defaults; the question is whether the defaults will be so numerous and the losses given default so large as to change the *likelihood* that any particular tranche will suffer a loss.[20] In the case of the top tranches in a pool—the 85–90 percent that are rated AAA or AA in most pools—the likelihood of a loss is very small, but when the number of losses in the pool is greater than might have been anticipated by the rating agency's model, the chances of a loss to the AAA tranches has almost certainly increased to some degree. That does not mean that these tranches will suffer or have actually suffered losses, but only that the chances of suffering a loss have increased. Indeed, in thousands of the pools that were downgraded by Moody's and Standard & Poor's, the AAA tranches have not yet—even in 2014—suffered a cash loss. Moreover, even if losses reach the AAA tranches in a pool, they represent a percentage loss, not a bankruptcy, as would be true in the case of a single obligor. That is, if a AAA-rated tranche is "impaired" because the losses have eaten through all the subordinate tranches, the holders of the AAA tranche may receive over time only 95 percent of what they expected.

Although it is difficult to assemble information on all the thousands of PMBS pools that were put together before 2007, it appears from a survey of Bloomberg data that very few of the AAA tranches in PMBS pools that were written down actually suffered cash losses. This finding is consistent with the conclusions of Moody's Investors Service in Table 3.3, which estimated the losses on AAA-rated PMBS tranches at 4.4 percent at the end of 2009. The point is significant because the AAA tranches were most likely to be acquired and held by banks, GSEs, and other financial institutions. The initial projected losses were much less than what was estimated. For a substantial period of time, the FHFA estimated that the GSEs' losses would exceed $300 billion, but in the end they were substantially less. Equally significant, many pools, after being downgraded and suffering substantial price reductions in the market, recovered almost completely and are now fetching prices close to what they brought in their initial issuance.[21] This is powerful evidence that the market in 2007–2009 was significantly oversold and that the write-downs required by fair-value accounting did not reflect reality. As Kevin Villani writes:

> Realized losses from bond defaults played no role in the subsequent failures, but regulatory enforcement of mark-to-market accounting for loans held for investment at a time when there were no markets due to regulatory actions did. The US regulatory system forced a nationwide liquidation that predictably forced prices to about half their intrinsic value based both on *ex ante* projections and verified *ex post* cash flows.[22]

If this is true, it raises serious questions about fair-value accounting, at least in the midst of a financial panic. It cannot be true that the market is receiving any useful information when the prices recorded by mark-to-market accounting diverge so far from reality. Indeed, a strong argument can be made that the market was being misled rather than informed.

An example of this is the Ace Securities Corporation Asset-Backed Pass-Through Certificates Series 2005-HE7. This Ace Securities vehicle was a $1.7 billion pool, consisting of approximately 9,000 first- and second-lien fixed- and adjustable-rate one-to-four family residential mortgage loans, offered for sale in November 2005 by Ace Securities, a subsidiary of Deutsche Bank. Figure 12.1 tells the pricing story of three of its top tranches—the kind that would have been bought by investors and intermediaries such as U.S. banks and investment banks before 2007. As shown in Table 12.1, each tranche was issued at a price of 100, but was downgraded at some point during the succeeding years, in some cases quite severely. Commensurate with the downgrades were declines in price,

TABLE 12.1. Downgrades by S&P and Moody's on 2005-HE7 AAA

	A1A		A1B2		A2D	
	Moody's	S&P	Moody's	S&P	Moody's	S&P
Nov. 30, 2005		AAA		AAA		AAA
Dec. 5, 2005	Aaa		Aaa		Aaa	
July 23, 2008		AAA–		AAA–		AAA–
Oct. 13, 2008		*AAA*		*AAA*		*AAA*
Oct. 15, 2008			Aa2		Aa2	
Feb. 26, 2009	Aaa–		Aa2–		Aa2–	
Mar. 16, 2009	*Aaa*		Baa2		Baa2	
Aug. 4, 2009				B		B
Jan. 13, 2010	Aaa–		Baa2–		Baa2–	
Feb. 2, 2010		AAA–		B–		B–
Mar. 2, 2010		AA–		*B*		*B*
Apr. 14, 2010	Aa1		B2		B2	
May 30, 2012			*B2+*		*B1+*	
July 20, 2012			*Ba3*		*Ba3*	
Aug. 15, 2012		AA+		B+		B+
Oct. 16, 2012		AA–		BB		BB

Source: Bloomberg.

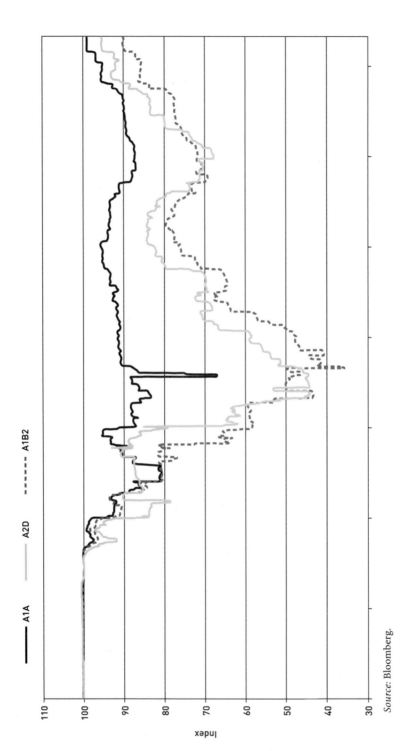

Source: Bloomberg.

FIG. 12.1. Ace Securities Corporation 2005–HE7 tranche pricing

which in some cases fell 60 percent. Yet none of these tranches has ever suffered a cash loss, and by the end of 2012, all had recovered to at least 90 percent of their original price. That was true despite the fact that the ratings from Standard & Poor's—the latest available— were AA–, BB, and BBB, respectively. This validates the point made earlier, that ratings downgrades for the top tranches of a pool do not mean that these securities are "toxic assets," or anything close to that. It simply means that their chances of suffering a loss of some kind has marginally increased. Nor does it necessarily mean, as the FCIC implied, that the rating agencies failed in their responsibilities.

Table 12.1 shows the downgrades of the top tranches that occurred between 2005 and 2012. In the panicky market atmosphere of 2007 and 2008, downgrades were shocking events, leading the unsophisticated media and some unsophisticated investors to believe that the downgraded AAA tranches in subprime mortgage pools were going to suffer serious losses. The practical effect of this was to further dry up the limited liquidity in the market, with many investors fleeing to safer ground. The prices for the Ace 2005-HE7 AAA tranches fell steadily. The top AAA-rated tranche, which was selling at 100.03 on December 1, 2005, was at 95.25 on October 30, 2008, and hit its low of 83.25 on March 27, 2009. After that, it began a slow recovery, ending on March 12, 2013, at 98.96. The third-highest AAA-rated tranche had a much more volatile history. It started on December 1, 2005, at 99.97, was downgraded to baa2 by Moody's on March 16, 2009, and reached a low of 44.21 on April 13, 2009. Thereafter it began its own recovery, ending at 95.4 on March 12, 2013. Despite these declines, neither of these securities could be called a toxic asset, and neither has yet suffered a cash loss.

The importance of this decline and recovery for a study of the effect of fair-value accounting is obvious. The data on the price declines in this particular non-agency PMBS during 2007 and 2008 were readily available and recorded on an almost daily basis by Bloomberg. Financial institutions that held one of the AAA-rated tranches of Ace 2005-HE7 would have been required to account for the decline in the prices of these securities in one of several ways. If they held the securities in a trading account, the sharp decline in market values would have caused a reduction in their reported earnings, even though they never suffered any cash loss. If they held the securities for sale, they would have been required to recognize a loss in the equity account designated as Other Comprehensive Income, and thus suffer an apparent decline in their capital position, even though the AAA tranches were flowing cash exactly as planned when they were acquired. Finally, if they had acquired the securities to hold to maturity, they would have had to determine whether, in 2009, the losses were other than temporary; if so, they would have been written down to their market value at the time and had an adverse effect on capital.

It is important to note that while Ace 2005-HE7 is representative of thousands of other securities, it was not by any means the worst. Many suffered even more significant price declines, and in some there may actually have been losses in the AAA-rated tranches. Still, those losses, if they occurred at all, were very likely to be percentage losses, not total losses. As the market began to adjust and take account of cash flows to these pools in 2010 and later, they probably recovered a substantial part of their value, just as happened to the third-highest AAA tranche in Ace 2005-HE7. What we can conclude from this is that a market panic drove down MBS prices well below their actual value. If we assume that these values were then recorded on the balance sheets and income statements of financial institutions in the United States and around the world, a substantial portion of the losses that these companies sustained in the financial crisis was not in any sense real; instead, the losses were caused by the tendency of fair-value accounting to embed the results of a market panic in the balance sheets of financial institutions.

Indeed, it is possible to compare how marking to market and historical cost accounting affected the same assets. It happens that the Federal Reserve required bank holding companies to report not only the mark-to-market or fair-value prices of their assets during this period but also the value of those assets under historical cost accounting. Figure 12.2 shows that at the peak of the panic in 2008 the value of available-for-sale non-agency MBS declined by almost 25 percent from the value they would have had under historical cost accounting.

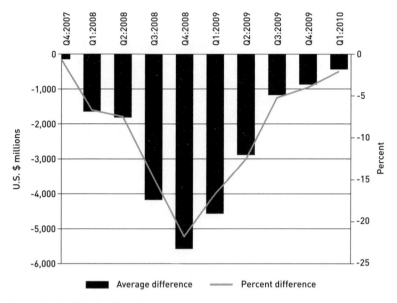

Source: Federal Reserve Board.
Note: Graph represents the average difference between historical cost accounting and fair value accounting for available-for-sale non-agency MBS assets. Data are collected from Form FR Y-9C. See Schedule HC-B, section 4, subsection b, and subsection 3 for data points.

FIG. 12.2. Average difference between historical cost accounting and fair-value accounting

Needless to say, if historical cost accounting (essentially, gradual amortization of the initial value of a financial asset over time) had been permitted at the time, it might have had a major stabilizing effect on public perceptions of the financial condition of many large financial firms.

EFFORTS TO CHANGE MARK-TO-MARKET DURING THE CRISIS

Companies required to write down the value of their MBS assets when they had not actually suffered any losses were desperately aware of the absurdity of their situation. Many complained publicly to Congress, to the FASB, and to the SEC, which had the authority to formulate accounting rules but had delegated that authority to the FASB. On

September 30, 2008, in the midst of the accelerating meltdown that followed the bankruptcy of Lehman Brothers two weeks earlier, the SEC's Office of the Chief Accountant, jointly with the FASB staff, put out its first significant statement on how the valuation process should work. Using a question-and-answer format, the document asked: "Can management's internal assumptions (e.g., expected cash flows) be used to measure fair value when relevant market evidence *does not exist* [emphasis added]?" The question itself is simply a restatement of the existing FASB rule, substituting "relevant market evidence" for "observable inputs" and was likely to leave accountants and auditors in the same position they had occupied before the SEC spoke. The SEC's answer was yes, but it was useless in moving the auditors who were refusing to certify the use of Level 3 for determining values. From the auditors' perspective, it was very difficult to determine that "relevant market evidence" does not exist. The AAA ABX.HE index described above, because it was derived from market activity, apparently qualified as relevant market evidence, even though—according to the academic work cited earlier—it was wildly off the mark when compared to the market value of AAA-rated tranches then and later. Relevant market evidence like that would not have provided much useful data for determining the value of a security, but would have prevented firms from using unobservable inputs such as cash flows.

But there was a more difficult question. Even if observable inputs such as the prices for the top AAA tranches of the ACE 2005-HE7 were available, should they be trusted? FAS 157 had described a fair-value measurement as involving an "orderly transaction between market participants on the measurement date." Without question, beginning in 2007 and continuing through early 2009, the market for MBS was in turmoil. Without steady buyers, and with many companies selling their MBS assets at distress prices to meet their cash needs, the market where orderly transactions were supposed to occur was not itself orderly. How could it be expected to produce orderly transactions? Even more troubling was the question of how firms and their auditors were supposed to find their way through this thicket when legal liability could attach for guessing wrong. It should have been obvious to policy makers at the SEC and elsewhere that, faced with difficult judgment questions about how billions of dollars in MBS assets should be valued, accountants and auditors would fall back on the most conservative methods, choosing the values that would get them in the least trouble. The clients might be enraged, but no investor was likely to bring an action against an auditing firm for *underestimating* MBS values. And so the downward slide continued largely unabated.

The SEC had the authority to call a halt to all this. Given the requirement for orderly transactions articulated in FAS 157, the SEC could have declared that the market was no longer functioning in a way that would enable orderly transactions. Therefore, the agency might have said, the requirement for fair-value measurement of assets and liabilities would be temporarily suspended; firms should value their MBS assets on the basis of their cash flows or some other reasonable method until further notice. Although the SEC had the authority to take this step, it continued to temporize. Accordingly, in the Emergency Economic Stabilization Act of 2008, Congress directed the SEC to study the issue of fair-value accounting and to report back with recommendations. The SEC's report, issued on December 30, 2008, largely endorsed fair-value accounting, but made some recommendations to the FASB, especially with respect to providing guidance about when a market was not active or when a transaction involved a distressed sale. In both cases, in theory, Level 3 valuations could be used. The FASB went back to the drawing board, but its recommendations were still not clear enough to move auditors from the conservative positions they had generally assumed. It was not that the FASB was unable to make itself clear; even in the face of the devastation it was causing, it seemed to be fighting a rearguard action to protect fair-value accounting against significant change.

Congress then stepped in. The House Financial Services Committee scheduled a hearing and called Robert Herz, the chair of the FASB, as a witness. Despite Herz's attempts to defend mark-to-market accounting, member after member warned that if the FASB persisted, the committee would respond with legislation. This was a terrible precedent; the worst way to establish accounting principles is through political pressure. But the situation was out of control, and things were getting worse. On March 10, 2009, the Dow Jones Indus-trial Average hit its lowest point in the crisis, about 6,600. Herz got the message. On March 17, 2009, the FASB issued further guidance on when a market is to be considered active, when a trade is con-sidered a distress transaction, and when a decline in the value of an asset held to maturity is to be considered an other-than-temporary impairment. These changes, which became effective on April 2, calmed the waters. It may be a coincidence, of course, but in this pe-riod of March–April 2009 the three top tranches of ACE 2005-HE7 hit their low points and began their gradual return to values close to the price at which they were issued. Even more compelling, the Dow began the long climb back to its current level. Those who argue that the market can see through the accounting to the ultimate reality have to consider what happened when the only thing that changed was the accounting.

In summary, over the entire period of the financial crisis, from the second half of 2007 through the first half of 2011, financial institu-tions incurred substantial losses, some of which were offset by raising capital. It seems likely, however, that if mark-to-market accounting had not been introduced by the FASB in 1993, just as the boom in housing prices was beginning, the bubble that grew between 1997 and 2007 would have been much smaller and the decline in housing prices less severe when the bubble deflated. In addition, assuming that the mortgage meltdown and the financial crisis had still oc-curred, it is likely that, in the absence of mark-to-market accounting, the losses to financial institutions would not have been so large, and the investor panic that characterized the period from 2007 to 2009 would not have reached crisis levels.

It is not a criticism of fair-value accounting in principle to say that it was the wrong policy to keep in place during a financial cri-sis. In normal conditions, fair-value accounting may be sensible ac-counting policy, but in order to tame its inherent procyclicality, it must be accompanied by suitable counter-cyclical provisions or by an emergency switch that will shut it off when it is creating an unstable bubble or a 2008-like crash. As Gary Gorton put it, "Accounting is supposed to produce information. How can that happen in a panic? In a panic, no one wants to trade; there are no markets. And hence there are no market prices."[23]

In the next Part, the discussion will turn to the government then and the government now. First, we will discuss how the government handled—and, as important, interpreted—the financial crisis that became suddenly real in August 2007. It gets failing marks for both. Its bumbling significantly exacerbated the crisis, but its effort to cover up its errors and shift blame to the private sector ultimately did the most damage. The result was a false narrative that the government didn't have enough authority to deal with the crisis—a narrative that fit perfectly with the intentions of the Democratic president and the Democratic supermajorities that controlled Congress after the 2008 elections. This narrative both produced the Dodd-Frank Act and, by failing to identify the true causes of the crisis, left the United States open to a return of the same policies in the future.

From Bad to Worse

The government's response to the crisis,
and why the crisis can happen again

13

From Bad to Worse

How Government Blunders Turned a Mortgage
Meltdown Into an Investor Panic and Financial Crisis

> Government is depicted as acting not in response to its
> own political incentives and constraints but because it is
> compelled to do so by concern for the public interest. . . .
> Such a tableau simply ignores the possibility that there are
> political incentives . . . to justify expansions of power as
> well as to use episodic emergencies as a reason for creating
> enduring government institutions.
>
> THOMAS SOWELL, *Knowledge and Decisions*

The financial crisis was precipitated by government housing policies, but it was made significantly worse by the panic and errors of
the officials who handled it. Then, in trying to minimize or justify
their own mistakes, these officials claimed that they had insufficient
authority to deal with the crisis. These exaggerated claims in turn
were used by Congress to justify provisions of the Dodd-Frank Act,
particularly Titles I and II, which were both unnecessary and harm-
ful. This chapter details how mismanagement of events, mistaken
judgments, and concern for personal reputations turned a mortgage
meltdown into a financial crisis.

WHY BEAR STEARNS WAS RESCUED

The first major U.S. victim of the mortgage defaults and the procyclical effects of mark-to-market accounting was Bear Stearns; with

assets of about $450 billion, Bear was the smallest of the five Wall Street investment banks that had grown large and powerful since becoming public companies in the 1980s and 1990s. (Merrill Lynch was the first in 1971, then Bear Stearns in 1985, Morgan Stanley in 1986, Lehman Brothers in 1994, and Goldman Sachs in 1999.) Not coincidentally, Bear was the investment bank with the largest percentage of commitment to private mortgage–backed securities (PMBS) backed by nontraditional mortgages (NTMs), and it gradually weakened as housing and mortgage values fell relentlessly through 2007 and into 2008. The investment bank business model was particularly vulnerable to the procyclicality of mark-to-market accounting. Unlike commercial banks, investment banks were traders. All of them had developed out of securities firms that were now their subsidiaries, and they continued to hold large portfolios of trading assets supported by short-term liabilities. The investment banks did not generally engage in maturity transformation, the inherent risk associated with commercial banks. As traders, they had and were intended to have a closer match between the maturities of their assets and liabilities than commercial banks, and thus they could justify somewhat higher levels of leverage.

In a 2010 study, two economists at the New York Federal Reserve Bank deconstructed the balance sheet of Lehman Brothers at the end of 2007. Their analysis, displayed in Figure 13.1, showed that 90 percent of Lehman's assets, as might be expected, were short-term. Short-term borrowing also predominated on the liability side of the balance sheet, but 18 percent was long-term debt, which would normally be a stabilizing factor. The major short-term vulnerability was not the collateralized borrowing, but Lehman's role as a prime broker for hedge funds. The funds it held in that capacity, 12 percent of its liabilities, were withdrawable on demand, and, according to the paper, "proved to be an important source of funding instability."[1]

Similar information on Bear Stearns is not available, but if Bear's balance sheet looked like a smaller version of Lehman's in 2008, its problem was obvious as the procyclicality of mark-to-market accounting played out. As mortgage values declined after the deflation of the housing bubble, losses in Bear's trading accounts went straight

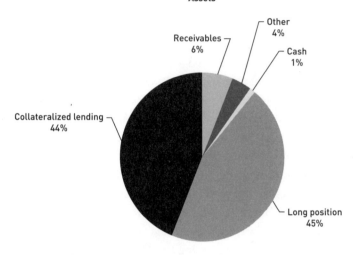

Assets

Other 4%

Receivables 6%

Cash 1%

Collateralized lending 44%

Long position 45%

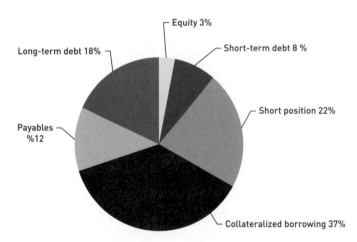

Liabilities

Equity 3%

Long-term debt 18%

Short-term debt 8 %

Payables %12

Short position 22%

Collateralized borrowing 37%

Adapted from: Tobias Adrian and Hyun Song Shin, "The Changing Nature of Financial Intermediation and the Financial Crisis of 2007–09," Federal Reserve Bank of New York, Staff Report no. 439, revised April 2010, p. 7.

FIG. 13.1. Assets and liabilities of an investment bank (Lehman Brothers, end 2007)

to its bottom line, resulting in significant operating losses. Bear began to report large losses as early as April 2007, and the company's shares fell 42 percent in 2007 alone. Operating losses and capital declines continued in 2008, and these spooked Bear's short-term creditors—especially those, like hedge funds, that had prime brokerage funds with Bear that were withdrawable on demand. As also noted in chapter 12, the decline in asset values raised the leverage ratios in the market generally, reducing liquidity and making it more expensive to borrow even if a firm with continuing losses could find credit. Finally, on March 12, 2008, rumors about Bear's lack of liquidity swept the financial markets, and the firm was unable to persuade investors that it could continue to meet its short-term obligations. In the end, it was reported, Bear could not even borrow on its Fannie and Freddie paper; no firm wanted a Bear Stearns asset on its balance sheet when creditors were withdrawing funds from any intermediary that might have previously unsuspected weaknesses. On March 16, with government support in the form of $29 billion in assistance from the Federal Reserve, Bear was acquired by JPMorgan Chase. Despite its illiquid position, Bear seemed to be solvent at that point; its officials told the Financial Crisis Inquiry Commission (FCIC) that it was profitable in the quarter in which it was taken over, and its shareholders were arbitrarily awarded $2 per share, later changed—after an outcry—to $10 per share. A year earlier, the stock had been worth $159 per share.

The government's action in rescuing Bear was seen by many as a turning point in financial history. In late March 2008, David Wessel, an economic writer for the *Wall Street Journal*, published an article titled "Ten Days That Changed Capitalism." The article's lead sentence, "The past 10 days will be remembered as the time the U.S. government discarded a half-century of rules to save American financial capitalism from collapse," effectively encapsulated the gravity that the government, the media, and the financial community attached to the developing crisis. Wessel quoted Edward Yardeni, another well-known economist, as telling clients, "The Government of Last Resort is working with the Lender of Last Resort to shore up the housing and credit markets to avoid Great Depression II."[2] The Bear Stearns rescue was important for reasons to be explained, but it was only the beginning of the crisis, not its end. The fact that informed commentators were already seeing a crisis of capitalism foreshadowed more hand-wringing to come. Anxiety was turning into panic. With the hindsight of six years, both economists might now have some misgivings about their heated prose. At this distance, the financial crisis itself seems less a crisis of capitalism than an investor panic induced by sudden unexplained and unfathomable mortgage losses, procyclical accounting policies, and ill-advised government moves. The first of these moves was the rescue of Bear Stearns.

Why was Bear Stearns rescued? There has never been a good answer to this question. Bear Stearns was an investment bank, not a commercial bank. The difference is crucial. Commercial banks are insured by the government because their unique role in the economy is to convert short-term liabilities—principally deposits withdrawable on demand—into long-term assets such as loans, a process called maturity transformation. This makes them inherently susceptible to depositor runs—emergency and panicked withdrawals—when and if depositors have lost confidence in the ability of the bank to return their money on demand. There is a value in runs; when a bank is weak, runs can close it down quickly, preserving its assets for an equitable division among all its depositors. However, runs are also socially disruptive and can induce runs on healthy institutions at times when panic is pervasive and there is insufficient information about the financial condition of the healthy firms. The government insures deposits in order to reassure depositors that their funds are safe and thus to make depositor runs less likely.

More important than these technical elements is the fact that bank deposits function as money; businesses and individuals use their bank deposits to make payments through the banking system, and that creates important interconnections between banks. The banking system functions through correspondent deposits. Small banks have deposits in larger banks, and larger banks have deposits in still larger banks. Eventually the largest banks have accounts in the regional Federal Reserve banks, which effect payments between these large banks by transferring funds between the banks' respective accounts on the books of the Federal Reserve banks. If a major bank is unable to make a payment because of a shortage of funds, the payment system can grind to a halt; its correspondent banks are caught short, and businesses and individuals are unable to meet their obligations because funds that they expected to have for payments have not arrived at their bank or have otherwise become unavailable. Payrolls are not met, closings do not occur, and accounts don't balance at the end of the day. In other words, there are compelling payment system reasons for the government to be concerned about the failure of a large bank.

No business, however, deposits its payroll in an investment bank. Bear Stearns, the investment bank, did not take checkable deposits, was not part of the payment system, and was not insured by the government. In March 2008, there was no expectation that if Bear Stearns were on the brink of failure, the U.S. government would ride to its rescue. It was not clear why that would be necessary. It is true that Bear had a lot of short-term overnight funds, but most of them were collateralized through repurchase agreements. If Bear were to fail, the AAA-rated securities that its lenders were holding as collateral could have been sold, although possibly not for their initial value. At that point, the value of these securities was in question, and the sales would have been unlikely to compensate Bear's creditors fully for their loss, but why should the U.S. government—or U.S. taxpayers—care whether Bear's creditors suffered losses? Moreover, since Bear was an investment bank, its assets were largely short-term—although, to be sure, not as short-term as the funds it held as a prime broker for hedge fund customers. These funds were withdrawable on demand. Still, unlike a balance sheet at a commercial bank, Bear's balance sheet was not made up of long-term loans that could not be easily sold. Finally, and remarkably, Bear was actually solvent; its shareholders were deemed to be entitled to $10 per share. Why did the government believe it was necessary to bail out a solvent investment bank?

THE INTERCONNECTIONS FALLACY
AND THE RESCUE OF BEAR STEARNS

In his book *On the Brink*, former Treasury Secretary Hank Paulson wrote:

A Bear bankruptcy could cause a domino effect, with other troubled banks unable to meet their obligations and failing. . . . I couldn't sleep . . . I worried about the soundness of balance sheets, the lack of transparency in the CDS [credit default swap] market, and the interconnections among institutions that lent each other billions each day and how easily the system could unravel if they got spooked. . . . A Bear Stearns failure wouldn't just hurt the owners of its shares and its bonds. Bear had hundreds, maybe thousands, of counterparties—firms that lent it money or with which it traded stocks, bonds, mortgages, and other securities. These firms— other banks and brokerage houses, insurance companies, mutual funds, hedge funds, pension funds, funds of states, cities and big companies—all in turn had myriad counterparties of their own.[3]

Thus, Paulson is suggesting that a Bear failure would drag down other large financial institutions because these large firms are all interconnected. Tim Geithner says essentially the same thing in *Stress Test*: " 'Too big to fail' has become the catchphrase of the crisis, but our fear was that Bear was 'too interconnected to fail' without causing catastrophic damage."[4] It is certainly true that interconnections exist among large financial firms, but the question is whether the exposures of one to another are so large that the failure of one would have the catastrophic effects Paulson and Geithner feared. In mentioning credit default swaps, Paulson was suggesting that this is one of the ways—perhaps the most important way—that this interconnection was established. Yet, as we will see, the rescue was a fateful mistake. Six months after Bear was rescued, another investment bank, Lehman Brothers, failed, and even though Lehman was almost 50 percent larger than Bear, the feared "interconnections" between Lehman and other firms had no role in the crisis that ensued.

Moreover, the Lehman bankruptcy came at a time when the market was in a state of near panic, much worse than it had been when Bear might have failed, with many large financial institutions thought to be unstable and possibly insolvent. Yet, despite the fact that Lehman was one of the largest financial institutions in the United States, with about $650 billion in assets, no other large bank, investment bank, securities firm, or insurance company failed or came close to failing because of the Lehman bankruptcy. Accordingly, although it is not often that one can test a proposition in social science the way experiments in natural science can be repeated and examined, here we have a test of whether Paulson and Geithner were correct. Would the failure of Bear have had the catastrophic consequences they feared? On the evidence of the Lehman bankruptcy, the answer is a resounding no. There was chaos after Lehman, to be sure—much of it the result of the government's sudden abandonment of the policy it appeared to have adopted when it rescued Bear—but Lehman had no knock-on consequences; it did not drag down any other large financial institution. Despite this fact, when the Dodd-Frank Act was enacted two years later, after the consequences of Lehman's bankruptcy should have been thoroughly understood, Congress still based the Dodd-Frank Act on the erroneous idea that Lehman's "interconnections" were the reason its failure was so consequential. Lehman's failure had no knock-on consequences, it is important to note, even though the firm was a major player in the credit default swap market, which apparently held particular terror for Paulson. This is one of the reasons that the Dodd-Frank Act should be seen as illegitimate; simply put, it did not respond to the real causes of the financial crisis, but only to groundless fears and, as we will see, *post hoc* rationalizations and exculpatory statements by key government officials.

In sum, the whole idea that the failure of a large financial institution will drag down others—a major underlying idea in Dodd-Frank—is wrong. Indeed, it is inherently implausible. Small firms can sometimes become so entangled with suppliers or customers that the failure of one or the other will be disastrous for the firm, but for large firms this scenario is highly unlikely. Because of their size and inherent diversification, large firms are seldom in the position of being financially dependent on other firms. The lack of a knock-on effect in the Lehman bankruptcy—even suddenly, shockingly, in the midst of a financial panic—proved this point.

What, then, if not interconnections, caused the losses to so many financial institutions in the financial crisis? The answer is what is known to scholars as common shock,[5] sometimes also called contagion—a financial event that adversely affects many firms at the same time. The banks, investment banks, and others that failed or came near to failing in the financial crisis were all heavy investors in PMBS backed by NTMs. As noted earlier, the Basel capital accords—by reducing the capital requirements for highly rated PMBS to 1.6 percent—herded banks and investment banks into these very instruments. The investment banks, as noted earlier, had become subject to Basel rules when they voluntarily accepted prudential regulation by the SEC in order to meet the requirements for doing business in the European Union. When the bubble deflated and housing prices declined throughout the country, all these institutions suffered losses at the same time.[6] Still, the continued viability of the interconnections idea gave rise to the creation of the Financial Stability Oversight Council in the Dodd-Frank Act. The Council, chaired by the secretary of the Treasury and made up of all the federal financial regulators, was given the unique authority to designate any non-bank financial institution as a systemically important financial institution, or SIFI. When so designated, the financial firm is turned over to the Federal Reserve for bank-like supervision and regulation. This special SIFI supervision is supposed to prevent the failure of one of these firms, which under the interconnections theory would bring down others and cause a financial crisis. But special regulation and supervision by the Fed will not prevent a financial crisis caused by common shock—another example of ineffective or erroneous policy prescriptions because of a failure to understand the real causes of the financial crisis.

Shortly after the Lehman bankruptcy, both Goldman Sachs and Morgan Stanley, the two largest investment banks, became bank holding companies subject to Federal Reserve regulation; Wachovia National Bank and Washington Mutual Bank were both taken over by the Federal Deposit Insurance Corporation (FDIC) and sold to larger institutions; and American International Group (AIG), the largest insurance holding company, was rescued from bankruptcy by the Federal Reserve. None of these events had anything to do with knock-on effects from Lehman's collapse. Goldman Sachs and Morgan Stanley became bank holding companies because they thought being regulated by the Federal Reserve would give the panicky market more confidence in their stability, not because they had suffered any serious losses as a result of Lehman's failure; Wachovia and Washington Mutual were insured depository institutions that got into trouble by making very low quality mortgages, but again not connected to Lehman's bankruptcy; and AIG was rescued by the Federal Reserve because it could not meet its obligations to provide the necessary cash collateral to its CDS and securities-lending counterparties when it was required to do so under the terms of its obligations. All of them, even AIG, were victims of common shock, not Lehman's failure. In the case of AIG, as discussed in chapter 3, its cash collateral obligations arose in part out of the requirement in CDS contracts for collateral to move between counterparties as the insured obligation strengthened or weakened. The PMBS that AIG's subsidiary had insured was losing value, increasing AIG's cash collateral obligation. Thus, the Lehman bankruptcy seems to demonstrate beyond question that the failure of a large non-bank financial firm—even in the midst of a financial panic—will not cause other financial firms to fail. Accordingly, the decision to bail out Bear Stearns was a serious error of judgment.

THE RESERVE PRIMARY FUND AND "BREAKING THE BUCK"

To be sure, one loss can be directly linked to Lehman's bankruptcy through interconnections, but it was a very special case: the loss involved was less than 2 percent, and it was not in any sense a bankruptcy or insolvency. Moreover, as discussed below, what happened to the Reserve Fund seems to be a direct result of the moral hazard created by the rescue of Bear. The Reserve Primary Fund, a mid-size money market mutual fund, lost so much on its holdings of Lehman commercial paper that it "broke the buck"—that is, it was unable to redeem all its shares at one dollar per share, as had become the standard promise for money market funds. This should not have been a surprise or even a problem. Since mid-2007, investors had been seeking safety by moving their funds to U.S. government securities. Some did it directly, controlling their own portfolios; others sold their shares in what were called primary funds (which, like the Reserve Primary Fund, invested largely in private-sector securities) and bought shares in money market funds that were invested heavily or entirely in government securities. When Lehman failed, this gradual movement over the previous year became a torrent, with many primary funds losing investors and government funds gaining them. Although this was called a "run," the term is a misnomer for what was essentially another manifestation of panicky investors changing their investment strategies in the face of uncertainty. A run on a bank is different; there, depositors pull out their funds because they fear that the bank will close when it runs out of cash. A money market fund doesn't close and doesn't run out of cash; it simply sells its assets—usually highly liquid—to meet investor requests for share redemptions. Those who redeem early may get 100 cents on the dollar, and those who redeem later may not (that's what "breaking the buck" means), but the same would be true if funds used a floating net asset value; the first out would get more than those who redeemed later. In any event, because the assets of money market funds are liquid and short term, the losses are unlikely to be substantial. Nevertheless, the Treasury set up an emergency insurance fund for money market funds in order to stop what the Treasury called a "run" on these funds, although no other funds broke the buck. Later, the Treasury and others claimed that the insurance fund was necessary because the Reserve Primary Fund's financial problems had caused the shutdown of the vital commercial paper market, through which many corporations met their short-term cash needs.[7]

The Treasury's insurance fund has the earmarks of another

panicky response by the Treasury and the Federal Reserve, similar to the rescue of Bear Stearns. There is little reason to believe that a "run" on the Reserve Primary Fund, the fact that it broke the buck, or withdrawals from other primary money market funds was a major cause of the shutdown of the commercial paper market. The market had been under stress and declining for a year before the Lehman bankruptcy and the problems of the Reserve Fund, and neither the Treasury nor the Federal Reserve had taken any action to stop it. As one academic paper has observed:

Commercial paper played a central role during the financial crisis of 2007–2009. Before the crisis, market participants regarded commercial paper as a safe asset due to its short maturity and high credit rating. Two events changed this perception. The first event began to unfold on July 31, 2007, when two Bear Stearns' hedge funds that had invested in subprime mortgages filed for bankruptcy. In the following week, other investors also announced losses on subprime mortgages. On August 7, 2007, BNP Paribas suspended withdrawals from its three investment funds because of its inability to assess the value of the mortgages and other investment held by the funds. Given that similar assets served as collateral for a specific category of commercial paper—asset-backed commercial paper—many investors became reluctant to purchase it. The total value of asset-backed commercial paper outstanding fell by 37 percent, from $1.18 trillion in August 2007 to $745 billion in August 2008.[8]

The decline in the size of the commercial paper market between August 2007 and the date of the Lehman bankruptcy in September 2008 was about $435 billion. During this period, interest rates in the asset-backed commercial paper (ABCP) market—the largest category by far—moved sharply higher, increasing 10 basis points between the beginning of July and the end of August 2007. This was 150 basis points over the Federal Reserve funds rate,[9] reflecting the additional risk that investors saw in commercial paper even before the Reserve Fund event.

However, *after* the Lehman bankruptcy, the AIG bailout, and the so-called run on the Reserve Primary Fund, the decline in the commercial paper market was much smaller, falling from about $670 billion to $420 billion. This was about half the decline that took place *before* the Lehman, AIG, and Reserve Fund events. In other words, the asset-backed commercial paper market was already in serious trouble well before the Lehman bankruptcy and before the Reserve Fund had broken the buck, and the decline during that period was far larger than the decline that occurred after those events had occurred. Nevertheless, the narrative about the period is that the Treasury was compelled to set up an insurance fund that would protect the $1-per-share stable value of money market funds and that this bold action stopped a dangerous run on other funds. A more accurate assessment of the Treasury's action is that the insurance fund was unnecessary; the decline in the size of the primary money market funds and the commercial paper market was simply an artifact of the general rush to safety that had been occurring in the market for over a year. As with the rescue of Bear Stearns, the Treasury's insurance fund left the false impression that money market funds needed government protection, an impression that has been and will be difficult to erase in the future.

Thus, it seems a bit of a stretch—to say the least—to attribute the "shutdown" of the commercial paper market to a supposed "run" on money market funds after the Lehman bankruptcy. There were plenty of other reasons for the commercial paper market to decline. But there is one possibility that seems plausible as an explanation of the Treasury's action. As described in chapter 1, by September 2008 the banks were under great pressure to find financing for their ABCP conduits. The Federal Reserve had permitted them to evade normal capital requirements by placing mortgages in these off-balance-sheet vehicles and issuing commercial paper backed by these assets to short-term lenders like primary money market funds. If the primary funds lost too many investors to government money market funds, the banks would have to find short-term funding from somewhere else, or they would have to take immediate losses by providing the financing themselves or bringing the loans back on their own balance sheets. Accordingly, the Treasury "rescued" the primary money market funds with an insurance system to keep the investors in place and allow the funds to continue financing the banks' ABCP conduits. This was seemingly confirmed in former Treasury Secretary Geithner's book, *Stress Test*, when he wrote: "The Reserve Fund debacle discouraged risk taking by other funds, which meant even less buying of commercial paper and less lending through repo, which meant an even *more intense liquidity crisis for banks and other institutions*. Basically, short-term short financing—whether secured by collateral or not—was vanishing" (emphasis added).[10] The Treasury and the Federal Reserve were not worried about the commercial paper market; they were worried about the liquidity positions of the banks and criticism of their own role in allowing the banks to set up ABCP conduits.

LEHMAN AND CREDIT DEFAULT SWAPS

Paulson's concern about CDS creating dangerous "interconnections" between Bear Stearns and other financial institutions was also shown to be invalid by a review of events after the Lehman bankruptcy. Lehman was a major player in the CDS market, and what happened after its bankruptcy proved that the CDS market was not as dangerous as he'd thought. This supports the views about the role of CDS in the financial crisis expressed in chapter 3. The CDS market continued without disruption after Lehman failed, and there is no known case where a major financial institution was brought down because of an interconnection with Lehman through the CDS market. The CDS that were written on Lehman—that is, for which Lehman was the "reference entity"—were settled in an auction procedure five weeks after the bankruptcy through the exchange of some $5.2 billion among hundreds of counterparties.[11] The CDS on which Lehman was a counterparty, protecting some other counterparty against a loss, went into the bankruptcy process. The transactions where Lehman was "in the money" were accepted by the trustee; the cases where it owed money were repudiated—as permitted in bankruptcy—and the counterparties became bankruptcy claimants. Again, there is no indication that any of the claimants was forced into insolvency by these losses. Those who had been counting on protection from Lehman were now compelled to go back into the market to buy substitute coverage—just like, as noted in chapter 3, homeowners who have to buy substitute fire insurance if their fire insurer fails—but the Lehman counterparties did not suffer any losses other than the additional cost of this substitute coverage. Most of all, they were not driven to insolvency. All this goes to show that Paulson's fears were unfounded. Neither CDS nor the interconnections that were causing Paulson to lose sleep were the problems he supposed, and to the extent that they were the reason for the rescue of Bear Stearns he made a serious misjudgment. Unfortunately, that was not the government's only error.

FEDERAL RESERVE LIQUIDITY
SUPPORT PROGRAMS AND TARP

Before and after the Lehman bankruptcy, many Federal Reserve programs were put in place to provide liquidity to a market from which liquidity had been drained by the decline in mortgage asset values.[12] These included the Primary Dealer Credit Facility, the Term Auction Facility, and the Term Securities Lending Facility. Many observers have argued that these Federal Reserve interventions, and particularly the Troubled Asset Relief Program (TARP), were what prevented the wholesale failures that Paulson thought would occur as a result of interconnections. But it is important to consider what these programs—other than TARP—actually were. All the Federal Reserve's programs were loans of various kinds and thus were made to address liquidity concerns rather than questions of solvency. They did not fill the holes, if any, in balance sheets of firms adversely affected by Lehman's bankruptcy; all of them were efforts to shore up liquidity positions. This is exactly what the Federal Reserve is supposed to do when there is a severe liquidity squeeze. The purpose of these programs was simply to restore public confidence in and liquidity to the financial system, not to replace any loss suffered because of Lehman.

TARP, a congressionally approved program in which the Treasury invested approximately $245 billion in the equity of the largest banks after Lehman's bankruptcy, could have filled holes in the balance sheets of the largest financial institutions, but the way it was implemented made it clear that this was not necessary. The funds were advanced in October 2008, six weeks after Lehman's filing, and were repaid by all the banks other than Citigroup six or eight months later, in April and June 2009. Citigroup made its final payment in December 2009. The six-week delay before funding and the early repayment indicates that the banks had not suffered serious losses from whatever interconnections they had with Lehman. It seems likely that the purpose of TARP was also to increase public confidence in the banks, not to shore them up because of losses from Lehman's default. Unfortunately, the idea has become embedded in the public consciousness that the TARP funds "bailed out" the banks that received them. This is incorrect. If the banks had been insolvent, it would have been true that the TARP funds saved them from closure, but there is no indication that any of the banks that received TARP funds were insolvent. In early 2009, only a few months after the crisis, the Federal Reserve and other bank regulators required the nineteen largest banks to take stress tests that would determine whether they were well enough capitalized at that point to withstand a serious economic downturn. The Federal Reserve's subsequent report in May 2009 was that none of them was insolvent under stress but that a few (not named) required additional capital in the aggregate amount of $75 billion.[13] Although this was after they had received TARP disbursements, it does not appear that any of them needed those infusions to stay solvent, and all of them were permitted by their regulators to return the additional capital within a few months of receiving it. Again, there is no indication that Lehman's bankruptcy had any knock-on effects through interconnections with other large financial firms, and if Lehman—50 percent larger than Bear—had no such effects, it seems clear that the rescue of Bear was unnecessary.

THE BEAR RESCUE AND THE POWER OF MORAL HAZARD

In his book, Paulson notes that securities firms like Bear have failed before without any adverse repercussions, but then concludes that this time was different:

We asked ourselves again what would happen if Bear failed. Back in 1990, the junk bond giant Drexel Burnham Lambert had collapsed without taking the markets down, but they had not been as fragile then, nor had institutions been as entwined. Counterparties had been more easily identified. Perhaps if Bear had been a one-off situation, we would have let it go down. But we realized that Bear's failure would call into question the fate of the other financial institutions that might share Bear's predicament. The market would look for the next wounded deer, then the next, and the whole system would be at serious risk.[14]

This was a key point, but Paulson doesn't seem to have understood the implications of what he was saying. If the other investment banks shared Bear's "predicament," they could be in jeopardy in the future. Rescuing Bear would be seen in the market as a U.S. government policy—a determination to rescue all of the large investment and commercial banks. Paulson, as well as his advisers Ben Bernanke and Timothy Geithner, certainly should have understood moral hazard and the implications of rescuing Bear. Why, then, did he come to the conclusion we will discuss later—that, after Bear, the government had no further obligation to rescue anyone?

I have spent a good deal of time on the rescue of Bear because that changed everything. It was a serious error—the original sin—and not simply because it was completely unnecessary. The consequences went far beyond that. As noted earlier, in rescuing Bear the Treasury and Federal Reserve sent an unmistakable message to the market—that they were prepared to rescue all large financial institutions in order to keep the market stable—and this in turn created a classic example of the power of moral hazard. Bear was by far the smallest of the investment banks. It would be irrational to rescue Bear and not rescue larger firms like Lehman or Goldman if they were threatened with bankruptcy. This perception had profound effects on the decisions by market participants thereafter. The managers of the Reserve Primary Fund, for example, undoubtedly thought that Lehman would be rescued; they saw no reason, then, to sell their Lehman paper and take a loss when all the Lehman creditors would ultimately be made whole, as Bear's were in the JPMorgan Chase acquisition. Richard Fuld, the chair of Lehman, probably thought that the rescue of Bear gave him a better bargaining position with any potential acquirer. After all, his creditors now had less to worry about; they would be protected; he could now get a better deal for his shareholders. The idea that their firm's creditors would be saved probably affected the CEOs and boards of all the large financial institutions that were then pondering what to do; their share prices were all at record lows, so raising more capital now would dilute their shareholders even more. With the government promising to protect the creditors, they would not need a lot of fresh capital to hold the firm together—a little would do. Considerations like these created a much different environment in the market after Bear was rescued. It was going to be harder to jawbone managements into raising more capital, harder to get them to believe they actually had to sell, and, most of all, it was going to be harder to find acquirers without holding out the promise of risk-sharing by the U.S. government. In other words, it was unnecessary, a blunder, to rescue Bear, but once that was done it was even a larger blunder—perhaps the greatest financial blunder ever—not to rescue Lehman. The Bear rescue changed the perceptions and ultimately the actions of all major financial players. Ultimately, it made them weaker and less prepared to deal with the enormous financial panic that occurred when Lehman was allowed to fail.

Some of the moral hazard consequences of the Bear rescue were noted by the Shadow Financial Regulatory Committee, a group of financial scholars sponsored by the American Enterprise Institute:

After Bear Stearns was rescued by a Treasury-Fed bailout in March, Lehman, Merrill Lynch, Morgan-Stanley and Goldman Sachs all sat on their hands for six months awaiting further positive developments (notably, an improvement in the market environment or a handout from the federal government). In particular, Lehman did little to raise capital or shore up its position not only because management thought financial conditions would improve, but also because its chief executive officer thought the government would never let it fail.[15]

Why, then, did creditors desert Lehman during the second week in September? If the market thought that all the large institutions would be rescued, why was there suddenly concern about Lehman's ability to meet its obligations? Let's look again at Fannie Mae and Freddie Mac. In August 2008, Standard & Poor's had cut the ratings for the preferred stock of Fannie Mae and Freddie Mac, and an article in *Barron's* predicted a government takeover that would wipe out the common stock.[16] The share prices of the GSEs went into free fall, persuading Paulson that something had to be done about the two GSEs. This was probably the correct decision. Their capital was depleted, and their losses would be substantial. Paulson pressed the GSEs' regulator, the Federal Housing Finance Agency (FHFA), to put them into a conservatorship—a legal status in which the FHFA, as conservator, would have the authority to operate them in lieu of their boards and managements. This action, however, on September 8, appears to have confirmed for market participants that the problems in the mortgage markets were even worse than they had thought. Fannie Mae and Freddie Mac were not—as far as anyone knew in August and September of 2008—involved with subprime mortgages. If they were driven to insolvency by the default of *prime* mortgages, there was no telling where the bottom was. Such thinking would have brought renewed concern not only about Lehman's viability but also about the viability of any other large financial institution that was heavily invested in the residential mortgage market. Accordingly, in the week following the federal takeover of Fannie and Freddie, creditors, counterparties, and customers began to pull their funds out of Lehman.

This in itself might not have been enough to cause the market's loss of confidence that the government would not follow through on its rescue policy. But despite the rescue of Bear, Paulson seems to have been doing whatever he could to undermine the idea that there would be a rescue of Lehman. He had been following a public strategy that specifically ruled out government support for a Lehman rescue, and he seems to have thought of this as part of a high-stakes negotiating process: "My team and I believed we should emphasize publicly that there could be no government money for a Lehman deal. To my mind, this was the only way to get the best price from a buyer, and the only way to prepare the industry to be fully ready for the likelihood that it would need to participate in any solution."[17] Yet he himself saw it as a bluff: "Tim [Geithner] agreed. He, too, favored an industry solution. But we both knew that if a Bear Stearns–style rescue was the only option, we would take it."[18] Geithner, however, was worried that Paulson was scaring off potential buyers with his continuing assertions that the U.S. government would not share any of a buyer's risk.[19] Paulson was aware of this: "Tim expressed concern about my public stand on government aid. . . . But I was willing to say 'no government assistance' to help us get a deal. If we had to reverse ourselves over the weekend, so be it."[20] To say the least, this was a confused strategy. Not only was it causing potential buyers to hang back, but it was creating uncertainty for his allies.

In a conference call with Bernanke and Geithner on Thursday, September 11, just before the fateful Lehman weekend, Paulson made a statement that seemed to be inconsistent with even this confused strategy, leaving both Geithner and Bernanke unsure whether Paulson would support a rescue: "By Thursday night," Geithner wrote, "when Hank forcefully repeated his no-public-money stand during a conference call with Ben [Bernanke] and SEC Chairman Chris Cox, I began to worry that he actually meant it. He declared that he didn't want to be known as 'Mr. Bailout,' that he couldn't support another Bear Stearns solution."[21] The same Paulson statement in that conference call apparently also spooked Bernanke, who, as chairman of the Federal Reserve, would be the source of the funding for any government risk-sharing. In David Wessel's book *In Fed We Trust*, which is told from Bernanke's point of view, Wessel reports that "in a conference call with Bernanke and Geithner, Paulson had stated unequivocally that he would not publicly support spending taxpayers' money—the Fed's included—to save Lehman. 'I'm being called Mr. Bailout,' he said. 'I can't do it again.' Though Paulson had no legal ability to stop the Fed, Bernanke and other officials would have been extremely reluctant to put money into any Lehman deal without the Treasury secretary's support—unless, as Paulson often did, he changed his stance."[22] Thus, as the fateful day approached, the U.S. government had no plan for what it would do if there were no buyer for Lehman, and the key official, the secretary of the Treasury, was unwilling to take the heat his job in the kitchen required. But it got worse.

The creditor withdrawals from Lehman induced by Paulson's own "strategy" began on September 8 and apparently caught him by surprise. But at this point he had relatively few options. There were potential acquirers for Lehman—the Korean Development Bank, Bank of America, and the large British bank Barclays. But it is likely that they all saw something in the Bear transaction that they thought was essential: the Federal Reserve had taken some of the risk with its $29-billion non-recourse loan to JPMorgan Chase. If the Federal Reserve was willing to put up $29 billion to help JPMorgan acquire a $450 billion company, what was it willing to do for a firm like Lehman, which was almost 50 percent larger? In at least two accounts, several potential acquirers were looking for the government to share some of the risk.[23]

Paulson knew the consequences of a Lehman bankruptcy: "We

knew a Lehman collapse would be a disaster. With roughly $600 billion in assets, the firm was bigger and even more interconnected [that word again] than Bear Stearns."[24] Yet, by his own account, he and the Treasury Department emphasized right up through the last weekend that there would be no U.S. government assistance to save the next investment bank or any other firm. Paulson and Bernanke seem not to have imagined that potential acquirers would be playing the same game, but with a different hand—withholding any formal offers until the government showed how much money it was willing to put up.

Paulson's strategy worked up to a point. On the last weekend, the major Wall Street institutions did come up with $29 billion to help with the rescue of Lehman. But it just wasn't remotely enough and came far too late in the process to make a difference. It is possible, of course, that Bernanke and Paulson thought that the contribution by the other large financial institutions—whatever its size—would be sufficient to rescue Lehman without any government contribution. But what would happen if it wasn't? Paulson and Bernanke had no fallback position—no Plan B or C—if the amount kicked in by the private sector was not enough by itself to rescue Lehman or to entice a third-party buyer to come into the game.

In the end, the only firms even slightly interested in Lehman were Bank of America and Barclays, but there is no way of knowing what other firms might have expressed interest in Lehman during the period after Bear's rescue if Paulson had not been telling the world that the U.S. government would not share some of the risk. As a professional deal maker, he had to know that after the Federal Reserve had put up $29 billion for a Bear rescue, it would be very difficult to get any buyer to come in for Lehman without any government risk-sharing at all. At the very least, a CEO would have trouble explaining to his board why he did not get any U.S. government support for an acquisition of a risky firm almost 50 percent larger than Bear. Later, as we will see, after the disaster of Lehman's bankruptcy, Bernanke would claim that Lehman was so deeply insolvent that the Federal Reserve could not have rescued it anyway. But at this point, somehow, Bernanke and Paulson were expecting some white knight to come in and buy Lehman without any government support. Accordingly, on the last weekend, the Treasury and the Federal Reserve were left with only two potential acquirers, both of which withdrew at the last minute; the excuses they gave were different, but it would not be surprising to learn in the future that if the U.S. government had come up with an offer to supplement what the Wall Street firms had kicked in, that might have made a difference. Unfortunately, by the weekend it would be too late. The real problem was that Paulson and Bernanke did not realize how much moral hazard they had created by rescuing Bear. That transaction had made the rescue of Lehman essential if a market meltdown was to be avoided.

It is hard to imagine that Paulson and Bernanke could have made this situation worse, but they did. After Lehman's bankruptcy caused a full-scale investor panic, they told the media and Congress that they failed to act because the government didn't have the legal authority to rescue Lehman. This *post hoc* justification was false, as will be shown below, but it provided the foundation for Title II of the Dodd-Frank Act, which gave the secretary of the Treasury and the FDIC extraordinary powers to take over and resolve failing financial firms. This would create yet more moral hazard and extend the errors of 2008 far into the future.

THE FEDERAL RESERVE'S AUTHORITY
TO RESCUE LEHMAN

As it became clear on the last weekend that Lehman would fail, Paulson and Bernanke considered where they were at that point: "Ben and I ran over our options for what to do if Lehman failed," Paulson wrote, "but the tough fact was, we didn't have many. . . . Ben reminded me [that] if Lehman filed for bankruptcy, we would lose control of the process, and we wouldn't have much flexibility to minimize market stress."[25] Note that there is no reference in these remarks to the idea that the Federal Reserve did not have the legal authority to provide financial assistance. Nor was there any reference to the Federal Reserve's lack of legal authority in its transcript of September 16, 2008, the day following the Lehman bankruptcy, when there was chaos in the markets, and people were asking why the Federal Reserve had rescued Bear Stearns and not Lehman Brothers.[26] Yet, in another interview with Wessel, reported in the *Wall Street Journal* on September 9, 2013, Bernanke said: "I will maintain to my deathbed that we made every effort to save Lehman, but we were just unable to do so because of a lack of legal authority."[27]

Nevertheless, it does not take much detailed analysis of a statutory text to find that the story Paulson and Bernanke confected to explain their failure to rescue Lehman has no basis in fact. Once again the media, which describes itself as holding officials accountable, failed to do the simple job of unpacking and examining this claim. Under Section 13(3) of the Federal Reserve Act, before its amendment by the Dodd-Frank Act, the Federal Reserve had authority, "in unusual and exigent circumstances," upon the affirmative vote of five members of the board of governors, to "authorize any Federal reserve bank" to make loans to "individuals, partnerships, or corporations" when such loans "are indorsed or secured to the satisfaction of the Federal Reserve bank."[28] So the Federal Reserve did have authority to lend to Lehman; the only issue is whether Lehman had sufficient collateral for a loan. Bernanke, in testimony before the FCIC and in subsequent statements, insisted that Lehman did not have sufficient collateral for a Federal Reserve loan, that the Federal Reserve would have been "lending into a run."[29] Even assuming that to be true, it is not inconsistent with the idea that the Federal Reserve had the legal authority. Whether Lehman had *sufficient collateral* is a practical judgment, within the discretion of the Federal Reserve, but not an element of the Federal Reserve's legal authority.

As it happens, I had an exchange with Bernanke about the Federal Reserve's authority when he testified before the FCIC on September 2, 2010. Before it was my turn to question him, he had said that "I believed deeply that if Lehman was allowed to fail or did fail that the consequences for the U.S. financial system or the U.S. economy would be catastrophic."[30] After first noting that Richard Fuld, Lehman's chair, had told the FCIC that Lehman was solvent and that no one had challenged that statement, I asked him why the Federal Reserve had not lent to Lehman. This was his response:

Bernanke: We are able to do so under the law so far as we have sufficient collateral. And we were prepared to do that. And I was in Washington ready to call the Board together to do that if that was going to be helpful. *However, what I was informed by those working on Lehman's finances was that it was far too little collateral available to come to our window to get enough cash to meet what would be the immediate liquidity runs on the company.* And therefore if we were to lend, what would happen would be that there would be a continued run. There was not nearly enough collateral to provide enough liquidity to meet the run, the company would fail anyway, and the Federal Reserve would be left holding this very illiquid collateral, a very large amount of it. So it was our view that we could not lend enough to save the company under the restriction that we could only lend against collateral [emphasis added].

Wallison: And you are saying then, that even if the collateral was illiquid, you could have lent against it, but you concluded—or someone in the New York Fed concluded— that there wasn't enough of such even illiquid capital— illiquid assets—for you to make this loan?

Bernanke: That is correct.

Wallison: Did you do a study of the collateral that was available? Does the New York Fed have a study of the collateral that was available so that we could see that?

Bernanke: Well I'd refer you to them. Remember we were working with the SEC to do these liquidity stress tests that we did over the summer. And then over the weekend there was 24-hour analysis going on that included not only the staff of the New York Fed but also assistants from the private sector companies that were gathered there. I don't have any—to my knowledge—I don't have a study to hand you *but it was the judgment made by the leadership of the NY Fed and the people who were charged with reviewing the books of Lehman that they were far short of what was needed to get the cash to meet the run. That was the judgment that was given to me.* So that was my understanding [emphasis added].[31]

My initial reaction to this was that Bernanke seemed awfully uninformed and passive about Lehman's condition that weekend. Now, it appears that much of what he said was not true. On September 29, 2014, the *New York Times* carried an article based on interviews with unnamed staffers at the Federal Reserve Bank of New York. According to the reporters, James B. Stewart and Peter Eavis, these staffers had done a study of Lehman's financial condition before the Lehman weekend and concluded that "Lehman might, in fact, be a candidate for rescue." Moreover, the "members of those teams said they never briefed Mr. Geithner, who said he did not know of the results."[32] If Geithner—who was then the president of the New York Federal Reserve—was not briefed, it is highly unlikely that any contrary results would have reached Bernanke, let alone results that indicated that Lehman's assets were "far short of what was needed to get the cash to meet the run." Nor would anyone at the New York Fed have told him that if the staffers there were doing the study.

Thus, we are left with this: even though Bernanke knew (or at least said that he knew) that a "catastrophe" would result if Lehman failed, he never made an attempt to find out whether or not Lehman had enough assets for a rescue. This is very difficult to accept. If Bernanke really believed that there would be a catastrophe if Lehman failed, it was grossly irresponsible not even to determine definitively whether a Federal Reserve loan was possible, and then—when the catastrophe actually occurred—to make up a story that the Federal Reserve didn't have the authority to rescue Lehman because Lehman did not have enough assets to support a Federal Reserve loan.

Also strange is Bernanke's passivity. Bernanke knew that Paulson would not support a bailout of Lehman; Paulson had said in a phone conversation with Geithner and Bernanke several days before the Lehman weekend that he would not support a bailout. But Paulson was known to change his mind, and had been following a strategy that if they got to the weekend without a buyer, he would support government financing. Bernanke knew that without the Treasury's support, the Federal Reserve would not be able to make the loan. Why, then, given what he thought would happen if Lehman went into bankruptcy, didn't Bernanke try to persuade Paulson to change his view? The first step would have been to show Paulson that Lehman's finances would support a loan. Instead, he seems to have decided to let the chips fall where they may.

It's not as though Bernanke's tale about the Fed's lack of authority had no consequences. It was one of the principal reasons that Congress adopted the Dodd-Frank Act, which gives the secretary of the Treasury extraordinary powers to seize non-bank financial firms and turn them over to the FDIC for liquidation if he believes that their financial distress will cause instability in the U.S. financial system. That power would not have been granted if the American people and Congress had been aware that the failure to rescue Lehman was simply an enormous blunder rather than a real example of insufficient government authority.

Moreover, if Lehman had actually been rescued, it's conceivable that the U.S. and the world could have avoided a financial crisis. As noted in chapter 12, the PMBS that looked like "toxic assets" in early 2009 eventually recovered much of their value. If the post-Lehman panic had been avoided through a Lehman rescue, and if the SEC had promptly resolved the mark-to-market issues that were causing financial firms to look unstable or insolvent, it is possible to imagine that the U.S. would have muddled through. There would not have been a Great Recession, and the Dodd-Frank Act would never have been enacted. History would have been very different.

Another reason that the Bernanke testimony is not credible is that after Lehman failed, the Federal Reserve reduced its collateral requirements for loans under the Primary Dealer Credit Facility to include non–investment grade bonds and even equities,[33] so the Federal Reserve doesn't seem to have had a problem with being flexible about collateral. If the Federal Reserve was willing to take equity—

as it did later in its rescue of AIG—Lehman's shares in its broker-age subsidiary would have been more than adequate collateral for a loan. No one has ever suggested that the Lehman broker-dealer was insolvent, and there were reports at the time that the Lehman broker-dealer had more than $60 billion in securities inventory, most of which were treasuries and other liquid securities. In addition, a consortium of financial firms—apparently not fearful that they were dealing with a hopeless case—had agreed over the weekend to ac-quire some of Lehman's more troubled assets for $29 billion.[34] That would have left the Federal Reserve with a much smaller loan and much less collateral to find and also bolstered the market's confi-dence in Lehman's ability to survive—if, of course, it wasn't deeply insolvent. Moreover, as we have seen, at the end of 2007, 90 percent of Lehman's assets were short-term. So even if the Federal Reserve had taken fixed-income assets, it wouldn't have been holding illiquid assets for very long; payment would have come when the loans ma-tured. Finally, there was a good chance that a Federal Reserve loan would likely have changed the psychology of the moment and given pause to the panic-stricken creditors and investors who were clam-oring for Lehman's cash. A loan from the Federal Reserve implies some degree of faith in the borrower, and it is not clear even now that Lehman was not solvent on a going-concern basis.

Richard Fuld, the chairman of Lehman, in his testimony to the FCIC, expressed nothing but puzzlement about why Lehman wasn't provided with the liquidity it needed on that last weekend:

> Lehman had the capital. We needed the liquidity. We went into that last week with over 40 billion of liquidity. We lost close to 30 of it in three days. It was a classic run on the bank. We needed the liquidity. I really cannot answer you, sir, as to why the Federal Reserve and the Treasury and the SEC together chose not to not only provide support for liquidity but also to not to have opened the window to Lehman that Sunday night as it did to all of our competitors. And I must tell you that when I first heard about the fact that the window was open for expanded collateral, a number of my finance

and treasury team came into my office and said, "We're fine. We have the collateral. We can pledge it. We're fine." Forty-five minutes later they came back and said that window is not open to Lehman Brothers.[35]

It has never been clear why the Fed did not make Lehman eligible for liquidity support under the Primary Dealer Credit Facility.

To further confuse things, in *On the Brink*, Paulson praised the FDIC's subsequent sale of Wachovia to Citigroup (a sale that was later reversed because of a better bid from Wells Fargo), because "all creditors would also be protected, a hugely important step that signaled to the markets the government's willingness to support our systemically important banks."[36] This explains the mindset that rescued Bear, and that's probably how the markets looked at it, but it certainly does not explain—other than as a matter of concern for his reputation as "Mr. Bailout"—why Paulson was willing to permit the world-historical mess that was made over Lehman. Could it really be that the 2008 financial crisis—perhaps the greatest financial crisis of all time—occurred because the Federal Reserve would not act without the support of the secretary of the Treasury and the secretary of the Treasury did not like the criticism he was receiving for the Bear rescue? And this when both of them said they believed there would be a financial catastrophe if Lehman failed? We'll probably never get the straight story. There is still no good answer, other than bungling, as to why the government rescued Bear and not Lehman.

LEHMAN AND THE FINANCIAL CRISIS

When Lehman filed for bankruptcy in the early morning of September 15, it produced a financial cataclysm. And why not? Until the weekend just before the filing, almost everyone believed that Lehman would be rescued as Bear had been. Afterward, many defenders of the Bear rescue stated that if Bear had not been rescued, chaos much like that which followed Lehman's bankruptcy filing would have happened with the bankruptcy of Bear. We'll never know the answer, of course, but there are many reasons to believe that the rescue of Bear was both unnecessary and the fateful step that set up the cataclysm of the Lehman bankruptcy filing. First, Bear was a much smaller firm than Lehman and was more heavily invested in the housing finance business. Its insolvency would likely have been interpreted as the result of its unusual risk-taking in housing rather than an example of how all the investment banks had been managed. Second, the rescue of Bear was completely unexpected and unprecedented; the U.S. government had never before laid out cash to rescue an uninsured financial institution. Accordingly, in a way that was quite different from Lehman, the market was not expecting a rescue and so was better prepared for the outcome. Third, as noted earlier, all the predictions about CDS and interconnections would have been proved wrong, as they were when Lehman failed, reducing the likelihood that the market would believe the failure of a large non-bank financial institution would have a systemic effect.

If Bear had been allowed to fail, all the moral hazard effects mentioned above would not have occurred—managements would have felt compelled to shore up their positions with new capital to hold their creditors in place; managements like Lehman's would not have driven hard bargains when approached by potential acquirers, realizing that an acquisition was likely to be better for their shareholders than raising the additional capital that would be required to satisfy their creditors; the Reserve Primary Fund would probably have sold its Lehman commercial paper, not expecting a bailout if Lehman were to approach bankruptcy; and no potential acquirer would have expected risk-sharing from the U.S. government.

Because it followed the rescue of Bear, the failure of Lehman was an entirely different matter. In the six months between the rescue of Bear and the bankruptcy of Lehman, the markets had been relatively calm; spreads in the CDS market in particular—the best index of market anxiety—were elevated but relatively stable. The reason for this lack of tension was probably the belief among market participants that the U.S. government had made its policy clear, and market participants believed it was unlikely that any large firm would be allowed to fail. The CDS spreads on Lehman, moving in a narrow range, tell the story. They were at about 250 basis points on June 17,

390 on July 15, 270 on August 5, and 300 on September 5. It was not until the Lehman weekend, September 13 and 14, when it became clear that the government had neither a buyer nor a Plan B, that the CDS market blew out, hitting 570 before the weekend and 707 on September 15.

At that point, from the perspective of firms, investors, and creditors, the world was turned upside down. Instead of a sense that the U.S. government knew what it was doing and had settled on a policy, there was now a sense that the government was winging it or simply incompetent. Instead of a sense of confidence that loans to the largest firms were likely to be repaid, there was a fear that no private firm of any size was a safe investment. So much money was withdrawn from the private market and invested in riskless U.S. Treasury securities that short-term Treasury rates turned negative. Panicked investors were willing to pay for the privilege of investing in a T-bill.

In these conditions, the worst thing that could happen to a financial firm was to have rumors circulate on the street that it couldn't meet withdrawal requests. When the market is in panic mode, investors, creditors, and others act on rumors. They don't ask questions, and they don't wait for verification. So financial institutions began to hoard cash, refusing to lend to one another, even overnight. This virtually unprecedented market meltdown *was* the financial crisis. As Alan Greenspan described it:

> One has to dig very deep into peacetime financial history to uncover similar episodes. The market for call money, the key short-term financing vehicle of a century ago, shut down at the peak of the 1907 panic, "when no call money was offered at all for one day and the [bid] rate rose from 1 to 125%." ... Even at the height of the 1929 stock market crisis, the call money market functioned, although annual interest rates did soar to 20 percent. In lesser financial crises, availability of funds in the long-term market disappeared, but overnight and other short term markets continued to function. The withdrawal of overnight money represents financial stringency at its maximum.[37]

The panic that was now in full cry certainly looked to people living through it as though the world was coming apart. Liquidity had
dried up completely, and the largest and best-known firms were having trouble meeting their cash obligations. Then, when it looked as
though things could not get worse, the Federal Reserve announced
that it was necessary to rescue AIG, the world's largest insurance
holding company. The AIG story is complex, beginning with the fact
that its problems were first described as stemming from credit default swaps, themselves little understood by the media, politicians,
and—one suspects—many people in the commentariat. In reality, as
described in chapter 3, a poorly managed securities lending business
was equally responsible for AIG's cash shortage. Nevertheless, AIG
soon became the poster child for the dangers of CDS, even though it
is the only firm that got into trouble while operating in that market.
AIG's problem was that its subsidiary, AIGFP, took only one side of
the CDS trade; it wrote protection, but—unlike others who wrote this
kind of insurance—did not hedge its risk. It is still not clear why the
Federal Reserve and Treasury thought they had to rescue AIG, but
after the failure to rescue Lehman and the chaos that followed, the
decision to rescue AIG looked like—and probably was—just more
government bumbling. "The rescue of A.I.G.," a *New York Times* col-
umnist reported, "further undermined confidence because, within
the space of several days, the government did a complete about-face.
The bailout suggested the Treasury Department was as confused
about what to do as the rest of us. So rather than help solve the crisis, the Treasury Department had actually contributed to the biggest
problem in the market right now: an utter lack of confidence."[38]

At the end of the fateful week that began with Lehman's bankruptcy, followed in a matter of days by the Federal Reserve's rescue of
AIG, there was yet another reversal of policy. Although Paulson had
been saying for months that there would be no government funds
made available for rescues, the Treasury now delivered to Congress a
three-page draft bill that would appropriate $700 billion for a whole-
sale rescue of the financial system. As Paulson explained to Congress, the idea behind the legislation was to give the Treasury the
necessary funds to buy the PMBS—now called toxic assets—from

the banks that were holding them. This was a good idea if the Treasury was willing to take the political heat for paying more than the market price for these assets. (Recall that at this time market prices had fallen to near zero because buyers fled the market when unprecedented numbers of mortgage delinquencies and defaults became apparent in 2007.) Although Paulson told Congress the Treasury intended to use the funds to acquire banks' toxic assets when he and Bernanke testified on September 23, that is not what the Treasury ultimately did. Whether the Treasury abandoned this idea because of questions about feasibility or because of the fearful politics of telling the public that it had paid billions of dollars for assets that were selling for virtually nothing in the market is not known, but at some point in October, even before Congress had approved the TARP legislation, the Treasury decided simply to buy preferred stock of the largest banks. This injected capital, but left the public with the false impression that the banks would have failed without this government support. The result was a degree of public resentment against the largest banks that has made it impossible for Congress to make any of the many necessary changes in the Dodd-Frank Act. With reason, any lawmaker who endorsed such a move will fear being accused of doing the bidding of the large banks.

Even after the injection of capital into the largest banks, the market continued to fall. Nothing seemed to be working.

However, when the Financial Accounting Standards Board, under pressure from the House Financial Services Committee, finally changed the mark-to-market requirements in March 2009, the stock market—measured by the Dow—finally began to recover. March 2009 was its lowest point in the post-Lehman crisis period. The Federal Reserve's announcement of the favorable stress test results in May also helped. By this time, the stock market was already above its March low, but its pace of recovery accelerated. Geithner, who was the chief proponent of the stress tests, had been correct; the tests had enough credibility to ease the anxieties of investors. Still, there is good reason to believe that there would not have been a financial crisis if Bear Stearns had not been rescued in March 2008 or if—having rescued Bear—the government went on to rescue Lehman as it rescued AIG. It's important to recall that the "toxic assets" that had driven down the capital positions and caused substantial operating losses among banks and other financial institutions eventually recovered much of their value. If Lehman had been rescued and the mark-to-market accounting problem had been resolved by timely SEC action, it's conceivable that the financial system would have been able to muddle through to a recovery without a panic and a financial crisis.

Unfortunately, Paulson and Bernanke made four major errors. The first and most consequential was the rescue of Bear. The moral hazard created by that single unnecessary action changed the calculations of all the other players in the market: it reduced the incentives for firms to restore their capital positions with additional equity, reduced the incentive for the Reserve Primary Fund to take a loss on its Lehman commercial paper, and reduced the likelihood that Lehman would take the necessary steps to save or sell itself. The fact that the U.S. government shared the risk of acquiring Bear made similar risk-sharing essential for any buyer of Lehman, the very opposite of Paulson's strategy. Thus, once Bear had been rescued, it was essential to rescue Lehman, and the failure to do so was the second major error and the precipitating cause of the panic and hoarding of cash that ensued.

Third, the failure of Paulson and Bernanke to own up to their mistakes, arguing that they did not have the legal authority to rescue Lehman, provided a foundation for congressional action—adopting the Dodd-Frank Act—that may prove in the long run to be more destructive than the financial crisis itself.

Finally, the TARP program accomplished little good, but left the American people with the false impression that the largest banks had been bailed out with taxpayer funds. The resentment that produced has made it difficult to enact major changes to the Dodd-Frank Act, because lawmakers don't want to be accused of taking the side of the undeserving banks that had been bailed out. As long as Dodd-Frank remains in place, economic recovery will be hampered.

There would not have been a field on which these errors of judgment could occur but for faulty government housing policies that had brought about the virtual collapse of the housing finance system in 2007 and 2008. As with most failed government policies, it's difficult to identify any one person or group that made key mistakes. This orphan had many fathers. Still, the most troubling fact is that the American public has no idea—or the wrong idea—why we had a financial crisis. As long as the American people believe that the government's housing policies had no role in the financial crisis, we are likely to repeat the same mistakes. As shown in the next chapter, there is evidence that this is already happening.

14

The False Narrative and the Future

Why the Failure to Understand the Causes of the Crisis May Lead to Another

> Only by understanding the factors that led to and amplified the crisis can we hope to guard against a repetition.
>
> BEN BERNANKE, Testimony to the Financial Crisis Inquiry Commission, September 2, 2010

The preceding chapters showed that government housing policy, implemented principally by HUD through Fannie Mae and Freddie Mac, reduced mortgage underwriting standards, built an unprecedented housing bubble, and—in combination with mark-to-market accounting and a blundering government response—was the principal cause of the 2008 financial crisis. Thus, the conventional narrative about the crisis—that it was caused by lax government regulation of private financial institutions—is false. In this chapter, I will show that this false narrative, by ignoring the real cause of the crisis, has opened the way for government policies that will again result in looser underwriting standards and another mortgage-based breakdown of the financial system. As Ben Bernanke's epigraphic remark suggests, we won't be able to prevent a repetition of the financial crisis unless we understand its causes.

A RUSH TO JUDGMENT

We frequently hear that the events of 2008 were the worst financial crisis since the Great Depression, and that only quick and decisive action by government officials prevented a complete meltdown of the world's financial economy. If that is true, and the world was as close to financial catastrophe as claimed, it is troubling that there was so little debate—in Congress, the academic world, or the media—about the causes of the crisis. The stakes, after all, were enormously high. However, almost from the moment of Lehman Brothers' bankruptcy, in September 2008, the U.S. government and other governments around the world concluded that they knew exactly what caused the financial breakdown and exactly what to do about it. Yet in 2008, as shown earlier, key facts about the housing market were unknown. Fannie Mae and Freddie Mac, for example, had not disclosed the true size of their exposure to nontraditional mortgages (NTMs), and there was little understanding that a housing price bubble of historic proportions had developed between 1997 and 2007.

In public policy, as in medicine, a prescription is only as good as the diagnosis. The first question policy makers should have asked is how the U.S. mortgage market came to be dominated by loans that failed in such unprecedented numbers as soon as housing prices stopped rising. Instead, the government and those that have an ideological stake in denying its role in the crisis asked no questions; despite the insolvency of both Fannie and Freddie, the government-backed firms that dominated the mortgage market, they simply asserted that the private sector, and particularly "Wall Street," was responsible. That narrative, later endorsed by the majority report of the Financial Crisis Inquiry Commission (FCIC), has not only remained largely unchallenged in the media but has become the principal conceptual underpinning for the restrictive regulatory legislation—the Dodd-Frank Act—that has since been enacted in the United States.

THE GROUP OF THIRTY REPORT

Only six months after President Obama took office, his administration sent to Capitol Hill the outlines of the legislation that would eventually become the Dodd-Frank Act, a law that was heralded as an essential series of steps to prevent another financial crisis. This legislative proposal, in turn, was based on a plan that had been advanced several months earlier, in January 2009, just after the president's inauguration, by the Group of Thirty—an international organization composed largely of former central bankers and bank regulators under the chairmanship of Paul Volcker.[1]

The Group of Thirty plan recommended that "systemically significant" financial institutions—based on size, leverage, scale of interconnectedness, and the importance of their services to the financial infrastructure—be subject to special prudential regulation, and that the boundaries of that prudential regulation be extended beyond regulated banks and bank holding companies to other nonbank financial institutions. Among the specific recommendations in the report were ideas that are in the Dodd-Frank Act today, or have been suggested as regulatory actions under the act, including special bank-like supervision of nonbank firms, a prudential regulator for money market mutual funds and other private pools of capital, and a special system for the resolution of failing nonbank financial institutions outside the bankruptcy system. In other words, the fundamental elements of what became the Dodd-Frank Act were proposed only four months after the onset of the crisis, without any serious discussion of whether the causes of the crisis had been correctly assessed. When the Obama administration immediately accepted these ideas and proposed legislation that embodied them, all attention thereafter was focused on the administration's proposal, effectively preempting what little discussion there was about what actually caused the crisis.

THE "INTERCONNECTEDNESS" ERROR

The importance that the Group of Thirty attributed to the idea of "interconnectedness" among financial institutions shows that the authors—and subsequently the Obama administration—had misdi-

agnosed the crisis. As discussed in chapter 13, interconnectedness refers to the knock-on effects of one firm's failure on its counterparties
or creditors; the central idea is that through their debts and other obligations to one another—their "interconnections"—the failure of a
large financial institution could bring down others, causing a broadly
based financial crisis like what occurred in 2008. This is superficially
plausible, but what happened after the failure of Lehman Brothers in
September 2008 showed clearly that it is wholly invalid as an explanation of the crisis. On the contrary, the Lehman case shows that significant knock-on effects from the failure of large nonbank financial
institutions are highly unlikely, at least with respect to their effects
on other large financial firms.

Lehman was one of the largest financial institutions in the world,
and it suddenly declared bankruptcy at a time when investors and
creditors everywhere were already in a state of high anxiety about
the financial condition of other large financial institutions. Yet no
other large financial firms failed because of Lehman's sudden collapse. In other words, Lehman's debts to other large firms, including
its obligations under credit default swaps—which were specifically
mentioned by Secretary Paulson as a source of dangerous interconnections—were not great enough to do material damage to its counterparties. If the interconnectedness idea had any validity, this would
have been the time for it to show up, and it did not. To be sure, there
was chaos after Lehman's failure, largely because the U.S. government had suddenly and unaccountably abandoned what investors
had thought was a policy—established by the rescue of Bear Stearns
—to prevent the failure of all large financial firms.

Nevertheless, following the architecture proposed by the Group
of Thirty, the Dodd-Frank Act based its entire nonbank regulatory
structure—intended to forestall systemic risk—on the interconnectedness idea, designating all banks and bank holding companies with more than $50 billion in assets as systemically important
financial institutions (SIFIs) and setting up a council of financial
regulators, called the Financial Stability Oversight Council (FSOC),
with the power to designate large nonbank financial institutions as
SIFIs. These firms were deemed to be systemically important because, through interconnections with others, their "material finan-

cial distress" could "pose a threat to the financial stability of the United States."[2] Firms so designated were to be turned over to the Federal Reserve for bank-like regulation of their capital and their risk-taking.[3]

THE CAUSE OF THE CRISIS WAS COMMON SHOCK

In reality, as shown in previous chapters, the financial crisis was caused not by interconnections among large financial firms, but by a phenomenon known to scholars as common shock or contagion.[4] A common shock to a financial market or system occurs when an asset held by many financial firms suddenly loses substantial value. Chapter 11 showed in detail how the decline in housing and mortgage values—brought on by the collapse of the massive 1997–2007 housing price bubble—seriously weakened most of the major financial institutions in the United States and Europe. The firms all had major exposures to the same assets—private mortgage–backed securities (PMBS) backed by NTMs. When these assets began to lose substantial market value, all the exposed firms were adversely affected at the same time. As outlined in chapter 12, mark-to-market accounting both weakened their capital positions and reduced their access to liquidity in the market. It was thus a common shock and not interconnectedness that caused the failure or near failure of Bear Stearns, Lehman Brothers, AIG, and the insured depository institutions Wachovia, Washington Mutual, and IndyMac. Many others were weakened but did not fail, or at least were not rescued. This is important because common shock cannot be addressed through the regulation of specially selected large institutions, as Dodd-Frank would do; it is dangerous specifically because, by definition, its effects are widespread and not limited to a few large institutions.

The Group of Thirty's focus on interconnectedness is to be expected from bank regulators, who are trained to regulate individual institutions rather than markets, and the Obama administration probably adopted the interconnectedness notion because of its bias in favor of increased regulation. If the next financial crisis is anything like the 2008 crisis, it would not be prevented—and might actually be made more likely—by heavier regulation of individual large financial firms. In general, there are two ways to prevent a similar mortgage-based crisis: maintain strong underwriting standards for mortgages or, more generally, prevent large financial firms from acquiring and holding the same assets. Neither is likely to be achieved by more stringent regulation of a few specific firms, as Dodd-Frank requires. Indeed, regulation tends to make regulated institutions more alike, diminishing the diversification in assets that is ultimately the only successful strategy for protection against market risks. As pointed out earlier, the Basel risk-based capital rules—a good example of how regulation can create bad outcomes—actually herded banks into PMBS by creating strong financial incentives to hold those assets. If the Dodd-Frank Act had been properly designed to address the real causes of the 2008 financial crisis, it would have directed the FSOC to look for excessive similarity in the assets of large financial firms. Instead, the Dodd-Frank Act set up a system for bringing nonbank institutions under the control of the Federal Reserve and subjecting them to stringent regulation in much the same way that banks are regulated—a system that has failed again and again in the past.

"YOU NEVER WANT A SERIOUS CRISIS TO GO TO WASTE"

Whatever the errors of the Group of Thirty, the Obama administration compounded them by adopting the Group of Thirty's proposal hastily and without apparent concern for whether these ideas would actually prevent a future crisis. In February 2009, the president's chief of staff told a television audience that "You never want a serious crisis to go to waste."[5] This remark speaks volumes about why the administration was rushing to judgment. The new president had said (erroneously) during the campaign debates that deregulation had caused the crisis, and the newly elected Democratic supermajorities in Congress were imbued with the idea—expressed often by Congressman Barney Frank—that what was necessary was a "New New Deal." The Obama administration was not going to wait for facts before acting, and the Group of Thirty proposal perfectly fit the bill for an administration and a Congress looking for a regulatory regime that would extend the government's control over more of the financial sector. From that point on, it was just a matter of time. Dodd-Frank initially passed the House without a single Republican vote and passed the Senate with only three Republican votes. It was signed into law on July 21, 2010, eighteen months after President Obama took office.

Along the way, Congress also set up the FCIC, which in theory could have been a locus of serious debate about the causes of the crisis, but, as described in chapter 3, it was not to be. From the beginning, the Democratic majority on the commission saw their role as confirming the narrative that underlay the Dodd-Frank Act, and they could not be persuaded to look in any other direction. In the end, as noted earlier, Congress did not consider the commission's report worth waiting for; it adopted the act six months *before* the commission reported. That didn't really matter. The commission was not set up for a debate; it was set up to concur in what Congress was going to do anyway. It just couldn't act as quickly as Congress—which is wryly funny when you think about it.

THE FALSE NARRATIVE BECOMES
THE CONVENTIONAL NARRATIVE

Because no extended debate about the causes of the crisis ever occurred, many people—including particularly the media—simply accepted the government's explanation, perhaps not realizing that it was an exculpation. In any event, the easy stories of greed and wrongdoing on Wall Street were too enticing, and most of the best-selling books about the crisis focused on that. Members of the media pride themselves on "holding the government accountable," but in this case they showed no interest in going more deeply into the issue of how the crisis came about.

Even the banks and other private institutions were confused about their responsibility for the crisis. There was no doubt that they had done many of the things they were accused of in the media, but having only media accounts to rely on they did not realize that the private sector's role in the crisis was relatively small when compared to what the government had done. A case in point is the evolution in the views of Michael Cembalest of JPMorgan Chase as more information about the government's role became available after 2009. Cembalest is the global head of investment strategy at JPMorgan Chase and writes a widely read financial newsletter called *Eye on the Market*. In 2009, surveying the wreckage left by the crisis, he had written that "the housing crisis was mostly a consequence of the private sector. Why? US Agencies appeared to be responsible for only 20% of all subprime, Alt A and other mortgage exotica." But in 2011, he retracted that view: "[O]ver the last 2 years," he wrote, "analysts have dissected the housing crisis in greater detail. What emerges from new research is something quite different: government agencies now look to have guaranteed, originated or underwritten 60% of all 'non-traditional' mortgages, which totaled $4.6 trillion in June 2008. What's more, this research asserts that housing policies instituted in the early 1990s were explicitly designed to require US Agencies to make much riskier loans, with the ultimate goal of pushing private sector banks to adopt the same standards."[6] In 2013, after additional study of the data, he went further, reporting that "the private sector descent into underwriting hell took place well after the multi-trillion dollar GSE [government-sponsored enterprises] balance sheets had gone there first. . . . There are many reasons to wonder how bad the former would have been had the latter not preceded it."[7]

By 2009, however, as a matter of the public's understanding, the narrative about the financial crisis had been settled and sealed. The crisis, it held, was caused by the failure to adequately regulate the greed and risk-taking of the private sector. Yes, Fannie Mae and Freddie Mac had become insolvent, but that was because they were seduced by the profits they could earn by acquiring and securitizing NTMs and by the desire to maintain their market share. As the secretary of housing told Congress, the GSEs had followed the pied piper of Wall Street down the road to perdition. Some were ideologically primed to accept this story. Joe Nocera of the *New York Times* said the FCIC's report was "utterly persuasive . . . conclusively showing that the two government-sponsored entities followed Wall Street and the subprime companies off the cliff, rather than the other way around."[8]

Earlier chapters of this book showed that this narrative was false. The affordable-housing goals had driven Fannie and Freddie to lower their underwriting standards. These lower standards, intended to assist low-income borrowers, had spread to the wider market, so many more mortgages were weak and of low quality than just the NTMs that Fannie and Freddie had acquired to meet the goals. There was no evidence that Fannie and Freddie had acquired NTMs because they were chasing profits or market share. Quite the contrary; as made clear in chapters 6 and 7 above, the documentary record showed clearly that the affordable-housing goals were the *only* reason for lowering their standards and acquiring NTMs, which as a group not only were unprofitable but drove Fannie and Freddie into insolvency. Chapter 8 then showed how the loosened underwriting standards Fannie and Freddie had to adopt in order to meet the affordable-housing goals inevitably spread to the wider market. The remarkable thing was that those who vehemently denied the role of the government's housing policies in the financial crisis got as far as they did with what was simply a just-so story, not an argument supported by data.

In the future, it may turn out that the most troubling feature of the false narrative about the 2008 crisis was its failure to acknowledge the need for policies that will prevent another collapse of the housing market. If the public believes that the financial crisis was caused by insufficient regulation of the private sector, and that the housing policies the government pursued between 1992 and 2008 had no role in the events of 2007 and 2008, a return of the same faulty policies are inevitable in the future. The real lesson of the financial crisis will not have been learned.

FANNIE MAE AND FREDDIE MAC BEFORE
THE AFFORDABLE-HOUSING GOALS

Chapter 4 contains a brief recounting of the government's role in the housing finance market since the Depression era. It shows that— whether employed by the government or the private sector—solid underwriting standards are the key to sustained housing market stability and do not appreciably reduce homeownership rates. Indeed,

in the few times in the past when the government has sought to stabilize the housing market, it has adopted and maintained these standards, reducing defaults and creating long periods of stability. Since
the late 1950s, however, the government's policies have often degraded mortgage underwriting standards and stimulated the growth
of credit bubbles and mortgage defaults by reducing underwriting
standards. The result has been continuing cycles of housing booms
and busts, culminating in the 2008 financial crisis. Even before the
enactment of the affordable-housing goals, Fannie Mae's experience
demonstrated that relaxing underwriting standards led to high rates
of default.

As discussed in chapter 4, when Fannie and Freddie were authorized to enter the conventional market in 1970, the charters they
received from Congress that year directed them to maintain underwriting standards "of such quality, type, and class as to meet,
generally, the purchase standards imposed by private institutional
investors." This language seemed to refer to high-quality mortgages,
and these standards were consistent with the traditional underwriting standards that prevailed in the conventional market at that time.
Despite seven recessions between 1953 and 1991, foreclosures on conventional mortgages had remained consistently below 1 percent and
were far more stable than Federal Housing Administration (FHA)
foreclosure rates during much of this period (Figure 14.1).

Figure 14.1 also shows that the conventional market began to deteriorate somewhat in the late 1980s. The cause in this case was likely
to have been Fannie's temporary abandonment, between 1981 and
1984, of the traditional prime mortgage standards it had previously
been following. The high market interest rates of the inflationary late
1970s had created serious problems for Fannie. Its portfolio of conventional and government-insured mortgages consisted of long-term
fixed-rate loans, which were yielding substantially less than even
Fannie's government-assisted cost of funds. Freddie was less affected
by interest rate conditions because it had already begun to securitize substantial amounts of its loans in the 1970s, so that investors
in Freddie's mortgage-backed securities were taking the interest rate
risks that were causing substantial losses for Fannie.

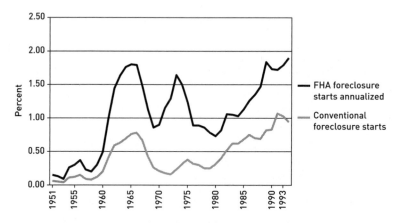

Source: Peter J. Elmer and Steven A. Seelig, "The Rising Long-Term Trend of Single-Family Mortgage Foreclosure Rates," FDIC Working Paper 98-2, 1998, www.fdic.gov/bank/analytical/working/98-2.pdf; and Mortgage Bankers Association.

FIG. 14.1. FHA and conventional foreclosure starts, 1951–1993

To avoid insolvency during this period, Fannie reduced its underwriting standards so that it could obtain upfront fee payments for acquiring riskier subprime and other low-quality mortgages. This defrayed some of its interest rate losses but resulted in serious credit losses from the mortgages it acquired between 1981 and 1984.[9] Accordingly, in succeeding years, Fannie completely revised its underwriting procedures, returning to the traditional standards that it had used through most of the 1970s: a down payment of 10 to 20 percent, a good to excellent credit record (FICO scores, which are now commonly used, were not in wide use at this time), and a debt-to-income (DTI) ratio of no more than 38 percent.

A study of the Atlanta area by the Government Accountability Office in 1990 showed that these standards were being applied there by both Fannie and Freddie.[10] Similarly, Fannie's 1992 Random Study, discussed in chapter 2, also showed that the mortgages acquired between 1988 and 1991, after the 1985 reforms went into effect, were again showing default rates of less than 1 percent.[11]

The importance of sound underwriting standards was also demonstrated recently in the dataset released by Freddie Mac in March

2013, and discussed in detail in chapters 2 and 8. The dataset consisted of 15 million 30-year, fixed-rate, fully documented loans. These mortgages represented 53 percent of all the loans Freddie acquired between 1999 and 2011. The 47 percent not disclosed were mortgages of lower quality, such as adjustable-rate mortgages (ARMs) or loans Freddie had acquired under special programs to meet the affordable-housing goals. Accordingly, the 53 percent were Freddie's best loans, and probably the best in the market at the time they were acquired, since the GSEs could outbid any private investor for the loans they wanted.

Table 2.2, in chapter 2, based on the Freddie dataset, compared the default rates through 2012 of the prime traditional purchase-money mortgages—borrower FICO scores of more than 660, down payments of at least 10 percent, and DTI ratios of at least 38 percent—in Freddie's 1999 vintage loans with purchase-money mortgages in the same dataset that did not meet one or more of these traditional standards. Table 8.1, in chapter 8, also based on the Freddie dataset, compared the default rates through 2012 of all the prime traditional purchase-money mortgages Freddie acquired between 1999 and 2007 with the performance of the loans that did not meet at least one of the traditional underwriting standards.

What we can see from the comparisons in these tables is that once traditional underwriting standards are abandoned, mortgage performance quickly deteriorates. This deterioration is particularly pronounced during stressful periods in the housing market. Both Tables 2.2 and 8.1 reflect performance during the boom years between 1999 and 2007. But boom years in the general economy and the housing market are inevitably followed by some period of decline or recession. Figure 14.2 shows the performance of the loans in Freddie's dataset with varying FICO scores and loan-to-value (LTV) ratios (down payments) in the seriously stressed period between 2007 and 2012. The figure makes clear that low FICO scores and high LTV ratios have an even greater effect on the performance of mortgages during times of stress. Thus, unless traditional mortgage underwriting standards are maintained through the business cycle, the ordinary patterns of boom and bust in the cycle will inevi-

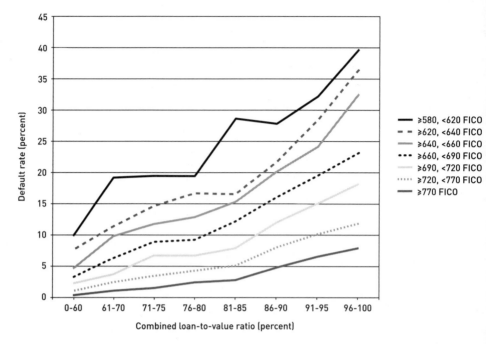

Source: Freddie Mac dataset.

FIG. 14.2. Effect of a combined loan-to-value ratio and FICO score on default rates of 2007 vintage home purchase loans between 2007 and 2012

tably bring about substantial losses. And if mortgage underwriting standards become as weak as they were between 1992 and 2008, and the government is involved in stimulating the market with financial support, a financial crisis like the one that occurred in 2008 is inevitable in the future. That is the lesson of the financial crisis, and the lesson we will be taught again if we accept the false narrative as the explanation for the crisis.

"THOSE WHO CAN'T REMEMBER THE PAST ARE CONDEMNED TO REPEAT IT"

This aphorism is often attributed to the philosopher George Santayana, but similar statements have been attributed to Edmund Burke, Winston Churchill, and other notables. Like all aphorisms, it is repeated because it carries an important grain of truth. How we view the past affects what we do in the future. If we have failed to correctly assess what caused the financial crisis, we will stumble blindly into another one in the future. And that, indeed, seems to be where we are headed.

As discussed in chapter 4, in the late 1950s, Congress sought to stimulate housing during a recession by reducing the FHA's down payment requirements. The result was a significant increase in defaults. Today, only a few years after the financial crisis, where perhaps as many as eight million homes were foreclosed—most of them belonging to low-income borrowers who were offered mortgages their income instability could not support—the FHA is doing it again. In 2014, for example, a firm called Carrington Mortgage advertised to potential lenders, "FICO Reduced to 550! We Deliver FHA Purchase: The low down payment program for your borrowers!" and another firm named HomeBridge advertised "FHA & VA Down to 580 FICO!" Many other subprime lenders are advertising the same concessionary rates based on FHA programs, even though a glance back at Figure 14.2 shows a 580 FICO score, even with a 10 percent down payment, has a default rate of higher than 30 percent in a period of market stress, and that, of course, would mean a family's painful loss of that down payment. Why is the FHA offering these loans? In part it may be to restart the housing market or to meet the political goals of the current administration, but it doesn't evince any awareness that making loans of this quality follows the path that caused the financial crisis only six years ago.

Similarly, in May 2014, the Federal Housing Finance Agency (FHFA), the regulator and current conservator of Fannie and Freddie, released a new "2014 Strategic Plan for the Conservatorships of Fannie Mae and Freddie Mac." In the plan's description, the FHFA noted:

> [H]ousing finance market conditions are far from what could reasonably be considered satisfactory or normal. One factor limiting access to credit is the change in credit standards required by mortgage market participants. Prudent standards

are essential to stable markets, as the excesses of the last decade made clear. . . . However, some originators and mortgage
insurers have placed *additional conditions—such as higher
minimum credit score requirements—on top of the acceptable
credit standards of each Enterprise. These credit overlays result
in the rejection of many loans that would otherwise meet Enterprise credit standards* [emphasis added].[12]

In this remarkable paragraph, the regulator and conservator of
Fannie and Freddie is asking lenders to make *lower-quality loans* because these would meet the standards of Fannie and Freddie. If there
is any single statement that shows the lessons of the financial crisis
have not been taken on board by the current administration, this is
it. The two GSEs became insolvent because of the poor quality of the
loans they had acquired, and now their regulator and conservator—
who should be focused on their safety and soundness and the protection of the taxpayers—is calling for originators to help them take on
more risk. The fact that this statement brought no outcry from Congress, the media, or the academic observers of the housing finance
market shows that too many in these groups, too, have accepted the
false narrative that the financial crisis had little to do with the government housing policies embodied in the affordable-housing goals.

Other examples abound. The sole effort of the Dodd-Frank Act
to prevent another mortgage meltdown was a provision that required
securitization sponsors to retain a portion of the risk in any pool
they securitize. This idea is based on the misconception that the
securitization process stimulated the origination and sale of risky
mortgages. As the FCIC described it, "The nonprime mortgage securitization process created a pipeline through which risky mortgages
were conveyed and sold throughout the financial system. This pipeline was essential to the origination of the burgeoning numbers of
high-risk mortgages. The originate-to-distribute model undermined
responsibility and accountability for the long-term viability of mortgages and mortgage-related securities and contributed to the poor
quality of mortgage loans."[13]

What the FCIC majority failed to understand, as discussed in chapter 3, is that the securitization process is no different from any supply chain and that it works the same way as supply chains for the manufacture of automobiles and the selling of cabbages. Each supplier along the way to the final buyer, including the final assembler of the parts, warrants the quality of the part or the product to the next person in the chain. If the warranty is violated, the responsible party must respond in damages or take the faulty product back and return the payment received for it. Exactly this, of course, has happened in the mortgage market in recent years, when the GSEs put back loans to the suppliers of mortgages they deemed to be faulty. In other words, everyone who touches the mortgage on the way to the final buyer is at risk of what is called in the housing market a "put back," and everyone, for good reason, has skin in the game.

The misplaced view that securitizers bore no risk led Congress, in Dodd-Frank, to require that securitizers must retain at least 5 percent of the risk of any securitization pool, unless the pool is made up entirely of what were called "qualified residential mortgages" (QRMs). A QRM was intended to be a mortgage of such high quality that it could be securitized without risk retention by the securitization sponsor. Congress set six agencies—the Federal Reserve, the Office of the Comptroller of the Currency, the FDIC, the FHFA, the Securities and Exchange Commission, and the Department of Housing and Urban Development—to the task of developing and proposing the terms of such a mortgage.

When the agencies' proposed rule was finally announced in March 2011,[14] it was roundly criticized—including by many members of Congress—because it included a 20 percent down payment on purchase money mortgages and several other relatively strict underwriting standards of the kind that were part of the traditional prime mortgage.[15] A down payment that high, many in the industry argued, would mean that large numbers of people would not be able to buy homes. Forgotten was the fact that the homeownership rate was approximately 64 percent for the thirty years before the affordable-housing goals were adopted, and for much of that period the traditional conventional mortgage required a down payment of that size.

The agencies had produced what was essentially a traditional prime mortgage, correctly judging that such a mortgage would not require risk retention because it would not produce significant losses through the cycle. But this was not acceptable to many in the housing industry who did not see the financial crisis as the result of reduced underwriting standards, and profited from the sale of homes no matter what ultimately happened to the buyers. Confused by this reaction and uncertain about what Congress wanted, the agencies went back to the drawing board and were not heard from again until 2013. But what happened then was truly appalling.

In addition to the QRM, the Dodd-Frank Act also authorized the Consumer Financial Protection Bureau, a new agency created by the act, to design the terms of a minimum-quality mortgage called a Qualified Mortgage, or QM. If the QRM was supposed to be a high-quality mortgage, the QM was intended to be the minimum-quality mortgage that would be acceptable in the market. The QM outlawed low- and no-documentation loans, interest-only loans, and several other kinds of mortgages that were deemed too risky for homebuyers, but it required no minimum down payment or FICO score (following the left's traditional objections to credit standards), although the DTI ratio of the borrower could not exceed 43 percent unless the loan was sold to the GSEs or FHA. The DTI ratio alone would not qualify as an underwriting standard; it was not even close. A DTI ratio only helps to determine whether the borrower has the resources necessary to pay, and 43 percent is a very high debt ratio; the down payment was intended to represent the borrower's commitment to the home, and the FICO score reflects the borrower's willingness or propensity to pay. People with low credit scores do not take their obligations seriously, even if they have the ability to pay.

The principal feature of the QM was that the lender was responsible for determining whether the borrower could repay the mortgage at the time the loan commitment was made. If it turned out that the borrower could not meet his or her obligations, the lender could be subject to substantial penalties, in addition to the losses on the loan. It was even possible that the borrower might have a defense to foreclosure if the lender failed to realize that the borrower could not meet the terms of the loan.

The QM, and the absence of any significant underwriting standards, was immediately popular with realtors, homebuilders, and others who argued that the loosening of underwriting requirements had nothing to do with the financial crisis, and without low down payments people wouldn't be able to buy homes. This popularity, in turn, put pressure on the six agencies to outline a QRM that was essentially the same as the QM, even though this would violate the spirit and the letter of the QRM that was specified in the Dodd-Frank Act. On August 19, 2013, President Obama met with all the financial regulators and urged them to complete their work in implementing Dodd-Frank.[16]

After all this pressure, the six agencies that were designated by Dodd-Frank to develop the QRM—a high-quality mortgage that could be securitized without the need for risk retention—simply gave up; in August 2013, after the meeting with the president, they released a proposed risk retention rule that would make the high-quality QRM essentially the equivalent of the minimum-quality QM. This meant that no risk retention would be required even for the securitization of mortgages with 3 percent down payments and 580 FICO scores, which, as shown in Figure 14.2, had a 40 percent default rate in the stress period between 2007 and 2012. Most remarkable of all, in taking this position, the agencies admitted that mortgages that complied with the QM standards and were originated between 2005 and 2008 had experienced a *23 percent* default rate through 2012.[17] In other words, the agencies that are supposed to be the guardians of the stability of the U.S. financial system agreed that a mortgage underwriting system that allowed a 23 percent rate of default did not trouble them.

This could never have happened if the narrative about the financial crisis had properly located the financial crisis in the reduction of mortgage underwriting standards brought on by the government's housing policies and implemented largely through the affordable-housing goals. In that case, the choice for policy makers would have been seen as a choice between increasing the availability of mortgage credit and a return to the conditions that produced the financial crisis.

Instead, the choice the agencies were led to see was much narrower—simply a choice between credit availability and mortgage defaults: "Academic research and the agencies' own analyses indicate that credit history [FICO score] and the LTV ratio [down payment] are significant factors in determining the probability of mortgage default. However, these additional credit overlays may have *ramifications for the availability of credit* that *many commenters* argued were *not outweighed by the corresponding reductions in likelihood of default*" (emphasis added).[18] Stating the choice that way, as a trade-off between real credit availability today and possible future mortgage defaults, the agencies were able to adopt a rule that would ultimately produce conditions in the mortgage market that were the same as those that preceded the events of 2008. Essentially the same language and reasoning were in the final rule, issued in October 2014.

Finally, as further proof that the false narrative has triumphed over the facts of the financial crisis, in May 2014 the Senate Banking Committee debated and ultimately passed, on a bipartisan vote, the Johnson-Crapo bill (after its sponsors, Senators Tim Johnson [D-S. Dak.] and Mike Crapo [R-Idaho]) to reform the housing finance market. The bill would have created a government-run housing finance market, with a government guarantee on all mortgage-backed securities. The official summary of the legislation called the QM rule a "robust" underwriting standard, even though it was no standard at all. Under the heading "Level Playing Field for Creditworthy Borrowers," the summary stated that "a new housing finance system must ensure that the American dream of homeownership is attainable for all creditworthy borrowers in all areas," and it contained provisions for obscuring how this would be done by using cross-subsidization to lower the costs of low-quality and risky mortgages by charging higher fees on high-quality prime borrowers. Although the bill was voted out of committee, as this book is being written it is given little chance to get to the floor for a vote. The reason is that the most "progressive" members of the committee were not satisfied that the legislation contained sufficient specificity about the amount of affordable housing that the bill would produce.

Unless at some point the narrative about the financial crisis is supplanted by an account of what really caused the financial crisis, it is only a matter of time before the ideas that produced the FHFA strategic plan, the QM/QRM rule, and the Johnson-Crapo bill will carry the day. If that happens, we can be sure that another financial crisis awaits us in the future.

NOTES

PREFACE

1. Public Law 111-203, July 21, 2010.

1. INTRODUCTION

1. See Jagdish Baghwati, "Critiques of Capitalism after the Crisis: Myths and Fallacies," *World Affairs Journal*, September 2009, http://www.columbia .edu/~jb38/papers/pdf/World_Affairs_Oct_2009.pdf; Joseph E. Stiglitz, *Freefall: America, Free Markets, and the Sinking of the World Economy* (Norton, 2010).

2. Federal Housing Finance Agency, "Enterprise Share of Residential Mortgage Debt Outstanding, 1990–2010," http://www.fhfa.gov/datatools/downloads /pages/current-market-date.aspx.

3. Fannie Mae Credit Policy memorandum, "Risk Pricing—Idea for August 3–4 meeting and Addressing Short-Term Pricing Opportunities," July 21, 1995.

4. U.S. Department of Housing and Urban Development, Office of Policy Development and Research, *Profiles of GSE Mortgage Purchases in 2005–2007*, Table 10a-2007, "Loan-to-Value Characteristics of Fannie Mae's Purchases, 2007."

5. Fannie Mae, 2005 Form 10-K, p. 36: "in reporting our subprime exposure, we have classified mortgage loans as subprime if the mortgage loans are originated by one of these specialty lenders, or for the original or resecuritized private label, mortgage-related securities that we hold in our portfolio, if the securities were labeled as subprime when sold."

6. Inside Mortgage Finance, *The 2013 Mortgage Market Statistical Annual* (Inside Mortgage Finance Publications, 2013), p. 17.

7. See, for example, Christopher Mayer, Karen Pence, and Shane Sherlund, "The Rise in Mortgage Defaults," *Journal of Economic Perspectives* 23, no. 1 (Winter 2009): 27.

8. Non-Prosecution Agreement between Fannie Mae and the Securities and Exchange Commission, December 13, 2011. See also Non-Prosecution Agreement between Freddie Mac and the Securities and Exchange Commission, December 13, 2011.

9. The FCIC staff interviewed Tom Lund, the executive vice president in charge of Fannie Mae's single-family business on March 4, 2010. Referring to housing price declines, Mr. Lund remarked, "If you told anyone that housing prices would decline 15% no less 40%, they wouldn't have believed you." Interview of Tom Lund, March 4, 2010, p. 10.

10. Bonnie Sinnock, "What Bank of America Actually Did Wrong," *National Mortgage News*, August 28, 2014, www.nationalmortgagenews.com/blogs /hearing/what-bank-of-america-actually-did-wrong-1042482-1.html (accessed September 18, 2014).

11. Viral V. Acharya and Matthew Richardson, "Causes of the Financial Crisis," *Critical Review*, May 12, 2009, p. 197.

12. See, e.g., Janet Yellen, "A Minsky Meltdown: Lessons for Central Bankers," presentation to the 18th Annual Hyman P. Minsky Conference on the State of the U.S. and World Economies, April 16, 2009.

13. Charles P. Kindleberger and Robert Z. Aliber, *Manias, Panics, and Crashes: A History of Financial Crises*, 5th ed. (John Wiley & Sons, Inc., 2005), p. 27.

14. Susan Wharton Gates, Vanessa Gail Perry, and Peter M. Zorn, "Automated Underwriting in Mortgage Lending: Good News for the Underserved?," in Fannie Mae Foundation, *Housing Policy Debate* 13, no. 2 (2002): 1.

15. Bank for International Settlements, "International Convergence of Capital Measurement and Capital Standards," July 1988, http://www.bis.org/publ /bcbs04a.htm.

16. Viral V. Acharya, Philipp Schnabl, and Gustavo Suarez, "Securitization without Risk Transfer," *Journal of Financial Economics* 107 (2013): 516.

17. Ibid.

18. Timothy F. Geithner, *Stress Test: Reflections on Financial Crises* (Crown Publishers, 2014), p. 136.

19. Acharya, Schnabl, and Suarez, "Securitization without Risk Transfer" (cited in n. 16), p. 516.

20. Larry Kudlow, "Barney Frank Comes Home to the Facts," GOPUSA, August 23, 2010, www.creators.com/conservative/lawrence-kudlow/barney-frank -comes-home-to-the-facts.html (accessed October 6, 2014).

2. THE DIFFERENCE BETWEEN PRIME
AND NONTRADITIONAL MORTGAGES

Epigraph: Sheila C. Bair, chair of the FDIC, remarks to the Wharton School, University of Pennsylvania International Housing Finance Program, Philadelphia, June 18, 2010, http://www.fdic.gov/news/news/speeches/chairman/sp jun1810.html.

1. Edward Pinto, "Three Studies of Subprime and Alt-A Loans in the US

Mortgage Market," February 5, 2011, http://www.aei.org/publication/three
-studies-of-subprime-and-alt-a-loans-in-the-us-mortgage-market.

2. Ibid., Study 1, Table 1.

3. Ibid., Study 2, Table 1.

4. Fannie Mae, "Serious Delinquencies by Demographic Characteristic,"
March 1992, document in author's files.

5. Thomas S. LaMalfa, "The Market for Non-Investment Quality Mortgages," *Wholesale Access*, December 1989, p. 1.

6. Mortgage Bankers Association, series on serious delinquencies of conventional mortgages, 1982–1991.

7. Robert B. Avery et al., "Credit Risk, Credit Scoring, and the Performance
of Home Mortgages," *Federal Reserve Bulletin* (July 1996), http://www.federal
reserve.gov/pubs/bulletin/1996/796lead.pdf.

8. Office of the Comptroller of the Currency, Federal Deposit Insurance
Corporation, Federal Reserve Board, Office of Thrift Supervision, "Expanded
Guidance for Subprime Lending Programs," January 31, 2001, http://www.occ
.gov/news-issuances/bulletins/2001/bulletin-2001-6.html and http://www.occ
.gov/news-issuances/bulletins/2001/bulletin-2001-6a.pdf.

9. Ibid., pp. 2–3.

10. Freddie Mac, "Freddie Mac Publishes Single Family Loan-Level Dataset," March 20, 2013, http://www.freddiemac.com/singlefamily/news/2013
/0321_loan_level_dataset.html.

11. Ibid.

12. The Federal Reserve, the Comptroller of the Currency, the Federal Deposit Insurance Corporation, the SEC, the Federal Housing Finance Agency,
and the Department of Housing and Urban Development, Proposal on "Credit
Risk Retention," August 28, 2013, p. 258, http://www.federalreserve.gov/news
events/press/bcreg/bcreg20130828a1.pdf.

13. Federal Reserve et al., "Credit Risk Retention," proposed rule, August
28, 2013, p. 263.

3. THE FINANCIAL CRISIS INQUIRY COMMISSION REPORT
AND OTHER EXPLANATIONS FOR THE CRISIS

1. Another favorite tack is to accuse anyone who cites the government's responsibility for the financial crisis of racism. An example of this is a blog entry by Edmund L. Andrews, "The Sarah Palinization of the Financial Crisis,"
Stan Collender's Capital Gains and Games, June 4, 2010, http://capitalgainsand
games.com/blog/edmund-l-andrews/1773/sarah-palinization-financial-crisis.
Again, name-calling of a particularly sleazy and dishonest kind substitutes for
facts or data.

2. Barry Ritholtz, "What Caused the Financial Crisis? The Big Lie Goes

Viral," *Washington Post*, November 5, 2011. See also Joe Nocera, "The Big Lie," Opinon, *New York Times*, December 23, 2011, where even the SEC became complicit in spreading The Big Lie; and Kevin Drum, "The Housing Bubble and the Big Lie," *Mother Jones*, December 24, 2011, http://www.motherjones.com/kevin-drum/2011/12/housing-bubble-and-big-lie; and, of course, Paul Krugman displaying his liberal conscience with this: "This isn't just a case where different people look at the same facts but reach different conclusions. Instead, we're looking at a situation in which one side of the debate just isn't interested in the truth, in which alleged scholarship is actually just propaganda"; Krugman, "Joe Nocera Gets Mad," The Conscience of a Liberal, *New York Times*, December 24, 2011, http://krugman.blogs.nytimes.com/2011/12/24/joe-nocera-gets-mad/?_r=0.

3. Ritholtz, "What Caused the Financial Crisis?"

4. Financial Crisis Inquiry Commission, *The Financial Crisis Inquiry Report: Final Report of the National Commission on the Causes of the Financial and Economic Crisis in the United States* (U.S. Government Printing Office, January 2011), http://fcic-static.law.stanford.edu/cdn_media/fcic-reports/fcic_final_report_full.pdf.

5. Ibid., p. xviii.

6. Ibid., pp. xviii–xxv.

7. Ibid., p. xxvi.

8. Robert G. Kaiser, " 'Act of Congress': How Barney Frank Foiled the Banking Lobby to Form a New Financial Watchdog," *Washington Post*, May 5, 2013: "Frank saw the Great Crash as a terrifying event that created a welcome chance to make historic changes in the regulations governing the financial industry, which had changed radically in recent decades. He wanted to write 'a new New Deal,' as he put it. Barack Obama's resounding victory in 2008, along with expanded Democratic majorities in the House and the Senate, seemed to make this a realistic possibility."

9. Edward Pinto, "Triggers of the Financial Crisis," memorandum to Staff of FCIC, March 15, 2010, p. 5, http://www.aei.org/publication/triggers-of-the-financial-crisis/.

10. Ibid., p. 12.

11. Edward J. Pinto, "Government Housing Policies in the Lead-Up to the Financial Crisis: A Forensic Study," draft manuscript, February 5, 2011, http://www.aei.org/publication/government-housing-policies-in-the-lead-up-to-the-financial-crisis-a-forensic-study/.

12. Financial Crisis Inquiry Commission, *The Financial Crisis Inquiry Report* (cited in n. 4), p. 219.

13. Ibid., pp. 123–124.

14. Ibid., pp. 124–125.

15. Ibid., pp. xxvi and xxvii.

16. FCIC staff report of statements by witnesses at a public hearing of the FCIC, April 9, 2010, quoted in a memorandum from Wendy Edelberg to the Commissioners, dated September 27, 2010, p. 25.

17. Fannie Mae, 2006 Form 10-K, p. 146.

18. The complete dissent was eventually printed in full by AEI as Peter J. Wallison, *Dissent from the Majority Report of the Financial Crisis Inquiry Commission* (AEI, January 14, 2011), http://www.aei.org/publication/dissent-from-the-majority-report-of-the-financial-crisis-inquiry-commission-2/.

19. Financial Crisis Inquiry Commission, *The Financial Crisis Inquiry Report* (cited in n. 4), p. 102.

20. U.S. Department of the Treasury, Resource Center, Daily Treasury Yield Curve Rates, 2000 to 2007.

21. Alan Greenspan, "The Crisis," *Brookings Papers on Economic Activity* (Spring 2010), p. 236, n. 47, http://www.brookings.edu/~/media/projects/bpea/spring%202010/2010a_bpea_greenspan.pdf.

22. John B. Taylor, *Getting Off Track* (Hoover Institution Press, 2009), pp. 1–14.

23. For the view from the left, see Paul Krugman, *The Return of Depression Economics and the Crisis of 2008* (W. W. Norton, 2009), chaps. 8–10; Joseph Stiglitz, *Freefall: America, Free Markets, and the Sinking of the World Economy* (W. W. Norton, 2010), chaps. 1, 3, and 6. For the right, see Richard A. Posner, *A Failure of Capitalism: The Crisis of '08 and the Descent into Depression* (Harvard University Press, 2009), chaps. 1, 3, 9, and 10.

24. See, e.g., Peter J. Wallison, "Deregulation and the Financial Crisis: Another Urban Myth," *Financial Services Outlook*, American Enterprise Institute (October 2009).

25. For additional discussion of this issue, see Peter J. Wallison, "Did the 'Repeal' of Glass-Steagall Have Any Role in the Financial Crisis? Not Guilty. Not Even Close," *Policy Briefs* (Networks Financial Institute) (November 2009).

26. This restriction was true in 2008. Section 608 of the Dodd-Frank Act, enacted in July 2010, adds restrictions on such things as securities lending that could increase a bank's theoretical exposure to its affiliates.

27. The Federal Reserve Bank of New York has a clear statement of eligibility for borrowing from the discount window at http://www.frbdiscountwindow.org/discountwindowbook.cfm?hdrID=14&dtlID=43.

28. Stephen Labaton, "Agency's '04 Rule Let Banks Pile Up New Debt," *New York Times*, October 2, 2008, http://www.nytimes.com/2008/10/03/business/03sec.html?pagewanted=all.

29. Erik R. Sirri, "Remarks at the National Economists Club: Securities Markets and Regulatory Reform," April 9, 2009, http://www.sec.gov/news/speech/2009/spch040909ers.htm.

30. U.S. Government Accountability Office, "Financial Markets Regulation: Financial Crisis Highlights Need to Improve Oversight of Leverage at Financial Institutions and across System," report no. GAO-09-739, 2009, p. 40.

31. Andrew W. Lo, "Reading about the Financial Crisis: A 21-Book Review," draft of January 21, 2012, p. 35.

32. Federal Deposit Insurance Corporation Improvement Act (FDICIA) of 1991 (Public Law 102-242, 105 Stat. 2236).

33. Jay W. Richards, *Infiltrated* (McGraw-Hill Education, 2013), p. 172.

34. See Financial Stability Board, "Strengthening the Oversight and Regulation of Shadow Banking: Progress Report to G20 Ministers and Governors," April 16, 2012, www.financialstabilityboard.org/publications/r_120420c.pdf.

35. Ben S. Bernanke, "Fostering Financial Stability," speech at the 2012 Federal Reserve Bank of Atlanta Financial Markets Conference, Stone Mountain, Georgia, April 9, 2012, www.federalreserve.gov/newsevents/speech/bernanke 20120409a.htm.

36. The report of the Special Inspector General for the Troubled Asset Relief Program (SIGTARP) is ambiguous on this point: "[T]he conclusion of the various Government actors that Citigroup had to be saved was strikingly ad hoc. While there was consensus that Citigroup was too systemically significant to be allowed to fail, that consensus appeared to be based as much on gut instinct and fear of the unknown as on objective criteria. . . . SIGTARP found no evidence that the determination was incorrect." Special Inspector General for the Troubled Asset Relief Program, "Extraordinary Financial Assistance Provided to Citigroup, Inc.," January 13, 2011, summary page.

37. The definitive work in this area has been done by Bert Ely, a bank regulation expert in Washington, D.C. Ely has kept track of every bank failure since 2007, along with the amount of the resulting loss to the FDIC. By his count, the aggregate loss to the FDIC was more than $90 billion, and the average loss, per bank, was 24 percent of the assets of the failed bank. An unpublished spreadsheet with these numbers is in the files of the author.

38. See, e.g., Peter J. Wallison, "Does Shadow Banking Require Regulation?," *Financial Services Outlook*, American Enterprise Institute (May–June 2012), http://www.aei.org/publication/does-shadow-banking-require-regulation/.

39. Colin Barr, "The Truth about Credit Default Swaps," *Fortune*, March 16, 2009, http://archive.fortune.com/2009/03/16/markets/cds.bear.fortune/index .htm (accessed October 10, 2014).

40. Roger Lowenstein, *The End of Wall Street* (New York: Penguin Press, 2010), p. 57.

41. Ben Protess, "Regulators Tighten Rules on Trading of Derivatives," *New York Times*, May 17, 2013, p. B8.

42. Gretchen Morgenson, "JPMorgan's Follies for All to See," Fair Game,

New York Times, March 17, 2013. See also Lynn Stout, "Regulate OTC Derivatives by Deregulating Them," *Regulation* (Fall 2009), p. 30.

43. Warren Buffett, testimony before the Financial Crisis Inquiry Commission, June 2, 2010, http://www.c-spanvideo.org/program/RatingAgen.

44. Hester Peirce, "Securities Lending and the Untold Story in the Collapse of AIG," Working Paper no. 14-12 (Mercatus Center, George Mason University), May 2014.

45. *Frontline* broadcast, October 20, 2009, http://video.pbs.org/video /1302794657/.

46. Financial Crisis Inquiry Commission, *The Financial Crisis Inquiry Report* (cited in n. 4), p. xxiv.

47. Senior Supervisors Group, "Observations on Management of Recent Credit Default Swap Credit Events," March 9, 2009, p. 2.

48. Fitch Ratings, "Global Credit Derivatives Survey: Surprises, Challenges, and the Future," August 20, 2009, p. 10.

49. Binyamin Appelbaum, "Days Before Housing Bust, Fed Doubted Need to Act," *New York Times*, January 18, 2013.

50. See Charles W. Calomiris, Robert A. Eisenbeis, and Robert E. Litan (US Shadow Financial Regulatory Committee), "Financial Crisis in the US and Beyond," in *World in Crisis: Insights from Six Shadow Financial Regulatory Committees*, on-line book (November 2011), p. 5.

51. Larry Cordell, Yilin Huang, and Meredith Williams, "Collateral Damage: Sizing and Assessing the Subprime CDO Crisis," Working Paper no. 11-30 (Research Department, Federal Reserve Bank of Philadelphia, May 2012).

52. Ibid., p. 2.

53. Ibid., p. 4.

54. Ibid., p. 8.

55. Ibid., p. 14.

56. Joseph Checkler and Emily Glazer, "Hedge Funds Are among the Winners of the Lehman Spoils," *Wall Street Journal*, September 13, 2013.

57. Cordell et al., "Collateral Damage" (cited in n. 51), p. 16.

58. Ibid., p. 7.

59. Ibid., p. 21.

60. Ibid., p. 7.

61. A more judicious discussion of why the rating agencies might have gone wrong is contained in Lawrence J. White, "Credit Rating Agencies: An Overview," *Annual Review of Financial Economics* 5 (2013), which contains an excellent review of the relevant academic literature on the rating agencies.

62. Thomas Sowell, *The Housing Boom and Bust* (Basic Books, 2009).

63. Financial Crisis Inquiry Commission, *The Financial Crisis Inquiry Report* (cited in n. 4), p. 417.

64. Alan S. Blinder, *After the Music Stopped: The Financial Crisis, the Response, and the Work Ahead* (Penguin Press, 2013), p. 84.

4. A SHORT HISTORY OF HOUSING FINANCE IN THE U.S.

1. Michael Cembalest, *Eye on the Market*, November 12, 2013, p. 4.

2. Homer Hoyt, *One Hundred Years of Land Values in Chicago* (Beard Books, 2000), p. 446.

3. "Rating of Borrower" (part II, section 3), in *FHA Underwriting Manual*, February 1936.

4. John P. Herzog and James Earley, *Home Mortgage Delinquency and Foreclosure* (Cambridge, Mass.: National Bureau of Economic Research, 1970), 12, http://www.nber.org/chapters/c3294.pdf.

5. Ibid.

6. Congressional Budget Office, "The Economic Effects of Recent Increases in Energy Prices," A CBO Paper, July 2006, p. 23: "In the 1970s' environment of rising inflation and interest rates, regulations on the mortgage market that had been in effect for many years—Regulation Q and usury laws for residential mortgages—turned out to be damaging to the economy. . . . When market rates exceeded those ceilings, the growth of deposits at commercial banks and savings and loan institutions slowed. . . . The result was a shortage of mortgage financing in the housing market. . . . Mortgage financing dried up, and home sales and home building collapsed. Such effects exacerbated the 1973–1975, 1980, and 1981–1982 recessions and contributed to the overall volatility of GDP throughout the 1970s and early 1980s."

7. See Appendix B, in Fannie Mae, "FNMA's Relationship with the Federal Government," undated [circa 1982].

8. Emergency Home Finance Act of 1970, Public Law No. 91-351, 84 Stat. 450.

9. U.S. Department of Housing and Urban Development, Office of Policy Development and Research, *1986 Report to Congress on the Federal National Mortgage Association* (1986), p. 6.

10. Peter J. Elmer and Steven A. Seelig, "The Rising Long-Term Trend of Single-Family Mortgage Foreclosure Rates," FDIC Working Paper 98-2, 1998, Table A, p. 21, http://www.fdic.gov/bank/analytical/working/98-2.pdf.

11. William R. Thomas, Jr., "A Standard of Quality," in *Secondary Mortgage Markets* (Winter 1985/1986), p. 23.

12. Ibid.

13. Fannie Mae (Richard Lorentz), "The Incidence of Foreclosure for 30-year FRMs" (all states as of September 30, 1991), document in author's files.

14. Federal National Mortgage Association Charter Act, Section 304(a)(1), http://www.fanniemae.com/resources/file/aboutus/pdf/fm-amended-charter

.pdf; Federal Home Loan Mortgage Corporation Act, Section 305(a)(1), http://www.freddiemac.com/governance/pdf/charter.pdf.

15. See Project I Mission Statement 1984 and Project I Concept Paper 1986, unpublished manuscripts in author's files.

16. Nathaniel C. Nash, "Fannie Mae to Sell New Securities," *New York Times*, April 22, 1987.

17. Leland C. Brendsel, "Great Expectations," *Secondary Mortgage Markets* 3, no. 1 (Spring 1986): 4.

18. Patric H. Hendershott and James D. Shilling, "The Impact of the Agencies on Conventional Fixed-Rate Mortgage Yields," National Bureau of Economic Research, July 1989, p. 1.

19. Andree Brooks, "Talking Fannie Mae; The Tight New Rules on Loans," *New York Times*, September 1, 1985.

20. Advisory Commission on Regulatory Barriers to Affordable Housing, "Not in My Backyard: Removing Barriers to Affordable Housing," HUD-5806, July 1991, p. 5-3.

21. Allen J. Fishbein, "Filling the Half-Empty Glass: The Role of Community Advocacy in Redefining the Public Responsibilities of Government-Sponsored Housing Enterprises," in *Organizing Access to Capital: Advocacy and the Democratization of Financial Institutions*, edited by Gregory Squires, chapter 7 (Temple University Press, 2003).

22. Gretchen Morgenson and Joshua Rosner, *Reckless Endangerment* (Times Books, 2011), pp. 22–24.

23. Timothy Howard, *The Mortgage Wars: Inside Fannie Mae, Big-Money Politics, and the Collapse of the American Dream* (McGraw-Hill, 2013), p. 65.

24. "History of Fannie Mae," http://www.alliemae.org/historyoffanniemae.html.

25. Fannie Mae, "Fannie Mae Chairman Commits Company to 'Transforming The Housing Finance System,'" press release, March 15, 1994.

26. Morgenson and Rosner, *Reckless Endangerment* (cited in n. 22), p. 26.

27. Michael Quint, "Racial Gap Detailed on Mortgages," *New York Times*, October 22, 1991.

28. Alicia Munnell, Lynn E. Brown, James McEneaney, and Geoffrey M.B. Tootell, "Mortgage Lending in Boston: Interpreting HMDA Data," Federal Reserve Bank of Boston, October 1992, http://www.bos.frb.org/economic/wp/wp1992/wp92_7.pdf.

29. Arnold Kling, "More on the Roots of the Bailout," *Library of Economics and Liberty*, August 2008, http://econlog.econlib.org/archives/2008/08/more_on_the_roo.html.

30. James A. Berkovec, Glenn B. Canner, Stuart A. Gabriel, and Timothy H. Hannan, "Mortgage Discrimination and FHA Loan Performance," *Cityscape:*

A Journal of Policy Development and Research 2, no. 1 (February 1996), www
.huduser.org/portal/periodicals/cityscape/vol2num1/index.html.

31. John Allison, *The Financial Crisis and the Free Market Cure: How Destructive Banking Reform Is Killing the Economy* (McGraw-Hill, 2013), p. 57.

32. Title XIII of the Housing and Community Development Act of 1992, Public Law 102-550, 106 Stat. 3672, H.R. 5334, enacted October 28, 1992.

33. Senate Report no. 102-282, at 34 (1992).

34. Fishbein, "Filling the Half-Empty Glass" (cited in n. 21), p. 114.

35. Federal Housing Enterprises Financial Safety and Soundness Act of 1992, Section 1332.

36. Ibid., Section 1333.

37. Ibid., Section 1335.

38. Ibid., Section 1354(a).

39. U.S. Department of Housing and Urban Development, "HUD's Regulation of the Federal National Mortgage Association (Fannie Mae) and the Federal Home Loan Mortgage Corporation (Freddie Mac)," *Federal Register* 65, no. 211 (October 31, 2000): 65106, www.gpo.gov/fdsys/pkg/FR-2000-10-31/pdf/00 -27367.pdf.

40. As this is written in late 2014, debate has begun in Washington over the structure of the housing finance system that will prevail in the future. The House Financial Services Committee, under the leadership of Jeb Hensarling (R-Tex.), voted out legislation that would create a largely private system. The Senate Banking Committee adopted legislation that is likely to include a structure controlled and insured by the government. Neither proposal has reached the floor of the House or Senate, and neither is likely to be acted on before the next Congress, which convenes in January 2015.

41. FDIC Regulations, Part 345, Community Investment, Section 345.22.

5. HUD'S CENTRAL ROLE

1. To illustrate the thuggish reputation that Fannie had earned in Washington, shortly after retiring from law practice and joining AEI in 1999, I had a phone conversation with a friend about what I planned to work on. I said that I thought Fannie Mae and Freddie Mac would be an interesting subject, because they seemed to be likely to have serious problems in the future. He replied, "You're going to criticize Fannie Mae?" I said yes, that's what I expected to do. There was a short pause on the phone, and then he said, "Do you have someone to start your car in the morning?"

2. Daniel Mudd, speech to Fannie Mae officers, 2004.

3. Oonagh McDonald, *Fannie Mae and Freddie Mac: Turning the American Dream into a Nightmare* (Bloomsbury Academic, 2012), p. xiii.

4. Harold L. Bunce, U.S. Department of Housing and Urban Development,

Office of Policy Development and Research, *The Funding of Affordable Loans: A 2000 Update* (April 2002), p. 3.

5. Ibid., p. 5.

6. U.S. Department of Housing and Urban Development, "HUD's Regulation of the Federal National Mortgage Association (Fannie Mae) and the Federal Home Loan Mortgage Corporation (Freddie Mac)," *Federal Register* 65, no. 211 (October 31, 2000): 65052, http://www.gpo.gov/fdsys/pkg/FR-2000-10-31/pdf/00-27367.pdf.

7. Ibid., p. 65092.

8. Department of Housing and Urban Development, "HUD's Housing Goals for the Federal National Mortgage Association (Fannie Mae) and the Federal Home Loan Mortgage Corporation (Freddie Mac) for the Years 2005–2008 and Amendments to HUD's Regulation of Fannie Mae and Freddie Mac; Final Rule," *Federal Register* 69, no. 211, Tuesday, November 2, 2004, Rules and Regulations, p. 63581, http://www.gpo.gov/fdsys/pkg/FR-2004-11-02/html/04-24101.htm.

9. Ibid.

10. Viral V. Acharya, Matthew Richardson, Stijn Van Nieuwerburgh, and Lawrence J. White, *Guaranteed to Fail: Fannie Mae, Freddie Mac, and the Debacle of Mortgage Finance* (Princeton University Press, 2011), p. 56.

11. Financial Crisis Inquiry Commission, *The Financial Crisis Inquiry Report: Final Report of the National Commission on the Causes of the Financial and Economic Crisis in the United States* (U.S. Government Printing Office, January 2011), p. xix, http://fcic-static.law.stanford.edu/cdn_media/fcic-reports/fcic_final_report_full.pdf.

12. U.S. Department of Housing and Urban Development, Office of Policy Development and Research, "Report to Congress on the Root Causes of the Foreclosure Crisis," January 2010, p. xii, http://www.huduser.org/portal/publications/hsgfin/foreclosure_09.html.

13. Testimony of Housing Secretary Shaun Donovan before the House Committee on Financial Services, April 14, 2010, http://portal.hud.gov/hudportal/HUD?src=/press/speeches_remarks_statements/2010/Speech_0414a2010.

14. Financial Crisis Inquiry Commission, *The Financial Crisis Inquiry Report* (cited in n. 11), p. xxvi.

15. U.S. Department of Housing and Urban Development, "Issue Brief: HUD's Affordable Lending Goals for Fannie Mae and Freddie Mac," January 1, 2001, p. 5, http://www.huduser.org/portal/publications/polleg/gse.html.

16. Department of Housing and Urban Development, "HUD's Housing Goals" (cited in n. 8), p. 63601.

17. David T. Rodda, Abt Associates, Inc., and Harley Advisors, for U.S. Department of Housing and Urban Development, Office of Policy Development

and Research, "Recent House Price Trends and Homeownership Affordability," HUD Contract C-OPC-21895, Task Order CHI-T0007, May 2005, p. 85.

18. See National Community Reinvestment Coalition (NCRC), "CRA Commitments," September 2007. The original report was removed from the NCRC's website, http://www.ncrc.org, after I called it to the attention of the FCIC staff, but can still be found at http://www.community-wealth.org/_pdfs/articles-pub lications/cdfis/report-silver-brown.pdf.

19. U.S. Department of Housing and Urban Development, "Na Hana Ku Aloha: 'Achieving through the Spirit of Aloha,'" *Honolulu Field Office Newsletter* (Fall 2001), http://webcache.googleusercontent.com/search?q=cache :http://archives.hud.gov/local/hi/newsletters/nlwfal2001.cfm.

20. Steve Cocheo, "Fair-Lending Pressure Builds," *ABA Banking Journal* 86, no. 12 (December 1994), http://www.questia.com/googleScholar.qst ?docId=5001707340.

21. U.S. Department of Housing and Urban Development, "Building Communities and New Markets for the New Century: 1998 Consolidated Report," Fiscal Year 1998 Report, p. 75, http://www.huduser.org/publications /polleg/98con/NewMarkets.pdf.

22. Tim Fears, "Questions and Answers from Countrywide about Lending," *RealTown*, December 11, 2007, http://articles.realtown.com/2007/12/11 /questions-and-answers-from-countrywide-about-lending/.

23. U.S. Department of Housing and Urban Development, "The National Homeownership Strategy: Partners in the American Dream," May 2, 1995, http://confoundedinterest.files.wordpress.com/2013/01/nhsdream2.pdf.

24. Ibid., chapter 4, action 35.

25. U.S. Department of Housing and Urban Development, Urban Policy Brief no. 2, August 1995, http://www.huduser.org/publications/txt/hdbrf2.txt.

26. Fannie Mae Foundation, "Making New Markets: Case Study of Countrywide Home Loans," 2000, http://content.knowledgeplex.org/kp2/programs /pdf/rep_newmortmkts_countrywide.pdf.

27. Federal Credit Reform Act (FCRA) of 1990, Title V of the Congressional Budget Act of 1990. Under the FCRA, HUD must estimate the annual cost of the FHA's credit subsidy for budget purposes. The credit subsidy is the net of its estimated receipts reduced by its estimated payments.

28. M. Carter McFarland for the Federal Housing Administration, "FHA Experience with Mortgage Foreclosures and Property Acquisitions," January 1963, p. 23, http://babel.hathitrust.org/cgi/pt?id=mdp.39015008723499;view=1 up;seq=36.

29. U.S. Government Accountability Office, "Federal Housing Administration: Decline in the Agency's Market Share Was Associated with Product and Process Developments of Other Mortgage Market Participants," report no.

GAO-07-645, June 2007, pp. 42 and 44, http://www.gao.gov/new.items/d07645 .pdf.

30. Ibid., pp. 42 and 44.

31. Fannie Mae Credit Policy Committee, "Summary Comparison of Proposed 3% CHBP Requirements with the FHA 203(b) Requirements," memorandum, July 22, 1993.

32. Integrated Financial Engineering, "Actuarial Review of the Federal Housing Administration Mutual Mortgage Insurance Fund (Excluding HECMs) for Fiscal Year 2009," prepared for U.S. Department of Housing and Urban Development, November 6, 2009, p. 42, http://portal.hud.gov/hud portal/HUD?src=/program_offices/housing/rmra/oe/rpts/actr/actrmenu.

33. Quicken press release, "Quicken Loans First to Offer FHA Home Mortgages Nationally on the Internet with HUD's Approval," January 20, 2000, http://web.intuit.com/about_intuit/press_releases/2000/01-20.html.

34. Integrated Financial Engineering, "Actuarial Review" (cited in n. 32).

35. U.S. Government Accountability Office, "Federal Housing Administration: Decline in the Agency's Market Share" (cited in n. 29).

36. Community Reinvestment Act (CRA), 12 U.S.C. 2901.

37. Original letter, dated January 2009, in author's files.

38. Randall S. Kroszner, speech at the Confronting Concentrated Poverty Forum, December 3, 2008, http://www.federalreserve.gov/newsevents/speech /kroszner20081203a.htm.

39. Board of Governors of the Federal Reserve System, "The Performance and Profitability of CRA-Related Lending," July 17, 2000, http://www.federal reserve.gov/communitydev/files/cra_cratext.pdf.

40. Fannie Mae, Follow Up to Urban Institute Meeting, undated, p. 2.

41. Sumit Agaarwal, Efraim Benmelech, Nittai Bergman, and Amit Seru, "Did the Community Reinvestment Act (CRA) Lead to Risky Lending?," NBER Working Paper no. 18609, December 2012.

42. Ben S. Bernanke, "The Community Reinvestment Act: Its Evolution and New Challenges," speech at the Community Affairs Research Conference, March 30, 2007, p. 2.

43. National Community Reinvestment Coalition, "CRA Commitments" (cited in n. 18), p. 4. This report discusses the principal amount of CRA loans that banks had committed to make in connection with merger applications. The report claimed that these commitments exceeded $4.5 trillion. Some of these commitments were in fact fulfilled through CRA qualifying loans that banks made in fulfillment of their commitments. This can be determined by looking for press announcements, but it is a time-consuming task and does not yield a complete inventory.

44. Ibid.

45. Financial Crisis Inquiry Commission, "The Community Reinvestment Act and the Mortgage Crisis," preliminary staff report, http://www.fcic.gov /reports/pdfs/2010-0407-Preliminary_Staff_Report_-_CRA_and_the_Mort gage_Crisis.pdf.

46. Edward Pinto, "Three Studies of Subprime and Alt-A Loans in the US Mortgage Market," February 5, 2011, Study 2, Table 3, http://www.aei.org /publication/three-studies-of-subprime-and-alt-a-loans-in-the-us-mortgage -market/.

47. Ibid., Study 2, Section G, pp. 29–32.

48. "Rules and Regulations," *Federal Register* 69, no. 211 (November 2, 2004): 63585, http://fdsys.gpo.gov/fdsys/pkg/FR-2004-11-02/pdf/04-24101.pdf.

49. Edward J. Pinto, "Housing Affordability: U.S. Is the Envy of the Developed World," *RealClearMarkets*, October 26, 2011, http://www.realclearmarkets.com /articles/2011/10/26/housing_affordability_us_is_the_envy_of_the_developed _world_99331.html.

50. Carol D. Leonnig, "How HUD Mortgage Policy Fed the Crisis," *Washington Post*, June 10, 2008, http://www.washingtonpost.com/wp-dyn/content /article/2008/06/09/AR2008060902626.html. Eventually, the number of families that lost homes to foreclosure was 8 million.

6. THE DECLINE IN UNDERWRITING STANDARDS

1. Abby Aguirre, "The Wrong Mortgage Derails a Mother's Plans," *New York Times*, November 8, 2008.

2. See Financial Crisis Inquiry Commission, *The Financial Crisis Inquiry Report: Final Report of the National Commission on the Causes of the Financial and Economic Crisis in the United States* (U.S. Government Printing Office, January 2011), http://fcic-static.law.stanford.edu/cdn_media/fcic-reports /fcic_final_report_full.pdf; for commentators, see, e.g., Bethany McLean and Joe Nocera, *All the Devils Are Here: The Hidden History of the Financial Crisis* (Portfolio/Penguin, 2011); Richard A. Posner, *A Failure of Capitalism* (Harvard University Press, 2009); and see Ben Bernanke, "Four Questions about the Financial Crisis," speech at Morehouse College, April 14, 2009.

3. Allie Mae, "History of Fannie Mae," http://www.alliemae.org/historyof fanniemae.html.

4. Martin D. Levine and Julie Gould, "Community Lending Review: Results and Recommendations," unpublished paper, November 14, 1995, p. 12.

5. Ibid., p. 2. The elements of the community lending program, many of which were carried forward as a means of meeting the affordable-housing goals, were described in a 1995 Fannie Mae brochure called "Opening Doors with Fannie Mae's Community Lending Products."

6. Richard W. Stevenson, "The Velvet Fist of Fannie Mae," *New York Times*, April 20, 1997.

7. Timothy Howard, *The Mortgage Wars: Inside Fannie Mae, Big-Money Politics, and the Collapse of the American Dream* (McGraw-Hill, 2013), p. 68.

8. 24CFR 81.16(c)(2)(ii)(B), adopted December 1, 1995. See also the letter from Sandra L. Fostek, Director, Office of Government Sponsored Enterprises Oversight, HUD, to Pamela F. Banks, Vice President, Fannie Mae, September 30, 2005, outlining how the GSEs can get goals credit for buying portions of a PMBS issuance. And see Carol D. Leonnig, "How HUD Mortgage Policy Fed the Crisis," *Washington Post*, June 10, 2008, http://www.washingtonpost.com/wp-dyn/content/article/2008/06/09/AR2008060902626.html.

9. Edward J. Pinto, "Government Housing Policies in the Lead-Up to the Financial Crisis: A Forensic Study," draft manuscript, February 5, 2011, p. 74, http://www.aei.org/publication/government-housing-policies-in-the-lead-up-to-the-financial-crisis-a-forensic-study/.

10. Statement of Ira G. Peppercorn of HUD, House Subcommittee on Capital Markets, Securities, and Government Sponsored Enterprises, Committee on Banking and Financial Services, July 30, 1998, http://democrats.financialservices.house.gov/banking/73098hud.shtml.

11. Fannie Mae, "Opening Doors with Fannie Mae's Community Lending Products," 1995, p. 3; and Fannie Mae, "CHBP Performance," memorandum from Credit Policy Staff to Credit Policy Committee, November 14, 1995, p. 1.

12. Inside Mortgage Finance, *The 2009 Mortgage Market Statistical Annual* (Inside Mortgage Finance Publications, 2009).

13. U.S. Department of Housing and Urban Development, Office of Policy Development and Research, *Subprime Markets, the Role of GSEs, and Risk-Based Pricing* (March 2002), p. 7.

14. Fannie Mae Credit Policy memorandum, "Community Lending Review," November 17, 1995, document contained in the author's files.

15. Robert B. Avery et al., "Credit Risk, Credit Scoring, and the Performance of Home Mortgages," *Federal Reserve Bulletin* (July 1996), http://www.federalreserve.gov/pubs/bulletin/1996/796lead.pdf.

16. Kenneth Temkin, George Galster, Roberto Quercia, and Sheila O'Leary, "A Study of the GSEs' Single-Family Underwriting Guidelines," April 1, 1999, http://www.urban.org/publications/1000205.html.

17. Department of Housing and Urban Development, *HUD's Regulation of the Federal National Mortgage Association (Fannie Mae) and the Federal Home Loan Mortgage Corporation (Freddie Mac)*, Congressional Record, October 31, 2000, p. 65093, http://www.gpo.gov/fdsys/pkg/FR-2000-10-31/html/00-27367.htm.

18. Edward Pinto, "Triggers of the Financial Crisis," memorandum to Staff of FCIC, March 15, 2010, p. 40, http://www.aei.org/publication/triggers-of-the-financial-crisis.

19. U.S. Department of Housing and Urban Development, "Cuomo

Announces Action to Provide $2.4 Trillion in Mortgages for Affordable Housing for 28.1 Million Families," press release, HUD no. 99-131, July 29, 1999.

20. Barry Zigas, "Fannie Mae HUD's Southwest Regional Office, Housing and Community Development and Minority Lending: Assessment and Action Plan," presentation to Southwest Regional Office, Housing and Community Development Advisory Council, November 16, 2000.

21. U.S. Department of Housing and Urban Development, Office of Policy Development and Research, Issue Brief no. 5, January 2001, p. 3.

22. Catherine Van Dusen, "Market Leadership Analysis Methodology: Treatment of Subprime Loans," memorandum, December 28, 2000.

23. U.S. Department of Housing and Urban Development, "HUD's Regulation of the Federal National Mortgage Association (Fannie Mae) and the Federal Home Loan Mortgage Corporation (Freddie Mac)," *Federal Register* 65, no. 211 (October 31, 2000): 65047, http://www.gpo.gov/fdsys/pkg/FR-2000-10-31/pdf/00-27367.pdf.

24. Jamie S. Gorelick, Remarks at American Bankers Association National Community and Economic Development Conference, October 30, 2000, http://web.archive.org/web/20011120061407/www.fanniemae.com/news/speeches/speech_152.html.

25. "Daniel H. Mudd's Responses to the Questions Presented in the FCIC's June 3, 2010, Letter," Answer to Question 6: How influential were HUD's affordable housing guidelines in Fannie Mae's purchase of subprime and Alt-A loans? Were Alt-A loans "goals-rich"? Were Alt-A loans net positive for housing goals?, http://fcic-static.law.stanford.edu/cdn_media/fcic-testimony/Subprime%20Lending%20and%20Securitization%20and%20GSEs/Dan%20Mudd%20Follow%20Up.pdf.

26. The information necessary was occupancy status (primary owner, second home, or rental); loan purpose (purchase or refinance); street address (including city, state, and ZIP); income; and loan amount in dollars. This allowed the GSEs to determine where the borrower was located, the borrower's income as a percent of the metropolitan statistical area median, whether it was a purchase or a refinance, and whether the home was a single-family or owner-occupied multi-family rental.

27. Kevin Villani, "How Politicians and Regulators Caused the Sub-Prime Financial Crisis of 2007 and the Subsequent Crash of the Global Financial System in 2008, and Likely Will Again," Working Paper, August 2010, http://chicagoboyz.net/archives/14624.html.

28. Department of Housing and Urban Development, "HUD's Housing Goals for the Federal National Mortgage Association (Fannie Mae) and the Federal Home Loan Mortgage Corporation (Freddie Mac) for the Years 2005–2008 and Amendments to HUD's Regulation of Fannie Mae and Freddie Mac;

Final Rule," *Federal Register* 69, no. 211 (November 2, 2004), Rules and Regulations, p. 63606, http://gpo.gov/fdsys/pkg/FR-2004-11-02/pdf/04-24101.pdf.

29. Fannie Mae presentation to HUD, March 2003, provided to the FCIC, slide 18.

30. U.S. Department of Housing and Urban Development, Office of Policy Development and Research, Profiles of GSE Mortgage Purchases, 1992–2000, 2001–2004, and 2005–2007.

31. Neil Morse, "Looking for New Customers," *Mortgage Banking*, December 1, 2004.

32. Rob Blackwell, "Two GSEs Cut Corners to Hit Goals, Report Says," *American Banker*, May 13, 2005, p. 1.

33. See, e.g., Peter J. Wallison, Thomas H. Stanton, and Bert Ely, *Privatizing Fannie Mae, Freddie Mac, and the Federal Home Loan Banks: Why and How* (AEI Press, 2004).

34. Barney Frank, Nancy Pelosi, et al., Letter to President George W. Bush, June 28, 2004.

35. See Edward Pinto, "Three Studies of Subprime and Alt-A Loans in the US Mortgage Market," February 5, 2011, Study 3, http://www.aei.org/publication /three-studies-of-subprime-and-alt-a-loans-in-the-us-mortgage-market/.

36. U.S. Department of Housing and Urban Development, "The National Homeownership Strategy: Partners in the American Dream," May 2, 1995, chapter 4, http://web.archive.org/web/20010106203500/www.huduser.org/pub lications/affhsg/homeown/chap1.html.

37. Pinto, "Three Studies" (cited in n. 35), Study 3, Table 2.

38. Ibid.

39. Federal Housing Finance Agency, "Data on the Risk Characteristics and Performance of Single-Family Mortgages Originated from 2001 through 2008 and Financed in the Secondary Market," September 13, 2010, p. 3. This report, among other things, compared the quality of the loans acquired by the GSEs to loans underlying the privately issued mortgage-backed securities, presumably to show through a favorable comparison that the FHFA's regulation was not remiss; but the FHFA did not then reveal the quality of the loans that underlay the PMBS that the GSEs actually acquired. For its part, HUD also did not report the effect of second mortgages on the LTV data it reported to Congress, also minimizing an element that substantially reduced the quality and increased the inherent riskiness of the mortgages the GSEs were acquiring.

40. Fannie Mae, "Fannie Mae's Role in Affordable Housing Finance: Connecting World Capital Markets and America's Homebuyers," presentation to HUD Assistant Secretary Albert Trevino, January 10, 2003, p. 25.

41. Pinto, "Three Studies" (cited in n. 35), Study 3, Table 3.

42. Ibid.

43. "The average estimated cost of guaranteeing single-family mortgages acquired by Fannie Mae and Freddie in 2007, as estimated by internal Enterprise costing models at the time of acquisition, was significantly higher than the average estimated guarantee fee charged by the Enterprises, reflecting the general market underpricing of mortgage credit risk in that year." Federal Housing Finance Agency, "Fannie Mae and Freddie Mac Single-Family Guarantee Fees in 2007 and 2008," p. 33, http://www.fhfa.gov/webfiles/14700 /GFees72009.pdf.

44. Fannie Mae, 2006 Form 10-K, p. 48.

45. Ibid., p. 126.

46. Pinto, "Three Studies" (cited in n. 35), p. 44.

47. Fannie Mae 2009 Credit Supplement, as of December 31, 2009, p. 6.

48. Pinto, "Three Studies" (cited in n. 35), Study 2, Table 1.

49. Ibid.

50. William J. Clinton, "Remarks on the National Homeownership Strategy," June 5, 1995, http://www.presidency.ucsb.edu/ws/?pid=51448.

51. George W. Bush, *Decision Points* (Crown Publishers, 2010), p. 449.

7. FORCE FED

1. See, e.g., Bethany McLean and Joe Nocera, *All the Devils Are Here: The Hidden History of the Financial Crisis* (Portfolio/Penguin, 2011), p. 50: "The real reason Fannie was willing to finally move into riskier territory was the same reason Countrywide did: profits." Nocera was particularly unhinged and irresponsible in his *New York Times* column "The Big Lie" on December 23, 2011, contending that Pinto and I had engaged in "The Big Lie" technique in describing the role of the affordable housing requirements in the 2008 financial crisis. See also Jeff Madrick and Frank Partnoy, "Did Fannie Cause the Disaster?," *New York Review of Books*, October 27, 2011: "The GSEs did generate large losses, but their bad investments in housing loans followed rather than led the crisis; most of those investments involved purchases or guarantees made well after the subprime and housing bubbles had been expanded by private loans and were almost about to burst."

2. See, e.g., Barry Ritholtz, "Get Me ReWrite!," *The Big Picture* (blog), May 13, 2010, http://www.ritholtz.com/blog/2010/05/rewriting-the-causes-of-the -credit-crisis/; Dean Baker, "NPR Tells Us That Republicans Believe That Fannie and Freddie Caused the Crash," *Beat the Press Blog*, Center for Economic and Policy Research, August 17, 2010, http://www.cepr.net/index.php/blogs /beat-the-press/npr-tells-us-that-republicans-believe-that-fannie-and-freddie -caused-the-crash; Charles Duhigg, "Roots of the Crisis," *Frontline*, February 17, 2009, http://www.pbs.org/wgbh/pages/frontline/meltdown/themes/howwe gothere.html.

3. Financial Crisis Inquiry Commission, *The Financial Crisis Inquiry Report:*

Final Report of the National Commission on the Causes of the Financial and Economic Crisis in the United States (U.S. Government Printing Office, January 2011), pp. xxvi and 123, http://fcic-static.law.stanford.edu/cdn_media/fcic -reports/fcic_final_report_full.pdf.

4. Daniel Mudd, speech to Fannie officers, 2004, slide 8.

5. Paul Weech, memorandum to Brian Graham, September 3, 2004.

6. Adolfo Marzol, memorandum to Daniel Mudd, March 2, 2005, FM-COGR_00267253.

7. Jody Shenn, "GSEs Accepting Higher Risks to Gain Housing Goal Credits," *American Banker*, June 27, 2006, http://www.americanbanker.com/issues /171_124/-281994-1.html.

8. Peter J. Wallison and Edward Pinto, "Senator Warren Gets Taken In by a False Analysis," *American.com*, March 17, 2014.

9. Freddie Mac External Risk Group, "Sub-Prime Market Share Strategy," memorandum, August 2, 2005, p. 2.

10. Letter from Sandra Fostek, Director of the Government Sponsored Enterprises Oversight, HUD, to Pamela Banks, Fannie Mae, September 30, 2005.

11. Fannie Mae, "HUD Housing Goals and the Subprime Market," unsigned and undated presentation, probably mid-2005, p. 4.

12. "Update on Fannie Mae's Housing Goals Performance," presentation to the U.S. Department of Housing and Urban Development, October 31, 2005, p. 9.

13. Fannie Mae, 2006 Form 10-K, p. 16.

14. Freddie Mac, Qs and As for upcoming announcement on PMBS, February 23, 2007, p. 1.

15. Office of the Comptroller of the Currency, Federal Deposit Insurance Corporation, Federal Reserve Board, Office of Thrift Supervision, "Expanded Guidance for Subprime Lending Programs," January 31, 2001, http://www.occ .gov/news-issuances/bulletins/2001/bulletin-2001-6.html and http://www.occ .gov/news-issuances/bulletins/2001/bulletin-2001-6a.pdf.

16. Freddie Mac, Financial Report for the Three and Nine Months Ended September 30, 2007, November 20, 2007, p. 8.

17. Daniel Mudd, letter to Brian Montgomery, assistant secretary of housing, December 21, 2007.

18. Freddie Mac, "Response to E-mail dated 12/13/2010 from Ron Borzekowski," undated. A footnote to the table states: "Regulatory guidance regarding housing goals required that GSEs receive pro rata housing goals credit for certain security purchases. Thus 'adjusted units' takes into account Freddie Mac's pro-rata share of each dwelling unit backing our security purchases, whereas 'unadjusted units' does not take into account Freddie's pro-rata share."

19. Financial Crisis Inquiry Commission, *The Financial Crisis Inquiry Report* (cited in n. 3), p. xxvi.

20. Fannie Mae, 2002 Form 10-K, Tables 30 and 33.

21. Edward Pinto, "Three Studies of Subprime and Alt-A Loans in the US Mortgage Market," February 5, 2011, Study 3, Table 3, http://www.aei.org/publication/three-studies-of-subprime-and-alt-a-loans-in-the-us-mortgage-market/.

22. Ibid.

23. Fannie Mae, 2002 Form 10-K, Table 34.

24. Inside Mortgage Finance, *Mortgage Market Statistical Annual*, 2011, vol. 2, p. 137.

25. Ibid., p. 136.

26. Ibid., p. 135.

27. McLean and Nocera, *All the Devils Are Here* (cited in n. 1), pp. 182–183.

28. See Pinto, "Three Studies" (cited in n. 21), Table 3.

29. Financial Crisis Inquiry Commission, *The Financial Crisis Inquiry Report* (cited in n. 3), p. xxvi.

30. Ibid., pp. 123–124.

31. Fannie Mae, 2005 Form 10-K, p. 37.

32. McLean and Nocera, *All the Devils Are Here* (cited in n. 1), p. 184.

33. David Min, "Faulty Conclusions Based on Shoddy Foundations," Center for American Progess, February 8, 2011, p. 9.

34. Financial Crisis Inquiry Commission, *The Financial Crisis Inquiry Report* (cited in n. 3), p. xxvi.

35. U.S. Department of Housing and Urban Development, "HUD's Regulation of the Federal National Mortgage Association (Fannie Mae) and the Federal Home Loan Mortgage Corporation (Freddie Mac)," *Federal Register* 65, no. 211 (October 31, 2000): 65106, www.gpo.gov/fdsys/pkg/FR-2000-10-31/pdf/00-27367.pdf.

36. McLean and Nocera, *All the Devils Are Here* (cited in n. 1), p. 50.

37. Department of Housing and Urban Development, Office of Policy Development and Research, "Report to Congress on the Root Causes of the Foreclosure Crisis," January 2010, p. xii, http://www.huduser.org/portal/publications/hsgfin/foreclosure_09.html.

38. Barry Zigas, "Fannie Mae and Minority Lending: Assessment and Action Plan," presentation to Southwest Regional Office, Housing and Community Development Advisory Council, November 16, 2000, FM-FCIC_00171953.

39. The occurrence of cross-subsidization within the GSEs was noted in a report by the Federal Housing Finance Agency, "Fannie Mae and Freddie Mac Single Family Guarantee Fees in 2008 and 2009," July 2010: "In both 2008 and 2009, cross-subsidization in single-family guarantee fees charged by the enterprises was evident across product types, credit score categories, and LTV ratio categories."

40. Fannie Mae, "The HUD Housing Goals," March 2003, slide 5, FM-FCIC_00172206.

41. Fannie Mae, "Costs and Benefits of Mission Activities, Project Phineas," June 14, 2005, slides 10, 17, and 20, FM-FCIC_00172093.

42. Barry Zigas, "Housing Goals and Minority Lending," September 30, 2005, slide 5, FM-FCIC_00172183.

43. "Update on Fannie Mae's Housing Goals Performance," presentation to the U.S. Department of Housing and Urban Development, October 31, 2005, FM-FCIC_00172185.

44. Rumfola, Parsons, and Kim (Single Family Business Product Management and Development), memorandum to Single Family Business Credit Committee, May 5, 2006, p. 6.

45. Fannie Mae, "2007 Housing Goal Plan," internal slide presentation, undated but probably January 2007, p. 1.

46. Charles Duhigg, "Pressured to Take More Risk, Fannie Reached the Tipping Point," The Reckoning, New York Times, October 4, 2008.

47. Fannie Mae, "Update on Fannie Mae's Housing Goals Performance," presentation for HUD, October 31, 2005, slide 9.

48. "Cash flow cost" equals expected revenue minus expected loss. Expected revenue is what will be received in guarantee fees; expected loss includes general and administrative expenses and credit losses. "Opportunity cost" is the guarantee fee actually charged minus the model fee—the fee that Fannie's model would impose to guarantee a mortgage of the same quality in order to earn a fair market return on capital. Fannie Mae, "Business Update—Headlines, Cost of Housing Goals," February 2007, p. 4.

49. Fannie Mae, "Housing Goals Briefing for HUD," April 11, 2007, p. 8.

50. Fannie Mae, "Housing Goals Forecast," Alignment Meeting, June 22, 2007, FM-FCIC_00172456.

51. Fannie Mae, "Plan to Meet Base Goals," Forecast Meeting, July 27, 2007, slide 4, FM-FCIC_00172469.

52. Daniel Mudd, letter to Brian Montgomery, December 21, 2007, p. 6, FM-FCIC_00171920.

53. Federal Housing Finance Agency, "Fannie Mae and Freddie Mac Single Family Guarantee Fees in 2007 and 2008," July 2009, p. 33.

54. Fannie Mae, 2006 Form 10-K, p. 146.

55. Freddie Mac, "Fourth Quarter 2008 Financial Results Supplement," March 11, 2009, http://www.freddiemac.com/investors/er/pdf/supplement_031109.pdf.

56. Freddie Mac, 2008 Form 10-K, p. 64, http://www.freddiemac.com/investors/er/pdf/10k_031109.pdf.

57. Freddie Mac, "Cost of Freddie Mac's Affordable Housing Mission," report to Business Risk Committee, Board of Directors, June 4, 2009, slides 2, 3, 7, 8.

8. GOING VIRAL

1. Carl Richards, "How a Financial Pro Lost His House," *New York Times*, November 8, 2011.

2. Faten Sabry and Chudozie Okongwu, "How Did We Get Here? The Story of the Credit Crisis," National Economic Research Associates, February 19, 2009.

3. Advisory Commission on Regulatory Barriers to Affordable Housing, "Not in My Backyard: Removing Barriers to Affordable Housing," HUD-5806, July 1991, p. 5-3.

4. James R. Barth, Tong Li, Triphon Phumiwasana, and Glenn Yago, "Surprise: Subprime Mortgage Products Are Not the Problem!," Milken Institute, December 2000, p. 1.

5. Noelle Knox, "First Rung on Property Ladder Gets Harder to Reach," *USA Today*, July 17, 2007.

6. Richard Syron, "Memorandum to Freddie Mac Board of Directors," February 22, 2007.

7. Freddie Mac, "Freddie Mac Publishes Single Family Loan-Level Dataset," press release, March 20, 2013.

8. U.S. Department of Housing and Urban Development, "National Homeownership Strategy: Partners in the American Dream," May 1995, p. 61, http://confoundedinterest.files.wordpress.com/2013/01/nhsdream2.pdf.

9. THE GREAT HOUSING PRICE BUBBLE

1. Randi F. Marshall, "Living on the Edge," *Newsday*, November 20, 2004, http://www.newsday.com/business/living-on-the-edge-1.587194.

2. James Grant, *Mr. Market Miscalculates: The Bubble Years and Beyond* (Axios Press), 2008.

3. See Ben Bernanke, testimony before the Financial Crisis Inquiry Commission, September 2, 2010; and Alan Greenspan, "The Crisis," second draft, March 9, 2010.

4. John B. Taylor, *Getting Off Track* (Hoover Institution Press, 2009), pp. 1–3; and John B. Taylor, testimony before the Financial Crisis Inquiry Commission, October 20, 2009.

5. Steven Gjerstad and Vernon Smith, "Monetary Policy, Credit Extension and Housing Bubbles, 2008 and 1929," in *Critical Review: Causes of the Crisis* 21, nos. 2–3 (2009): 272.

6. Dr. Michael J. Lea, testimony before the Subcommittee on Security and International Trade and Finance of the Senate Committee on Banking, Housing, and Urban Affairs, September 29, 2010, pp. 6–7.

7. James MacGee, "Why Didn't Canada's Housing Market Go Bust?," Economic Commentary, Federal Reserve Bank of Cleveland, December 2, 2009, pp. 3, 4.

8. U.S. Department of Housing and Urban Development, Office of Policy Development and Research, "Recent House Price Trends and Homeownership Affordability," May 2005, p. 46.

10. FLYING BLIND INTO A STORM

1. Henry M. Paulson, Jr., *On the Brink: Inside the Race to Stop the Collapse of the Global Financial System* (Business Plus, 2010), p. 61.

2. Fannie Mae, 2005 Form 10-K, p. 39.

3. Fannie Mae, 2007 Form 10-K, p. 129.

4. Ben S. Bernanke, "The Economic Outlook," testimony before the Joint Economic Committee, U.S. Congress, March 28, 2007.

5. Stephen Wisnefski and Jesse Thomas, "Bernanke Plays Down Threat from Subprime Defaults," *Wall Street Journal*, May 18, 2007, http://online.wsj.com /article/SB117940879677706211.html.

6. Ben S. Bernanke, "The Subprime Mortgage Market," speech at the Federal Reserve Bank of Chicago, May 17, 2007.

7. Federal Reserve, Federal Open Market Committee, press release, August 7, 2007.

8. Federal Reserve, Federal Open Market Committee, conference call, August 10, 2007, p. 8, http://www.federalreserve.gov/monetarypolicy/files/FOMC 20070810confcall.pdf.

9. Alan Greenspan, *The Map and the Territory: Risk, Human Nature, and the Future of Forecasting* (Penguin Press, 2013).

10. Scott Frame, Andreas Lehnert, and Ned Prescott, "A Snapshot of Mortgage Conditions with an Emphasis on Subprime Mortgage Performance," August 27, 2008, p. 2, http://www.clevelandfed.org/our_region/community _development/pdf/mf_knowledge_snapshot-082708.pdf.

11. Michael Lewis, *The Big Short: Inside the Doomsday Machine* (W. W. Norton, 2010).

12. Greenspan, *The Map and the Territory* (cited in n. 9), p. 68.

13. David Lawder, "Strong World Econ Containing Subprime Risk," Reuters, August 1, 2007, http://www.reuters.com/article/2007/08/01/us-usa-paulson-sub prime-idUSBJC00005820070801.

14. Vikas Shilpiekandula and Olga Gorodetsky, "Who Owns Residential Credit Risk?," *Lehman Brothers Fixed Income U.S. Securitized Products Research*, September 7, 2007.

15. Fannie Mae, "2012 Second-Quarter Credit Supplement," August 8, 2012, p. 6.

16. "Moody's Projects Losses of Almost Half of Original Balance from 2007 Subprime Mortgage Securities," January 14, 2010, http://seekingalpha.com /article/182556-moody-s-projects-losses-of-almost-half-of-original-balance -from-2007-subprime-mortgage-securities.

17. BCA Research, "Special Report: The U.S. Housing Train Wreck: An Update," September 20, 2007, p. 2.

18. Ibid., p. 6.

19. See, e.g., Frame, Lehnert, and Prescott, "A Snapshot of Mortgage Conditions with an Emphasis on Subprime Mortgage Performance" (cited in n. 10); and Christopher Mayer, Karen Pence, and Shane Sherlund, "The Rise in Mortgage Defaults," *Journal of Economic Perspectives* 23, no. 1 (Winter 2009): 27–50.

20. Paul Krugman, "Fannie, Freddie and You," Opinion, *New York Times*, July 14, 2008.

21. Amazingly, even as late as June 2010, some Fannie Mae employees still believed that the firm did not buy subprime loans. In an FCIC staff interview with William Brewster, the director of Fannie's Mortgage Fraud program, he was asked his definition of a subprime loan. "This is circular," he said, "but it's any loan that Fannie or Freddie wouldn't buy. Fannie didn't buy subprime loans, so we don't have a firm idea what it was." Interview of William Brewster, June 11, 2010.

22. Office of Federal Housing Enterprise Oversight, Report to Congress, 2008.

23. Ibid., p. 6.

24. Fannie Mae, 2005 Form 10-K, filed May 2, 2007.

25. Fannie Mae, 2008 Form 10-K Credit Supplement.

26. Fannie Mae, 2007 Form 10-K, pp. 129 and 155.

27. Ibid., p. 129.

28. Ibid., p. 130.

29. Fannie Mae, 2008 Third Quarter Form 10-Q, p. 115, http://www.fannie mae.com/ir/pdf/earnings/2008/q32008.pdf.

30. Financial Crisis Inquiry Commission, "Securitization: Misleading Disclosure," Topical Investigative Report, November 30, 2010.

31. Non-Prosecution Agreement between Fannie Mae and the Securities and Exchange Commission, December 13, 2011. See also Non-Prosecution Agreement between Freddie Mac and the Securities and Exchange Commission, December 13, 2011.

11. 31 MILLION NONTRADITIONAL MORTGAGES PRECIPITATE A CRISIS

1. Ben Bernanke, "Four Questions about the Financial Crisis," speech at Morehouse College, April 14, 2009, http://www.federalreserve.gov/newsevents /speech/bernanke20090414a.htm.

2. According to the Mortgage Bankers Association's National Delinquency Survey, as the bubble flattened in 2006 and began to deflate in 2007, the serious delinquency rate on conventional fixed-rate subprime loans began to

rise. Although it began at a low .16 percent in the first quarter of 2000, it had risen to 2.82 percent in the first quarter of 2006, and then to 4.41 percent in the last quarter of 2007; during the same periods, serious delinquency rates on adjustable-rate mortgages, which started in 2000 at .30 percent, had risen to 2.55 percent by the first quarter of 2006 and then to 7 percent. Eventually, the delinquency rates peaked at 12.7 percent on fixed-rate loans and at 18.4 percent among adjustables. Although prime loans in general did far better, by 2009 they were still well outside their usual rates of serious delinquency in normal times. Fixed-rate prime loans had a serious delinquency rate of .34 percent in the first quarter of 2006 and .44 in the last quarter of 2007, peaking at 2.91 in the last quarter of 2009. Prime adjustables were .33 percent in the first quarter of 2006 and 1.63 percent in the fourth quarter of 2007, peaking at 7.72 percent in the first quarter of 2010.

3. Sheila C. Bair, "Systemically Important Institutions and the Issue of 'Too-Big-to-Fail,'" testimony to the Financial Crisis Inquiry Commission, September 2, 2010, p. 3.

4. Financial Crisis Inquiry Commission, "Investigative Findings on Bear Stearns (Preliminary Draft)," April 29, 2010, p. 16.

5. Ibid., p. 45.

6. Daniel O. Beltran, Laurie Pounder, and Charles Thomas, "Foreign Exposure to Asset-Backed Securities of U.S. Origin," Board of Governors of the Federal Reserve System, International Finance Discussion Papers no. 939 (August 2008), pp. 11–14.

7. Institute of International Finance, "IIF Board of Directors—Discussion Memorandum on Valuation in Illiquid Markets," April 7, 2008, p. 1.

12. FAIR-VALUE ACCOUNTING
SCALES UP THE CRISIS

Epigraph: William M. Isaac, "How to Save the Financial System," Opinion, *Wall Street Journal*, September 19, 2008, http://online.wsj.com/article/SB122178603685354943.html.

1. Sebastian Boyd, "BNP Paribas Freezes Funds as Loan Losses Roil Market (Update 5)," *Bloomberg*, August 9, 2007.

2. Alan Greenspan, letter to Richard Breeden, chairman of the Securities and Exchange Commission, November 1, 1990.

3. Sanders Shaffer, "Evaluating the Impact of Fair Value Accounting on Financial Institutions: Implications for Accounting Standards Setting and Bank Supervision," Federal Reserve Bank of Boston, Working Paper no. QAU 12-01, December 31, 2011, p. 25.

4. Financial Accounting Standards Board, "Statement of Financial Account-

ing Standards No. 115: Accounting for Certain Investments in Debt and Equity Securities," May 1993, p. 4.

5. Ibid.

6. Ibid., p. 15.

7. Ibid., Appendix, p. 28. One of the key questions, not addressed in this book, was how to treat liabilities under the fair value system. In theory, liabilities should be treated the same way as assets, but that gives rise to an anomalous result. If a firm's credit condition weakens, and as a result the market value of its liabilities declines, the result is an increase in its net assets.

8. William A. Longbrake and Clifford V. Rossi, "Procyclical versus Countercyclical Policy Effects on Financial Services," The Financial Services Roundtable, July 2011, p. 38.

9. John Allison, The Financial Crisis and the Free Market Cure: How Destructive Banking Reform Is Killing the Economy (McGraw-Hill, 2013), p. 104.

10. Tobias Adrian and Hyun Song Shin, "The Changing Nature of Financial Intermediation and the Financial Crisis of 2007–09," Federal Reserve Bank of New York, Staff Report no. 439, revised April 2010, p. 17.

11. Financial Accounting Standards Board, "Statement of Financial Accounting Standards No. 157: Fair Value Measurements," September 2006, p. 2.

12. Ibid., p. 11.

13. Ibid.

14. "Credit Crisis Timeline," Credit Writedowns, http://www.creditwrite downs.com/credit-crisis-timeline/, accessed March 14, 2013.

15. Richard Stanton and Nancy Wallace, "The Bear's Lair: Index Credit Default Swaps and the Subprime Mortgage Crisis," The Review of Financial Studies (Oxford) 24, no. 10: 3250–3280, 3251, http://rfs.oxfordjournals.org /content/24/10/3250.short.

16. Gary B. Gorton, Slapped by the Invisible Hand: The Panic of 2007 (Oxford University Press, 2010), p. 130.

17. Ibid., p. 116.

18. Ibid., p. 130.

19. Calculation by the staff of the Financial Crisis Inquiry Commission. See The Financial Crisis Inquiry Report: Final Report of the National Commission on the Causes of the Financial and Economic Crisis in the United States (U.S. Government Printing Office, January 2011), pp. 121–122 and p. 574n121, http://fcic-static.law.stanford.edu/cdn_media/fcic-reports/fcic_final_report _full.pdf.

20. See, for example, Richard S. Berg, testimony to the U.S. House of Representatives Committee on Financial Services, March 29, 2009, www.markto marketdebate.com/testimony-032509.pdf.

21. See, for example, Michael Corkery and Al Yoon, "A Toxic Subprime Mortgage Bond's Legacy Lives On," Wall Street Journal, September 13, 2013;

Joseph Checkler and Emily Glazer, "Hedge Funds Are among the Winners of the Lehman Spoils," *Wall Street Journal*, September 13, 2013.

22. Kevin Villani, "How Politicians and Regulators Caused the Sub-Prime Financial Crisis of 2007 and the Subsequent Crash of the Global Financial System in 2008, and Likely Will Again," Working Paper, August 2010, p. 19, http://chicagoboyz.net/archives/14624.html.

23. Gorton, *Slapped by the Invisible Hand* (cited in n. 16), p. 130.

13. FROM BAD TO WORSE

1. Tobias Adrian and Hyun Song Shin, "The Changing Nature of Financial Intermediation and the Financial Crisis of 2007–09," Federal Reserve Bank of New York, Staff Report no. 439, revised April 2010, p. 7.

2. David Wessel, "Ten Days That Changed Capitalism," *Wall Street Journal*, March 27, 2008.

3. Henry M. Paulson, Jr., *On the Brink: Inside the Race to Stop the Collapse of the Global Financial System* (Business Plus, 2010), pp. 97–99.

4. Timothy F. Geithner, *Stress Test: Reflections on Financial Crises* (Crown Publishers, 2014), p. 151.

5. Hal S. Scott, "Interconnectedness and Contagion," November 20, 2012, Committee on Capital Markets Regulation, http://www.capmktsreg.org/pdfs/2012.11.20_Interconnectedness_and_Contagion.pdf; see also George G. Kaufman and Kenneth E. Scott, "What Is Systemic Risk, and Do Bank Regulators Retard or Contribute to It?," *Independent Review* 7, no. 3 (2003): 371–391.

6. See, e.g., Hal S. Scott, "Interconnectedness and Contagion" (cited in n. 5), and Peter J. Wallison, "Magical Thinking: The Latest Regulation from the Financial Stability Oversight Council," *Financial Services Outlook*, November–December 2011.

7. Financial Stability Oversight Council, "Proposed Recommendations Regarding Money Market Mutual Fund Reform," November 2012, p. 4.

8. Marcin Kacperczyk and Philipp Schnabl, "When Safe Proved Risky: Commercial Paper during the Financial Crisis of 2001–2009," *Journal of Economic Perspectives* 24, no. 1 (Winter 2010): 29.

9. Viral V. Acharya, Philipp Schnabl, and Gustavo Suarez, "Securitization without Risk Transfer," *Journal of Financial Economics* 107 (2013): 516.

10. Geithner, *Stress Test* (cited in n. 4), p. 195.

11. Peter J. Wallison, "Everything You Ever Wanted to Know about Credit Default Swaps—But Were Never Told," *Financial Services Outlook*, December 2008.

12. See ibid. for a detailed account of these programs.

13. Peter J. Wallison, "Stress for Success: The Bank Stress Tests Buy Time," *Financial Services Outlook*, May 2009, p. 1.

14. Paulson, *On the Brink* (cited in n. 3), p. 102.

15. Charles W. Calomiris, Robert A. Eisenbeis, and Robert E. Litan (U.S. Shadow Financial Regulatory Committee), "Financial Crisis in the US and Beyond," in *World in Crisis: Insights from Six Shadow Financial Regulatory Committees*, on-line book (November 2011), p. 20.

16. Jonathan R. Laing, "The Endgame Nears for Fannie and Freddie," *Barron's*, August 18, 2008.

17. Paulson, *On the Brink* (cited in n. 3), p. 181.

18. Ibid.

19. Geithner, *Stress Test* (cited in n. 4), p. 180.

20. Ibid., p. 187.

21. Ibid., p. 179.

22. David Wessel, *In Fed We Trust: Ben Bernanke's War on the Great Panic* (Crown Business, 2009), p. 14.

23. See DealBook, "48 Hours That Reshaped Wall Street," *New York Times*, September 15, 2008; and Bill Stacey and Julian Morris, "How Not to Solve a Crisis," International Policy Network, November 2008, p. 4 : "Early talks apparently failed because management held out for a higher price. Later talks failed because the government refused the guarantees sought by potential purchasers."

24. Paulson, *On the Brink* (cited in n. 3).

25. Ibid.

26. Binyamin Appelbaum, "The Fed's Actions in 2008: What the Transcripts Reveal," *New York Times,* February 21, 2014.

27. David Wessel, "Financial Crisis: Lessons of the Rescue: A Drama in Five Acts," *Wall Street Journal*, September 9, 2013.

28. Federal Reserve Act, section 13(3). The entire provision read as follows before it was amended by the Dodd-Frank Act in 2010: "In unusual and exigent circumstances, the Board of Governors of the Federal Reserve System, by the affirmative vote of not less than five members, may authorize any Federal reserve bank, during such periods as the said board may determine, at rates established in accordance with the provisions of section 357 of this title, to discount for any individual, partnership, or corporation, notes, drafts, and bills of exchange when such notes, drafts, and bills of exchange are indorsed or otherwise secured to the satisfaction of the Federal reserve bank: Provided, that before discounting any such note, draft, or bill of exchange for an individual or a partnership or corporation the Federal reserve bank shall obtain evidence that such individual, partnership, or corporation is unable to secure adequate credit accommodations from other banking institutions. All such discounts for individuals, partnerships, or corporations shall be subject to such limitations, restrictions, and regulations as the Board of Governors of the Federal Reserve System may prescribe." See also Alexander Mehra, "Legal Authority in Unusual and Exigent Circumstances: The Federal Reserve and the

Financial Crisis," *University of Pennsylvania Journal of Business Law* 13, no. 1 (March 2, 2011).

29. Ben Bernanke, testimony before the Financial Crisis Inquiry Commission, September 2, 2010, http://www.c-span.org/video/?295300-1/2008-finan cial-crisis-systemic-risk-ben-bernanke-testimony.

30. Jim Puzzanghera, "Bernanke Says Fed Had to Let Lehman Fail," *Los Angeles Times*, September 3, 2010.

31. Financial Crisis Inquiry Commission, hearing on September 2, 2010, http://www.c-span.org/video/?295300-1/2008-financial-crisis-systemic-risk -ben-bernanke-testimony.

32. James B. Stewart and Peter Eavis, "Revisiting the Lehman Brothers Bailout that Never Was," *New York Times*, September 29, 2014.

33. U.S. Government Accountability Office, "Federal Reserve System: Opportunities Exist to Strengthen Policies and Processes for Managing Emergency Assistance," report no. GAO-11-696, July 2011, p. 215.

34. Paulson, *On the Brink* (cited in n. 3), p. 210.

35. Richard Fuld, testimony to the Financial Crisis Inquiry Commission, September 1, 2010.

36. Paulson, *On the Brink* (cited in n. 3), p. 317.

37. Alan Greenspan, "The Crisis," *Brookings Papers on Economic Activity* (Spring 2010), p. 217, http://www.brookings.edu/~/media/projects/bpea /spring%202010/2010a_bpea_greenspan.pdf.

38. Joe Nocera, "Hoping a Hail Mary Pass Connects," Talking Business, *New York Times*, September 19, 2008.

14. THE FALSE NARRATIVE AND THE FUTURE

1. Group of Thirty, Report of the Working Group on Financial Reform, January 15, 2009, http://www.group30.org/images/PDF/Financial_Reform-A _Framework_for_Financial_Stability.pdf. See also Peter J. Wallison, "Regulation without Reason: The Group of Thirty Report," *Financial Services Outlook*, American Enterprise Institute (January 2009).

2. Dodd-Frank Act, section 113.

3. Ibid., section 115.

4. See Hal S. Scott, "Interconnectedness and Contagion," November 20, 2012, http://www.capmktsreg.org/pdfs/2012.11.20_Interconnectedness_and_Conta gion.pdf; see also George G. Kaufman and Kenneth E. Scott, "What Is Systemic Risk, and Do Bank Regulators Retard or Contribute to It?," *Independent Review* 7, no. 3 (2003).

5. Rahm Emanuel, YouTube video, February 9, 2009, http://www.youtube .com/watch?v=1yeA_kHHLow.

6. Michael Cembalest, *Eye on the Market*, May 3, 2011, p. 3.

7. Michael Cembalest, *Eye on the Market*, November 12, 2013, p. 5.

8. Joe Nocera, "Inquiry Is Missing Bottom Line," *New York Times*, January 28, 2011.

9. Department of Housing and Urban Development, Office of Policy Development and Research, *1986 Report to Congress on the Federal National Mortgage Association* ([Washington, D.C.]: U.S. Department of Housing and Urban Development, Office of Policy Development and Research, 1987), p. 6. See also Timothy Howard, *The Mortgage Wars* (New York: McGraw-Hill Education, 2013), pp. 25–29.

10. U.S. Government Accountability Office, "Secondary Mortgage Market: Information on Underwriting and Home Loans in the Atlanta Area," report to congressional requesters, November 1990, www.gao.gov/products/RCED-91-2.

11. Fannie Mae, "Serious Delinquencies by Demographic Characteristic," March 1992 (document in author's files).

12. Federal Housing Finance Agency, "The 2014 Strategic Plan for the Conservatorships of Fannie Mae and Freddie Mac," May 13, 2014, p. 7, http://www
.fhfa.gov/AboutUs/Reports/ReportDocuments/2014StrategicPlan05132014
Final.pdf.

13. Financial Crisis Inquiry Commission, *The Financial Crisis Inquiry Report: Final Report of the National Commission on the Causes of the Financial and Economic Crisis in the United States* (U.S. Government Printing Office, January 2011), p. 125, http://fcic-static.law.stanford.edu/cdn_media/fcic-reports
/fcic_final_report_full.pdf.

14. Federal Reserve, the Comptroller of the Currency, the Federal Deposit Insurance Corporation, the Securities and Exchange Commission, the Federal Housing Finance Agency, and the Department of Housing and Urban Development, "Credit Risk Retention," March 2011, *Federal Register* 76, no. 83 (April 29, 2011): 24090–186, http://www.gpo.gov/fdsys/pkg/FR-2011-04-29/pdf/2011
-8364.pdf.

15. See, for example, North Carolina Association of Mortgage Professionals, "NCAMP's Comments for Federal Register on QRM," July 22, 2011, http://www.federalreserve.gov/SECRS/2011/July/20110728/R-1417/R-1417
_072211_83812_424740059535_1.pdf.

16. White House, Office of the Press Secretary, "Readout of the President's Meeting with Independent Financial Regulators," August 19, 2013, http://www
.whitehouse.gov/the-press-office/2013/08/19/readout-presidents-meeting-inde
pendent-financial-regulators.

17. Federal Reserve et al., "Credit Risk Retention," August 28, 2013, pp. 257, 259, http://www.sec.gov/rules/proposed/2013/34-70277.pdf?utm_
source=page&utm_medium=/financial-reporting-network/insights/2013
/agencies-comment-risk-retention-rule.aspx&utm_campaign=download.

18. Ibid., p. 258.

INDEX

and Best Practices Initiative,
138–139
Countrywide Home Loans, Inc.,
138, 142
Cox, Chris, 327
CRA. *See* Community
Reinvestment Act
Crapo, Mike, 360
credit, 9, 31, 60, 107, 111;
easy, 238–239; and FHA
requirements, 144, 374n27;
under GSE Act, 117–118;
and loss predictions, 255–
257; and subprime borrowers,
32, 34
credit default swaps (CDS), 74,
80, 81, 82–83, 92, 293; at
AIG, 77–79, 338; at Lehman
Brothers, 320–321, 336–337;
as risks, 75–77
Credit Policy Committee (Fannie
Mae), 161–162
credit profiles, 54–55 (table), 211,
212–213 (table), 255–256
credit rating agencies, failures of,
93–96
cross-subsidization, of subprime
and Alt-A loans, 210–211,
382n39
Cuomo, Andrew, 130, 165

debt-to-income (DTI) ratios, 7,
9, 15, 31, 32, 35, 51, 95, 110,
111, 214, 353, 358; and non-
prime mortgages, 227–228;
and prime mortgages, 38–39;
and qualified residential

mortgages, 37–38; and
traditional mortgages, 29–30
default rates, 31, 32, 35–36, 51,
110, 161, 200, 245, 354 (fig.);
at Freddie Mac, 227–228, 233
(fig.); house prices and, 241
(fig.), 247, 270–271; housing
bubble and, 58, 267–268; on
NTMs, 34, 206, 265–266, 276–
277; on prime loans, 220–221,
231–232, 266–267
delinquency rates, 34, 156, 191
(table), 216, 241 (fig.), 247,
386–387n2; and housing price
bubble, 267–268; of NTMs,
200–201, 202 (table), 276–277;
of prime loans, 220–221,
266–267
Democrats, 47; on FCIC, 43–44;
and GSEs, 70, 172
Department of Agriculture, Rural
Housing Service, 5, 180
Department of Housing and
Urban Development (HUD),
26, 37, 109, 161, 247, 357,
374n27; and affordable-
housing goals, 45, 52–53, 85,
113, 118, 130, 131–132, 180–
181, 183–190; and affordable
lending, 156–157; and Best
Practices Initiative, 137–139;
on down payments, 229–230,
239; and financial crisis,
134–137, 157–159; and GSE
performance goals, 133–134,
166; and GSEs, 70, 85, 112,
203; and low- and moderate-

Federal Reserve Act, 73, 390–
391n28
Federal Reserve Bank of Boston,
115
Federal Reserve Bank of
Cleveland, on subprime loans,
246–247
Federal Reserve Board, 115; and
CRA lending, 152, 153–154
Federal Reserve System, xiv, 4,
37, 47, 72, 75, 275, 327, 338,
346, 357; and bank deposits,
311–312; bank holding
companies and, 315–316; on
bank liquidity, 20, 22–23; and
commercial paper market,
318, 319; and CRA loans, 148,
150–151, 155; on determining
risk, 83–85; on discount
window, 64–65; economic
forecasting by, 250–251; on
economic slowdown, 249–250;
interest rates and, 59, 60, 239,
279; and Lehman Brothers
failure, 329–335; liquidity and,
73, 279, 287–288, 321–323;
moral hazard created by,
21–22; and Reg Q, 104–105; as
regulator, 44–45; on subprime
loans, 252–254
FHA. See Federal Housing
Administration
FHFA. See Federal Housing
Finance Agency
FICO scores, 30, 31–32, 33
(table), 95, 110, 141 (table),
144, 353, 354 (fig.), 360;

and mortgage rating, 34, 35,
36–37, 38, 39, 50–51, 173, 194,
216, 258, 259
financial accounting, 280;
standards for, 281–288
Financial Accounting Standard.
See FAS 115; FAS 157
Financial Accounting Standards
Board (FASB), 280, 289, 302,
303, 339; rules, 300–301; on
securities assets, 282–283
financial crisis, 3, 24, 244,
343; causes of, xii, xiii, 57,
132–133; CDOs and, 89–93;
CDS and, 74–83; common
shock and, 315–326, 346–347;
credit rating and, 93–96;
false narrative about, xiv, 26,
304, 342, 350, 354, 356, 360;
government role in, 348–349;
HUD and, 134–137; and
Lehman Brothers bankruptcy,
335–336; liquidity and, 337–
338; low interest rates and,
57–61; perfect storm theories
for, 97–99; predatory lending
and, 96–97; risk-taking and,
61–71, 83–85; securitization
and, 86–89; "shadow banks"
and, 71–74
Financial Crisis Inquiry
Commission (FCIC), 25, 41,
59, 78, 80, 83, 87, 94, 133,
135, 155, 161, 197, 214, 251,
262, 343, 348; on affordable-
housing goals, 198–199; on
Bear Stearns near-failure,